Drawing *and* Sketching *in* Pencil

Drawing *and* Sketching *in* Pencil

ARTHUR L. GUPTILL

WITH A PREFACE BY HOWARD GREENLEY

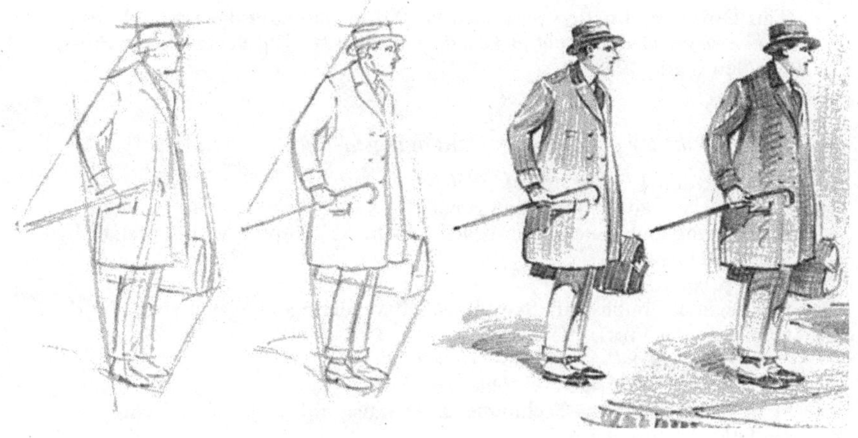

DOVER PUBLICATIONS, INC.
MINEOLA, NEW YORK

To

ALBERT E. MOORE

WHO TAUGHT THE AUTHOR THE VALUE OF TRUTH
IN REPRESENTATION AND PERSEVERANCE
IN EFFORT. THIS BOOK IS DEDICATED
IN GRATEFUL ACKNOWLEDGMENT.

Bibliographical Note

This Dover edition, first published in 2007, is an unabridged republication of *Sketching and Rendering in Pencil,* published by The Pencil Points Press, Inc., New York, 1922.

Library of Congress Cataloging-in-Publication Data

Guptill, Arthur Leighton, 1891–1956.
[Sketching and rendering in pencil]
Drawing and sketching in pencil / Arthur L. Guptill; with a preface by Howard Greenley.
p. cm.
Originally published: Sketching and rendering in pencil. New York: Pencil Points Press, 1922.
ISBN-13: 978-0-486-46048-2 (pbk.)
ISBN-10: 0-486-46048-7 (pbk.)
1. Pencil drawing—Technique. 2. Architectural rendering—Technique. I. Title.

NC890.G8 2007
741.2'4—dc22

2007017033

Printed in Canada
46048707 2025
www.doverpublications.com

PREFACE.

AN ARTISTIC conception is susceptible of translation into graphic expression through a variety of media, but by a certain universality of custom, or perhaps more accurately of convenience, the familiar lead pencil has achieved a significance derived from its immediate association with all forms of pictorial delineation. One may speak of it as a kind of staff upon which the artist or the draftsman leans most heavily. But this popular acceptance or recognition has, curiously enough, failed to carry with it an equivalent degree of appreciative comment or of authoritative instruction in the technique of its individual employment. Therefore, an examination of the text and illustrations contained in this volume must be of special and compelling interest to any one of artistic profession or aspirations, for in his accomplished and excellent interpretation of the potentiality existent within the pencil, Mr. Guptill is practically a pioneer.

By far the greater acknowledgment must be given, however, to the very definite stimulus contained in this volume toward a really effective educational development among architectural draftsmen. The atelier system which offers an inexpensive means of acquiring certain architectural training, based on the general principles of instruction at the Ecole des Beaux Arts in Paris, nevertheless, stops short of completeness from the lack of stress placed on the important element of free-hand drawing. Great emphasis is properly laid on the solution of the plan and its presentation but the adherence to the mechanical method more or less predicated in the drawing of the two-dimensioned plan, has been carried with almost equal insistence into the study of the three-dimensioned elevation. Out of this practice has grown a kind of formalized T-square and triangle "indication," much in vogue, and with scarcely more suggestive value than the working drawing produced with the other mechanical paraphernalia of ruling pens, compasses and dividers.

Most draftsmen avoid the blunted pencil point as they would a plague. A large part of their time is spent in sharpening the pencil to the length and sharpness of a needle. With such an implement their horizon is narrowed down to the production of scale drawings and the conventionalized sectional hatchings indicative of various materials. Form expressed in the graceful, flowing suavity of line becomes a remote possibility under such conditions.

If I am dwelling with some insistence upon the value of free-hand drawing, it is not in disparagement of instrumental drawing, nor with any view to its neglect. It is rather in the desire to build something more vital and engaging on this foundation of mechanical skill which will result in the draftsman becoming ever increasingly more of a draftsman that I most earnestly recommend this book. Mr. Guptill has with every evidence of success endeavored to assist the draftsman out of this automatic conventionalized indication into the realm of appreciation of the greater artistic possibilities lying within himself. To suggest to others a way of increasingly beautiful accomplishment is obviously no slight contribution. This volume is a plea for better instruction in free-hand drawing and for the thorough perception of its value.

The illustrations accompanying the text, by their variety and excellence of selection and their orderly arrangement, furnish in themselves a basis of suggestion to students which should awaken the most enthusiastic response.

The initial and almost certain discouragement which the making of a drawing from life connotes, inevitably becomes an emotion of compelling interest once a grasp of the elements of form and contour has been accomplished. I know of no way in which artistic capital, in the sense of facility and sureness of drawing, can be obtained better than by drawing from life and the transition from the plastic model to the rendering of the static architectural ornament enables the student to embody in his drawing the spirit of the design with a sureness and a refinement of detail not possible to one who has not passed through the former experience.

There is some distance to be travelled along the road of artistic endeavor before the student can express his personality in the composed statement of the artist. Mr. Guptill has, I think, in pointing out the road and contributing to its illumination, wisely kept away from the indication of style. His insistence has been in the line of encouragement of a greater fluency of speech in the language of pencil technique and of the assistance that intelligent conventionalization can render in the presentation of form and of color and of materials.

New York City.

HOWARD GREENLEY.

CONTENTS

Part I.

Part II.

LIST OF ILLUSTRATIONS

LIST OF ILLUSTRATIONS (*Continued*)

ILLUSTRATIONS BY THE AUTHOR

Drawings by the author, illustrating points brought out in the text, are found throughout this work and are designated as Figures 1 through 53.

It is a pleasure for the author to express here his grateful appreciation of the co-operation of all those who have contributed towards the making of this volume—especially to Walter Scott Perry, under whom, as Director of the School of Fine and Applied Arts, Pratt Institute, Brooklyn, New York City, the lectures upon which this work is based were prepared, and to the artists who have kindly given permission for the reproduction of the drawings shown in the supplementary illustrations.

FOREWORD.

IN VIEW of the popularity that the pencil has long enjoyed as a medium of artistic expression, it seems rather strange that so little has been written relating exclusively to it. For it is certainly true, whatever the reasons may be for this apparent neglect on the part of our writers,—reasons on which it is idle and irrelevant to speculate here, —that though there is a wealth of material dealing with kindred subjects, contributions bearing directly on the uses of this universal medium are few and meagre indeed.

This dearth of material became clearly apparent to the author when he was called upon, some ten years ago, to teach pencil sketching and technique in the art and architectural classes at Pratt Institute, for at that time a book was sought which might be employed as a text and reference work for his students. As nothing seemed available complete enough to satisfactorily meet all the requirements, a series of lectures was prepared by the author, based on his own training in art and architecture, which, after having been revised and amplified from time to time to meet the needs of the various classes under his instruction, forms the basis of this present volume.

Some of these lectures were arranged for pupils seeking a general art education; others were especially for architectural students, while a few, taking up the representation of furniture, draperies and the like, were used for the classes in interior decoration. As records were kept in all of these classes from year to year of the difficulties most frequently encountered and of points which seemed to require the most thorough explanation; also of the mistakes most commonly made by the pupils, it was possible to so revise the lectures as to anticipate and cover in advance many of the questions and problems which might otherwise have given trouble. An effort was made to guide the student step-by-step through the work, explaining each part with the greatest care.

When arrangements were made in 1920 to prepare a serial article on the subject of "Sketching and Rendering in Pencil" for "Pencil Points" it obviously became necessary to approach the whole subject from the standpoint of the architect and the architectural draftsman and student, so arranging the facts presented as to make them of the greatest value and interest to persons connected with the architectural profession. It seemed advisable, therefore, to exclude considerable material of a general nature, but in its place several additional sections were prepared, based on the professional experience of the author as architect and architectural illustrator and dealing especially with the uses of pencil in the free-hand rendering of architectural subjects.

This article, based on the lectures mentioned above, appeared in "Pencil Points" from August, 1920, to December, 1921, inclusive, in seventeen instalments, and met a much warmer reception than was expected by either the author or the publishers. Because of the rapid growth of the magazine, the back numbers of each issue were soon exhausted—it became impossible to meet the demand for the early installments; therefore the publishers, taking into consideration the fact that the inquiries received were not only from those connected with the architectural profession, but from artists and teachers and art students as well, decided that it was advisable to republish the entire series in some permanent form so as to make it available to all. The present volume is the result of this decision, and as it now stands contains in revised form the material published in "Pencil Points," to which has been added much material which was omitted from the magazine mainly because it approaches the subject entirely from the art rather than the purely architectural standpoint. Then, besides many new illustrations by the author drawn especially for this purpose, we are able to include through the kind cooperation of many well known artists, numerous examples of pencil work, showing a wide range of subject and great variety of technique. All these various reproductions are presented not merely as excellent examples of pencil drawing, however, but each is selected to illustrate some principle of composition or some suggestion for technique given in the text, thus adding, we believe, to the usefulness of the whole.

In preparing this volume we have presupposed that our readers would be, in the main, students of art or architecture or some allied subject, on the one hand, and architects or draftsmen, artists and art teachers on the other. We have endeavored to offer suggestions of value to all these classes of individuals and to do so it is plainly necessary to include much that is too elementary for the experienced man and much that is a bit too advanced for the novice. Therefore let the former omit or hurry over the rudimentary portions and the latter seek advice from his teacher as to the parts best suited to his state of progress. For the beginner needs a teacher and no book or books can take the place of personal instruction,—in fact, a book of this sort can do little but offer general instructions and suggestions, a bit of knowledge and a little inspiration;—if the reader gains a few thoughts that are new or has ideas which were partly forgotten brought back to him or is made to see familiar things from an enlarged viewpoint, this work will have served a useful purpose.

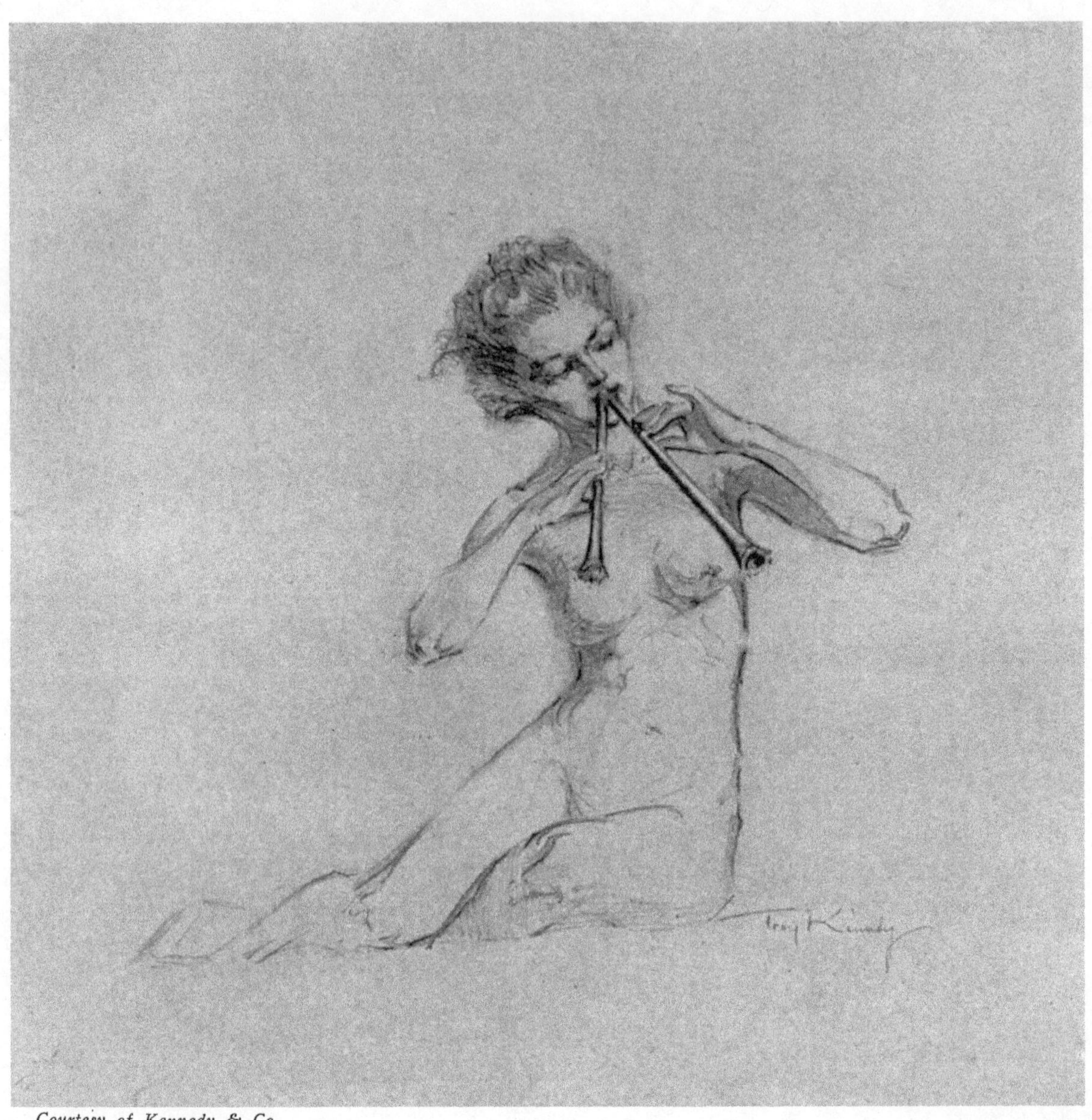

Courtesy of Kennedy & Co.

A FIGURE STUDY BY TROY KINNEY FOR HIS ETCHING "PROVOQUANTE"

DRAWING AND SKETCHING IN PENCIL

PART I.

CHAPTER I.

FIRST CONSIDERATIONS

UNDOUBTEDLY the ready availability and low cost of the pencil and materials needed for use in conjunction with it are partly responsible for its popularity among artists, while the ease with which it can be carried from place to place and prepared and kept in condition for work are in its favor, also.

But aside from these intrinsic merits of the pencil itself, it has other advantages of a different sort,—for instance its common employment for writing and similar purposes has given us all a certain familiarity with it, so that the beginner, having become accustomed from earliest childhood to these everyday uses to which it is put, finds it a natural and simple matter to learn to hold and manipulate it properly when drawing, which is, of course, highly important as it leaves him free to give his attention to other difficulties less easily avoided.

Yet the advantages we have mentioned, great as they are, seem insignificant when put into comparison with the one leading fact which has given the pencil its place in the world of art,—the fact that it is suitable for any kind of a drawing from the roughest outline sketch or diagram to a complete rendering of an elaborate subject. What other medium is there which responds so readily to any demand made upon it? Sharply pointed it will give us a line as fine and clean-cut as that of the pen; bluntly pointed it can be used almost as a brush. It will make strokes sufficiently light and delicate or bold and vigorous to suit the most exacting, or tones so smooth that in them no trace of any line can be found. It is responsive to the slightest touch, allowing us to grade at will from light to dark or from dark to light. What other medium will do all this? What other medium permits so great freedom in correcting and erasing at any time during the progress of the work? What medium permits of such rapid manipulation when speed is desired and still proves suitable for the most careful and painstaking study? It should not be supposed that it is only in the making of drawings in light and shade or outline that it is of value, either, for when color is desired there are excellent colored pencils to be had by the use of which wonderful effects are obtainable, either on white paper or on tinted surfaces,—furthermore light washes of water-color can be run over pencil work satisfactorily, charming combinations of such mediums being frequently seen.

Nor should it be forgotten that aside from all these various types of work in which the pencil plays a leading or a most conspicuous part, there are many drawings in which it serves a less prominent but by no means less important one, for it is employed with great frequency in the preparation of drawings to be completed in other mediums;—pen drawings, for example, are almost invariably blocked out in pencil before any ink is applied, while its use is not infrequent for the same preliminary preparation for paintings in wash, water color or oil as well as for making the numerous studies which are usually done before a large or important composition is finally executed. Therefore, even though the student intends to become a painter, pencil facility should prove invaluable to him. In fact, practice with this instrument helps greatly to fit one for work in all other mediums—drawings done in fine line train one for pen-and-ink, broad line shading being more like charcoal or crayon or brush work helps one in the use of these mediums, while pencil shading in mass or full tone prepares one directly for painting in wash or color.

With these various facts before us, it is not difficult to see that the pencil is an instrument which no artist or art student can afford to ignore; especially is it of value to the beginner for as has been pointed out it is hard to find another medium that approaches the pencil in permitting the same speed and accuracy in drawing, coupled with ease in correction. It is unfortunate if the student allows his impatience to attempt work in pen-and-ink or pastel or water-color or oils to cause him to proceed to the use of any of these mediums before he has mastered the pencil, for if he does so he will face unnecessary difficulties.

But if the pencil is valuable to the artist or art student it is absolutely indispensable to the architect and his assistants, for whereas the artist has numerous mediums from which to choose the one best suited to his particular needs or individual taste, the architect has nothing that can take the place of the graphite point for a major portion of his work. What other medium would answer for laying out his accurate plans and elevations and sections, and what else would do for all the various detail drawings which must be carefully made to scale? Yet the pencil serves the architect in other ways than these, for aside from this instrumental work which is hardly within the scope of this volume, many drawings of a free-hand nature are required, such as details of carved stone and wood, ornamental iron, lettered inscriptions and the like, and what is still more important the pencil is particularly valuable for making rendered presentation sketches of the kind submitted to a prospective client to show how a proposed structure will appear when completed, these sketches frequently serving to bring new work into the office. Then, too, the architect finds a knowledge of free-hand perspective sketching of great value in other ways, for he can by means of a few strokes of his pencil make some point clear to his client or express his ideas satisfactorily to his draftsmen, or help his contractors to visualize some matter not readily understood from the working drawings.

The architect's indebtedness to this little instrument which helps him to get work and to execute it is plain then, but if he feels a debt to this constant friend, so indeed should the architectural draftsman or student, for the pencil perhaps offers him more assistance in learning architecture and in advancing in this profession than does any other one thing.

For it is natural that the draftsman who gains proficiency in the use of an instrument so frequently employed by the architect stands in line for promotion, especially if he is able to do all the free-hand work which the average draftsman is so often unqualified to handle.

And even though a man may never reach a point where he stands out among his fellows because of his pencil sketches, he can gain much benefit in many ways by practising sketching during his spare moments. Drawing from photographs or buildings always increases a student's knowledge of architecture, but it does far more than this. It improves his powers of observation and retention, for he is forced to observe in order to draw at all and in drawing he unconsciously assimilates not only knowledge of the buildings drawn, but also a sense of relative proportions and shapes applicable to original problems in design. The more such drawings he makes, too, the greater will be his power to visualize the appearance of a proposed building long before a single study on paper has been made. The ability to thus form in the mind an image of the completed structure is most desirable, but the average draftsman gives so much time to working in elevation or plan only that he is likely to lose sight of the fact that the building is to be finally judged by its appearance in three dimensions and not by the drawings from which it is built. The draftsman who has the power to visualize does not forget this fact and so makes all his drawings with greater intelligence.

There are some men, on the other hand, who are able to see in their minds a building exactly as they wish to erect it, yet they are unable to freely express their ideas on paper. To such men a knowledge of free-hand drawing would be of the greatest benefit. In fact a man who can sketch well is able not only to express his own thoughts on paper but can draw from a description given him by someone else.

Then there are others connected with the architectural profession besides the architect and his draftsmen and designers who find a knowledge of sketching of value, for engineers and construction superintendents can often explain to others or make clear in their own minds certain obscure points in construction by means of quick sketches.

And just as the architect and his assistants find skill in pencil handling advantageous, so do those connected with such professions as interior decoration and landscape architecture, and in much the same way—this is not difficult to see. What is not so commonly understood, however, is that skill in pencil sketching often proves of practical value to the layman, though he may make infrequent use of his accomplishment. There are problems which sometimes come up in the daily life of any person difficult to express or explain by oral or written word but which can be easily made clear by even the crudest sketch.

Does it not seem rather strange, then, when we reflect on these various advantages of skill in sketching, that of all the millions of people in this country using pencils every day, and of the thousands of men in the architectural and similar professions alone who work from morning till night throughout the year with the pencil as their principal tool, that so few ever attempt to make anything but the crudest sort of free-hand sketch and that among those who do seriously try to make finished pencil drawings a still smaller number have the perseverance to reach any real degree of success? For taken all in all there is much of a practical nature to be gained through free-hand pencil work, and in addition to this a great deal of pleasure to be obtained,—in fact, the satisfaction of being able to draw well is worth in itself the time spent in acquiring the necessary knowledge.

Chapter II.

THE ESSENTIAL EQUIPMENT

THERE is nothing, perhaps, which so kindles the interest and enthusiasm of the student as to surround himself with the required drawing materials, while even the experienced man who is accustomed to the everyday use of these accessories can hardly gaze upon a new clean sheet of paper and pencils pointed ready for his hand without an itching to commence, a desire to seize a pencil and be at it, for there is something about such materials to lure one on—to urge one to do his best.

In fact the appeal of all such things is so strong that the beginner is almost sure, unless guided by his instructor, to buy too great a variety and quantity of materials and is inclined to attach too much importance to them, for important as they are (and no man can do good work with poor tools), the truth of the matter is that few and comparatively inexpensive things are needed for such work, and especially for the earlier problems. But these few should be the best of their respective kinds, for the difficulties that beset the beginner are so many and great that it would be a grave mistake for him to handicap himself by using anything of an inferior nature, as even the best materials are none too easily mastered.

If the student has no teacher to aid him in his selection he is usually safe in securing the standard drawing pencils and papers and the like which are carried in stock by reliable dealers in artists' supplies. After a time he will develop a liking for certain kinds for certain purposes and will eventually choose without hesitation the pencil and paper best suited to the subject to be drawn and the sort of drawing to be made. And whether one works with an instructor or without, his personal preferences will become more and more marked from year to year, and the more difficult it will be for him to adapt himself to materials with which he is not perfectly familiar. This unfortunately causes some artists of mature years to heartily condemn everything to which they are unaccustomed, which is hardly fair, for that which is worthless to one may be excellent for another. After the early problems are over, then, it is often well to experiment until a certain familiarity with all the standard materials is gained. Those which are here recommended will do for most of the problems of the beginner while others are discussed in later chapters.

Materials

Pencils—Drawing pencils are usually graded from 6B, the softest and blackest, to 9H, the hardest and firmest, with fifteen grades between, or seventeen in all, arranged as follows:—6B, 5B, 4B, 3B, 2B, B, HB, F, H, 2H, 3H, 4H, 5H, 6H, 7H, 8H, 9H. Of these the soft pencils are best suited to freehand work, though some papers demand much harder pencils than others. In fact, the choice of pencils depends almost entirely on the character of paper to be used, a smooth, glossy paper demanding a much softer pencil than is needed for work on rough paper which has considerable "tooth." For quick sketches, one soft pencil, perhaps a 2B or B or HB, will sometimes do for the whole drawing, but a carefully finished sketch showing considerable detail may require as many as seven or eight pencils grading all the way from 3B or 2B to 4H or 5H. In such a drawing most of the work would be done with the softer pencils, the harder ones being used for the light, transparent tones and fine detail. A little experimenting will usually show what pencils are best suited to the paper to be used and to the subject to be drawn. The fact that the weather makes a great difference in the pencils required is not usually recognized, but it is true that pencils that are just right on a dry day will prove too hard when the air is damp and the paper filled with moisture. Pencils of different manufacture vary in their grading so it is generally best to use those of one make on a drawing. Cheap pencils seldom prove satisfactory as the lead is variable and often so gritty as to scratch the paper.

Paper—Almost any drawing paper will do, but the choice depends mainly on the size and character of the drawing to be made. For small sketches it is best, as a rule, to use smoother paper than for large work,—in fact it is almost impossible to draw fine detail on extremely rough paper. A glazed paper, however, is seldom desirable as the shiny surface is dulled in an objectionable manner if the eraser is used. Sometimes, however, very crisp, snappy sketches are made on glazed paper, but a soft pencil is required for such work. Extremely rough paper is occasionally satisfactory for a large drawing, but a medium-rough surface is best for general work. Some tracing papers are very good and have the advantage that the sketch can be first blocked out on one sheet and then rendered on a second sheet placed over the first. The drawings by the author illustrating this text were made for the most part on "kid finish" Bristol Board, which has the advantage of being stiff and durable, with a firm surface.

It is often well to have several standard sizes for sketch sheets, one small enough to slip into the pocket, and one or two larger sizes. Drawing paper of the Imperial size of 22 in. x 30 in. can be cut without waste to several convenient proportions, such as 15 in. x 22 in., 11 in. x 15 in. and 7½ in. x 11 in. Some draftsmen prefer to have punched sheets to be used in a standard notebook cover, 8 in. x 10½ in., being satisfactory. The sketch books and pads for sale in all art stores are good for small work.

Erasers—As a rule it is best to avoid the use of erasers so far as possible, as erasing often injures the paper surface, but art gum or a soft white eraser is necessary for removing construction lines and for cleaning the sheet. A fairly hard red or green eraser may be required sometimes for correcting errors, and a soft "kneaded" rubber is very useful in lifting superfluous tone from a portion of a drawing. An erasing shield is an essential if changes are to be made.

Brush—A soft brush is needed for keeping the drawing free from dust as tiny specks often cause spots and streaks as the pencil passes over them. The paper should always be dusted with care after erasing is done.

Boards—It is usually well to fasten the drawing to a board of convenient size with thumb tacks. Be sure that the board is very smooth, for unless it is so or the paper very thick, the grain of the wood may show in the final drawing. When using thin or medium-weight drawing paper it is best to put an extra sheet or two under the drawing to insure a good surface.

Fixatif—Sketches done with soft pencils rub and soil so easily after they are completed that it is customary to spray or "fix" them. An atomizer and bottle of fixatif can be obtained in any art store but the fixatif usually sold tends to turn the drawing slightly yellow and also causes a gloss or shine if too much is applied. A French fixatif made for spraying pastels has the advantage of being more transparent and of causing less shine, but is quite expensive.

Sandpaper Block—A scratch pad of sandpaper is essential as an aid in pointing the pencils. These are sold in a convenient form with handles so attached as to make their use possible without soiling the hands. A sheet of fine sandpaper or a file may be substituted for the block if desired.

Knife—Obviously a sharp knife will be useful for trimming the paper, sharpening the pencils, lifting thumbtacks, etc.

The above materials are needed for all problems. Drawing tables, easels, etc., will be described in later chapters which take up the kinds of work for which they are essential.

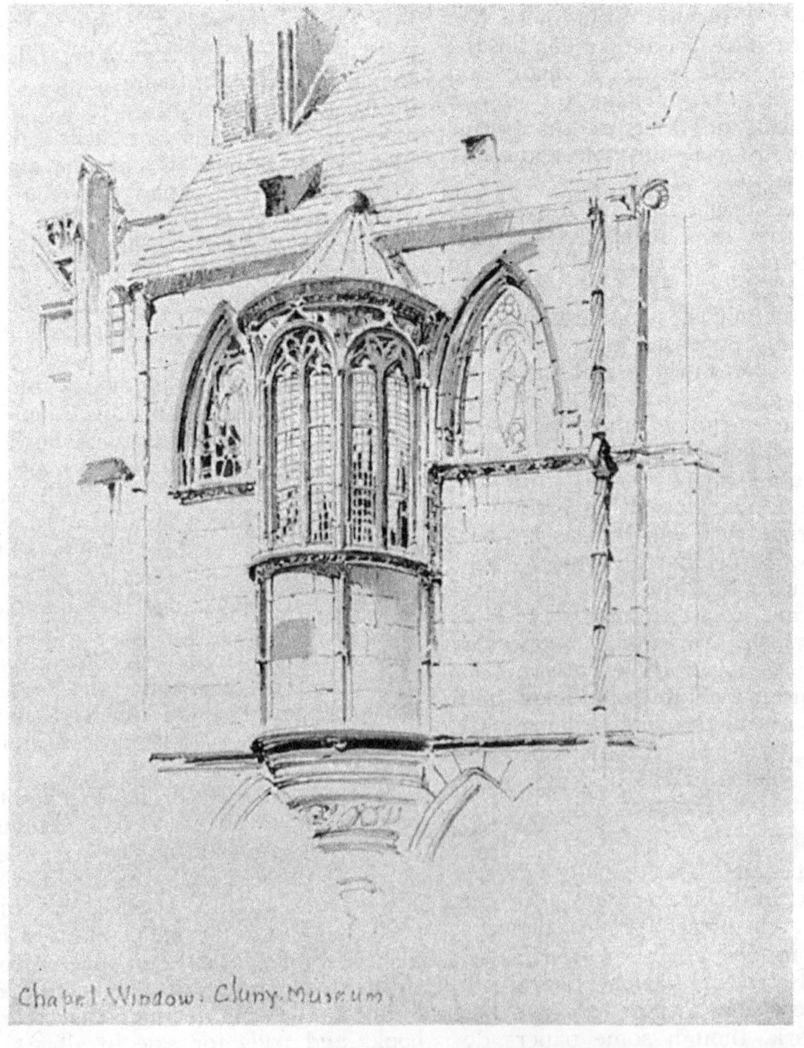

Pencil Sketch by Otto R. Eggers.

Chapter III.

OBJECT DRAWING IN OUTLINE

When one studies drawing he usually does so because of his personal inclination,—hence when the necessary materials have been selected and prepared he is anxious for his first instruction, and if his early problems prove interesting he is quite sure to become so enthusiastic as to make rapid progress. But this is an age of rush and hurry; perseverance and thoroughness seem to have been almost superseded by impatience and superficiality. Therefore progress, however rapid in reality, often seems painfully slow to the beginner, who is all too frequently so blinded by his desire to hasten on to the sort of thing which is way beyond him that it is hard for him to realize the importance of thorough mastery of the elements. If he is given problems which he considers beneath him he becomes resentful but if he is allowed to attempt difficult subjects of his own choosing and then fails to get the results hoped for he is apt to give up the whole matter in disgust,—blaming the instructor oftimes for his lack of success. Is it not, then, part of the duty of the teacher to point out the reasons why it is necessary for one to advance slowly enough to permit thorough mastery of each fundamental as he goes along? For if the student can be made to see the need for first learning to draw simple things well,—if he can be brought to realize that his progress will be all the more rapid in the end for having done so, problems which might otherwise prove irksome will be approached, if not with enthusiasm, at least with patience born of understanding.

Even cubes and cylinders and pyramids are interesting to draw if one takes the proper attitude towards them, and there is often no better starting point for the beginner than just this class of subjects. If we select a wooden cube, for instance, stripped bare of everything which might detract attention from its simple geometric form, and study it from various angles and make many sketches of it (as will be explained more at length later on) its appearance will be fixed forever in the memory so that one can recall it at any time and represent it on paper. "But," the student may ask, "what is the advantage of spending so long on a simple block of wood? I want to draw ships and street scenes and buildings and not blocks such as children use for toys." The advantage is clear if we pause to consider that most large objects like buildings and trolley cars and chairs and tables are based, so far as their general form is concerned, on just such elementary shapes as cubes, prisms, cones and pyramids. Once skill is acquired in drawing these, a big step has been taken towards learning to do larger and more complex subjects. If one starts with a cylinder and masters that and then tries pails, barrels, logs, tree trunks, smoke stacks, reservoirs and the like, as well as such architectural features as round buildings, circular towers, columns and archways, he will be surprised at the ease with which all these last may be proportioned, for these things differ little in basic form from the simple cylinder. If one can draw in addition triangular and hexagonal prisms and pyramids and cones, he can do all sorts of roofs and dormers and things of that kind, as well as innumerable small objects.

It is often advisable, then, for the beginner to start with such simple objects, drawing each one over and over again, attempting as has been pointed out above to memorize its shape so that it may be sketched at any time without reference to the object itself.

One will be helped greatly if he studies along with his practice in object drawing the principles of perspective as applied to freehand work, so the reader is referred to Chapter V, which deals directly with this phase of our subject, and which should, therefore, be read in conjunction with this.

When one has become thoroughly acquainted with the appearance and with the methods of representation of such objects (and has gained familiarity with the perspective principles involved) the next step is to apply this knowledge to the drawing of objects showing greater variety of form and surface and color,—such everyday things as books, dishes, fruit, or old shoes. Here the architectural student may ask why it is essential for him to know how to draw books, for "what have books to do with the sketching of architecture?" But indirectly they and kindred objects have much to offer, for aside from the skill in form representation and the perspective knowledge gained from their study (directly applicable to larger problems such as buildings), one learns also in the quickest way from these small things which are easily seen as complete units by the eye, how to express all sorts of textures of materials. When one has learned to show the leather of shoes and the glass or porcelain of dishes and the cloth or metal or wood of other objects it is not difficult for him to represent brick and stone and shingles and slate. Columns and balusters and all like architectural forms have much the same play of light and shade and gradation of tone, too, as is found on dishes and similar objects and it is much easier to draw from these little things which are near at hand than from features like columns which are usually so large that a confusing amount of detail is visible to prove troublesome to the beginner. Let him feel confident, then, that when spending his time as we have suggested, it will not be wasted.

Arranging the Working Space. Now if one is to gain the greatest advantage from his practice, whether the subject is a geometric solid or a bit of still life, he must seek a place where he can work undisturbed, and must have his equipment well chosen and arranged in a convenient way.

A room where one can be alone is ideal, or where the other occupants are engaged in similar pursuits as in an artist's studio or a class room. North light is desirable, for if windows face the east or south or west there will be sunlight streaming in at times during the day, which will cause the shadows and reflected lights on the objects to shift in position and to change in value constantly. North light, on the other hand, is a sort of indirect light, coming not straight from the sun but being largely reflected from the sky. It is more diffused, therefore, and gives softer and less changeable shadows and remains more constant during the whole day, being not so much affected by shifting in the sun's position or by the passage of clouds. And north light is purer in hue, too, less yellow than the direct rays of the sun, though this is of especial advantage only when working in color. Light from too many sources is disturbing, as it causes complexity of shadow and reflection. It is best to have the illumination from one window only, the shades being so arranged that the light may be cut off at either the top or the bottom as desired. (See Figure 1, which is designed to show a practically arranged room for this type of work.) Generally it is the lower half or two-thirds of the window that should be shaded, as light from above gives more pleasing shadows. Many studios are for this reason provided with overhead light from skylights or dormers, though for our purposes the upper half or third of the ordinary window will do very well.

The objects to be drawn should not be too far from this window for if they are they will not only lack sufficient light but the shadows will be too much elongated. If rays fall downward at an angle of about 45 degrees from the left they should prove satisfactory, the objects being from three or four to eight or ten feet from the window.

Object stand. There should be some sort of stand on which these objects may be placed and usually a small table of average height (about 30″) will do very well. One painted white or with a white cover is good. If a dark table is used it will be necessary to cover it with a white or very light cloth or paper on which the objects may rest and show good contrast. A background of the same material should be provided so that sharp relief can be obtained, and the surroundings cut off from view. The diagram Figure 2 shows a method of making a convenient folding object rest or shadow box of heavy cardboard which may be used on any table. Thin wood or wall-board may be substituted if desired. Cut two cardboards "A" and "B" of equal size, about 15″ x 22″, next binding them together with tape in such a way that "A" can be raised to a vertical position while "B" remains horizontal to rest on the table. Flaps "C" and "D," each 15″ square, are attached to "A" in the manner shown. Figure 2 gives at "B" and "C" two of several positions in which the box may be used, the first being the best for the early problems.

Chair or seat. A simple chair with a rather straight back and no arms is the best—one which though permitting freedom, will at the same time

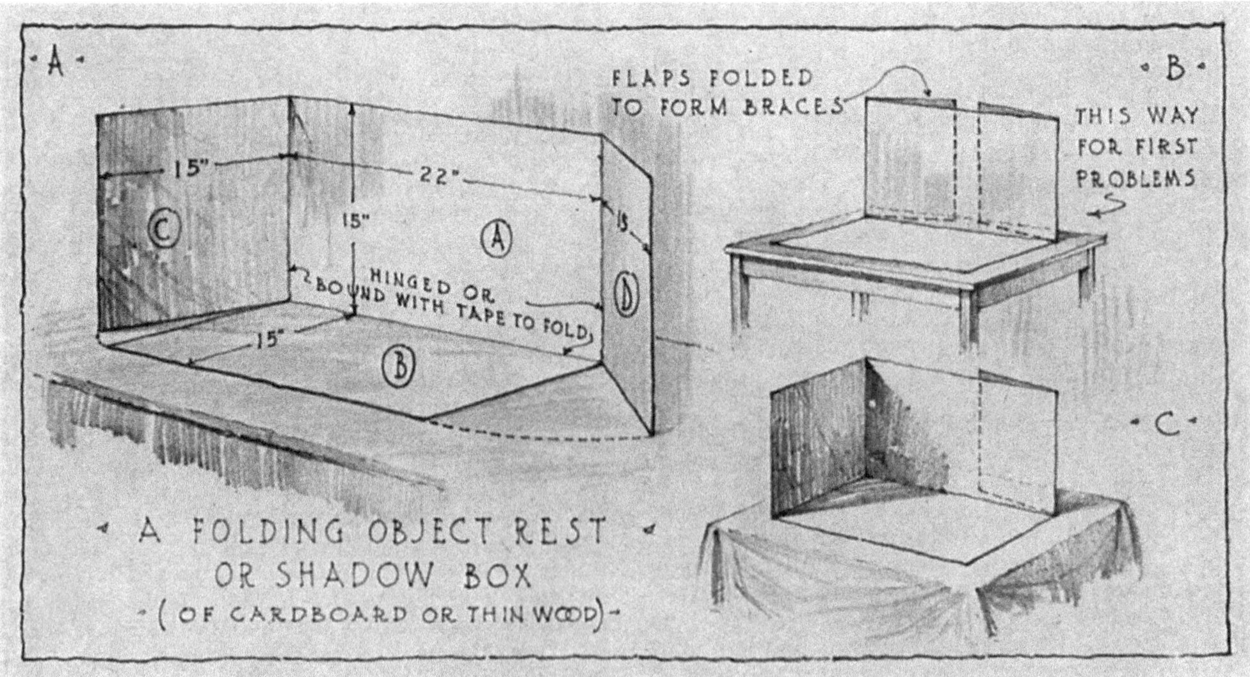

Figure 2. Illustrating a Method of Making an Object-Rest or Shadow Box.

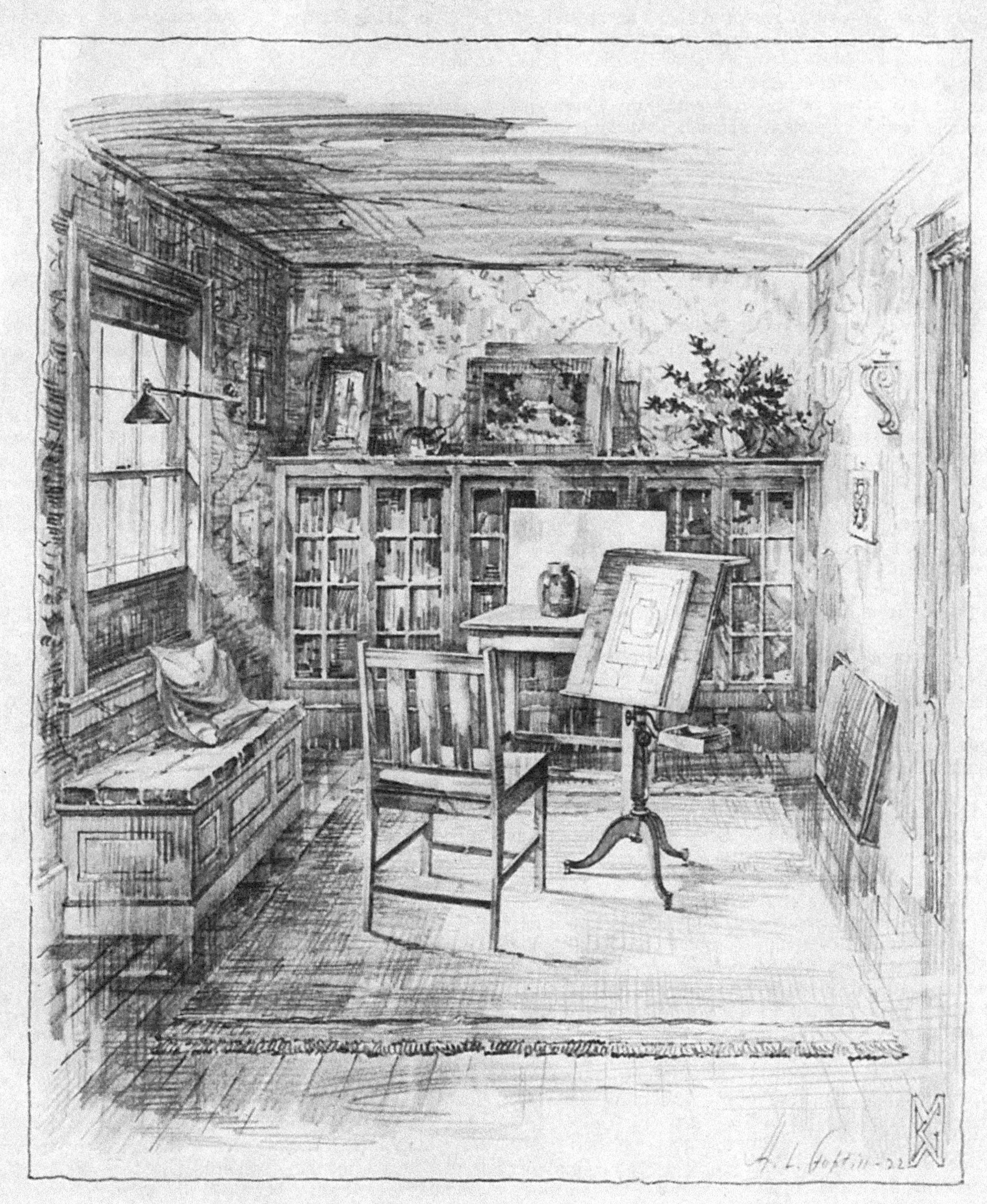

Figure 1. A Room Arranged as a Studio for Object or Cast Drawing.

not prove so comfortable as to invite laziness. For in object drawing it is essential that one should sit upright all the time. The chair should be so placed that the student will sit directly facing the objects.

Easel or adjustable drawing table. An easel or adjustable drawing table is essential on which the drawing board may rest. Usually this should be kept in an almost vertical position so the sketch is at right angles to the line of sight from the eye. If the board is tipped in some other manner the paper will be so foreshortened as to prevent accurate work, unless one changes his own position so as to still view it at right angles. The type of adjustable table shown in the sketch, Figure 1, has some advantages over the customary easel, especially for the architectural student, for it can be used not only in a great variety of positions as an easel but will also serve as a drafting board or as a table when placed horizontally or nearly so. Easels such as are available in any well stocked artists' supply house will do very well, however, those which permit of easy raising or lowering of the drawing to any desired height being the best. Whether table or easel is chosen it should be placed slightly to the right of the student as he faces the objects, just enough to one side to keep it from obstructing the view. This position and the height from the floor should be such as to make it easy to glance from the objects to the drawing and back again.

These three things, then, the stand on which the objects are to rest, the seat, and the easel or adjustable table, are most important and taken together with such smaller necessities as paper and pencil constitute the essential equipment. Cases or drawers or folios in which new paper, finished drawings and the like may be kept are convenient, and in addition there should be some provision made for taking care of the pencils, erasers and knives which must be near at hand. Attachments may be purchased for the type of table pictured in Figure 1, specially designed to accommodate such accessories, whereas the easel is usually equipped with a shelf to serve the same purpose. Some of the stands made for smokers are convenient if we substitute pencils and sandpaper pad for pipe and tobacco. As an added improvement to the studio a shelf should be provided where the drawing may be placed from time to time for comparison with the objects drawn. The top of the cases shown in Figure 1 would answer for this purpose (these cases, by the way, allow for storage of still-life, casts, etc., as well as books and drawings) though a rest or shelf right beside the objects would be still better. Students sometimes have a portable music rack such as musicians use placed near the object stand so they are able to set the drawing side by side with the subject for study and comparison.

If one plans to work by artificial light it will be advisable to arrange it to take the place so far as is possible of the natural daylight. The lamp near the window in Figure 1 is an adjustable one of telescopic nature which is excellent for the purpose as it may be shifted instantly to any desired position. Some artists prefer kerosene to electricity, claiming it gives a softer light. The kind of lamp is perhaps of less importance than its placement, however, as great care is necessary to avoid unpleasant glare or reflection. The light should be secured against so swaying or moving as to change the shade and shadow.

And last but not least a wastebasket proves a desirable adjunct to the studio.

Selecting the Subject. When this equipment has all been assembled and arranged we can select our first subject and start to draw. But there are various kinds of drawings of objects which may be made and it seems advisable to consider these for a moment for they are all useful, and one's training in still-life is incomplete until he has done drawings illustrating each of these different types.

First come the drawings in outline only, in which special attention is given to correct proportion and perspective; next we have studies in full value, in which all the tones are worked out with the utmost care so that each drawing gives as truthful a representation of the objects as it is possible to get with pencil. Then we have drawings in which some tone is added to outline,—a sort of combination of these other two methods, and others in which tone is built up by successions of fine lines or broad lines or both. All of these types are careful studies but there are still others in which speed is a leading consideration, a time limit being set before the drawing is commenced. These are frequently called time sketches. Aside from all these studies and sketches in which truth is sought, drawings are sometimes made in which the objects simply serve as a motive for a somewhat original composition for which a rather decorative treatment usually seems appropriate.

Of all these various classes of drawings we will discuss in the next chapters the first two quite fully,—the drawings in outline and the studies in full values. Much that we say concerning these will relate also to the others, which will, therefore, be more briefly described.

So let us select our subject and be at it.

We have already mentioned that there is nothing better for the beginner who is just ready to start his first practice than some simple object with which he is already quite familiar, something small enough so that it can be seen easily at a glance and yet large enough so that little effort is required to see it. And it should have a certain amount of individuality or distinctive character rather than mere prettiness, for one of the first things that we should learn is how to so analyze the subject as to discover its leading characteristics, and record them on paper with a few deft strokes. It should be of a simple color scheme, too, for the beginner has enough to occupy his attention if the colors are few and these few not too brilliant and distracting. To meet these requirements common, everyday objects are often the best that we can have. Geometric forms have been previously mentioned as desirable but as the representation of these will be especially considered in Chapter V we will turn to objects having less regularity or symmetry of form, such as old shoes or dishes. Bear in mind, however, when Chapter V is read that much which is given here relates as well to the representation of the geometric forms.

So let us take as our first subject an old shoe, quite the worse for wear, for this will give us variety of shape in abundance as well as individuality (for no two old shoes look just the same).

Beginning the work. Now that our equipment is arranged and our subject is selected, we are nearly ready to begin, but must first place the shoe on the object stand in a natural position with the light falling upon it in an interesting way (though the lighting is less important for outline work than for the later shaded studies). Thumbtack a sheet of paper about 11" x 15" or larger to your drawing board (see Chapter II in regard to the selection of paper) remembering that if several additional sheets are placed beneath the drawing, the surface will be better. Whittle a medium soft pencil such as an HB to a fairly sharp point, and place your chair and easel in a position which will permit of comfort and a clear view of the object and good light on the paper. Then when seated there are certain things to be decided before touching pencil to the paper. We must determine what sort of a drawing we are about to make. Is it to be in outline or in black and white? Is it to be a rough sketch or a carefully finished study? Are we to attempt to accurately represent the subject as we see it, every spot and line, every infinitesimal detail that we are able to discover on close search, or are we to work more for the general impression that one gets on looking at such an object in the usual way? As a rule it seems best for the beginner to confine his early attempts to outline, getting the main proportions as accurate as he can, seeking to bring out in his sketch the individual characteristics of the object. If the drawing is to be of a shoe, let it represent that particular shoe and not some other. Perhaps it may be well if the writer here digresses for a moment to relate his own experiences when making his first drawing under instruction. It was in the studio of Mr. Albert E. Moore at Portland, Maine —to whom this volume is dedicated, and whose influence is felt in every page. The drawing materials had been prepared and the author was eagerly waiting to see what the subject was to be. And then it was brought out,—an old, ragged felt hat. And a block of wood a few inches long, and two or three inches high. And that was all. And the hat was raised at one side on the block and arranged to form an interesting composition. Then the work was started, the directions being to make an outline drawing of that hat, expressing its individuality, getting right at the essentials, considering the whole thing in a big way. A half hour later the drawing was finished,—perfect, according to the personal opinion of its youthful author,—an improvement on the original in every way. And then came Mr. Moore! In the light of later understanding his patience seems truly remarkable. For he pointed out how the drawing was wrong here and wrong there, was, in fact, (though commendable for a first attempt) wrong in all its larger proportions, but especially how it failed to express the character of *that particular hat.* So the sheet was wiped clean and a new drawing made, and again, until the end of the morning found a somewhat discouraged youth whose pride in his newly acquired materials had received quite a setback. Finally after three or four half-days' time the drawing was finished (and what a feeling of satisfaction this accomplishment gave), the first of many similar studies, each of which brought added emphasis to the need of truthfully expressing the leading characteristics of the subject drawn.

We should perhaps try to make clear to the student just what is meant by "truthfully expressing the leading characteristics of the subject." To do so takes us back to a consideration of what a drawing is or should be. A drawing is simply an explanation. The best drawings which we have are those which tell their story directly and simply and which do not confuse us with multitudinous and irrelevant details. It is seldom that the artist attempts to tell in one drawing all the facts about the subject represented, but the leading truths are sought for,—the characteristics which appeal to him as being the most valuable and interesting. Just as individuals differ from one another in their choice of clothes, so artists differ in their selection and interpretation of the characteristics of any subject, so if several skilled men were to depict certain objects as viewed from the same point under the same conditions the resulting pictures would be quite different, though it is perfectly possible that all might be of equal merit and all considered as equally truthful; far more truthful than a photograph of the same objects. This may sound a bit strange as the student is often under the impression that the drawing which comes the closest to a photographic representation is the best and the most true. But this is not so. The tiny details of nature are without number and if we study any object minutely we are almost overwhelmed with the small parts which close inspection reveals. A clear photograph shows many of these things. When we glance at an object in the usual way, however, we are not aware of each tiny detail for it is only when we focus our attention upon one portion after another that we see the smallest of the visible parts at all,—the usual impression that we get is the one which we should attempt to transfer to our paper; not a photographic likeness which seeks and records every fact.

As the student gradually develops his perceptions he will be able to choose that which is essential according to the purpose for which the drawing is made from that which is superfluous, so that when we look at his drawings we will be conscious with little mental effort of the subject drawn and its principal attributes. It is undoubtedly largely this ease in understanding a good drawing which causes us to enjoy it in preference to a photograph of the same subject.

So the beginner must strive to retain in any subject such elements as have the greatest significance, in some cases even exaggerating them, sacrificing at the same time some of the lesser truths if by so doing the drawing as a whole will be easier to read or understand. It will be no less honest because of this.

To learn what to look for and what to overlook is as important as the improvement of draftsmanship, and there is perhaps no better way to begin to do this than to start with outline, as an outline

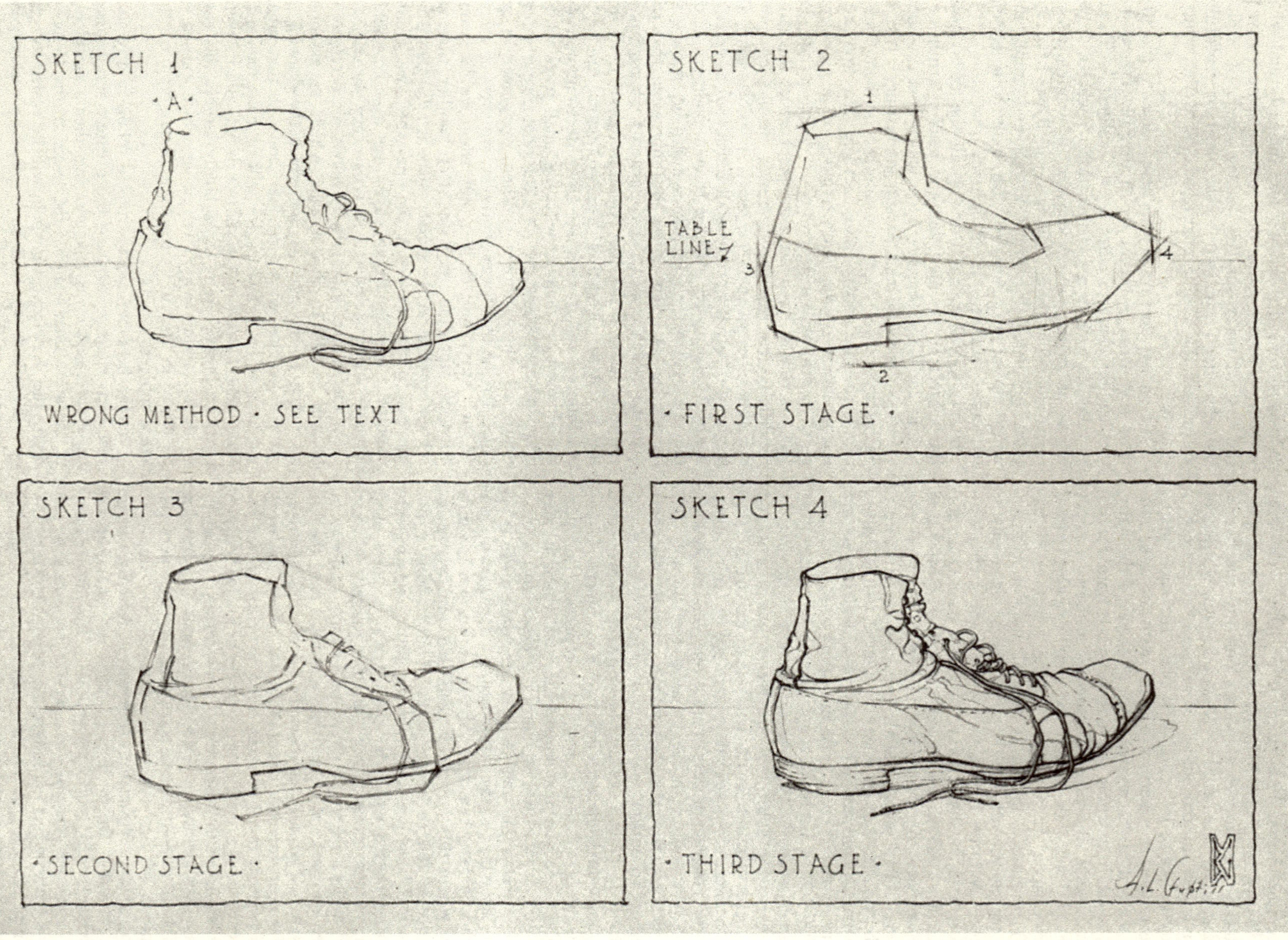

Figure 3. Showing the Various Stages in Making an Object Drawing in Outline.

drawing is the simplest that we can make, for as light and shade is largely disregarded in such work, concentration can be given to representing proportions and contours. It is for this reason that we assume that we are to draw the shoe in outline, attempting to honestly delineate it in a simple way.

It is here that the student, if left to his own devices, will often make the mistake of starting to draw at one point (such as "A," Sketch 1, Figure 3) at the top of the shoe, work down one side, completing the entire outline as he proceeds, next going across the bottom and up the other side and finally back to the starting point. Should an expert artist choose to do so he might employ this method successfully, but it is not to be recommended to the beginner as it is a very difficult way in which to work, for however careful one may be in drawing each small portion as he goes along, the larger forms are almost sure to be wrong, which in turn means that the smaller proportions are wrong too, in relation to one another. Sketch 1 shows the incorrect result that the employment of such a method is quite sure to bring. At first glance this drawing perhaps seems as correct and as interesting as does Sketch 4, made by the method which we are about to describe, but its chief fault lies in its proportions, for Sketch 4 gives the correct shape of the shoe as viewed from the one position from which it was drawn. If we start at "A" and compare the contour of the shoe in Sketch 1 with that in Sketch 4, bit by bit, we find them much the same. That is the danger of the system, it leads us astray almost without our knowing it. For when we get to drawing the sole and glance across at the heel we find the sole is too low, the sole and heel coming to a horizontal line, whereas at 4, the sole is higher. Compare the height of the toe in the two sketches with the table line at the back and note that this height in 1 is too low. Then as we go on up to the top we find the ankle much larger at 1 than at 4. Now in drawing a shoe such inaccuracies are not wholly disastrous but if the same method were applied to drawing the portrait of a person and as many mistakes crept in, a correct likeness would surely fail to materialize.

So instead of working in this way one should go at the whole matter very methodically. First of all, as soon as the object is in place and the easel and chair are in position, mark the location of the chair and the model stand on the floor in some way. A chalk mark around each leg of the easel and of the chair will do very well. Otherwise it is possible that some change will be made in their position and even the slightest shift is often enough to prove very confusing and cause inaccurate results. Then when you sit on the chair, sit right in the middle and keep erect. This is most important. For if you shift a bit to one side or the other or slump an inch or two, the object will present quite a different appearance (the change being particularly noticeable when one is drawing books and boxes and the like). So all the while that you are working hold the same position. As an aid to remaining stationary some instructors go so far as to have the student sight across some mark or point along the top of the object stand to some coinciding mark which can be made on the wall. Then the student, sighting from the first point to the second point, will establish his position and if he finds at any time that the points are not in line, one behind the other, he will know he is out of position. The same marks will prove useful to the instructor when he sits to give criticism, as they will enable him to view the objects from exactly the same point used by the student; in fact if he is of different height it may otherwise be very difficult for him to assume the correct position and unless he does so he cannot give the proper criticism.

As soon as the student has taken his position he should study the object for a few minutes before starting to draw. Notice the general shape of the mass, forgetting the detail but considering the simple form. Compare the height with the width. Is the mass taller than it is wide or is the opposite true? Is the general form square or round or oval or triangular? What are its most individual characteristics? Is it flat or rounded? Are its edges regular or irregular? Are the surfaces rough or smooth? When the subject has been analyzed with the greatest care the next step is to determine how large the drawing is to be and to locate the extreme limits of the object on the paper. If the subject is higher than its length it is best to place the paper in a vertical position so that the picture space will be in proportion to the object (or objects). Usually the size of the drawing will be less than that of the subject itself. Place a light mark towards the top of the paper to locate the extreme limit of the drawing in that direction, next another for the same purpose at the bottom, followed by others at the sides. These marks are shown at 1, 2, 3 and 4. Sketch 2, Figure 3. Next block out very lightly with a few sweeps of the pencil the larger proportions, the point barely touching the paper surface. Now set the drawing back near the objects. Compare. Is the height right in relation to the width? If it is hard for the student to determine this there is a test which may be applied here which is commonly used by artists, not only in object drawing, but in life drawing, nature sketching, etc.,—namely, thumb measurement.

Thumb Measurement. This test is known as thumb or pencil measurement. One eye is closed and the arm outstretched at full length towards the object, the hand grasping the sharpened end of a pencil held at right angles to the arm (more properly at right angles to the line of sight from the eye to the object). The pencil can then be used as a measure for comparing width and height or the length of one line with another (just as a ruler might be applied directly to the objects themselves), the thumb nail being allowed to slide along on the pencil until it marks any desired point. It is best to take the smaller dimension first and use it as a unit of measure for the larger. As the various proportions are compared in this way the corresponding dimensions on the drawing can be tested either by the eye or by laying the pencil directly upon them. If they are not relatively the same the differences will be obvious and corrections can be made. The value of this test is lost unless the pencil is kept at exactly the same distance from the eye,

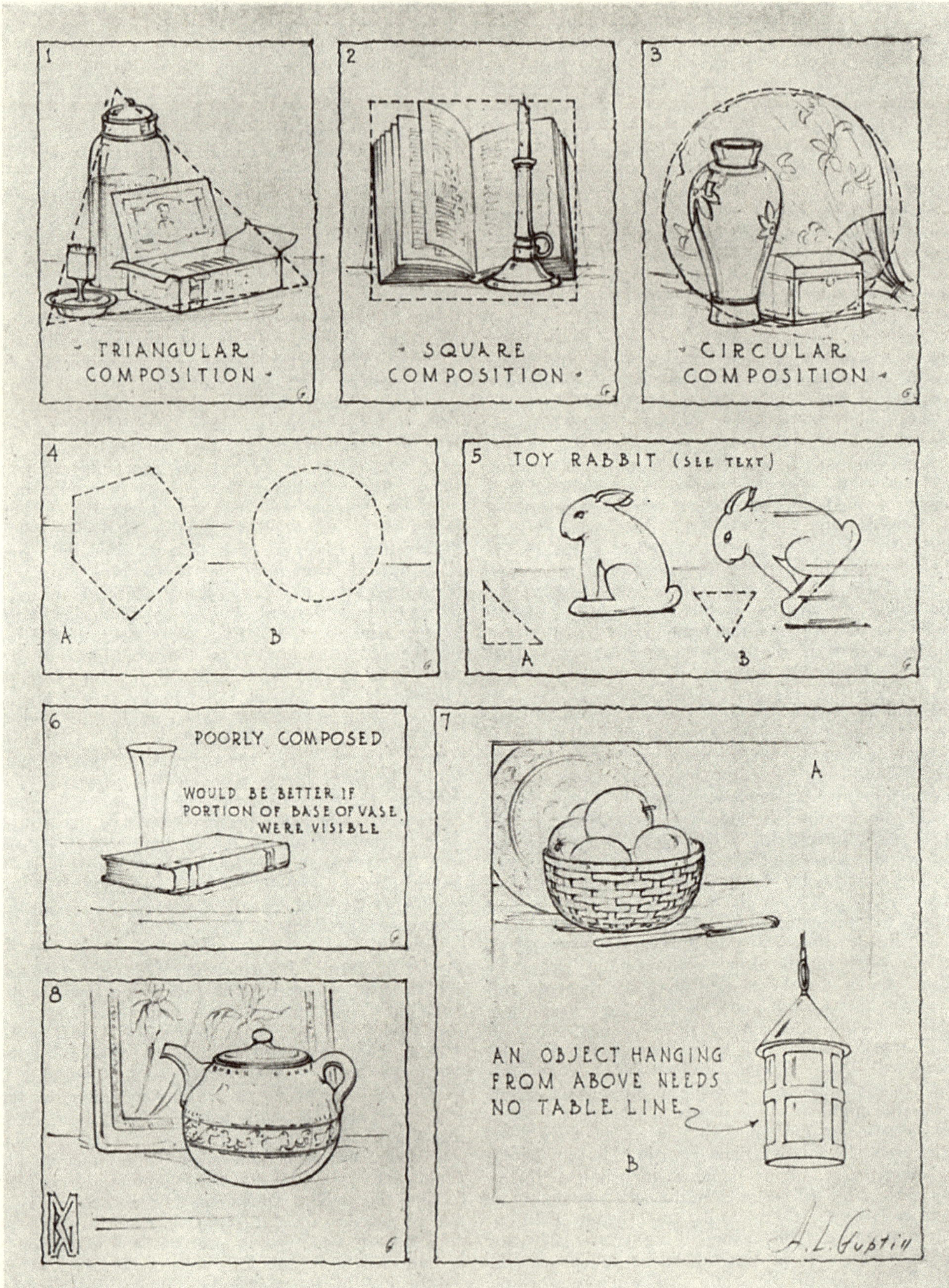

Figure 4. Offering Some Suggestions on Composition, for Use in Object Drawing.

so the elbow must not be bent or the body turned; therefore, keep the shoulders firm against the chair back. At best this method of measurement is useful merely as a test as it is only approximately accurate, so the student should not employ it too frequently but should, instead, learn to depend on the eye, especially for the smaller proportions. If the drawing is frequently set back near the object he will soon learn to see and correct his own mistakes. In making corrections it is not always necessary to erase the incorrect lines, for if they are very light the new strokes can be made a bit heavier and will be easily distinguished. If the wrong lines prove confusing, however, erase them by all means.

It is not enough to compare the height of the object with the width, or the relative lengths of different lines as is done by the thumb measurement, but the slant of the lines should be studied also, to make sure that they are pitched correctly. Hold the pencil at arm's length in such a position that it hides, or coincides with, some important line in the object,—then do the same with the same line on your drawing. Or hold the pencil vertically or horizontally and sight across it at some sloping line. Compare the angles formed by the various intersecting edges, too, and make corrections wherever necessary.

As soon as the main proportions have been properly established and the larger subdivisions blocked in and corrected in turn, we have completed the first stage of our work as illustrated in Sketch 2, Figure 3. At this time the larger characteristics or peculiarities of the subject should be clearly expressed.

In the second stage, pictured in Sketch 3, the larger parts are still further subdivided and more of the small details are added. In this stage the drawing should be set back several times, too, for comparison with the subject. Here, as in the first stage, it is not necessary to erase all the construction lines or incorrect strokes unless they prove distracting. This second stage expresses the smaller or minor characteristics, retaining at the same time most of the larger. At this point the drawing is really a construction diagram over which it is intended to work. For shaded problems drawings are often brought only to this second stage before the values are added.

Now, before going on to the third and last stage illustrated in Sketch 4, get away from the work entirely for a few moments. In fact it is advisable to rest the eye every fifteen minutes or half hour by doing something else. One can even save time in the end if he goes to the window and looks out, or walks about a bit, forgetting the drawing completely. After such relaxation mistakes will usually be evident at the first glance and the brief respite will make it easier to resume and hold the correct position. This is important. Every time you take your seat you must be sure you are viewing the object from the right spot for, as we have said, the slightest difference in position will make a marked difference in the appearance. In this last stage remove all wrong or unnecessary lines. Then partly erase with a soft or kneaded rubber or art gum the correct lines until they are barely visible, showing just enough to afford a guide for the final relining. A great deal of thought should be given to this last work for the final line should not be a perfect and mechanical one but should be expressive of the shapes and textures represented. For some parts the pencil will need a rather sharp point, —for others it must be quite blunt. The pressure should be varied, too, as certain lines need to be so light and delicate as to be barely visible while others will be bold and strong. In places gradation will take place from light to dark or from dark to light. No rules can be given for obtaining satisfactory results; it is a matter of taste and feeling. But draw thoughtfully and observe before you draw. This third stage expresses many of the smaller peculiarities of the subject, being a subdivision of the lines of the second stage, carefully refined, preserving, however, the big characteristics of the first stage.

Table Line. In order to make an object appear to rest on something solid instead of to merely hang in the air it is usually advisable to draw a horizontal line, often called a table line, which frequently represents the back of the object stand. Such a line gives some evidence of material support. If graded to light as it disappears behind the object or objects, it will add also to the feeling of detachment and space. This line should never be just half way between the margin lines. A second table line representing the front edge is sometimes advisable.

Margin Line. A freehand line drawn an inch or so from the edge of the paper all around, thus acting as a frame, adds to many compositions. Sometimes this line is carried only part way around as at "A," Sketch 7, Figure 4.

As soon as the sketch is completed, sign it with your name, date it, and put on approximately the amount of time required from start to finish. Then spray the drawing with fixatif, if you wish, or clip a piece of paper over it for protection and place it in your folio or some safe place for preservation. Don't make the mistake of destroying these early sketches, thinking they are of no value, for though they may not be beautiful pictures, it is often both interesting and instructive to look them over later, the comparison of a number of them done at different times showing just what progress has been or is being made.

When the sketch of the shoe is signed and laid to one side select another similar subject and draw it in just the same way, striving to truthfully express the individuality as before. Proportion the object as you see it and not as you think it ought to be—there will be time enough to use your originality later on, for remember it is truth we are seeking now, as a knowledge of truth is a foundation for all the rest to follow.

Marginal Notes or Sketches. When a subject has been selected for a drawing it is often advisable to make very quickly a tiny sketch of it on the margin of the paper before going ahead with the final drawing. A few minutes will do for such a marginal sketch or note, just time enough to allow for a blocking in of the larger proportions,—the main lines of construction. When making this tiny sketch one is observing the subject and acquainting himself with it as preparation for the larger work. Figure 5 shows a number of these trial sketches.

Time Sketches. As a means of acquiring skill to grasp and delineate the leading characteristics of an object quickly, time sketches are valuable. These are nothing more or less than drawings done in a limited time, which is often set in advance. For a simple subject to be left in outline, five minutes is allowed, or fifteen or whatever seems advisable (this depending partly on the subject and partly on the skill of the artist). As good a drawing is made as is possible within the limits set. In such work it is especially important to block out the main proportions first, adding as many of the smaller details as time permits. Then there is another sort of time sketch (often referred to as a time study) in which a drawing is pushed to completion as quickly as is possible and the required time noted. The speed and dexterity gained through all such training will prove indispensable when it comes to working from the living model or sketching moving objects. Animals, people, vehicles, boats and clouds do not always remain still to suit the convenience of the artist. Although all this "speed work" is essential and a pleasant change from the usual form of drawing where time is not a leading consideration, too much of it leads to carelessness and inaccuracy, being detrimental rather than beneficial. Alternate your problems, then, making some quick sketches and some painstaking studies, and progress should be steady and consistent.

Memory Drawings. When one has acquired a fair amount of skill doing the types of work described above, let him try a few drawings of the same objects from memory, for the ability to draw from memory or the imagination is a great asset to the artist. When you have finished a drawing of an old shoe, for instance, done from the object itself, leave the shoe in the same position on the object stand but hide it from view, temporarily, with a cardboard or sheet of paper and lay the study just finished to one side. Then on a fresh piece of paper try to draw the object from memory. When the main lines have been blocked out, look at the shoe again and compare your drawing. Hide the shoe once more, correct your drawing and push it nearer to completion and again compare it with the object itself. Go on in this way until the drawing is completed. Then try some quick sketches of the shoe from memory, looking at it first until you get a fresh impression of it in your mind, next drawing swiftly and freely, working for only the larger proportions and individual characteristics. This sort of work is of the greatest value in training one to observe carefully and to retain that which is observed. It may not be out of place to say that the student who looks at an object for a long time, forming sort of a photograph of it in the brain, is usually better able to memorize the form than is the student who glances back and forth constantly from the object to the drawing as he works, forgetting the impression of each line once it is represented on paper. This is only a general rule, however, and has many exceptions as some students have the power to really observe and memorize more at a glance than do others in several minutes.

Outline Drawing of Several Objects. The drawing of two or three objects instead of one is logically the next step. It involves few new principles, though the matter of arrangement or composition now needs our attention, for it is not always easy to choose and arrange several objects to form a satisfactory whole. The reader is referred to Chapter V, Part II, which offers suggestions of assistance at this time. Study what is said there about unity and balance. In order to obtain unity it is essential that the objects chosen should be well related by use,—objects which we find associated for one reason or another. We have already mentioned that such things as are frequently found in the cellar or shed or attic often have more character than objects which are merely pretty. Objects that grow are often interesting, especially if the forms are irregular.

It is not enough, however, to have things of a kind or things associated by use unless they also offer variety of form and surface and texture (and if drawings are to be shaded, variety in light and dark). Little pleasure would be taken in a sketch showing several objects of equal roundness grouped together, or several others based on cubes of like size. Instead we look for dissimilar forms. We look for dissimilar edges, too, some that are soft, broken or indefinite and some that are sharp and clean-cut. An ink bottle with stationery and pen might be pleasingly arranged, or a hat and gloves and grip, or any of the many combinations to which we have referred at the end of Chapter IV. An enormously large object fails to harmonize in size with something much smaller unless they are arranged with the utmost care and even then such a composition is difficult, so too much difference in form or size is as bad as too little. Thought and care must be used, then, in both the selection and arrangement.

When two or three objects have been chosen place them on the stand and shift them about until they compose satisfactorily. A view-finder such as described on page 95 in Part II will be of use in this work. It is often advisable at this point to make a little trial marginal sketch to see how the arrangement will look on paper. Then try some different grouping of these same objects. If some object does not seem to fit, substitute another for it. Make a new marginal sketch. Go through this process two or three times and the best arrangement will be found. Figure 5 shows at "A," "B" and "C" several such sketches blocked out as a study of grouping. Considering the fact that still life objects are always shown in repose and bearing in mind that a triangle resting on its base always seems to express this feeling as much as any shape, many compositions of objects conform to a triangular proportion. Sketches "A" 3, Figure 5 and "1," Figure 4, are triangular in general mass and are, therefore, restful. When a triangle is placed on its apex, however, or any of its vertices, the opposite is true. The two sketches of the little toy rabbit in Figure 4 are shown to illustrate this point. At "A" the toy seems stationary; at "B" it seems to be running off the paper, showing action rather than repose, and the latter effect is obtained mainly by the position of the triangular mass. Sketch 2, Figure

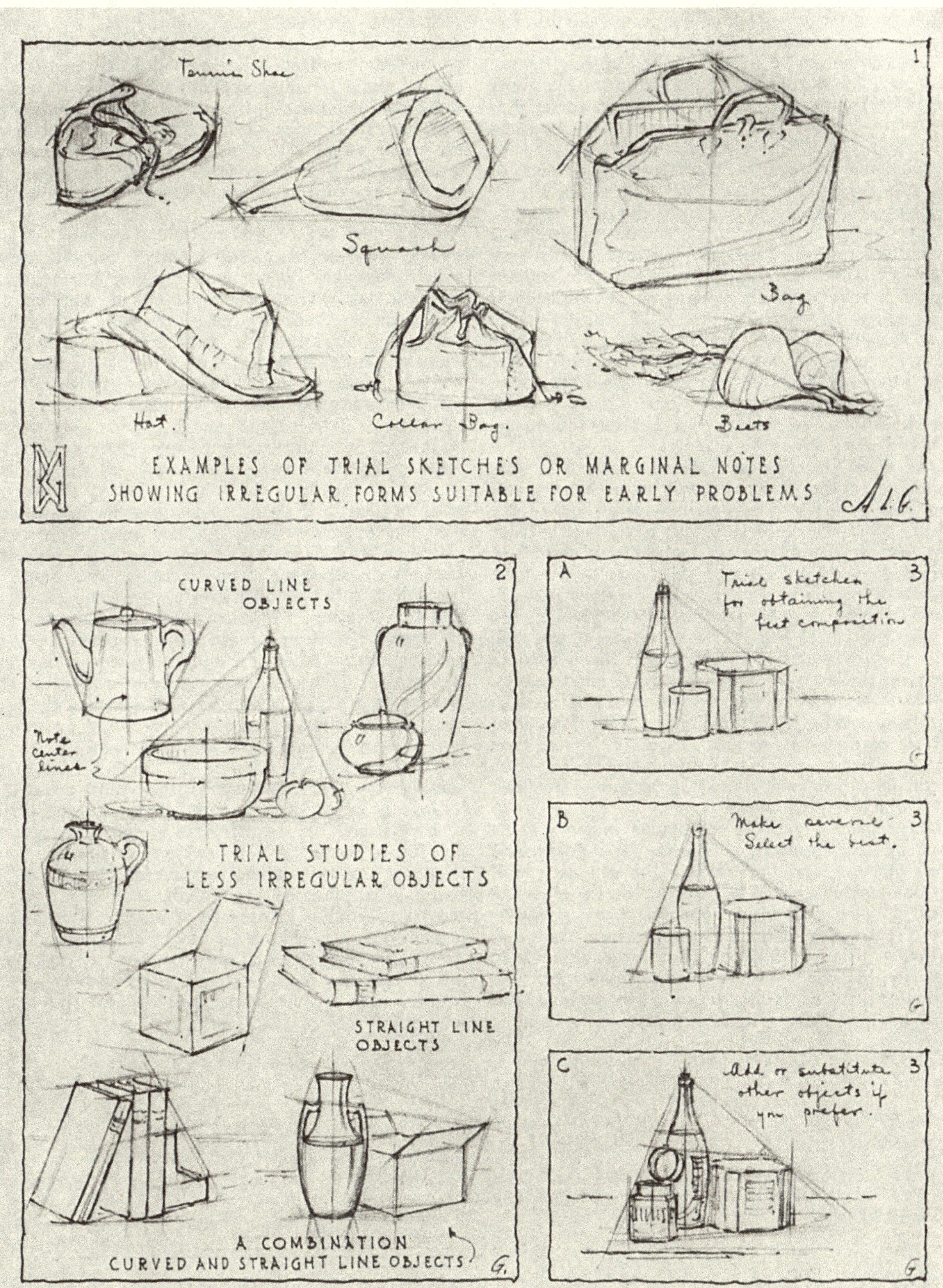

Figure 5. Illustrating Some of the Uses of Marginal Notes and Trial Sketches.

4 shows a square composition; Sketch 3 one which is circular. Rectangular compositions frequently seem restful; when using circular or oval masses care must be taken that the objects do not seem inclined to roll out of the picture. The more nearly horizontal the base is, the better, for if it is too round in form the objects give an impression of instability, seeming to have a desire to rock back and forth or fall over. Both the irregular mass at "A" and the circular mass at "B," Sketch 4, Figure 4, have an unstable appearance, the first seeming to rest on too sharp a point at the base. As a further illustration of the principle that objects seem more satisfactory if resting firmly on some support we call attention to the feeling of incompleteness and restlessness that one notices in objects which show no portion of their bases. The vase in Sketch 6 for instance, disappearing behind the book, gives us a sense of something lacking. Another point worth considering is that objects should not be placed so far below the eye that they seem to tip up, as this always seems disturbing.

The other sketches on Figures 4 and 5 explain themselves, and as experience will soon teach the student how to get a satisfactory arrangement of the objects, it seems needless to say more here. Once they are in position the outline drawing should be carried forward by gradual steps just as we have explained for single objects, using care that in each drawing there is good relative proportion between all the different objects. When it comes to the final stage greater variety of outline may be needed to represent the larger number of surfaces and textures.

When the student has learned to draw well in outline it is time for him to start his work in light and shade and this will be discussed in the next chapter. Before turning to this, however, attention should be called to a means of learning freehand work which is growing in favor.

Drawing on Glass. If one stands facing a china closet or dish cupboard which has glass doors, and closes one eye, and then takes a lithographic pencil or china marking pencil he can trace on the glass the form of some dish inside, and this tracing will be a correct drawing of the dish as it appears from that particular point. Of course, it is rather difficult to draw in this way well for it is no easy matter to maintain just the same position throughout the work, and neither is it easy unless one's hand is well trained, to follow the outline with sufficient accuracy to produce a perfect drawing. Nor would there be any particular advantage in being able to do so. But students who have difficulty in perceiving or understanding certain facts in perspective can sometimes find help by using glass, making sure that it is at right angles to the line of sight from the eye to the object. One can sketch on a window, drawing, or more correctly, tracing, buildings or trees or any objects in repose which may be visible through the glass.

Occasional use of this method may help the beginner, but there is another far more valuable use to which glass may be put as a drawing surface, and with this use every beginner should be familiar.

A sheet of glass is placed on the easel or drawing table as a substitute for the usual paper, with a sheet of paper or white cloth beneath so the lines will be plainly visible when they are drawn. Then the objects are sketched on the glass with the china marking or lithographic pencil just as they would be blocked in with pencil on paper. When the main proportions are drawn as accurately as the student is able to get them the glass is raised to such a position that the drawing comes between the eye and the objects drawn, using one eye only. When the glass has been shifted to just the proper position the lines of the drawing should coincide with those of the object, this method therefore being an excellent test for accuracy. If errors are noted, return the glass to the table and erase the incorrect lines with a damp cloth. Make the necessary corrections and test again in the same way as before. Repeat the process as often as is necessary; then when the proportions are right wash off the drawing and try a new one of a different subject.

There is perhaps no way in which the beginner can learn to see his own mistakes and acquire a knowledge of perspective foreshortening more easily than this, and the use of glass is especially recommended to those who are unable to secure the services of a teacher. The glass invented by Anson K. Cross is a patented one having a spirit level in the frame, and it is used in somewhat the manner described above. Many well-known artists and educators advise the use of this glass, which has been introduced into some of the leading schools of the country. A crayon is especially prepared for use with it.

Chapter IV.

OBJECT DRAWING IN LIGHT AND SHADE.

WE NOW come to the making of shaded drawings of objects in which we wish to represent the exact amount of light and shade found in the objects themselves.

In this work no outline will appear for we are to make as truthful a representation of the tones seen in nature as is possible with a lead pencil, and nature shows us no outline. A little observation will prove that we are able to tell one object from another by its light or shade or color. Most areas of light or of shade have clearly defined shapes which explain to us the forms of the objects and all these shapes seem to have boundaries where one tone stops against another. In elementary work and for certain types of explanatory drawings lines may be used to represent these contours or boundaries, the light and shade being omitted or merely suggested, and the eye is satisfied with the result. But the result is a wholly conventional one. Now we must stop thinking of lines but must think of tones instead. We must learn to think of the exact degrees of light and shade found in the objects and to represent them correctly. We must learn to translate the values of color into values of light and dark. For the value of a given color must be represented by a tone of gray which has the same degree of light and dark that the color has. These tones will vary all the way from the white of the paper to the pure black of the softest pencil. We have white tones, and light tones, and middle tones and dark tones and black tones, and though there are in reality many more than these five groups (in fact the tones in nature are innumerable), it is best in drawing to simplify the values, not attempting to break up a tone to express every slight difference in value which may be discovered on close inspection.

For the first problems it is suggested that some object or objects be chosen with little color, confining the choice to such things as are white or gray of black or of dull tints or shades, for with these the relative values can be seen quite easily. The student will be helped in judging a value if he compares it with white. So take a small sheet of white paper a few inches in size and compare it with the various objects to be drawn. Is there any tone in the objects as light as the paper? Select the lightest tone that you can find. You may discover two tones of different color but the same value. Now hold your sheet of white paper in bright light and compare its tone with that of similar paper in some darker place. Now take a piece of black paper and compare that with the objects. Is there any tone as dark as the black paper? Select the darkest tone that you can find in the objects. Now place the dark paper in brilliant light and compare its tone with that of another piece of the same paper in some darker place. Such experiments will prove that even though a surface is white it will not always appear white, and though black, its value will change in effect as it is moved from place to place—the less light a surface receives the darker its values will seem to be.

It should be remembered also, that if we have two objects of exactly the same form under the same lighting conditions, but one light and the other dark, the darker one will have darker values all over as its local color is added to the shade.

So the lightest value on the objects will usually be found in that one having the lightest local color and in that part of it receiving the brightest light (usually that portion nearest the window). There are some exceptions to this; highly glazed dark objects will sometimes reflect a value so light as to be the lightest in the whole composition, being even more brilliant than the paper on which the objects are being drawn.

When we intend to do shaded work in full values we prepare first of all an outline drawing just as was described in the preceding chapter, though the final accented outline is not needed,—instead the outline should be softened with an eraser until it becomes simply an inconspicuous guide for the work in shading. Next we lightly add the contours or boundaries of the most clearly defined areas of light or shade. Now we determine the lightest light and the darkest dark and make a comparison of the other values. Then sharpen a medium soft pencil to a fairly sharp point (a softer one may be necessary for extremely dark tones) and we are ready to begin. There are several methods of procedure open. Some teachers feel that it is best to first draw the darkest tone, then the next lighter, and so on up through the values, leaving the lights for the last. Others start with the lightest tones, next add the grays, working down to the darkest values. Really everything depends on the individuality of the artist and the type of drawing desired. Assuming that we are to make as correct a representation as we know how, it will probably be easiest to work over the whole drawing, not attempting to bring any one portion to the proper tone at first, but building up all the various tones gradually. In this way unity will be obtained. Set the drawing back frequently, and get away from it once in a while for a few minutes' rest.

We have already mentioned that as a rule such surfaces as are receiving the brightest light (which means they are turned directly towards the source of light), will be the brightest. If we have an object which is rounded in form (such as a cylinder) we will usually find it the lightest in value towards the window. Those portions which are turned away from the light will of course be rather dark. There may be a gradual change of tone from the lightest

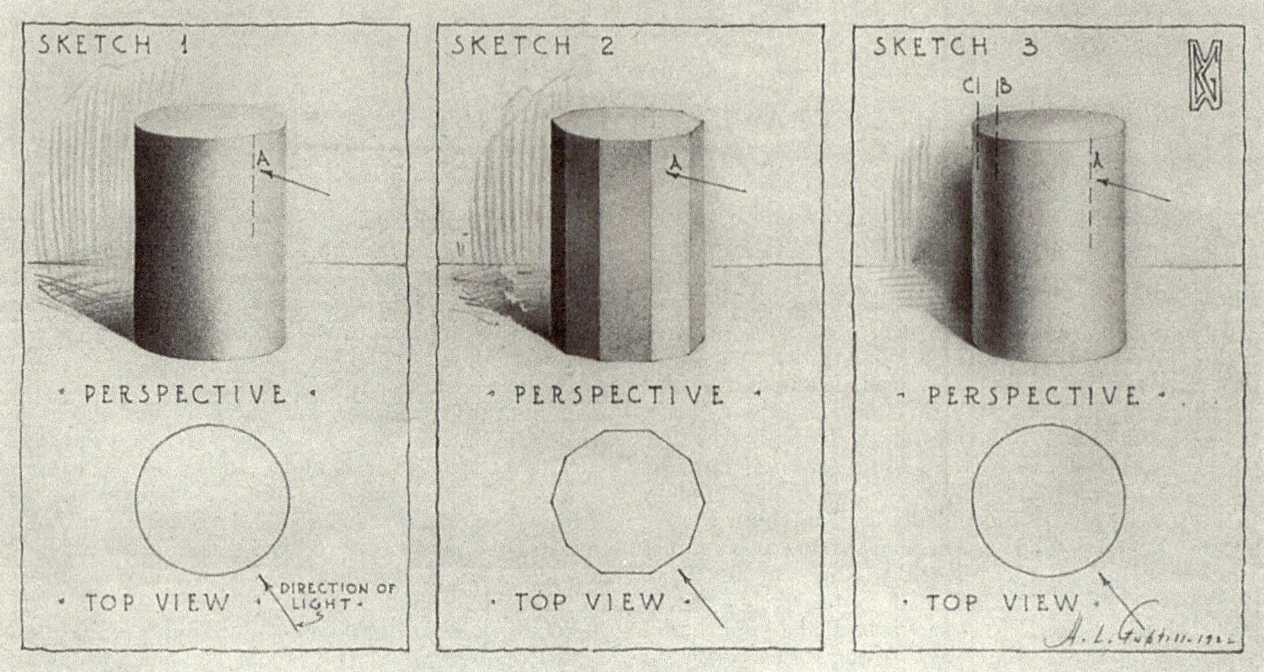

Figure 6. Modelling or Shading of Objects.

parts to the darkest,—see Sketch 1, Figure 6,—or if the object has a somewhat irregular surface such as the decagonal prism, shown at Sketch 2 in the same diagram, the values may change gradually plane by plane from the lightest plane to a slighter darker plane, to a still darker one, and so on around to a point on the back opposite the lightest plane. It is not always true, however, that the darkest plane or portion of curved surface will be the one farthest from the source of light, for there is sometimes a certain amount of illumination from some other direction, and even if there is not, there are frequently rays of light reflected onto the parts in shade or shadow, thereby neutralizing the otherwise dark values. Sketches 1 and 3, Figure 6, will serve to illustrate this point (the reader is referred also to Chapter VI, Part II, on graded tones). At "1" the brightest value is on that portion of the cylinder receiving the strongest rays of light. Then as the surface curves more and more away from the source of illumination the darker it gets. At "3" a different condition exists. The brightest part of the surface is at "A" as in "1"; then the tone gradually darkens until it reaches "B," which is the darkest. Then at "C" a lighter value is found, caused by the reflection of light rays from some other object.

Planes. Now few objects which we draw have surfaces curving as gradually as those of the cylinder just illustrated or planes so mechanically arranged as those of the prism. More often the objects are so irregular that the light and shade varies from part to part; there may be many portions turned towards the light and many turned more or less away. These various areas of light and shade which are seen in an object, caused by its irregular form and its position in relation to the source of light, are usually referred to as "planes," even though they do not fully meet the geometric definition of the word.

Edges of Planes. In some irregular objects there is quite a definite line of demarkation between the various planes. In gradually curving objects there is no such line—the tone simply grades as we have noted in the case of the cylinder, with no sudden, perceptible change in value. In most objects both of these two conditions exist; in parts the planes seem quite definite, in others they merge together. There is nothing more important than to draw these edges correctly, sharpening them or losing them as the case may be. In the same way there is great difference in the edges of the objects themselves as they come in contrast with the background or with other objects. Some stand out in sharp relief, others are indistinct. Some dark objects become so lost in shadow on their shade side that it is hard to distinguish the form, hence it should not be over-accented in the drawing.

Shadows. Shadows out-of-doors and shadows in-doors are entirely different in their appearance. In-doors they are softer and more indefinite;—whereas some edges of shadows seem sharp, many are almost lost. Hold the end of your pencil on a sheet of paper and the shadow will seem sharpest right at the point of intersection. Bear this in mind when shading. Correctly drawn shadows have much to do with the effect of modelling or projection. Needless to say, unless the objects are arranged with care and the whole group well lighted the shadows may prove very distracting; considerable experimenting will be necessary to compose a group to the best advantage. If light is coming from several sources the shadows will surely be unfortunate, for the complex forms cast in different directions will tend to restlessness and confusion.

Now when your drawing seems finished set it back for a final comparison. Have you the exact degrees of light and dark in the drawing as in the

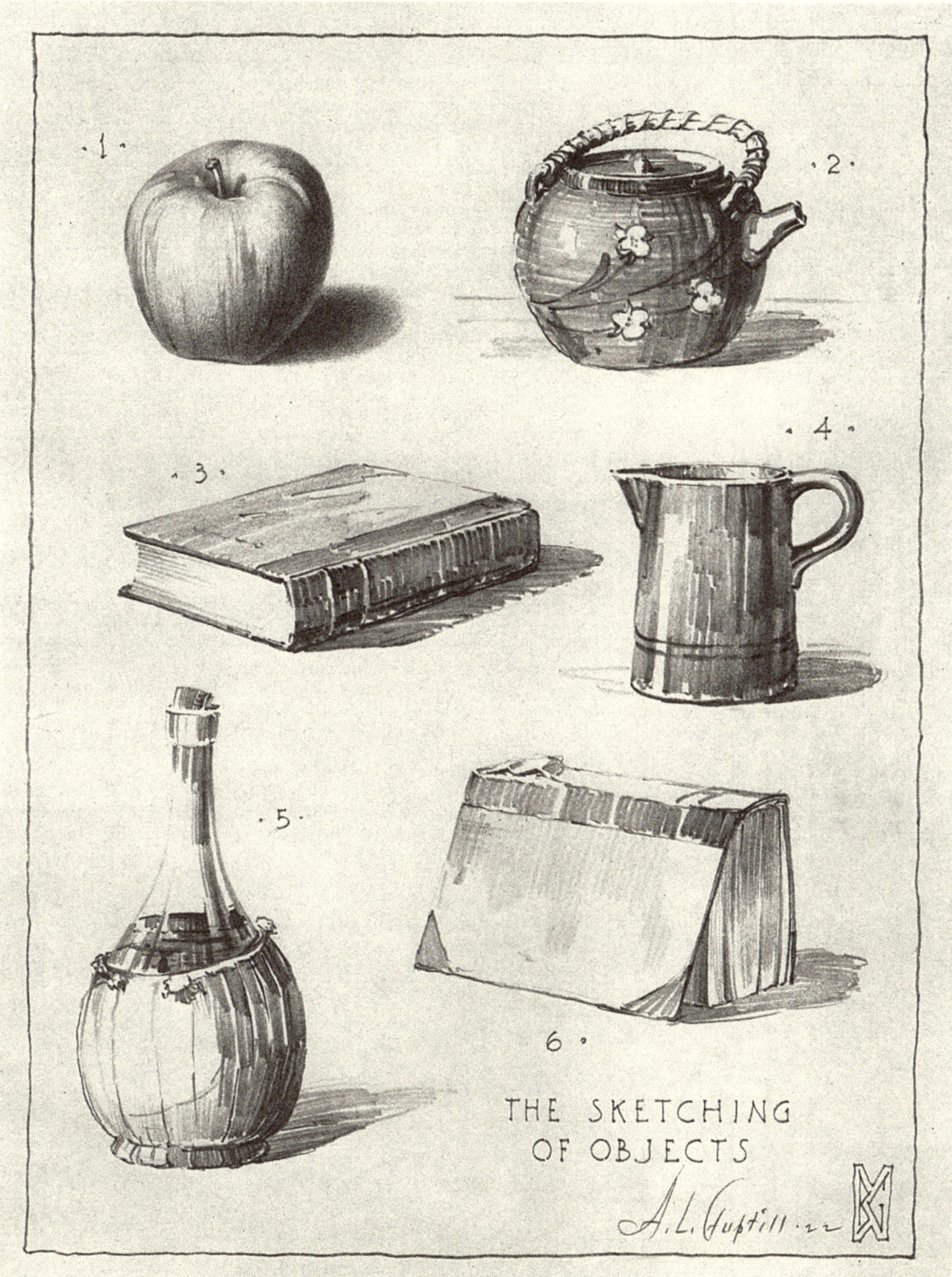

Figure 7. Illustrating the Representation of Objects in Light and Shade.

objects themselves? Have you the correct degrees of sharpness and softness in the edges? Is there too much dark on one side or at the bottom or the top, or does the whole hold together nicely? Are the tones clear and transparent, or heavy and dead? Have you succeeded in expressing space, depth, weight, texture? Have you practiced economy of tone or is the drawing confusing because of too many different values? Have you lost the outline as you should in drawing in light and shade, remembering that the mere contrast of tones as in nature will bring out what you wish to express?

Now partly close the eyes and study your drawing reduced to its simplest elements. Do the nearer parts seem to come forward properly and the farther parts to go back? If not, force the nearer parts a bit and sacrifice the distant portions. We must get a feeling of projection and distance. Is there a complexity of high light? If so, tone down all lights a bit, leaving one to be the strongest of them all, for a picture is better with one lightest light and one darkest dark. Too much emphasis cannot be attached to the importance of studying the objects drawn and the drawing itself through partly closed eyes, not only when it is completed but from time to time as the work progresses. For in this way one shuts out all but the essentials, and hence is not led into complication and restlessness of effect.

Now we have said little about the kind of stroke to be used for this work, for it is better that there be no definite line showing. The tone should be built up by going over and over it with a comparatively sharp point, merging the various lines together until they are lost. Naturally the textures represented make a difference in the manner of working, but to make such studies of the greatest value each tone should be as nearly perfect as possible, the student striving for transparency and luminosity. The drawing of the apple at 1, Figure 7, was done in this manner. Sometimes tones are rubbed smooth with the finger or with a stump, but this method has little to commend it for this class of work.

There is another type of shaded still life drawing, however, which is more sketchily done, where a few strokes of the pencil are used to express a great deal. This type of work has been illustrated in Figure 7 which shows separate strokes in many places rather than continuous tone. The student should practice this kind of work, too, so drawing the strokes as to best express the surfaces represented, using some fine and some broad lines. In line work the strokes should as a rule follow the direction of the surface.

In types of work sometimes seen the still life becomes a motif for a decorative scheme or combinations of tone and outline are found, or washes of color are added to the pencilling, but there are many elementary text books which show examples of such work, therefore the interested student can find a great deal of material to help him, if he desires to do so. The student's drawings opposite illustrate some of these possibilities for decorative work and on page 23 is an excellent example of a type of drawing frequently made in which a few very dark, crisp accents are added to a clean-cut outline. Notice the direct and economical way in which the various materials are suggested, and the commendable simplicity of the whole.

Objects for Drawing—Objects having distinct character are best as subjects for drawings. Quaint and old-fashioned things are particularly interesting, or things which are worn or broken. Rummage the attic or stable or cellar. Look in the garage or garden. Even the kitchen and laundry will yield many simple and useful implements and utensils excellent for our purpose. The following list may guide the student in his search.

Objects for elementary or comparatively small compositions: Garden trowel and flower pots; hammer, box of nails; screwdriver and screws; basket

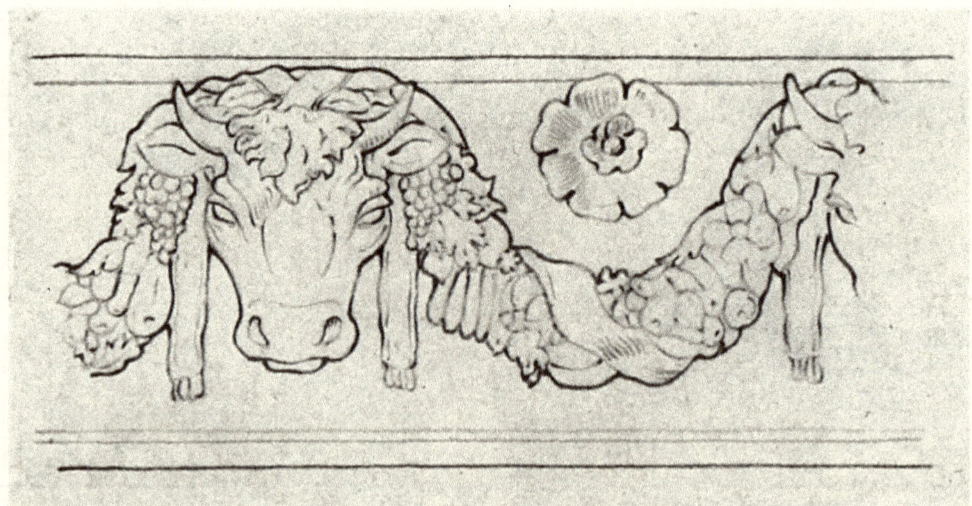

Courtesy of Pratt Institute *Ethel M. Weir*

Accented Outline Drawing by Student at Pratt Institute.

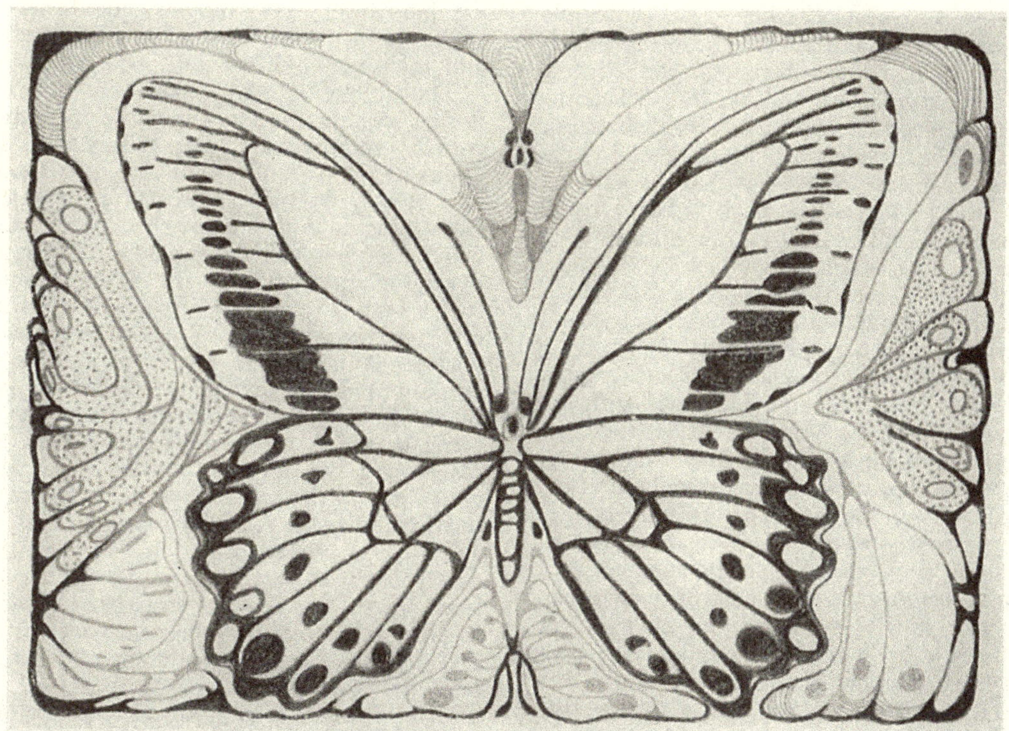

Courtesy of Pratt Institute *A. Mershon*

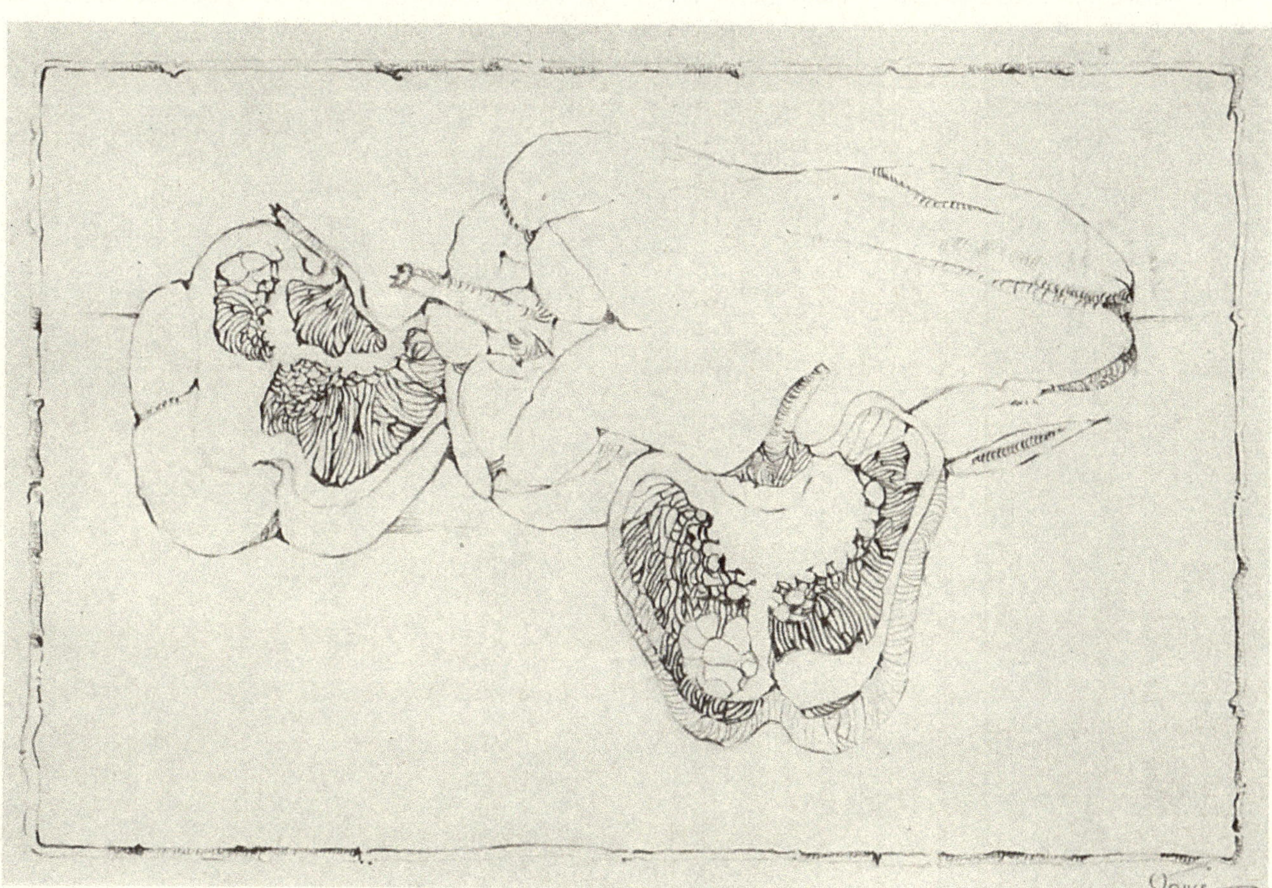

Courtesy of Pratt Institute *Marjorie House*

DRAWINGS BY STUDENTS AT PRATT INSTITUTE

of clothespins, coil of clothesline; pail with cloth hanging over side, scrub brush and scouring powder; old battered coalhod; tack hammer, box of tacks, etc.; flatirons with stand and holder; whet stone with knife and piece of wood half whittled; sponge, soap and basin of water; dust pan and brush, feather duster; ice-cream freezer, bag of salt, etc.

Among larger objects we have: Snow shovel, rubber boots and mittens; shovel and tongs; wash tubs on bench with basket of clothes; wheelbarrow, rake and basket; broken box with axe; watering pot, trowel, broken flower pots; hat and coat on nail; old trunk partly opened, etc.; old hats and hatboxes; umbrellas in various positions, opened, closed and half closed; brooms and mops with dustpans and pails; chopping block, sticks of wood, axe; basket of kindlings and hatchet; old churn with chair beside it; baseball bat, mitt and ball.

Books can always be arranged effectively, piled up, tumbled down, spread out, open or closed.

Book, candle stick and matches; old novel partly opened, apple between leaves; half open newspaper with books; book with reading glass or with spectacles; ink bottle with copy book and pen; books, paper weight, half-open letter and envelope.

Then there are other objects which can be found around the house, such things as are in every-day use: Glove box and gloves; collar bag; photograph in frame, bowl of flowers; cribbage board and cards; pipe, tobacco jar, matches, etc.; opera glasses, bag and program; slippers, gloves and fan; hats or caps; hat, grip and gloves; shaving mug, brush, razor, etc.; basket or bag with sewing or knitting; brush, comb and mirror; children's toys and dolls.

The following suggestions are for the uses of fruits, vegetables, etc. Such combinations are of course innumerable: Paper bag with fruit, vegetables or candy falling out and at the side; bananas half peeled on plate with knife; lemons, squeezer, glass, sugar and spoon; box of sardines, sliced lemons and plate of crackers; cocoanut, broken open; bunches of beets or carrots or similar vegetables with tops; several apples, one cut in half, another partly pared; tea pot, tea cups, plate of sandwiches; fruit bowl or basket filled with fruit; pineapple with knife and plate; squash or pumpkin cut open, partly sliced; pumpkin made into jack-o-lantern; bread on plate, some sliced, with knife; salad plate with lobster and lettuce, mayonnaise bowl, spoon and fork; roast of meat on platter with carving knife; plate of beans, bottle catsup, napkin; sugar bowl, cubes of sugar, sugar tongs; box of candy open or partly open; crackers in box or bag, bowl of milk, spoon; strawberries or grapes in basket; bunches of grapes with bit of vine, leaves, and tendrils; apples, pears or peaches hanging on branches with leaves; heads of lettuce, cauliflower and bunches of celery; sliced meat on platter, garnished with parsley. And bowls and vases of flowers are always good, too, or branches of leaves or berries. For more elaborate studies, views of room corners or portions of a yard or street offer many possibilities.

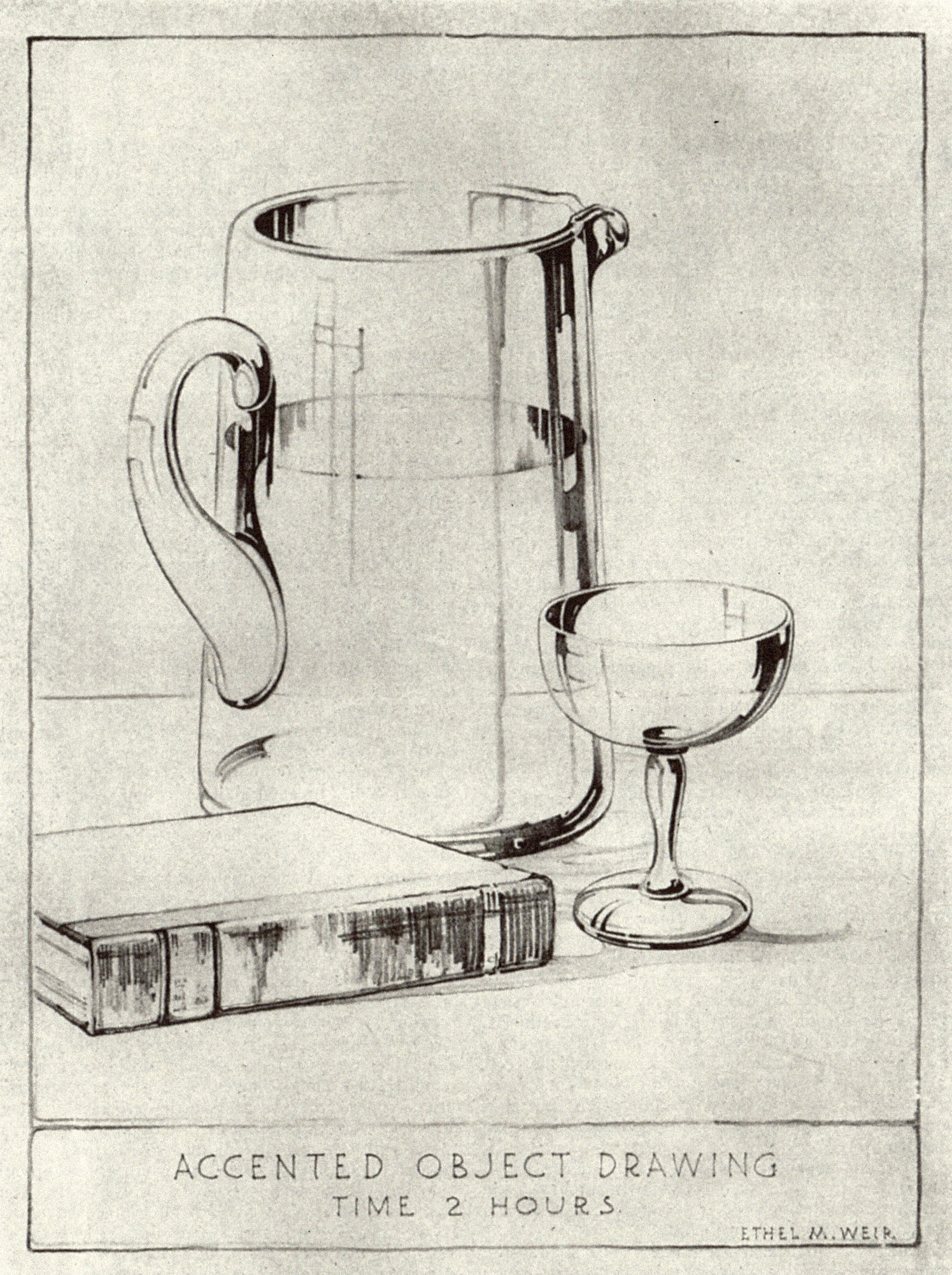

OBJECT DRAWING BY ETHEL M. WEIR

Chapter V.

FREE-HAND PERSPECTIVE.

OBJECTS usually appear different in shape from what we know them to be, or, in other words, the appearance seems contrary to the facts which we know regarding these objects. We are aware, for instance, that a cube has six equal faces and that each of them is square. If we draw six squares, however, or a smaller number, combining them in any and every possible way, the final result will certainly not give us the same impression as the cube itself. We also know that the top of a right cylinder is a circle, yet it is seldom indeed that we see a cylinder in such a position that the top appears as a true circle. We think of it as a circle simply because we know it to be one; not because it seems really circular; for unless we look straight at the end of the cylinder it appears elliptical or even as a straight line.

So when we are in doubt as to how things should be drawn in order to have them look right, we not only study the things themselves but we also turn to the science of perspective which gives us principles that are helpful to us in drawing objects correctly, not as they actually are, but as they appear from the point from which they are viewed. Free-hand perspective trains us especially in the application of these principles to the practical problems of free-hand sketching.

For the purpose of this book it seems desirable to discuss very briefly only a few of the more important of these principles. Nothing short of a complete volume could do justice to the subject, and as there are already many excellent works available it seems needless to duplicate here that which has already been so successfully and completely handled elsewhere. The reader who really desires to thoroughly master the subject should read some such book as "Free-hand Perspective and Sketching" by Dora Miriam Norton, not forgetting, however, that the reading itself will do little good unless sketches are made to illustrate each point as the student goes along. And one should learn to be observing of the perspective appearance of objects all about him; if he is studying circles and ellipses, let him take notice of every circular arch, or clock face, or barrel, or other similar form which he sees.

Now fundamentally these principles which have to do with the appearance of things are few, and among them the following are perhaps the most important.

First, the apparent size of an object decreases in proportion to its distance from an imaginary plane which passes through the eye at right angles to the direction in which one is looking.

Second, a surface appears in its true shape only when parallel to this plane, or, in other words, when at right angles to the line of sight from eye to surface.

This first principle can be easily tested if one stands close to a window and looks straight through it;—an entire building in the distance will appear only a few inches in size on a single pane of glass. If there are several objects of equal size at varying distances from the eye it will be noticed that the nearest one appears to be the largest and the others seem smaller and smaller in proportion to their distance away.

By way of illustration of the second principle it will be easy for the student to demonstrate for himself that when a surface (take a circular end of a cylinder, for example) is not so placed as to be at right angles to the line of sight it appears smaller in one dimension because of being turned away, and the farther it is turned the smaller this dimension seems, until when turned so far as to cause the surface to coincide with the direction of sight it will appear simply as a line. This apparent change of shape is called foreshortening.

Now in order to give a working knowledge of the application of these principles in the quickest and most direct way we will discuss the appearance and methods of representation of a few typical geometric forms. Elsewhere we have explained that once the simple forms are understood it will not be difficult to do objects which are more complex, applying exactly the same principles.

The Horizon Line or Eye Level—This is an imaginary horizontal line at the level of the eye. In object drawing or other small work, the latter term is the more commonly used; for buildings and outdoor work in general, the former is customary.

The appearance of any object will vary according to whether it is at or above or below the eye level and to the right or in front or to the left of the spectator. To observe just what variation does take place in the appearance of objects as viewed from various points, it is advisable for the student before doing any drawing, to take simple things and to hold them in different positions, noticing just how they look when moved from place to place, nearer or farther from the eye and higher or lower in relation to the horizon line.

The Sphere—Take, for example, a sphere, or an apple or orange or some other object of spherical form. When held above the eye it appears as a circle,—below the eye and at the eye level its contour is practically the same. If it is a true sphere there will not be the slightest variation. If we take an apple, however, with the stem at the top, and hold it level but below the eye, not only is the stem visible but so is a portion of the surface beyond it. If we raise it until the top of the apple is at the height of the eye, still holding it level, the stem is still seen but none of the surface beyond is visible. A bit of the "blossom" below may now show. As we raise it above the eye the stem will gradually disappear as will a portion of the top surface, and as

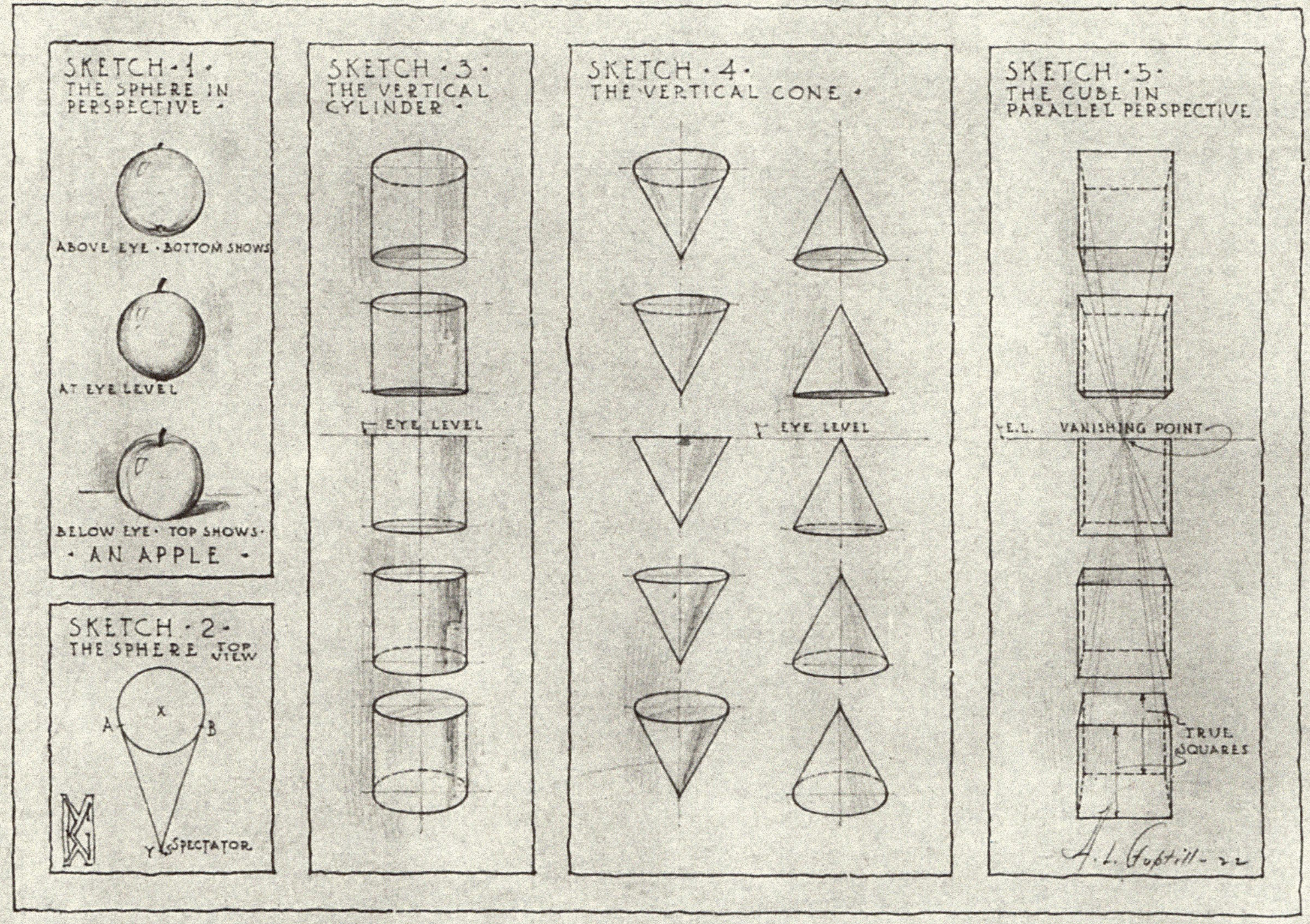

Figure 8. Illustrating Perspective Principles.

this is lost to view more of the lower part will become visible, so if it is held some distance above the eye we will see the entire "blossom" and the surface beyond. In other words, whereas a sphere remains the same in profile regardless of its position, we see different portions of its surface as it is moved up and down, and the same is true if it is shifted to the right or to the left, or spun round and round. Sketch 1, Figure 8, illustrates this point. Study this and then draw several objects of spherical form placed in a variety of positions.

Attention should be called to the fact that we seldom see half way around a sphere. Sketch 2 perhaps explains this more clearly. If "X" represents the top view of the sphere and "Y" the position of the spectator, the lines drawn from "Y" tangent to the sphere, mark at "A" and "B" the limits of the visible portion of the sphere at the plane of its greatest circumference. The larger the sphere or the closer the spectator the smaller this distance becomes.

The Cylinder, Vertical—Now take a right cylinder and hold it vertically, and with one eye closed raise it until the top is level with the other eye. In this position the top circle will appear as a straight line, the circular plane being so greatly foreshortened that only its edge can be seen. Now lower it a bit. The circular top is now visible but still so much foreshortened that it is elliptical instead of circular in appearance. Lower it still farther and the rounder the ellipse becomes. Now just as this top ellipse appears rounder as it is dropped below the eye, it is evident that if the bottom of the cylinder could be fully seen it would appear still rounder than the top, as it is even farther below the eye. Experience will prove that the degree of roundness of the ellipse will be in proportion to its distance below the eye. Next raise the cylinder vertically until the lower end is at the eye level; this now appears as a straight line just as did the top end before. Raise it still higher and the bottom comes in sight as an ellipse, the top of the cylinder being now hidden. And the higher the cylinder is raised, the rounder the ellipse of the bottom becomes, its fullness being in proportion to its distance above the eye level. If the cylinder is lowered until the bottom and top are both equi-distant from the eye level both will be invisible but the visible edges of each will have like curvature, and if the cylinder were transparent so both the top and bottom could be seen, the ellipses representing both would be identical in size and shape, as both circles are the same distance from the level of the eye.

Transparent cylinders of glass are convenient for such experiments or the student can make one of celluloid or some similar material.

What is true of the perspective appearance of the top or bottom of a cylinder is true of any circle, and if the student wishes to prove this, let him cut a circle from a sheet of heavy paper or cardboard and experiment with this. When held horizontally and level with the eye does it not look like a straight line? And when raised above or dropped below the eye level does it not appear as an ellipse? Note the apparent change in roundness of this ellipse and in the length of its short axis as the circle is raised or lowered. Only the long axis will appear of the same proportionate length regardless of the position of the circle. Is it not true, also, that when a circle appears as an ellipse the ellipse is always perfectly symmetrical about its long and short axis lines, and is it not divided by these axis lines into four quarters which appear exactly equal?

Go back to the cylinder again and see if this, too, does not, when held vertically, appear symmetrical about a vertical central axis line at all times, every element of the cylindrical surface being vertical also? As in the case of the sphere we seldom see half way around the circumference; hence less than one-half of the cylindrical surface is visible at any one time.

Now try a number of sketches of the vertical cylinder and the horizontal circle as viewed from different positions (Sketch 3 shows a few). Practice drawing ellipses, too, until you can do them well; this is no easy matter.

The tipped or horizontal cylinder will be discussed later.

The Vertical Cone—While we still have the horizontal circle in mind let us consider the right circular cone placed vertically. Sketch 4 shows the cone in this position. It will be seen that the appearance of the circle is the same as in the case of the cylinder. Also that if the apex of the cone is at the top and the cone below the eye, we can see more than half way around the conical surface. If raised above the eye we see less than half way around. And if the cone is inverted the opposite is true. Note also that a right circular cone will always appear symmetrical, the long axis of the ellipse of the base being at right angles to the axis of the cone. Make several drawings of the vertical cone;—the horizontal or tipped cone will be discussed later.

The Cube in Parallel Perspective—We now turn to the cube. Hold it with the top at the eye level and the nearer face at right angles to the line of sight so it is seen in its true shape. Only one face of the cube is visible now, and that appears as a square. Lower the cube a few inches and the top appears, greatly foreshortened. The farther horizontal edge, being a greater distance away than the nearer one, seems the shorter of the two. The parallel receding edges of the top seem to slant. If these slanting edges were continued indefinitely they would appear to meet at a point and that point would be on the eye level. Lower the cube a few inches farther. The top now appears wider and the two receding edges have still greater slant. If continued they would still meet at a point on the eye level, the same one as before. The front face still appears square. Now raise the cube above the eye, still holding it vertical. The top goes out of sight and the bottom becomes visible. The front face looks square as before. Now the higher the cube is raised the more the bottom shows. The receding lines now seem to slant downward towards the eye level; if continued they would meet the very same point on the eye level as when the cube was below the eye.

Now in order to convince yourself that these same facts are true of other objects, take a box or any form similar to the cube, and study it in various horizontal positions above and below the eye, keeping the nearest vertical plane so turned that it is always seen in its true shape. When the object is below the eye do not the horizontal receding lines seem to slant upward with an appearance of convergence? And when the object is above the eye do not these horizontal receding lines seem to slope downward in the same way? And whether above or below the eye is it not true that all the horizontal surfaces appear to slope towards the eye level as they recede? It is interesting to note as mentioned above that such parallel edges as recede would, if continued far enough, appear to converge towards the same point on the eye level, exactly opposite the eye itself, this being termed the vanishing point for that set of edges. Such edges as do not recede have, of course, no appearance of convergence and hence no vanishing point.

All the time that you are studying the object ask yourself such questions as the following, for it is by personal observation and analysis that one can best gain a knowledge of perspective appearances. Is it true that every set of parallel receding horizontal lines has a common vanishing point of its own? And that of two parallel lines of same length which do not recede the one nearest the spectator appears the longer? And that any parallel edges which are at right angles to the line of sight actually appear parallel?

When an object is placed like the cube or box which we have mentioned, so its principal face is at right angles to the line of sight from the eye, we say that it is viewed in parallel perspective. Sketch 5 shows cubes in parallel perspective in various relations to the eye level.

The Cube in Angular Perspective—We now purpose to turn the cube into a new position, placing it in a horizontal manner below the eye and turned at an angle with all four of the edges of the top receding. None of the edges now appears horizontal. Now sketch the top of the cube in this position. It will be noticed that if the cube is so turned as to make equal angles with the line of sight as at "A," Sketch 6, Figure 9, we will see equal portions of the lines marked "a" and "b" and they will have equal slant. The same will be true of "c" and "d." Now if we turn the cube so that it makes unequal angles with the line of sight, as at "B," Sketch 6, we find that line "a" will seem shorter and line "b" longer than before.

Now to more firmly fix these thoughts in your mind shift the cube from place to place and question yourself in this way. If two edges of the square top of the cube recede from you at unequal angles, which of the two appears the longer? Which the more nearly horizontal? And considering the complete cube, turned at an angle so that two or more of its faces are visible, can any one of these appear in its true shape? Will all parallel edges receding towards the left appear to converge or vanish to one point and those towards the right to another? And if so will these points be on the eye level?

Continue your analysis in this thorough way and you will observe many interesting things. You will see that such edges of the cube as are truly vertical appear so and hence should be drawn so. You will notice that the nearest vertical edge will be the longest and that the others will decrease in length as they get farther away.

When a cube or other object is so placed that no surface is seen in its true shape, or that its principal planes are at other than a right angle with the line of sight, it is said to be in angular perspective. As it is rather difficult for the beginner to draw in angular perspective well, he should work for some time from a cube itself, placing it in different positions above and below the eye. In drawing such an object it is usually advisable to actually locate and draw a line representing the level of the eye on the paper, making sure that the various receding lines are converging to the proper vanishing points on this eye level. It is sometimes wise in these early problems to actually continue such receding lines indefinitely, allowing them to meet at the proper points, as at "C" and "D," Sketch 6. As an aid in testing for correct drawing of a cube in angular perspective it is occasionally helpful to draw diagonal lines on the top foreshortened square as we have done with the dotted lines at "A" and "B," Sketch 6. At "A" with the cube turned at equal angles, the long diagonal is horizontal, the short perpendicular. Let the cube be swung around as at "B," however, and the diagonals immediately tip. Point "g" drops lower than "e," and "h" moves to the right of "f" instead of remaining above it. If the vertical faces are turned at unequal angles, then, we not only see more of one than of the other but the diagonals of the top plane will always be tipped; never vertical or horizontal. Rules of this sort are of comparatively little help, however; the thing that counts in all these objects is the observation and practice from the things themselves.

The Cylinder, Not Vertical—Now that the drawing of the cube has given one a little knowledge of receding lines, it is well to go back to a consideration of the cylinder, only this time we will not place it vertically. Hold it, instead, in a horizontal position at the level of the eye (closing one eye) and turn it so that the circular end appears in its true shape. In this position nothing is seen but the end. If we then swing it or tip it so that the end and some of the curved surface are both visible, the end will appear as an ellipse. The less of the curved surface shows, the rounder this ellipse will be. Then swing the cylinder until one end appears a straight line. In this position the other end is invisible but if the cylinder were transparent it would be found that this end would appear as an ellipse. Study the cylinder in all sorts of positions above and below the eye, making observations of this sort. Such study and comparison will prove that the right cylinder, regardless of position, will always appear symmetrical about its long axis line; that the long diameters of the ellipses forming the ends will be at right angles to the axis of the cylinder. One will notice, too, that it is never possible to see quite half way around the cylindrical surface. And when the farther end of the horizontal or tipped cylinder is a greater distance from the eye than the nearer end it will appear smaller, which means in turn that the elements of the cylindrical surface will appear to converge, and these elements being all parallel lines they will seem to vanish towards a point. If the cylinder is placed horizontally this point will be on the eye level; if tipped in some other position the point will be above or below the eye. To this same vanishing point the axis of the cylinder will also recede if produced. And it will be noticed, too, that regardless of the placing of the cylinder those elements of the surface which form the straight boundaries will appear tangent to the curves of the bases. At "A," Sketch 7, the cylinder has been drawn within a square prism. To do so gives one a knowledge of the relationship between objects based on the square and the circle.

The Cone, Tipped—And if we turn to the cone once more for further consideration and look directly at its apex we will find that it appears as a true circle. And when so held that its base becomes a straight line it has the contour of a triangle. The visible curved surface of a cone may range from all to none. The bounding elements of the cone are always represented by straight lines tangent to the ellipse which represents the base. And the right cone, like the cylinder, will always appear symmetrical, being divided by its long axis into two equal parts.

Study the little sketches of cylinders and cones in Sketch 7, Figure 9. Then make many of your own.

Now in just the same way consider other geometric forms, such as the triangular prism placed vertically and horizontally, and the pyramid and the hexagonal prism in various positions. Though our space does not permit full discussion of these here, it seems essential to call attention to a few facts in regard to the appearance of the triangle, the hexagon, etc. But first, let us say another word or two about the square. We have drawn a square at Sketch 8 and have crossed its diagonals. Doing this locates the true center of the square "o" as it appears in perspective. It seems more than half way back, for the farther half of the square, being a greater distance from the eye than the first half, seems smaller. For the same reason, line "bo" seems longer than "od," though in top view we know they would be equal. This will perhaps make more clear the fact that equal distances on any receding line seem unequal, the farther seeming the shorter. Now suppose that at the end of this square we draw a triangle, as at "B," Sketch 8, locating its apex by drawing a line horizontally from center "o" to line "bc," erecting a vertical altitude at the point of intersection "f,". choosing point "e" arbitrarily on the altitude and then drawing "ec" and "eb." This triangle illustrates the truth that the apex of a vertical isosceles or equilateral triangle having a horizontal base appears in a vertical line erected in the perspective center of the base. As it is easier to judge the correct proportion of a square in perspective than of a triangle, a square is sometimes drawn first as a guide as in Sketch 9. At Sketch 10 we have shown a hexagon. It will be noticed at "A" that the two short diagonals "bf" and "ce" and the long diagonals "be" and "cf" divide long diagonal "ad" into four equal parts. For in a correct drawing of a hexagon it is always true that any long diagonal when intersected by two short and one long diagonals will be divided into four equal parts. When a hexagon is sketched in parallel perspective as at "B" they all appear equal. Now in drawing polygons, especially those which are regular such as the hexagon just mentioned, it is often easiest to first draw an ellipse representing a circumscribed circle. In drawing the decagonal prism in Figure 6, for instance, an ellipse was first drawn just as for the cylinders, then the decagon was drawn within it. So try a number of polygons, and later prisms and pyramids built upon polygonal bases.

Concentric Circles—Even in so brief a treatise on perspective it seems necessary for us to make some reference to concentric circles, as they must be frequently drawn and as they often cause trouble. Students sometimes are under the mistaken impression that circles in perspective do not appear as true ellipses. They argue that as the nearer half of the ellipse is not so far from the spectator as the other half it appears larger and hence must be drawn so. Whereas this may sound logical on the face of it, it is not true. For if you test actual objects you will find the circles always appear in perspective as true ellipses. We can make this more clear by referring to Sketch 11. We have already mentioned that one cannot see half way around a cylinder. At "A," we have drawn the top view of a cylinder. The spectator is standing at "s." Lines of tangency from "s" to the cylinder give us at "1" and "2" points representing the extreme limits of the cylindrical surface visible from "s." If we draw a straight line across from "1" to "2" it marks the greatest width of the cylinder as it appears from "s." This line really does not pass through the true center of the circle, represented at "o," but is between this center and the spectator, and becomes the major axis of the ellipse representing the circle. The shaded portion back of this line on the sketch will appear from "s" exactly the same size at that portion left white; hence the ellipse must appear truly symmetrical about this line. At "B" the spectator stands closer, and sees less of the cylindrical surface. Now suppose we have two concentric circles representing the tops of two concentric cylinders as indicated at "C," the spectator still standing at "s." If we treat these independently as before, drawing tangents to the curves, these tangents will measure off visible surfaces from 1 to 2 on the larger and from 3 to 4 on the smaller. This shows that the eye will see relatively more of the cylindrical surface of the smaller cylinder. Line 3-4 is nearer the center "o" than line 1-2 but does not pass through it. Now the easiest way for the student to draw such circles in perspective is to assume that they are inscribed in squares. At "D" two squares having a common center are shown in perspective. The crossing of the diagonals gives us the true center of the circle at "o," correctly located in perspective. At 1, 2, 3 and 4 are points through which the larger ellipse must pass. Line "x," just half way from points 1 and 3 will be the long axis of the large ellipse, which will be drawn symmetrically about this line, passing through points 1, 2, 3 and 4. The smaller ellipse will be drawn in exactly the same way, passing through points 5, 6, 7 and 8, and drawn symmetrically about axis "y," which is half way from 5 to 7.

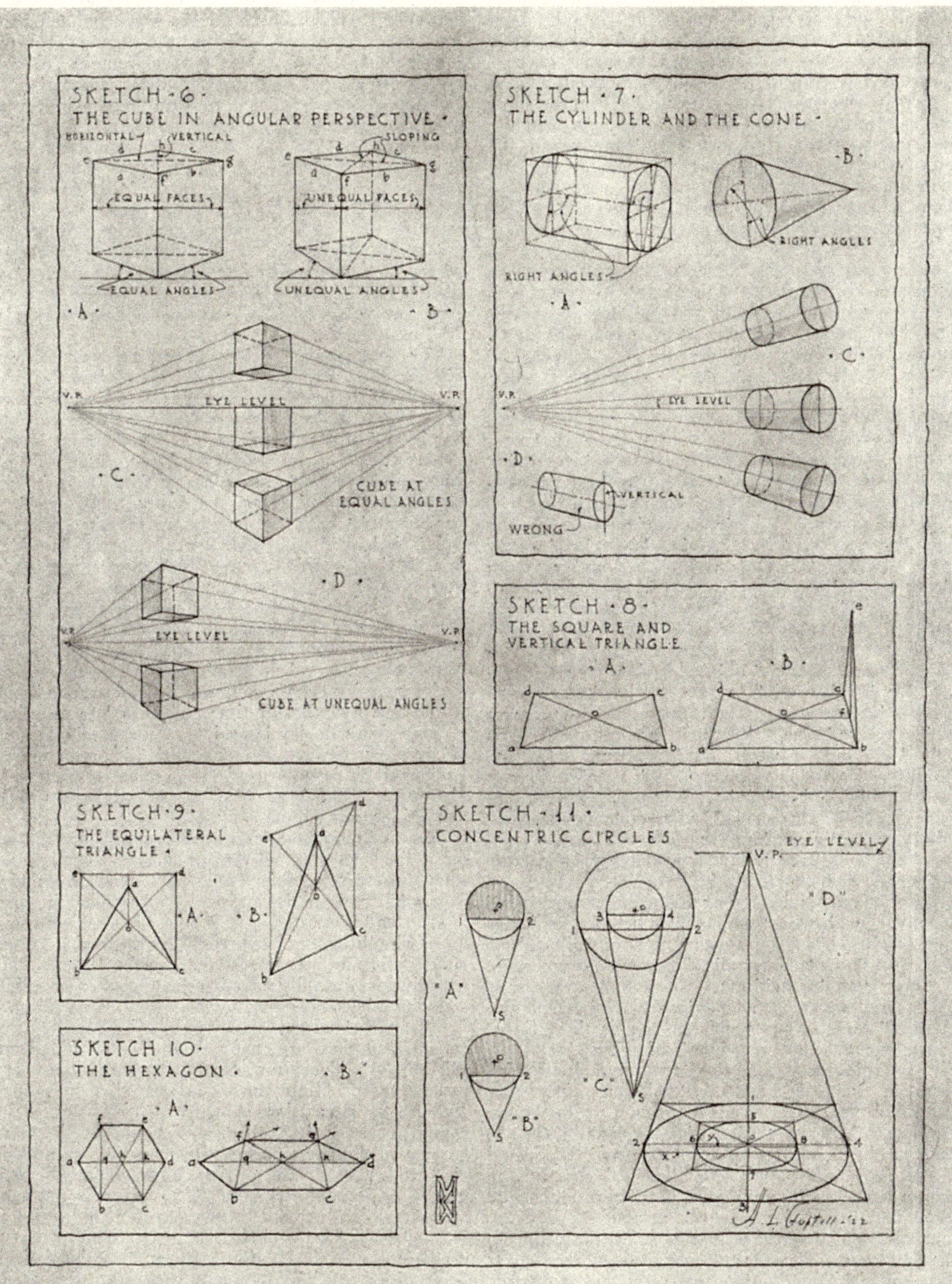

Figure 9. Illustrating Some Further Perspective Considerations.

Study these circles at "D" and examine objects in which other concentric circles are found. Is it not true that foreshortened concentric circles appear as ellipses? And would not the short axis lines of these ellipses coincide? It will be noticed, too, at "D," that distances 3-7, 7-0, 0-5 and 5-1 on the short axis seem to decrease gradually though actually the same as the unforeshortened distances on the long axis, 2-6, 6-0, 0-8 and 8-4. So in drawing such ellipses remember to have the space between them widest at the ends as at 2-6 and 8-4, and a little wider between the near curves as at 3-7 than at the farther side as at 5-1.

When one feels able to do all the more common of the geometric forms individually in every possible position let him draw combinations of several. This work should be followed by a practical application of the same principles to the drawing of objects of all sorts and sizes based on the same forms, as discussed in the chapter on object drawing. And as one draws he should analyze and memorize.

And one should attempt to make free-hand perspective sketches from memory or the imagination or from actual working drawings prepared instrumentally such as a front and side and top view.

In the chapter on object drawing some of the advantages of studying certain things by drawing them on glass have been pointed out and we have also described the glass invented by Mr. Cross specially for this purpose. Either the common or the patented glass might be of great help to the student in his perspective studies, particularly if this subject proves difficult. Training in instrumental perspective is often of help, too, though instrumental perspective sometimes shows apparent distortions which mislead one. A certain amount of help is gained from it, however, and students who are familiar with the instrumental work usually advance more rapidly in free-hand work because of the training. Likewise the student who understands free-hand perspective will find a great deal in the subject to help him to do instrumental problems more artistically than he otherwise could.

We have several times mentioned that once skill is gained in drawing cubes and other simple forms such as we have just described, it is not difficult to apply the knowledge acquired to the representation of more complex subjects.

The architectural student desires to sketch buildings and so let us consider the application of the principles stated above to work of this nature.

Let us assume that we are to draw a house, for example, which is twenty feet wide and forty feet long, and twenty feet from the ground to the eaves, the house being so turned that we look more directly at the long face than at the end. The land is assumed to be level. At Sketch 1, Figure 10, such a house has been drawn. As the eye is usually from four to five feet above the ground, the horizon line has been drawn one-quarter of the way up on the building. The nearest cube was worked over first until its proportion and perspective convergence seemed satisfactory. Then lines "D" and "E" were produced indefinitely (See "A," Sketch 1) and a diagonal line AC was carried through point "B," exactly half way from the ground to the eaves, thus automatically marking off at "C," the end of a second cube. When the two cubes were completed the roof was added. By crossing the diagonals of the square ends of the house proper, centers "o" and "p" were located and through these, vertical lines "s" and "t" were erected, and on these points were taken to mark the height of the ridge "F," which was converged towards its correct vanishing point at the right. Sketch "B" is the same with the exception of the roof which is here hipped instead of gabled. The ends of the ridge were located by erecting "A" and "B" perpendicularly through the points of intersection of the diagonals of the tops of the two cubes forming the main house. And Sketch "C" shows a different roof of the gambrel type, the gable having been drawn first just as at "A" as a guide.

The student may feel that these are unusual conditions; that few houses would be of just the proportion of two cubes,—and this is of course true. It is not a difficult matter, however, when a cube has been drawn as a unit, to add one or several more in any direction, or portions of one. If the house just considered was to be thirty feet long, for instance, instead of forty, the second cube could be easily cut in half, the correct perspective distance being judged by the eye, or the diagonals of its nearest face could be crossed which would give the correct point of intersection for the cut.

Once the main proportions have been established the doors and windows, roof overhangs, etc., can be added and the whole completed. Experience will show many uses of diagonal lines in locating centers and measuring distances, and other short cuts which will prove a saving of time and an aid to accuracy.

Sometimes it is desired to show buildings entirely above the eye, as on a high hill or mountain, and again it is a part of the problem to represent them below the eye. Sketch "2" illustrates these conditions in a simple way.

Now whether buildings are above or below the eye or at its level and whether simple or complex, the same general principles hold. But when a building is complicated in its masses, or irregular in plan, it is usually best to think of it as inclosed within a more simple mass, drawing this mass first, and then subdividing it into the smaller parts. Sketch "3" was designed to illustrate this thought, the dash lines showing the simple mass which was drawn first.

When the larger proportions of a building are established there are many details to be added and Sketch "4" pictures a few typical ones in a very meager way. Many towers are based on pyramids and cones such as those shown at "A" and "B." One should practice these, then, and should try his hand at steps, chimneys, arches, dormers, etc., until he feels able to sketch any of the more commonly seen details easily and well, either from the objects themselves (which is excellent practice) or from memory.

Sketch "5" is to show that when furniture is to be represented it is often well to first block it in very simply so far as mass is concerned, just as we did the building in Sketch 3. For the chair at "A" two cubes were drawn as shown by the dotted lines, and the seat below was sketched within a square prism. When objects are thus inclosed

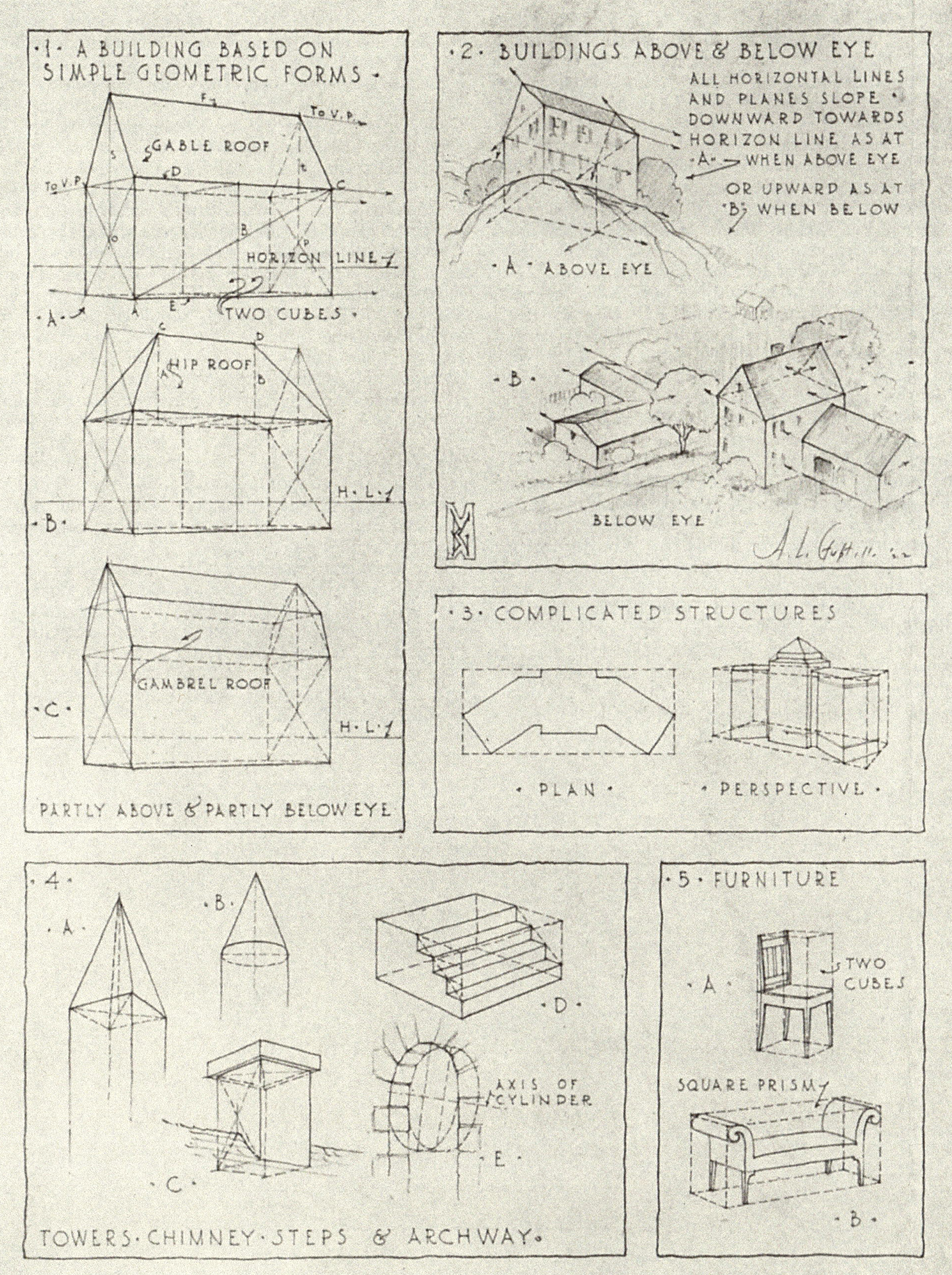

Figure 10. Illustrating the Application of Perspective Principles.

within simple forms or "frozen into a block of ice" one is less likely to get them incorrect in perspective. It is suggested that as a means of adding to one's ability to do this well he cut out prints of buildings and pieces of furniture and sketch simple shapes around them with a few lines, preferably straight, for this will help one to realize that all objects are comparatively simple in basic form.

Photographs or prints can help us in another way in the study of perspective, for we can lay a ruler on them or a T-square or triangle and produce with a pencil the various series of parallel lines to or towards their vanishing points, locating and drawing the eye level or horizon line first of all. This will help one to understand the perspective phenomena more quickly, perhaps, than any other one thing.

We should not close without some reference to the perspective of interiors, though a brief word will suffice, for it is hardly necessary to say more than that interiors are done in just the same way as are exteriors, only we are looking at the inside of the cubes and prisms instead of at the outside, which means that we simply remove those faces which are the nearest to us. Rooms themselves are usually very simple as to form; it is in the furniture, turned at various angles and of irregular shape, that one encounters the greatest difficulty. A little practice, however, will give one considerable proficiency in all of this work.

One should be cautioned, nevertheless, that the difficulties are not few, for whether one is drawing interiors or exteriors or small objects it must be borne in mind that in theory he is supposed to look in the same fixed direction constantly until the drawing is finished, and although in practice this is not especially hard to do when an object is so small as to come entirely within the range of vision without the gaze being shifted, when it comes to large objects or entire rooms or buildings we are so accustomed to glancing about from place to place that it is not easy to keep from making a sort of composite sketch in which the various small parts may be correct in themselves, but wrong when considered in relation to one another and to the whole. When drawing a room, for instance, it is easy to go astray by looking first at a window and drawing that, and next doing a door, and so on, one thing at a time.

When this method is followed the whole is quite sure to look distorted. For this reason one should locate a horizon line on the drawing whenever possible and if vanishing points would naturally come within the paper area find them also, and in sketching the main lines try to give them the right proportion and perspective convergence, for if a sort of framework can be correctly built up for the whole it will not be hard to add the detail; therefore spend plenty of time on this first work. If too much trouble is encountered when drawing from actual buildings sketch from photographs for a while as this will be much easier to do. Then go on to portions of interiors and exteriors before attempting them in an entirety.

The excellent drawing by Mr. Watson on page 33 shows a type of subject which would prove extremely difficult to block out because of the great number of converging lines, unless one was familiar with the perspective principles involved; and if a subject of this nature is not correctly constructed the errors will usually be glaringly apparent, regardless of the quality of the technique.

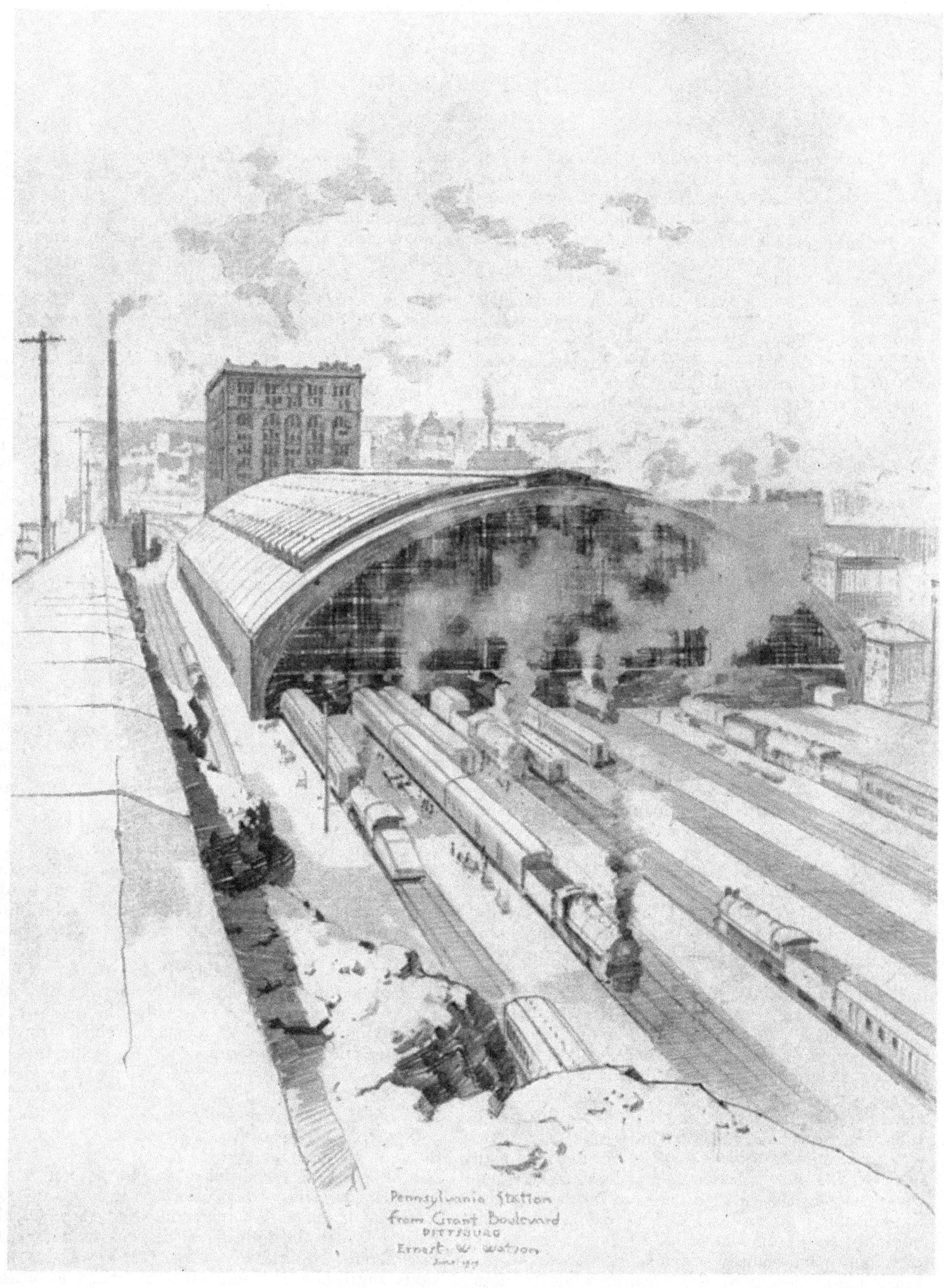

PENCIL SKETCH BY ERNEST W. WATSON PENNSYLVANIA STATION, PITTSBURGH, PA.

Chapter VI.

CAST DRAWING

WE NOW come to another important phase of our work—cast drawing, for as soon as the student has gained facility in object drawing, the next logical step is to turn to plaster casts for his subjects; in fact, many teachers make cast drawing a starting point for the beginner.

If one is to work at home a few casts may be purchased, and the expense of obtaining the smaller ones is not great. One is more fortunate, however, if he has access to a museum or school collection which will give him the opportunity to make such a choice for each drawing as will best meet his needs, for there are casts of many kinds and sizes, ranging all the way from tiny ones of coins and medals and jewelry to huge plaster representations of sculptured groups, too enormous to be housed in any but the larger museums.

The student will be wise in selecting first a cast of medium size, say a foot or so in its greatest dimension, and of a simple subject. The architectural student will find it extremely beneficial to make a series of drawings of architectural ornament, and there are casts available of all of the better-known forms. A good starting point would be the lotus flower or palmette or something of the sort which has come down to us from the earliest times. This might be followed by others of like nature, one or two typical forms being selected from each well-known period. There would be the acanthus and anthemion of the classical work, perhaps, or some of the incised patterns of the Byzantine, or the roughly carved grotesques of the Romanesque, while the Gothic is particularly rich in ornamentation, showing not only many geometric forms but naturalistic and conventionalized carving of ivy, oak and grape leaves, the ball flower, etc. Then comparative sketches might be made of capitals of different styles of architecture and of mouldings; these last are especially important and every draftsman should be familiar with such moulded members as are in common use, enriched with the well-known egg and dart, leaf and dart, guilloche, dolphins and acanthus, bay leaf, etc., etc. Let him study these and not only his knowledge, but his appreciation of architecture will be strengthened. For advanced studies the orders of architecture might be drawn from the cast, correctly represented in perspective and with all the metopes, triglyphs, mutules, modillions, etc., carefully represented:—it is doubtful if there is a better way to master the orders than to work in this manner. Nor is there a better way of learning to design carved wood or stone or ornamental terra cotta than by working from casts of antique examples, as one not only stores up knowledge of the forms of the past but unconsciously assimilates a sense of proportion and design of the greatest value in doing original work.

If casts of ornament are chosen for the first problems let them be simple, as we have indicated above, and comparatively low in relief, as these are the easiest to do. Then the later problems should be so arranged that high relief decoration and incised ornament are also represented and that not only geometric patterns are shown but conventionalized and naturalistic representations of plant and animal life and the human form as well. Some casts that are delicate in detail should be done and some which are bold and vigorous in character;—in short, one should not rest content until he feels that he has quite successfully mastered every type of ornamental subject.

The art student, however, may find a few of these ornamental casts enough and then go on to the type of subject which will prepare him more directly for later work in drawing from the living model. Here as before it is best to select something which is not complex, a cast of a foot or hand or arm offering a good starting point. After a while heads may be attempted and the complete human figure.

One is hardly wise to attempt to draw from the living model until he has spent considerable time in working from these inanimate objects, which will hold the pose until a drawing is finished, something which the living model can hardly be expected to do. And neither do these casts have hues of color to add to the difficulties of the student.

Then there are anatomical casts, especially designed to show the various bones and muscles, and these should be studied at this time, for the art student cannot begin too early to learn anatomy and its application to problems in art.

This practice from casts of the human form is to the art student absolutely indispensable. And it is hardly less essential for those of the architectural profession, for from the earliest times the human figure has been used in connection with architecture, sometimes merely as applied ornament or decoration and sometimes structurally, as, for example, the caryatids of the Erechtheion at Athens. So no architect can afford to neglect this part of his training. He should study especially the use of the human figure as applied to such architectural features as friezes, the tympana of the pediments, the spandrels of arches, and the pendentives of vaults; also the free-standing figure as used in connection with or as a part of architecture.

Now regardless of the type of cast selected for the first subject, the method of procedure is exactly the same as for the drawing of objects, and as this has been described fully elsewhere it seems needless to repeat it here. We might mention, however, that in order that the lighting shall be satisfactory, the cast should be shifted, if possible, to various positions until one is found which brings a pleasing relation of light and shade. Then the form should be sketched and the shading started.

Figure 11. An Example of Cast Drawing in Light and Shade.

It should be understood that the appearance of a cast will vary greatly under different lighting conditions, and at various times of the day, for even though north light is used it will be more or less changeable from time to time. Therefore it is best to work for only an hour or two daily until the drawing is finished, these hours being in the morning, for example, or in the afternoon. For the light is usually about the same for a few hours in succession at any given time of day, dark or rainy days being, of course, exceptions.

We have explained before that the darkest tone on light objects is usually lighter than the darkest tone on dark objects, though, strange to say, it does not often appear so, therefore even though the cast is light, its deeper tones will seem quite dark in contrast with those areas receiving their illumination more directly.

In the first problems it is usually best to work in full values with a fairly sharp pencil, completing each drawing with the greatest care, modelling until the nearer parts seem to come forward, and the farther portions retreat, subordinating the unimportant, but emphasizing the essentials. Caution must be used not to force those darks too strongly which are found in the lighter areas or the lights within the shade tones; instead simplicity should be sought just as in object drawing, all unimportant tones being suppressed. Figure 11 is an example of cast drawing in full values of light and shade.

In later problems separate lines may be used in building up the tones; in fact there is no harm in experimenting in various ways of working, trying out any ideas which suggest themselves. The architectural student can perhaps improve his draftsmanship if he does a few cast drawings on tracing paper, mainly in accented outline or entirely so if he wishes, using a rather clean-cut line which is suitable for blue-printing; in fact, prints may be made of each drawing when completed. Such work trains one to make better scale or full-size details of ornament and the like. It is helpful also for one to occasionally select some cast of an architectural subject and instead of drawing it in perspective just as it appears, to make instead an elevation of it (using instruments, perhaps, for some of the straight lines) and a section or two or a side elevation, all so drawn as to correctly express the form and modelling of the object. These drawings may be shaded or left in outline.

On page 20 is a drawing of ornament in accented outline only, while at the top of page 37 parallel strokes of shading are combined with accented outline effectively. The drawing at the bottom of the same page has strokes of shading following the lines of growth.

Casts based on the human figure seem more difficult to the average beginner than do those of ornament, and like them should be most carefully drawn, painstaking effort being expended on every part. For the first portrait drawings such casts should be selected as show the greatest amount of individuality; those which have certain marked peculiarities which can be clearly grasped and represented. Study the various planes of light and shade and shadow as to form and value, giving particular attention to the edges of the planes, sharpening them or softening them truthfully. As the values are being built up it is often well to over-accent or force such edges a bit, as this will help one to retain the virility and strength expressed in the cast. The reason for so doing is to safeguard the student against having everything too soft and round, a common failing of the beginner. In giving a drawing its final touches, edges which have been made too sharp must of course be lifted or softened until they become less definite.

In portrait work we have a real test of skill. One may make errors when sketching an old hat or shoe and they may not be conspicuous,—even in ornament drawings mistakes are not always evident when the work is completed. But when one does a portrait, whether from photograph or cast or life, unless proportions and modelling are true there will not be a perfect likeness and unless a student is able to get a likeness he knows that his drawing is faulty. If a good likeness is lacking the drawing should be compared frequently with the original and corrected and changed until the desired effect is gained and the modelling brought to as near perfection as is possible. This work from cast should never be hurried over or neglected, for one cannot hope to cope with the difficulties of drawing from the living model until skill has been acquired in representing well that which has no disturbing hues of color and which holds a steady position.

When one has acquired considerable skill in working on white surfaces, tinted paper may be tried, the tone of the paper representing the middle values, the lights being added with white pencil or chalk or paint, and the darks built up with pencil. Such sketches are often very effective and results may be obtained quite quickly in this way, but one should not neglect the painstaking studies on white paper in order to make time for this sort of thing. Aside from all the other advantages which careful work has, it prepares one for work in other mediums; it is an easy step from pencil to wash and from wash to color, while pen drawing is much like the line shading which is often done with the pencil. The architectural student is called upon to render much ornament in wash, such as the details used in the Class B Analytique problems in the course of the Beaux-Arts Institute of Design, and in renderings of a competitive nature done in the offices, and the making of carefully shaded drawings from the cast will prepare one directly for this class of work.

Now by way of a final suggestion, it should be made clear that unless a student really has unusual ability he should not attempt this advanced work without a competent instructor, and any student, regardless of his ability, should get criticism from others from time to time, for even though one may develop by himself tricks of technique and a certain cleverness of handling, such things do not offset faulty drawing, although they may hide it from the student himself. Now we will pass on to a consideration of life drawing, not without admonishing the student, however, to attempt no work from life until his skill warrants it; remembering that unless one can draw a good likeness from the cast he surely cannot do so from the living model.

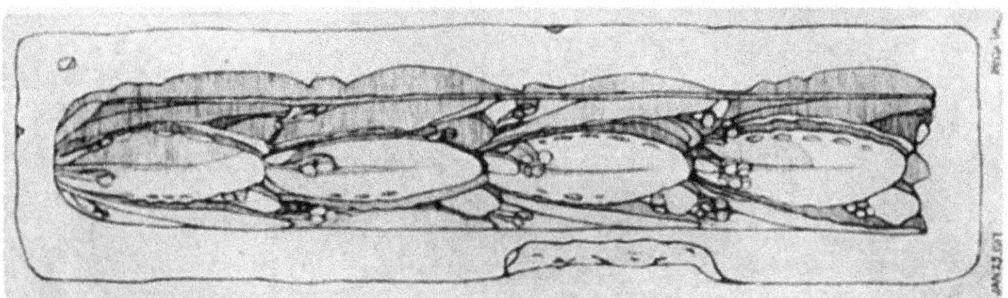

Courtesy of Pratt Institute *Freda Uhl*

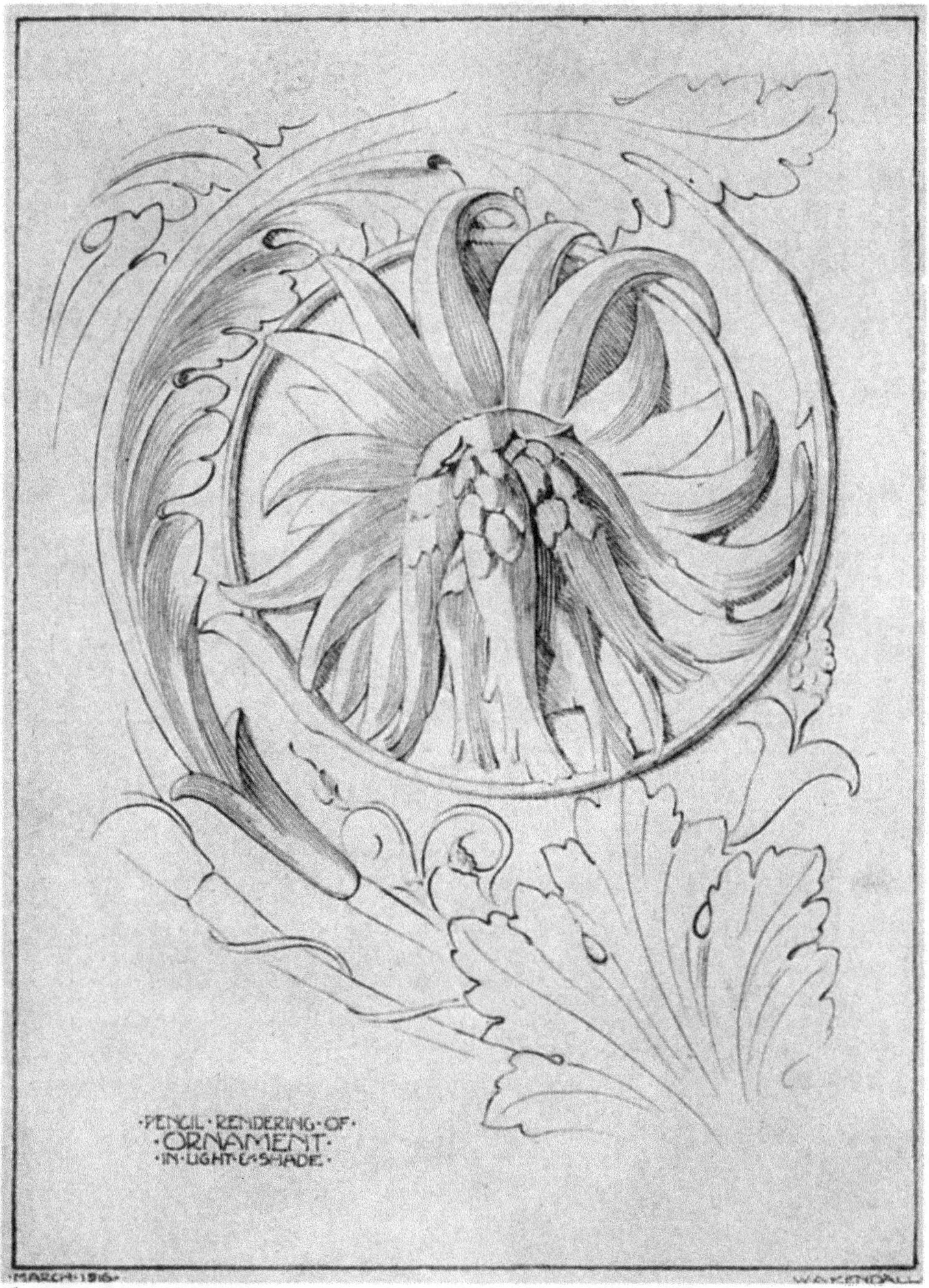

·PENCIL·RENDERING·OF·
·ORNAMENT·
·IN·LIGHT·&·SHADE·

·MARCH·1916· W.A.KENDALL

Courtesy of Pratt Institute *W. A. Kendall*

ORNAMENT DRAWINGS BY STUDENTS AT PRATT INSTITUTE

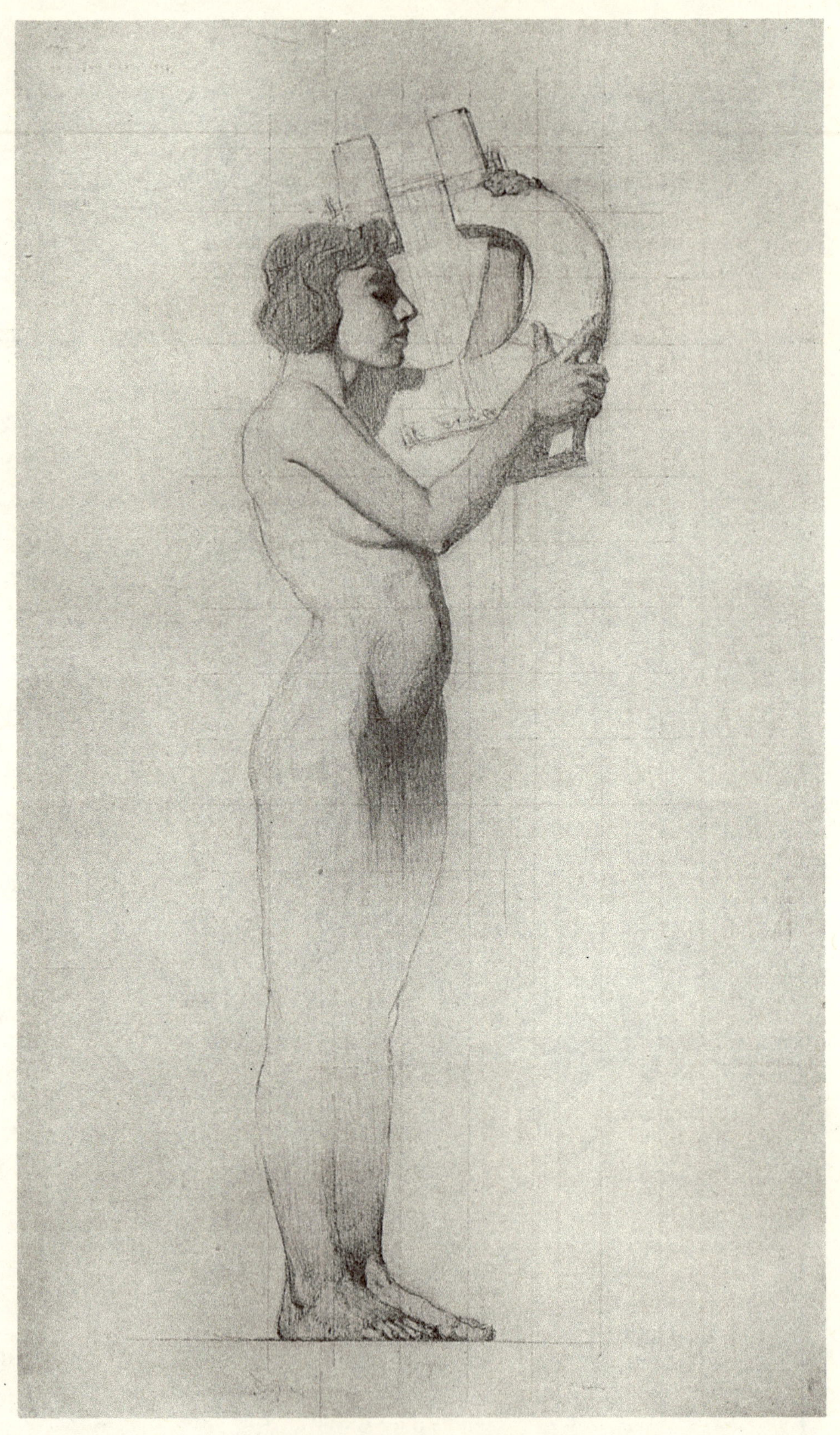

PENCIL STUDY BY JULES GUERIN FOR ONE OF THE FIGURES IN HIS MURAL DECORATIONS IN THE LINCOLN MEMORIAL, WASHINGTON, D. C.
HENRY BACON, ARCHITECT

Chapter VII.

LIFE DRAWING

THERE seems to be a general desire on the part of art students to hurry on through all the preliminary work of practice strokes and tone building, and object drawing and cast drawing to the subject which is now before us,—life drawing. When one starts to draw from real living people he feels that he is about to get somewhere, that he is really on the road to becoming an artist. And the importance of drawing from the living model cannot be denied. So large a percentage of all of the drawings and paintings which we see about us every day make some use of the human figure,—(many of them, and especially the work of an illustrative nature such as we find in our books and magazines, giving figures the position of primary importance), it seems plainly evident that unless the art student learns to draw them well his place in the art world will be considerably restricted.

So the students of sculpture, mural painting, portrait painting, illustration and commercial art need no urging to study life drawing, as they realize fully to what extent their success will depend upon it. The architect, or more especially the beginner in architecture, is often slow, however, in perceiving the advantages to be gained from pursuing such a course, especially those of that profession who lean towards the practical rather than the æsthetic. And it is not our contention that life drawing is the one thing of primary importance to the architect. What we do wish to point out is that it offers enough of advantage to make its study well worth the while, and we can give no stronger proof that this opinion is quite general than by stating that in nearly all of our larger architectural schools the students are given life work as a regular part of their prescribed courses of study. It is not merely that the architect is sometimes called upon to draw a few figures to add interest or give scale to a drawing of some proposed building, (for such work can be done well enough to serve the purposes without particular skill) —neither is it because he may find it necessary to draw sculptured figures as a part of his design, as in a pediment, for instance, or flanking a doorway, for though this second reason is more important than the first, sculptors or trained modellers are usually called in to actually execute such work on the building itself, and they are capable of correcting errors and going ahead with the whole thing sympathetically once the architect has given them his general idea. The study of life drawing is important more because it gives such excellent training in light and shade and proportion, and an appreciation and understanding of design than for these other reasons. For if one acquires the fine perception which will enable him to note and analyze and understand the subtle variations between one tone and another which one finds, especially when working from the nude, his architecture will be the better for it; and if one assimilates, as he should, a feeling for rhythm and balance and symmetry and other characteristics of good composition, it may be applied advantageously to his daily work;—more than this, his improved skill in draftsmanship will be always worth the effort expended to obtain it, for if one acquires such dexterity as enables him to draw figures in correct proportion he will have no great trouble sketching the most complicated architecture.

So the architect should be encouraged to take up life work and the art student's enthusiasm should not be curbed. Both should be cautioned, nevertheless, that it should not be attempted until proper preparation has been made for it, and it is for this reason that we have given so much space to urging thoroughness in the preliminary work in object drawing, still life, perspective, cast drawing, etc. And both should be cautioned, too, against the folly of attempting to do life drawing without proper instruction and criticism. Fortunately, there are evening courses in most of the larger cities which give the students who lack the time or means of taking day courses the opportunity of learning at night. To supplement such training there are many excellent books on all branches of the subject which can be studied as time permits.

Because there are so many books available and so many classes open to students, it seems scarcely necessary for us to go into the matter at any length here,—in fact, we could hardly do so without going beyond the scope of our subject, for whereas the pencil is used frequently for figure work it is perhaps more often employed in preliminary sketches and studies than for the final execution. Then, too, there are so many kinds of life drawings that to describe them all would require a good-size volume.

Whenever we start to erect any sort of a building it is essential to have a firm foundation and framework on which to build the superstructure. In the same way in studying the human figure it is necessary to have our framework; in this case the human skeleton. So the student should learn about the skeleton first; he should study anatomy until he becomes familiar with the different bones, individually and in their relation one to another. He should learn the names by which they are known. He should know the different positions which they assume when one walks or runs or sits or reclines, and the acquisition of such familiarity with them will require conscientious study, and practice with the pencil. In fact, there is no part of life drawing which should be carelessly done; too much emphasis cannot be given to this point.

Once the bones are well understood, attention must be directed to the muscles and to the flesh which rounds out the body. One should learn in just what manner the muscles are attached to the

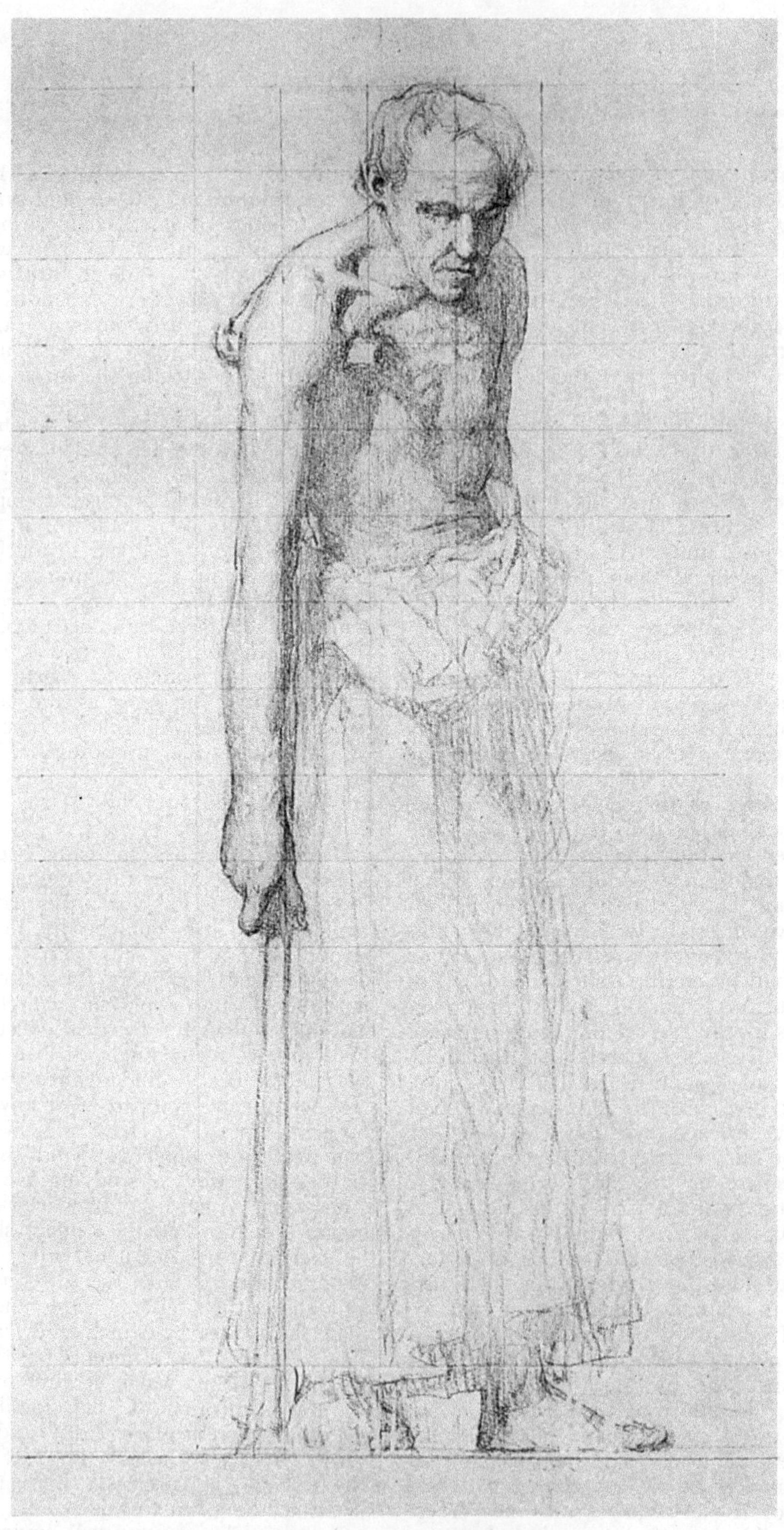

PENCIL STUDY BY JULES GUERIN FOR FIGURE IN HIS MURAL DECORATIONS IN THE LINCOLN MEMORIAL, WASHINGTON, D. C.
HENRY BACON, ARCHITECT

bones themselves, just how they appear when at rest and when in action. And it is necessary to not only study each important muscle by itself, but to also learn its relation to every other muscle and to the body as a whole. When the larger groups of muscles are mastered attention should be given to some of the more important of the smaller ones, such as those of the face. The sculptor or portrait painter or illustrator will, of course, give special thought to these, for unless they are well understood it will be difficult for him to properly express such emotions as sadness, joy, fear, surprise. For although the entire pose of the figure varies with these emotions, it is not enough to have the proper action in the body as a whole; much depends on these smaller parts. To learn them well one must study the action of the muscles when people talk or eat or smile or whistle, special studies being made of the eye, the ear, the nose and the mouth. Then, too, one must study the various characteristics of youth and of old age, and of the different races. It is not only the faces which should be carefully analyzed, however. Hands, too, are very expressive; the clenched fist tells a far different story than does the hand extended for a clasp of friendship. Even feet are very important; some artists who seem quite familiar with the rest of the figure have much difficulty with them or consider them too unimportant to be studied with care.

Now needless to say it is best before studying all of these smaller parts in detail to learn to draw well the figure as a whole, so as soon as one has had some practice from the skeleton placed in different positions, he should start working from the nude model. In line with what we have said above, the models should be varied not only as to sex but as to age, size and race. Then, too, the lighting should not always be the same. As to posing the model it seems almost needless to remark that the student should work from a great variety of poses; the figure should be shown at rest, sitting or standing or reclining, and in action. Action poses are often hard for the model to take and to hold, but they should be attempted, especially after the student has gained enough practice from the figure in repose to enable him to work swiftly and directly, so that the main lines of action may be swept in while the model is still fresh. In these let the model be doing something in a natural way; give a boy a baseball bat for instance and let him put as much action into the pose as though he intended to make a home run; give an aged man a wheelbarrow (or as a substitute for it—two sticks will do) and let him pretend to trudge across the garden. In these poses the model will, of course, remain as nearly as possible in the one set position, resting and resuming the pose as often as seems necessary. There is another type of action pose, however, in which the model repeats some motion a great number of times, rather slowly, so the student is able to study the muscles as they assume different positions. Quick sketches can be made showing these changes in a comparative manner. Boxing, fencing and the like offer excellent movements for this type of action sketch, especially if one motion is repeated over and over again. Too little of this work is given in most of our schools.

The architectural student has less need, perhaps, for these action sketches, than the artist, for the nude or partly draped figure as used in architectural sculpture and ornament is more often shown at rest; too much motion would be disturbing to the design as a whole. So in posing the model, horizontals and verticals should be worked for to harmonize with the structural lines of the architecture, many of the lines being straight or nearly so, and the whole arranged to express strength and solidity.

In drawing from the nude there is no principle which is at all different from those already described under object and cast drawing. The placing on the paper is arrived at in just the same way, points being located to mark the extreme limits of the figure. The student must learn to work quickly for even the easiest poses cannot be held for over a half hour and a new pose is seldom quite the same, even if intended to be. The student who has the necessary foundation for this work will be able to do away with many of the construction lines which are needed by the beginner in object drawing, but he will, instead of making so many trial lines, locate only a few salient points, comparing these with the model carefully and correcting them until they are just right, for the model is likely to sway and slightly change the pose at any time. On the first drawings forget all such small details as the features, fingers, etc., but above all be sure that the action of the figure and the general masses are correct. A half hour or an hour is usually enough for each subject;—it is better to do a number of them and get the essentials of each pose than to spend too much time on one. The shading may be almost neglected or merely suggested on the early problems, but carefully finished studies should be made later with special attention to the values.

The amount of time given to the study of the nude figure will, of course, depend largely on the aim of the student, whether he is to take up illustration or portraiture or sculpture or some other form of art work.

Then when one has gained a certain facility in drawing the nude figure, the draped figure would be a natural subject, and here, too, the problem is difficult. For it is very easy when representing the folds of drapery to lose the proportions of the form underneath; hence, it is often desirable to sketch the main lines of the figure first exactly as though it were undraped, adding the drapery later. In fact, in all work where people are drawn (or painted for that matter) it is necessary to have in mind constantly the correct proportion of each complete figure, so expressing or suggesting it that the effect will be correct, for no amount of work on the clothing itself will make up for faulty construction.

When it comes to the figure in full costume new difficulties are encountered, for the expression of the forms and textures of the various fabrics is not easy. But work from the costumed figure is very interesting, especially if the model is posed to tell some story. Students of illustration should get a great deal of work in which the problems are made as real as possible, illustrating incidents in actual life or some character in literature, the model being so dressed and posed as to express the idea to the best advantage. Backgrounds may be added from the imagination.

And aside from this work from the posed model there is no better practice in figure drawing than to sketch members of one's family and his friends, or people passing in the street. Catch them unawares if you can and the sketches will be all the more lifelike for it. When you have no sketch book at hand or no opportunity to use one, study people all about you, and imagine that you are drawing them, for this will help more than would be supposed.

Of all these types of drawings which we have touched upon, it is hard to say which is the most important, for everything depends on the purpose for which each study is made. The architect needs one kind of work, the sculptor another, the commercial illustrator a third, and so on. Needless to say the portrait painter or illustrator will follow the work in pencil with more advanced study in pen or wash color, and there is no harm if the others do too; these other mediums can usually be handled quite easily, however, once the pencil has been well mastered. And it is equally true that whether one does object or cast drawing or outdoor sketching or anything of this sort in pencil, he is doing far more than mastering this medium;—he is building a strong foundation for all other work in art.

The illustrations are shown as typical examples of life work from the nude, done in pencil.

Those by Jules Guerin on pages 38, 40, 51, 52 and 54 are reproduced from some of his original studies for the symbolic figures in his mural decorations recently put in place in the new Lincoln Memorial at Washington, D. C., of which Henry Bacon was the architect. These drawings are all made from life and are excellent examples to study, being unusually interesting in technique.

The study on page 43 by Eugene F. Savage is for one of the figures in his decorative painting "Idealism" in the Polytechnic Preparatory School, Brooklyn, N. Y. This drawing is the one from which this figure was sketched into the picture: previously a number of studies had been made from the model. A formal character was given to this figure to fit it for incorporation in the picture, and though the model was used this has not the naturalistic character of the customary life drawing. The horse was first sketched in from the full-size cartoon, then the figure was added.

The drawings by Taber Sears reproduced on pages 44, 47 and 50 are also studies from life for mural paintings. Mr. Sears' paintings of religious subjects are especially fine in conception and embody much of the spirit of Mediaeval times. They have a character and a manner that fit them especially well for their places in juxtaposition to the architectural detail of the churches for which they are made.

On pages 45 and 53 are excellent studies by Barry Faulkner for figures in the mural decorations which he has done for the great Cunard Building, New York City, B. W. Morris, architect. These are both extremely fine examples of technique.

The reproductions on pages 46 and 48 are of studies from life by H. I. Stickroth for his mural painting "The Valley of Contemplation" drawn while a Fellow of the American Academy in Rome. The originals are in pencil on buff paper. This technique, too, is well worthy of the most careful study on the part of students of drawing.

On page 49 is a different type of subject, a study by Frank Vincent DuMond for one of his mural decorations for the Panama-Pacific Exposition. These decorations represent the influx of the widely different human elements that went to make California:—the Spanish adventurers and the missionaries, the scholars, the "forty-niners" and all the others. In this spirited sketch we see a group of homeseekers pressing on across the plains to the new land of promise. The study is in pencil on gray paper, size about 30 in. by 40 in.

The sketch of Vera Fokina by Troy Kinney on page 55 is a figure study of unusual power. It is one of many rapid sketches Mr. Kinney makes in studying the movements of a dancer as a preliminary to the execution of one of his notable etchings of the dance. By means of these studies Mr. Kinney makes definite many impressions of movements of the dance preceding and following the movement which he chooses to represent in his etching. In this way he fixes his impressions of the character of a momentary action and this undoubtedly helps him to embody in his etchings the sense of life that is one of their most admirable qualities. The frontispiece to this volume is another of Mr. Kinney's delightful sketches.

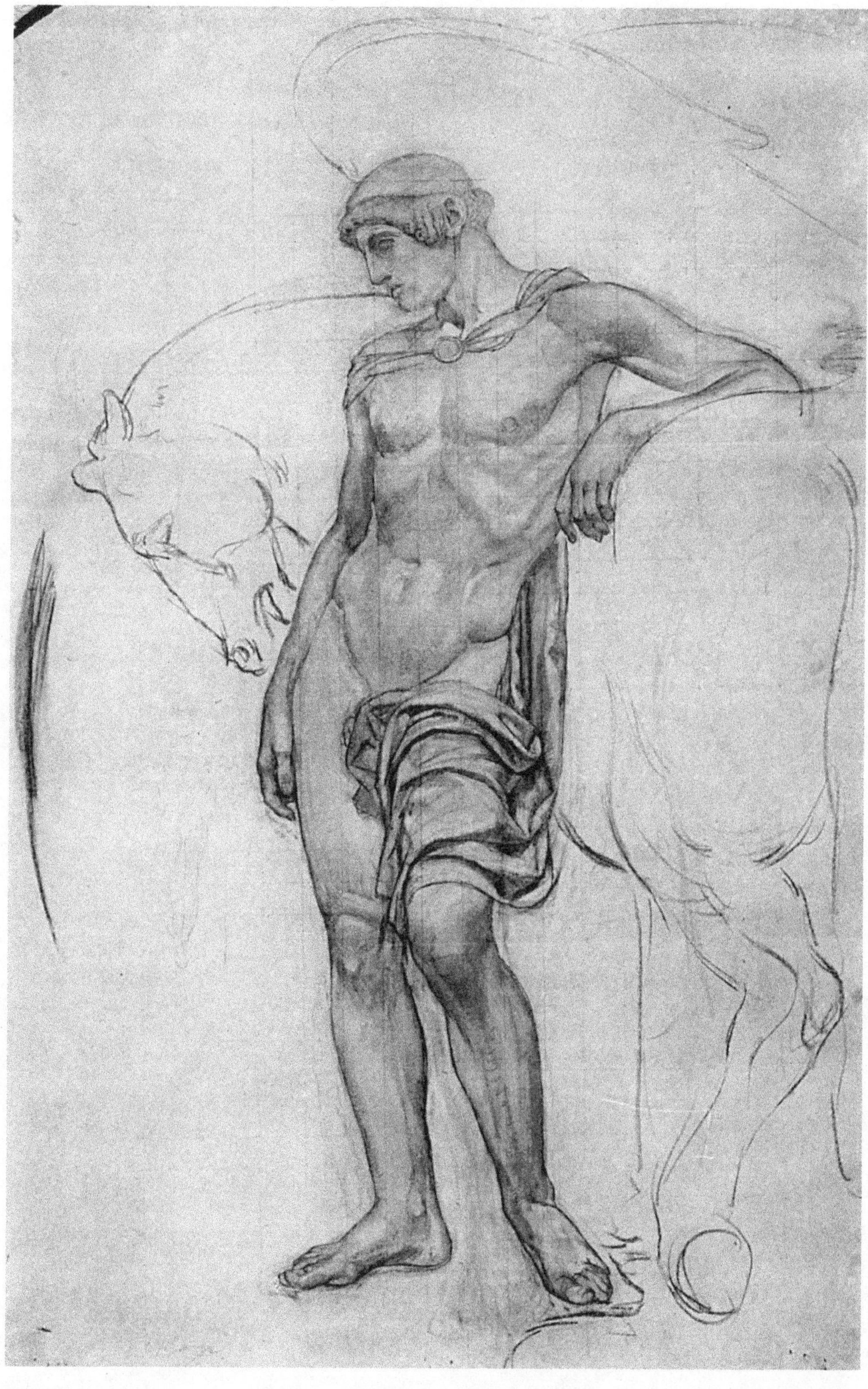

STUDY BY EUGENE F. SAVAGE FOR FIGURE IN HIS DECORATIVE PAINTING "IDEALISM" IN THE POLYTECHNIC PREPARATORY SCHOOL, BROOKLYN, N. Y.

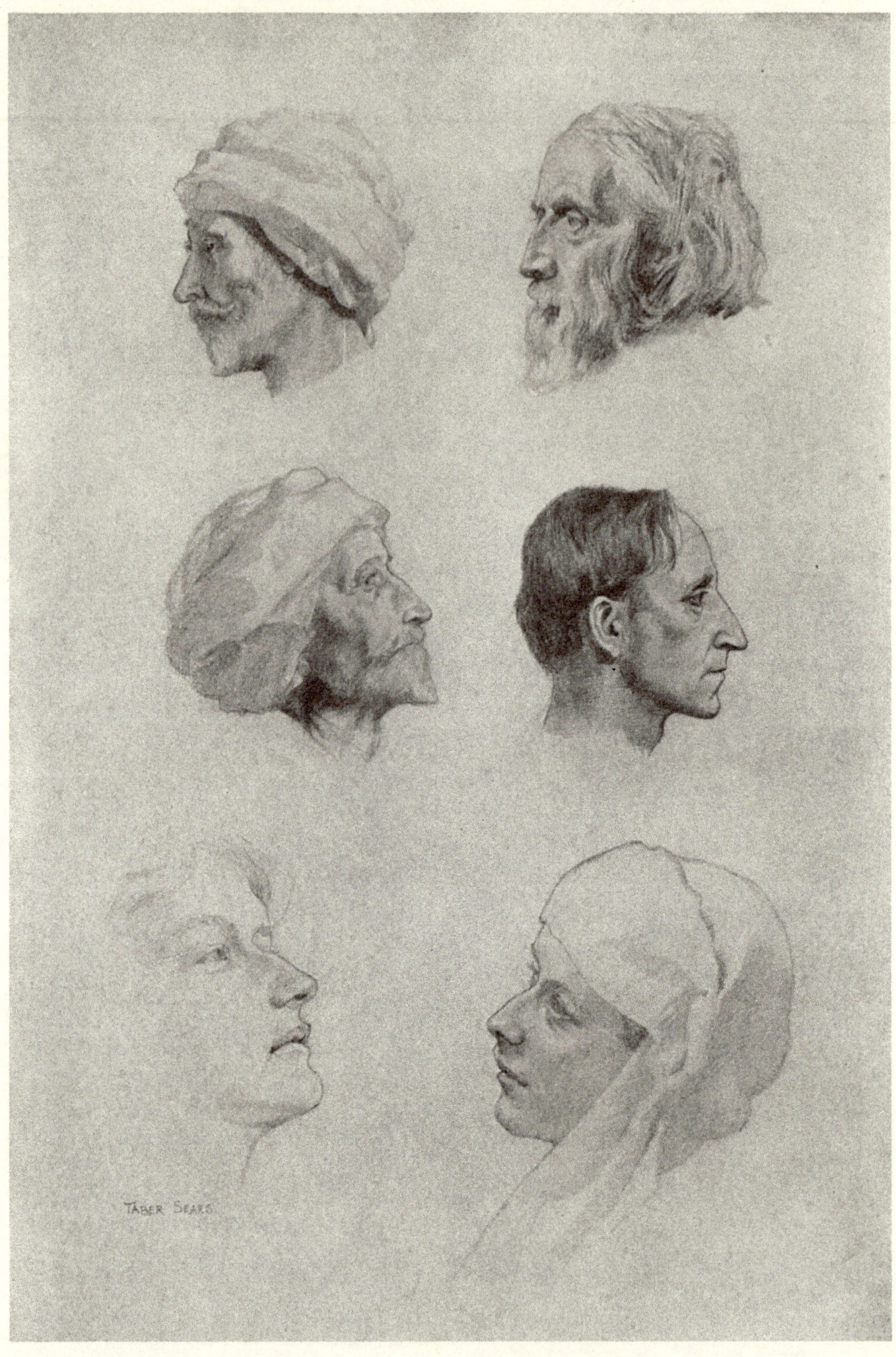

STUDIES OF HEADS BY TABER SEARS FOR ALTAR PAINTING IN TRINITY CHURCH, BUFFALO, N. Y.
BERTRAM GROSVENOR GOODHUE. ARCHITECT

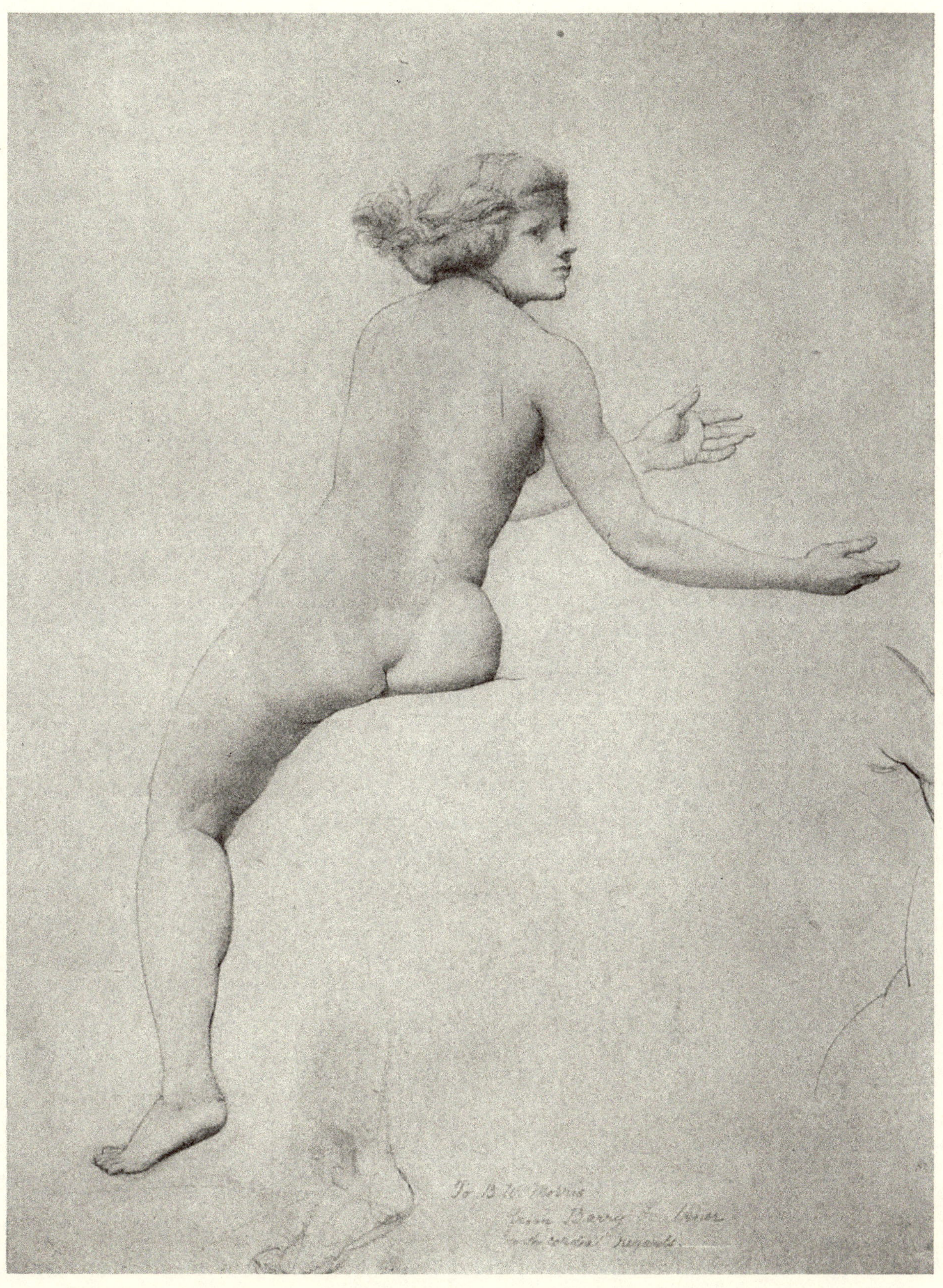

FIGURE STUDY BY BARRY FAULKNER, FOR ONE OF HIS MURAL PAINTINGS IN THE CUNARD BUILDING. NEW YORK CITY

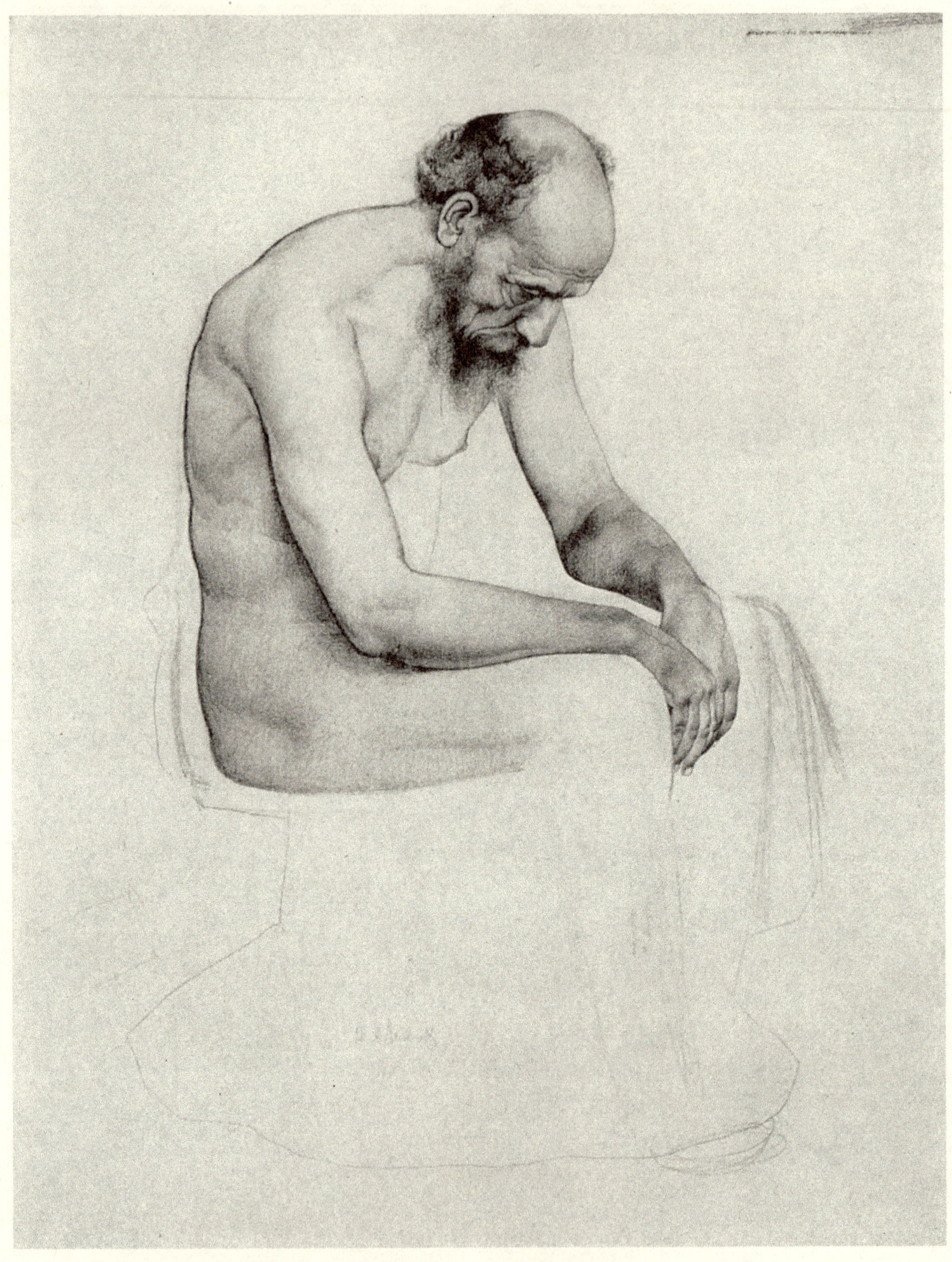

PENCIL STUDY BY H. I. STICKROTH FOR ONE OF THE FIGURES IN HIS MURAL PAINTING "THE VALLEY OF CONTEMPLATION"

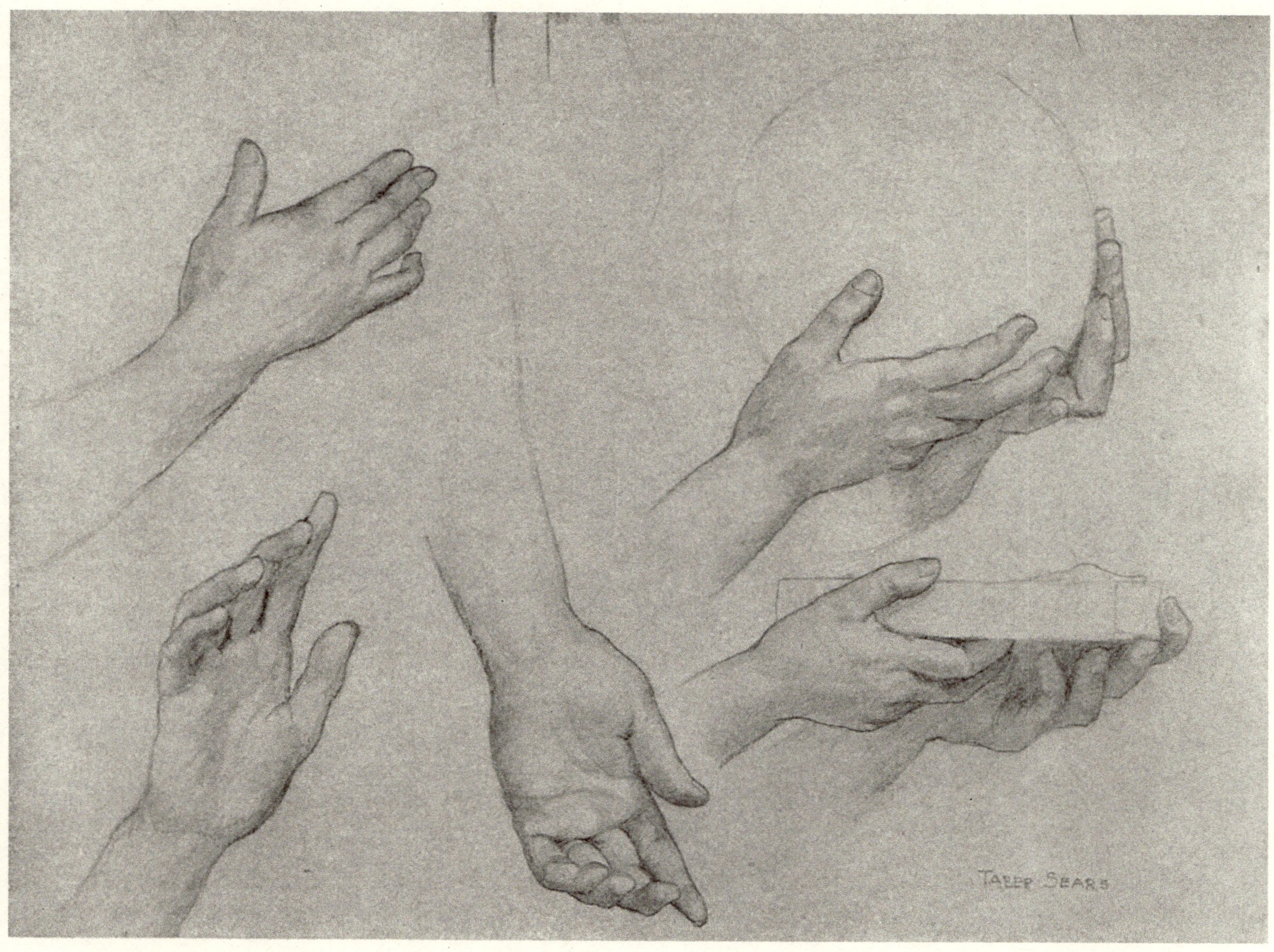

STUDIES OF HANDS BY TABER SEARS, FOR CHANCEL DECORATION IN THE FIRST PRESBYTERIAN CHURCH, NEW YORK CITY

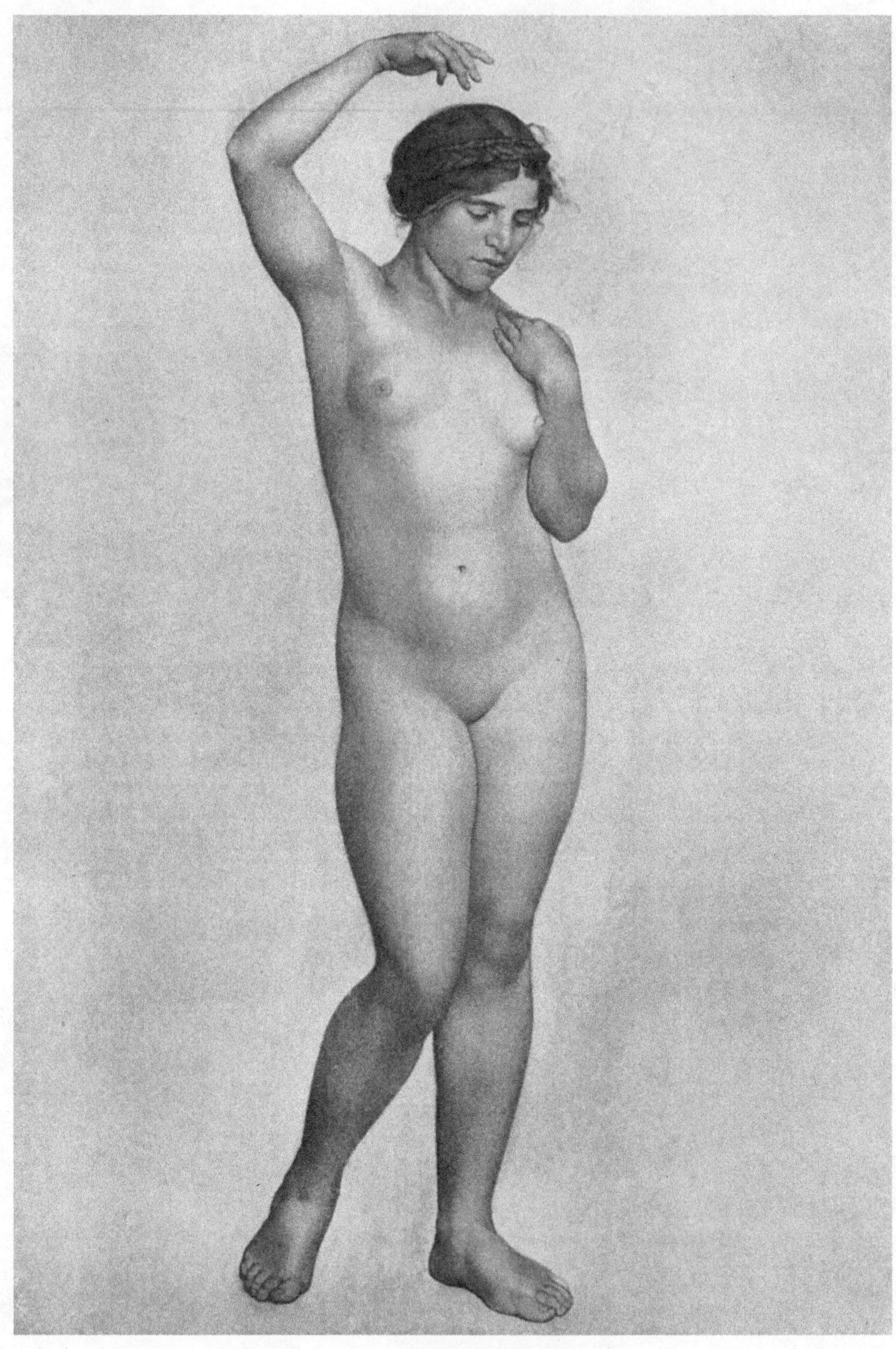

STUDY BY H. I. STICKROTH FOR ONE OF THE FIGURES IN HIS MURAL PAINTING "THE VALLEY OF CONTEMPLATION"

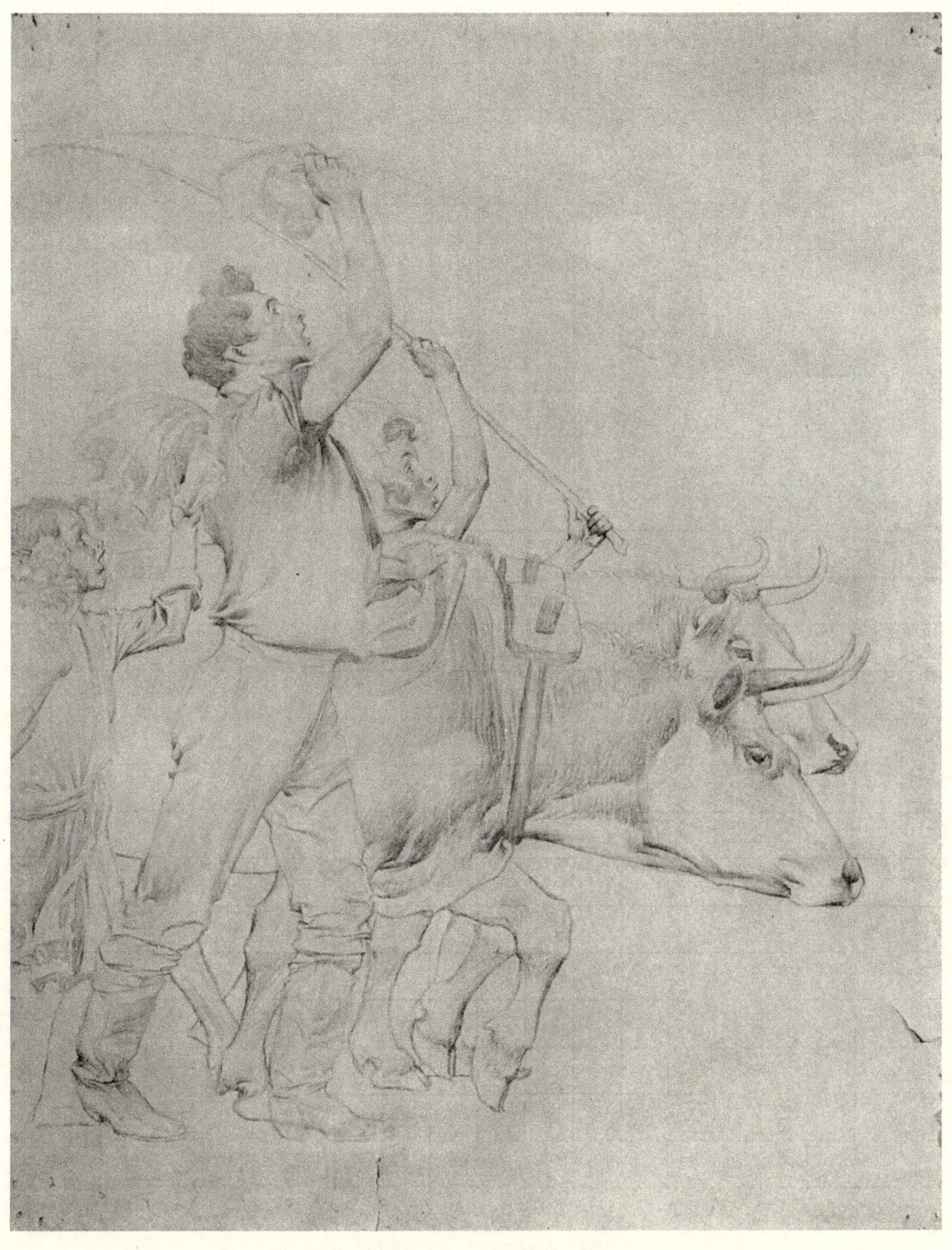

STUDY BY FRANK VINCENT DU MOND FOR A MURAL DECORATION
FOR THE SAN FRANCISCO EXPOSITION

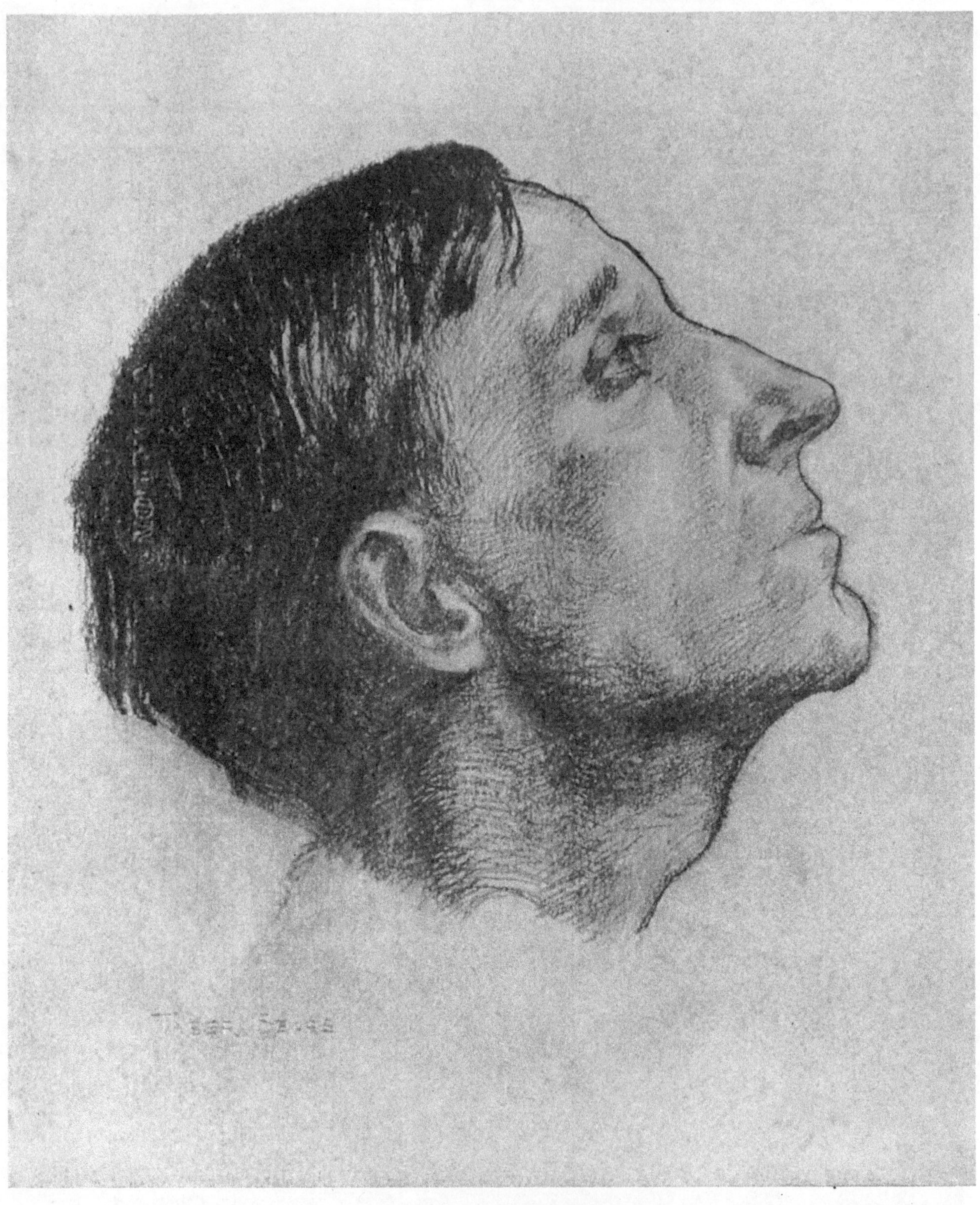

STUDY OF HEAD BY TABER SEARS FOR MURAL DECORATION IN GRACE CHURCH CHOIR SCHOOL, NEW YORK CITY
YORK & SAWYER, ARCHITECTS

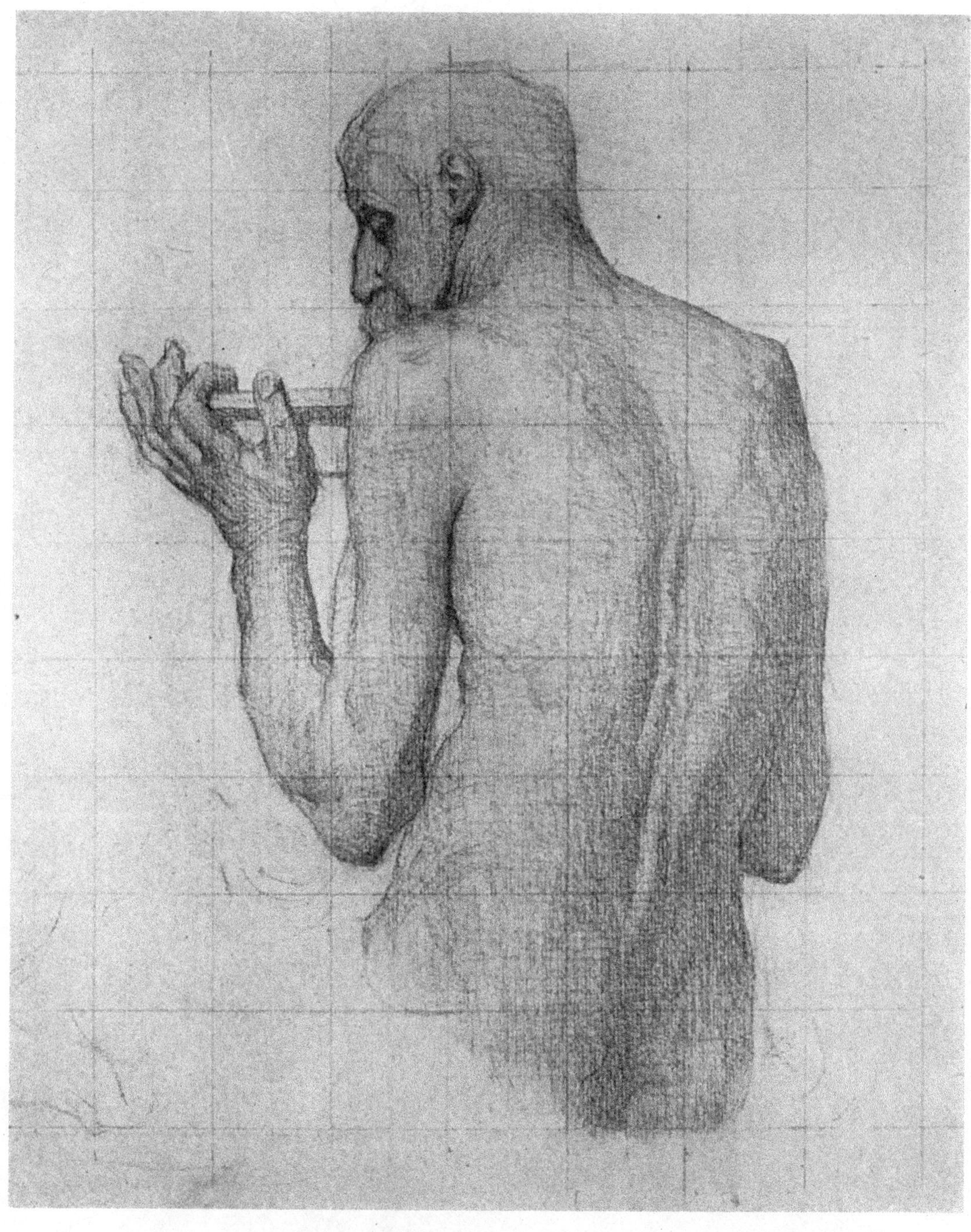

STUDY BY JULES GUERIN FOR FIGURE IN MURAL DECORATION IN THE LINCOLN MEMORIAL, WASHINGTON, D. C.

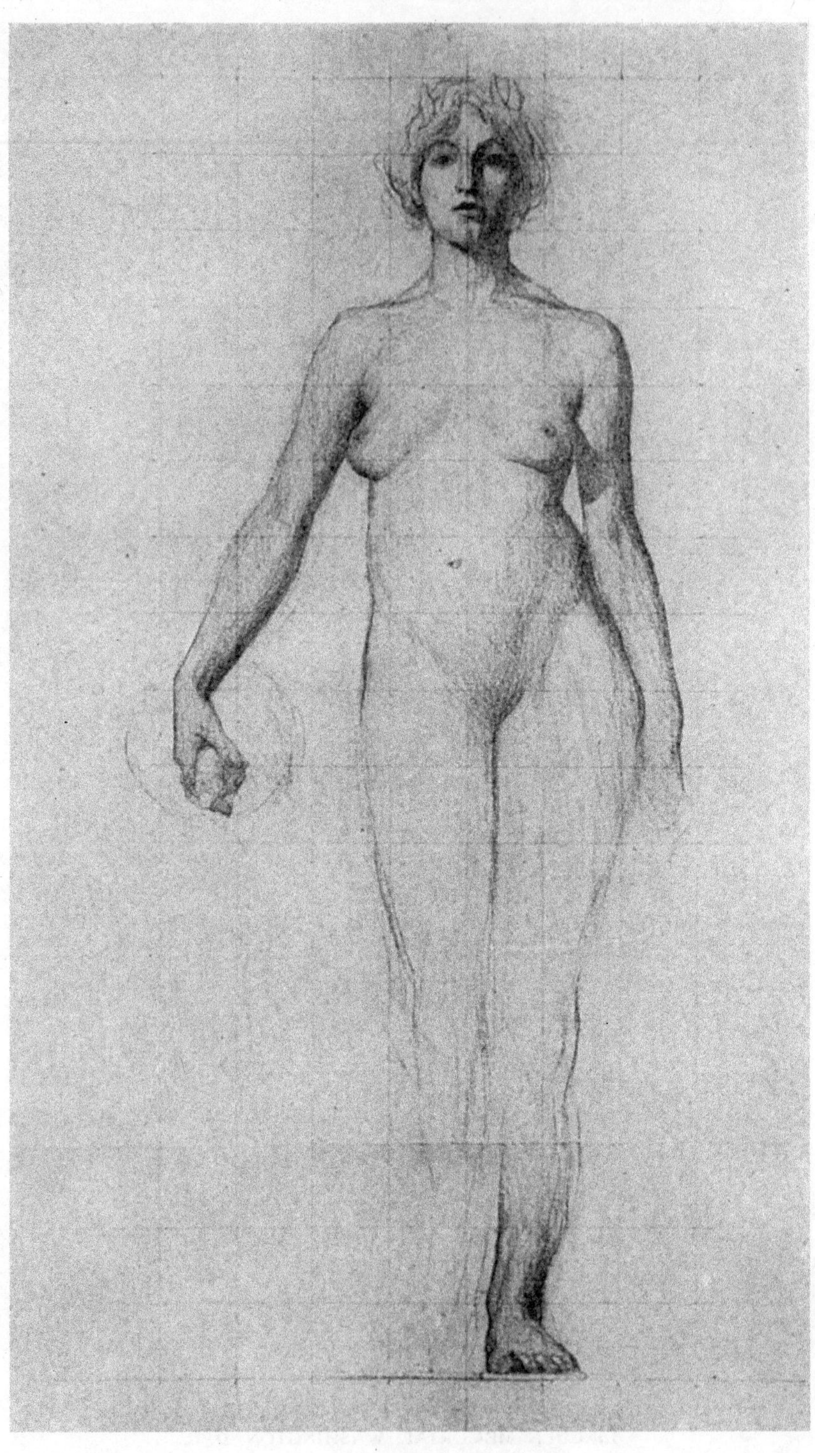

STUDY BY JULES GUERIN FOR FIGURE IN ONE OF HIS MURAL DECORATIONS IN THE LINCOLN MEMORIAL. WASHINGTON, D. C.

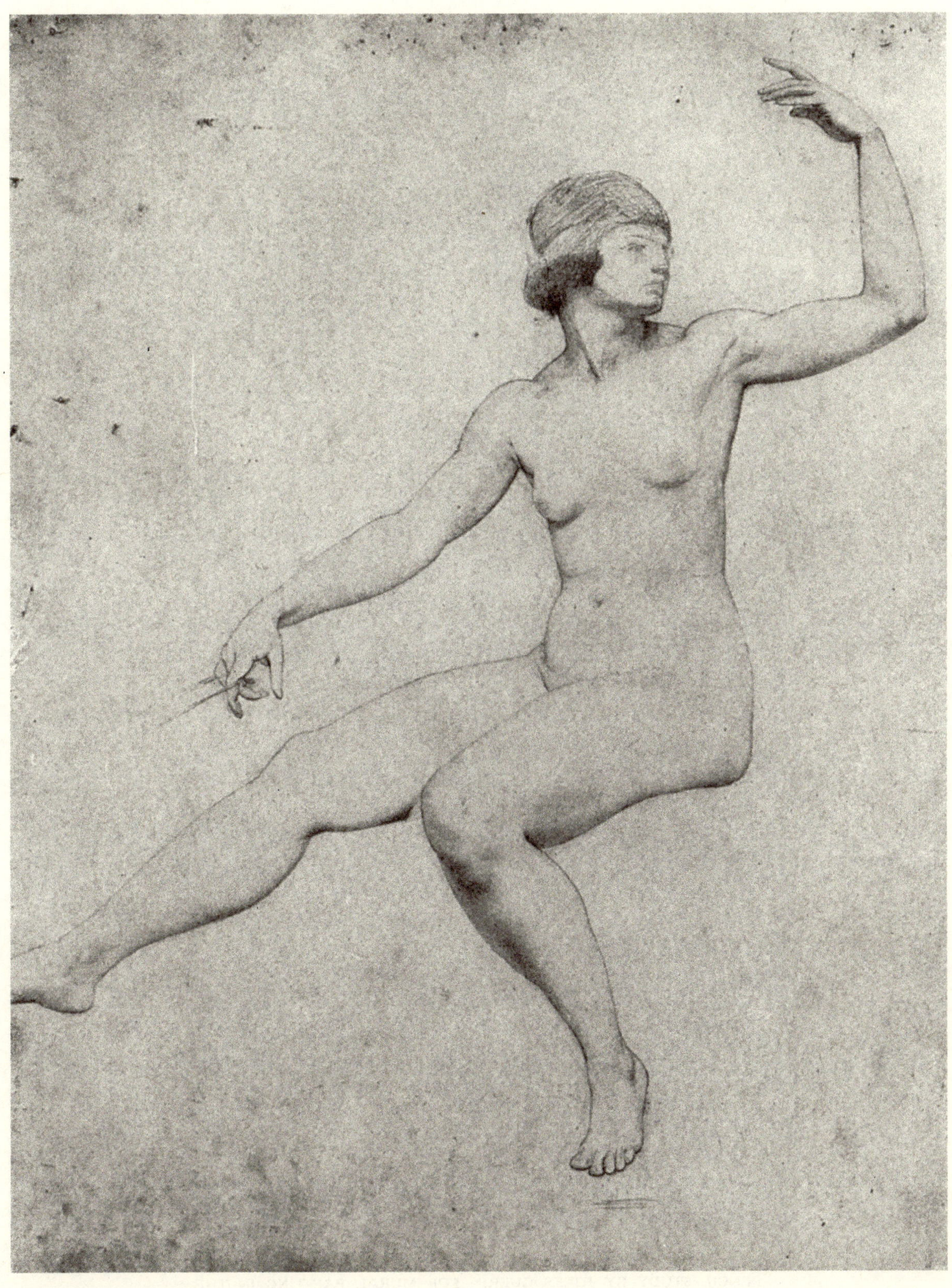

DRAWING BY BARRY FAULKNER FOR MURAL DECORATION IN THE CUNARD BUILDING, NEW YORK CITY

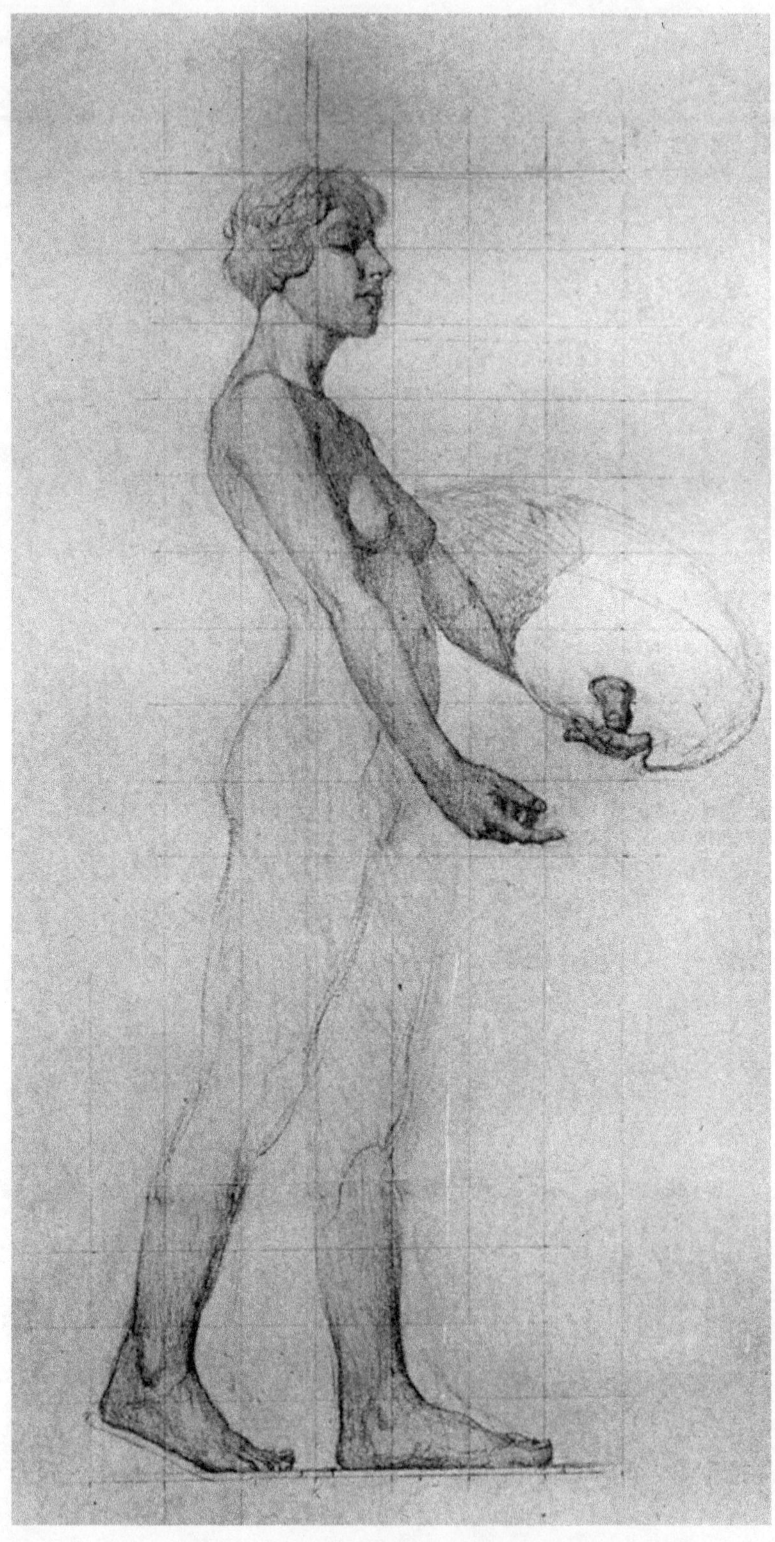

PENCIL STUDY BY JULES GUERIN FOR MURAL PAINTING IN THE LINCOLN MEMORIAL, WASHINGTON, D. C.

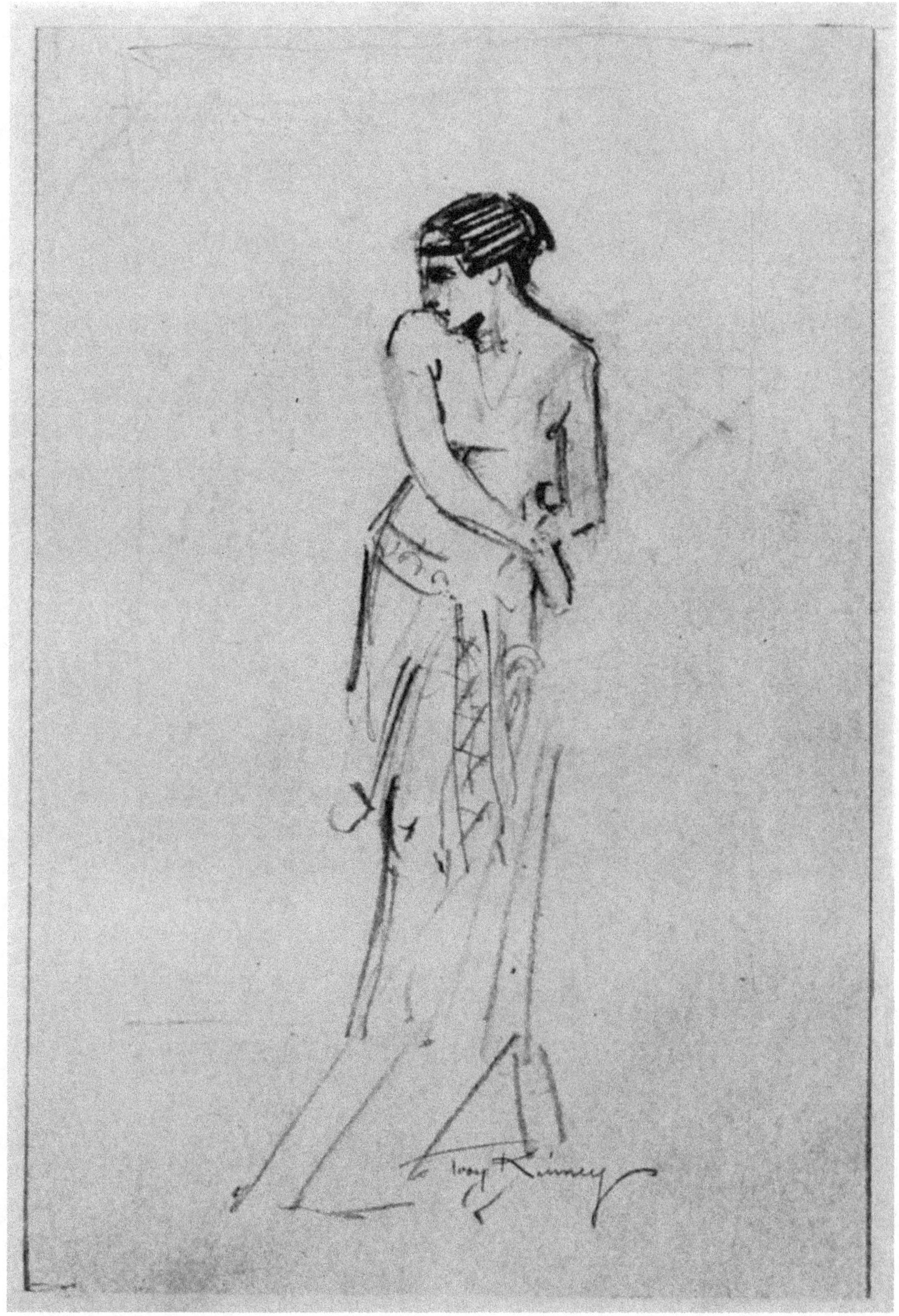

Courtesy of Kennedy & Co.

STUDY BY TROY KINNEY.
FOKINA IN HER DANCE OF SALOME

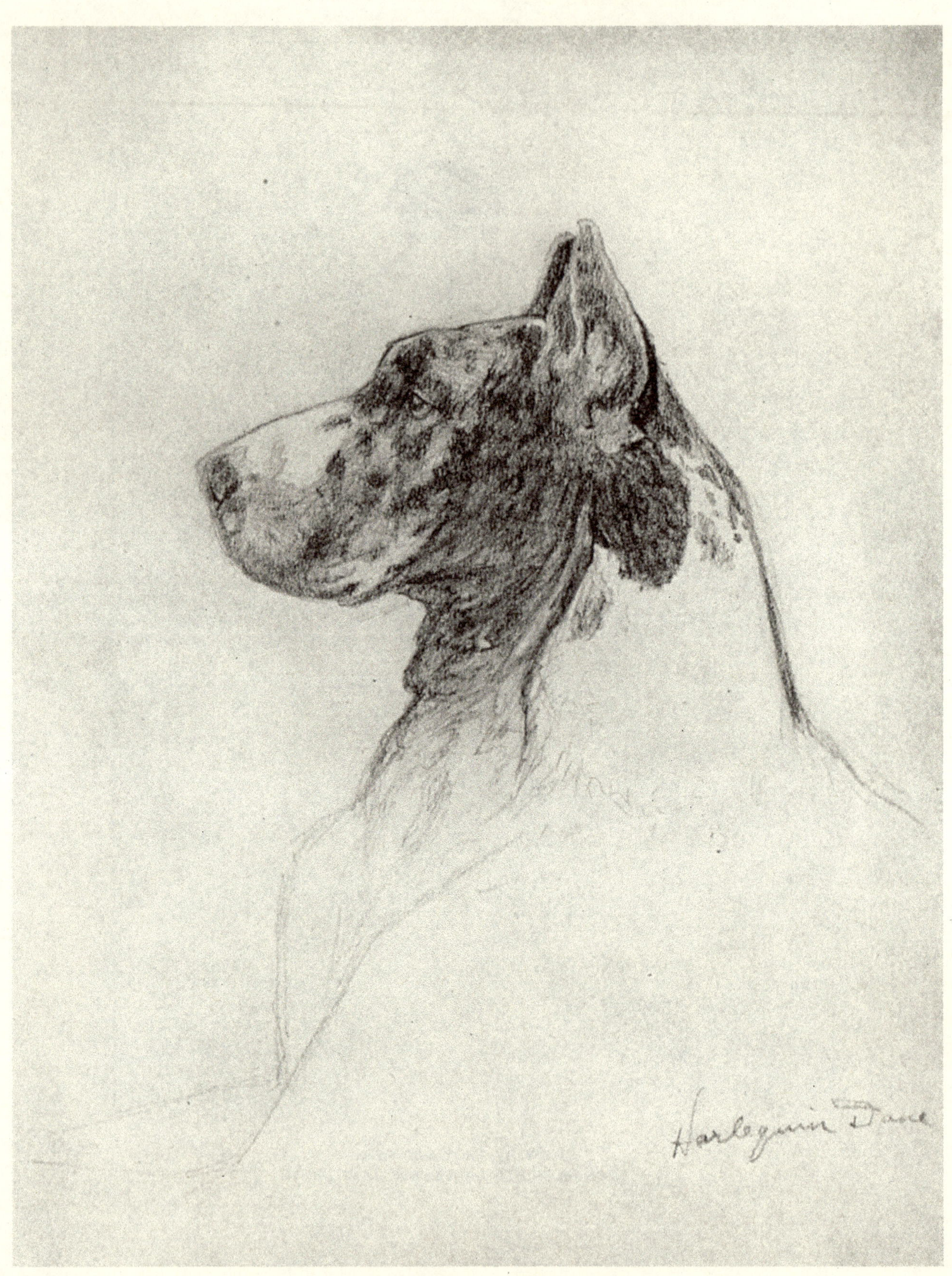

SKETCH OF A GREAT DANE BY CHARLES LIVINGSTON BULL

Chapter VIII.
SKETCHING ANIMALS

AMONG artists there are many specialists; men who give attention to the representation of some one type of subject only. We have our portrait painters, for instance, and our landscape painters. There are those who do nothing but marine views or who select city streets or gardens and flowers or some other kind of thing which appeals to them individually.

Included in these special groups of men are those whose interest lies wholly or mainly in the picturing of animals,—who devote years to the acquisition of knowledge on this particular class of subject; who go on expeditions far afield seeking first hand information; who travel the world over, perhaps, sketching and drawing and painting all the time, wherever animals are found.

But we do not purpose to consider our subject here from the standpoint of these specialists; instead we simply wish to point out to the reader some of the benefits which the average student of art may gain from animal sketching in pencil, and to offer a few suggestions regarding such work.

Animal sketching combines some of the advantages of drawing from the human figure with those of outdoor sketching, for as the subjects to be pictured are often in motion, one gains an ability to grasp the most significant of their characteristics instantly and a facility to rapidly represent them on paper, and as animals are found out of doors, as a rule, one must go into the open to draw them, which should add to his enjoyment and afford a beneficial change from the class room or studio. Aside from these considerations, however, which do not always exist, as the beginner frequently works indoors from photographs or stuffed specimens which can be drawn at leisure, there is another point worth mentioning, for it should not be forgotten that the more things one learns to draw and the greater his mental collection of facts of form and of light and shade and of color becomes, the easier it will be for him

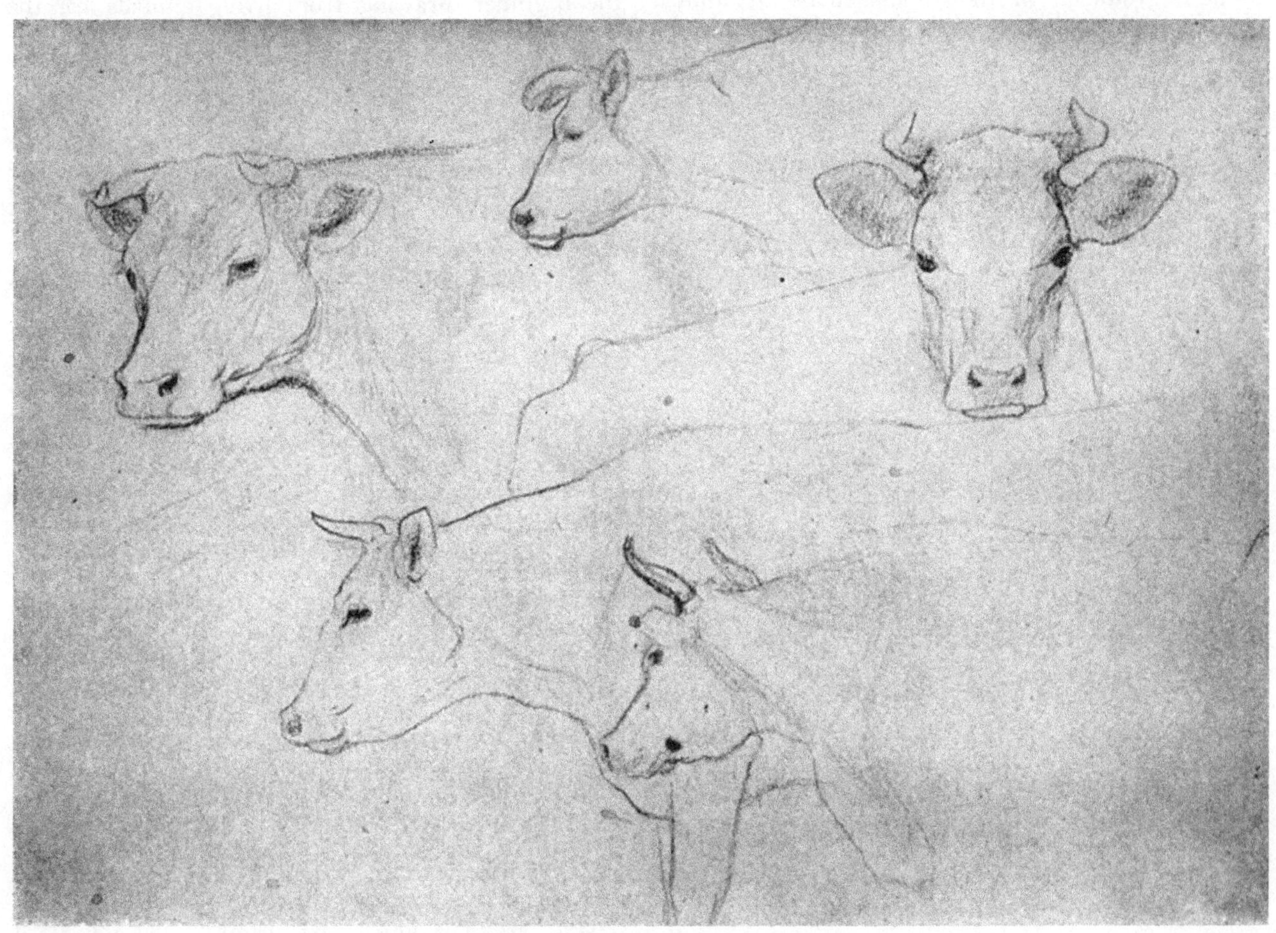

Pencil Sketch by Charles Livingston Bull.

to advance, especially if he wishes to become an illustrator or turns to the usual types of commercial art for a livelihood. And the more one knows about animals, the more he will wish to know, as a rule, for his life will be the richer because of his knowledge.

It is seldom that living animals can be used to advantage for indoor classes, so the beginner in animal sketching is more often provided with photographs or with stuffed specimens from which to draw. Through these things he gains a fundamental knowledge of his subject before he ventures to attempt the more difficult task of working from living things. In many of our cities it is possible to obtain sketching permits which allow one to work in the museums, and the student who has this opportunity should avail himself of it, not only because it will fit him for his later work, but because he can find in such collections mounted specimens of a rare or unusual nature, such as animals from the tropics or the polar regions.

It would hardly be wise for the student who has not advanced some distance in his art studies to spend much time drawing from living animals, yet there will be no harm if he occasionally does so, and once he has gained a certain amount of skill in working from still life and casts and the like, he can profitably give considerable time to it. Then as soon as he is grounded in the fundamentals of animal sketching through the work from photographs or stuffed specimens as described above he should take every opportunity for such practice and make the most of it. We say "take every opportunity" because one soon learns that he must get this practice when he can;—we do not always have animals about us and even if we do they sometimes fail to show a willingness to pose. In fact, it is often necessary to follow animals from place to place in order to sketch them at all. This is of course difficult, so the beginner, drawing from living animals for the first time, should try to catch them asleep or busy eating or at rest; even then they will offer difficulties enough.

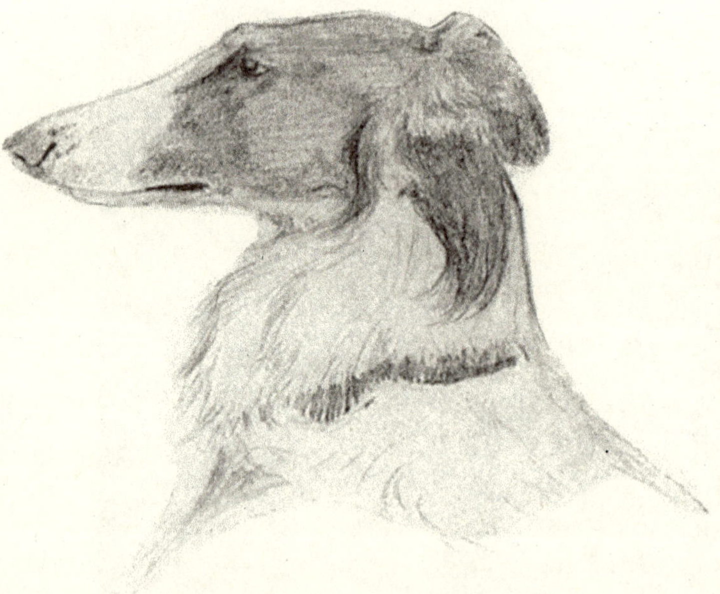

Head of Russian Wolf Hound, Sketch by Charles Livingston Bull.

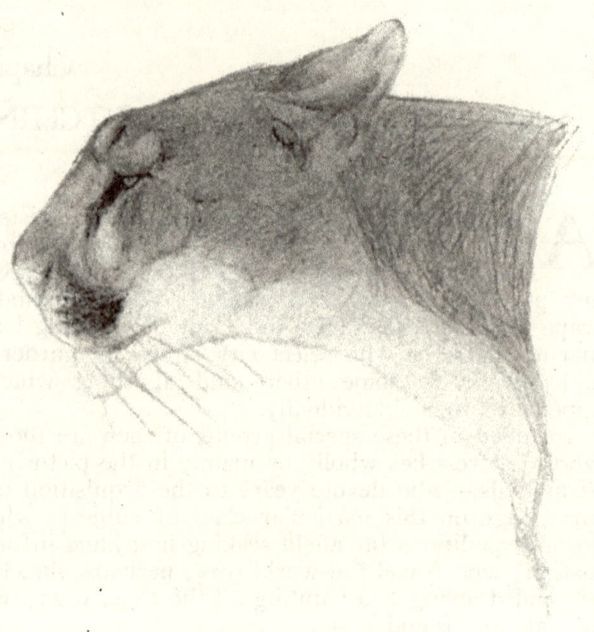

Head of Puma, Sketch by Charles Livingston Bull.

Domestic animals usually afford us the most satisfactory subjects for our first sketches, partly because they are more often available, partly because we are already more or less familiar with them, and partly for the reason that they have little fear of man and so assume natural positions. Cats and dogs are good and they offer a wide variety of subjects, and horses and cows and other quadrupeds common to our farms are excellent, too. The beginner will also find that as a rule cows or oxen or sheep or other slow moving creatures are easier to sketch than such restless or quick moving types as horses or dogs or kittens, but this is not always so, for when they are at rest one is about as easy to do as another.

When the student has his paper ready and the subject selected, the method of working will be about the same as for drawing from the human figure. Of course the different kinds of animals differ more in appearance than do people, and this means that even greater attention must be given to the interpretation of the individual characteristics of each subject, which in turn means that before starting to draw, one should analyze his subject thoroughly, searching especially for such characteristics as are not common to other animals. Then when the first strokes are made on the paper they must be direct, for there is little time for fumbling or erasing. Of course if the animal is at rest the work may be carried on more leisurely, but it is well to get the habit of drawing quickly and positively. Animals move so constantly that the artist can seldom draw more than a few lines before some change in position is noted. In this case it is often better to begin anew, and if another move is soon

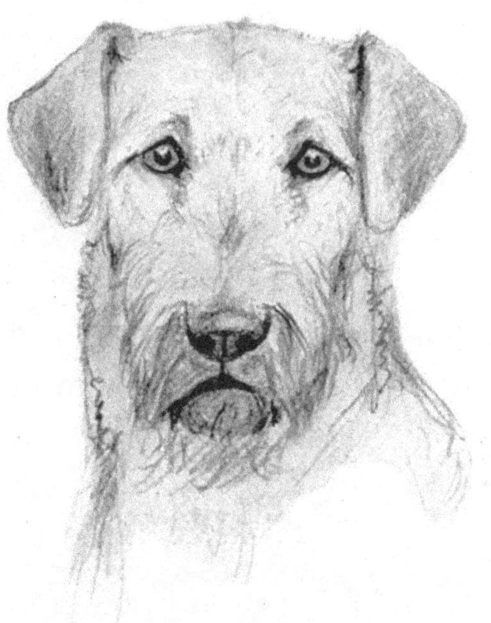

Head of Airedale, Sketch by Charles Livingston Bull.

made of enough importance to prove disturbing start still another sketch, until there are possibly a half dozen or more small ones begun on the same sheet. Then these can be carried along simultaneously, for the animal will probably either resume a previous pose sooner or later, or the artist can change his own position until his subject appears relatively the same as before.

Usually the first sketches are done in outline only, though this outline should be made as expressive as possible,—an entirely different line is needed for the shaggy coat of a Saint Bernard dog than would be used for some short haired type like the hound. If the animal remains fairly still it will not be difficult to add some shading to the outline, and if time permits, it may be possible to put in enough surrounding detail so that the sketch tells some story, for the animal can be shown as if doing a special thing,—a kitten can be sketched, for instance, as if playing with a spool of thread, or a dog gnawing a bone may be shown, or a calf drinking from a pail.

It should not be supposed that domestic animals are the only ones suitable for this free-hand work, for if one has the opportunity to sketch wild things in the woods—though one seldom does—or caged animals as in a zoo, he should make the most of it, and will sometimes find them even more interesting than the domestic species, not so much that they are different in themselves but more because they are less familiar to us. Needless to say, such animals as these would be drawn by the same method which we have already described for those of a domestic nature.

Now the student cannot make these sketches too frequently for the practice will always be beneficial, but if one wishes to become really proficient in animal sketching, he should not stop with work of this kind. He should learn something of the anatomy of animals and this is by no means simple; he should learn to interpret and express their emotions, for animals, especially the more sensitive types such as dogs, will show fear or surprise or pleasure just as plainly or even more plainly than a human being. He should study their habits. He should learn what animals have the most strength or alertness or agility and in what manner they display these characteristics; and he should bear in mind, too, that just as animals have individuality considered singly, so do groups of animals have certain characteristics common to a given species. If we study such groups we will notice these differences in many ways; let a number of horses and cows and sheep out to pasture and they will collect in formations of different sorts and these formations will change under varying conditions. Some groups of animals if driven to fight will make a circle with their heads towards the outside; others will separate and each go his own way. It seems hardly necessary to more than touch on such differences here and it would take much space to do so, but let the student make observations for himself.

Now when it comes to sketching groups of animals it will be found that one can scarcely work without some recourse to his memory and imagination, for even though a few in a group may retain their position for some time it is more than likely that others will be moving. This means that it often proves necessary to sketch them one or two at a time, putting them into natural arrangements on the paper later.

The most difficult thing of all, perhaps, is to successfully picture animals in rapid motion. One must learn by observation and study the impression given by such movements and then attempt to put this impression on paper.

The excellent sketches of animals by Mr. Charles Livingston Bull, accompanying this text, are taken directly from his own sketch books and are worthy of the most careful study.

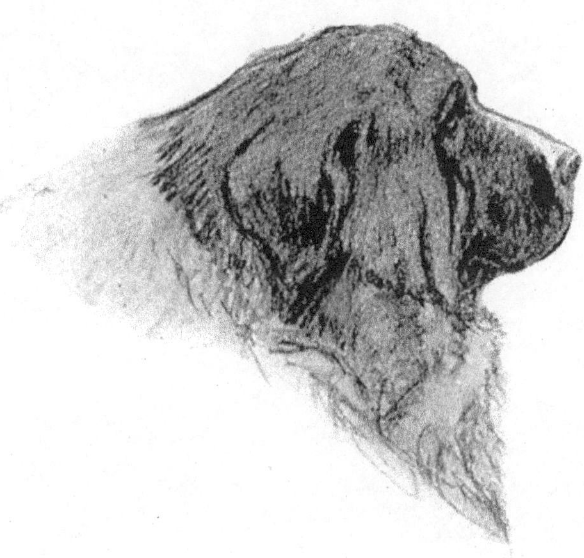

Head of Red St. Bernard, Sketch by Charles Livingston Bull.

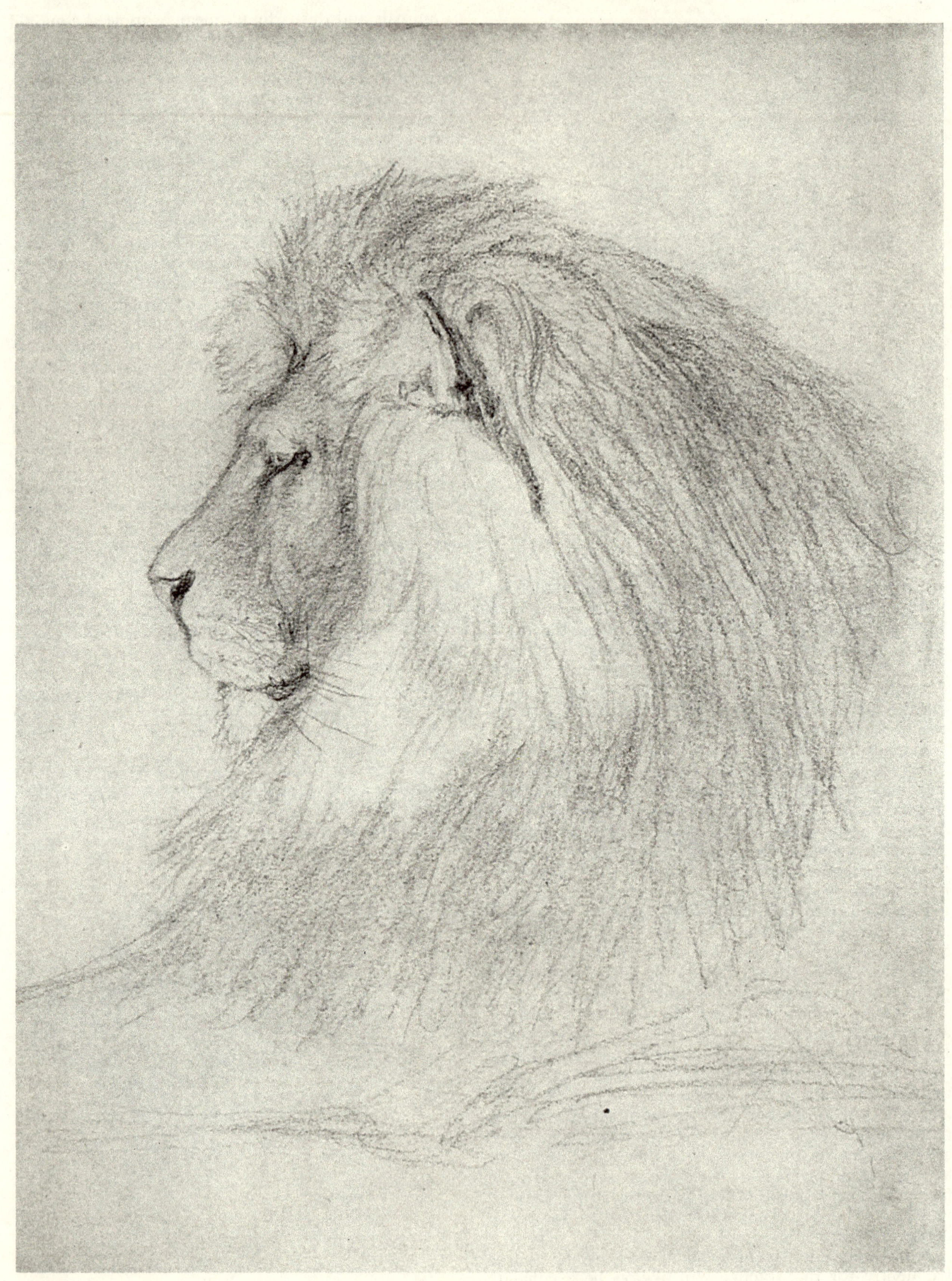

HEAD OF A LION. SKETCH BY CHARLES LIVINGSTON BULL

PART II.

Chapter I.

ARCHITECTURAL CONSIDERATIONS

WHEN the student has obtained a sound fundamental knowledge of the subjects treated in Part I, namely—Object Drawing in Outline, Object Drawing in Light and Shade, Free-hand Perspective, Cast Drawing, Life Drawing and Sketching Animals, it would seem that he might find little difficulty in sketching buildings, street scenes and the like.

Yet every new subject presents its peculiar problems;—there are many things that the beginner will hardly know how to approach. A street scene or a landscape or a building, for instance, needs a far different treatment than a posed model in the life class, but the artist should be trained to do all of these well, especially if he hopes to become an illustator or commercial artist. If typical book or magazine illustrations, or free-hand drawings of almost any sort in which figures appear, are studied, it will be seen that buildings or portions of buildings or bits of landscape are given almost as much attention as the figures themselves,—one could hardly hope to become successful in such a line of work if he lacked skill in the representation of any of these things.

Among the following chapters the art student will find many valuable hints to help him draw these subjects for some have been especially prepared to offer suggestions on the drawing of buildings, both in whole and in part, as well as all sorts of accessories such as water and clouds; then there are other chapters presenting many facts regarding technique, composition, decorative drawing, the uses of tinted paper, etc., for one should master these, too, in order to gain versatility.

If skill in the representation of buildings is important to the artist or the art student it is indispensable to the architect and his assistants, and it is mainly to meet their requirements that the following chapters have been prepared. If the time for drawing practice is limited, the work in object drawing and cast drawing and life drawing described in Part I may be omitted by the reader of architectural inclination and he may turn directly to the problems discussed in these coming pages, where the subject of Sketching and Rendering in Pencil is considered mainly from the standpoint of the architect. But unless the reader is well grounded in drawing it is desirable that he study Part I and before going further it is advisable to study at least the first two chapters of Part I, and Chapter V on free-hand perspective. A knowledge of perspective is essential to anyone who paints or draws, and especially to those who find the representation of buildings or street scenes a part of their work.

Selecting the Subject—In Part I emphasis was placed on the importance of selecting a suitable subject for each drawing, and it is equally essential for the work to be done at present that the choice be as carefully made;—it is as much of a problem to learn to select as it is to learn to draw. Now the architectural draftsman or student wishes to learn architecture as well as how to draw, so it is usually best for him to choose some architectural object of merit. The drawing may be made directly from some interesting portion of a building, if the student feels capable of attempting this, or from a photograph. In either case it is well not to attempt too much at one time.

When the subject has been chosen it is necessary next to decide exactly how much of the object is to be drawn. If one works from the photograph this is comparatively easy, for by using strips of paper or cardboard as a frame, suitable compositions can be found. One has more difficulty, however, when drawing directly from a building for it is then necessary to determine the point from which the best view can be obtained. If you were to photograph such an object as you have selected to draw, the view-finder of the camera would help you to determine the best point at which to stand and would frame for you any number of interesting views from which you might select the best. The same idea may be carried out by the student of sketching, either by using a camera view-finder or, what is more commonly done, by making a view-finder by cutting a rectangular opening about 1½ in. x 2 in. through a sheet of stiff paper or cardboard, which, when held near the eye, will help you to decide the point from which the drawing can best be made. Once the subject has been chosen and the point from which it is to be drawn decided upon, we are ready to block in the proportions of the sketch.

At this point it is as well to remind the student that it is more difficult to learn what to leave out of a drawing than what to put in. As we minutely examine any object in nature we see an overwhelming mass of small detail. Even as we sit in our rooms and glance around we find, if we search, thousands of spots of light or shade or color. These tiny spots are the many lines of the delicate graining of the wood, the hundreds of partly-visible threads from which the hangings and upholstery materials are woven, the myriad indentations and projections of the masonry and plaster.

It is hardly necessary to point out that it would be impossible to correctly indicate each of these spots on a small sheet of paper, even if it were desirable to do so. Instead we must try to represent the

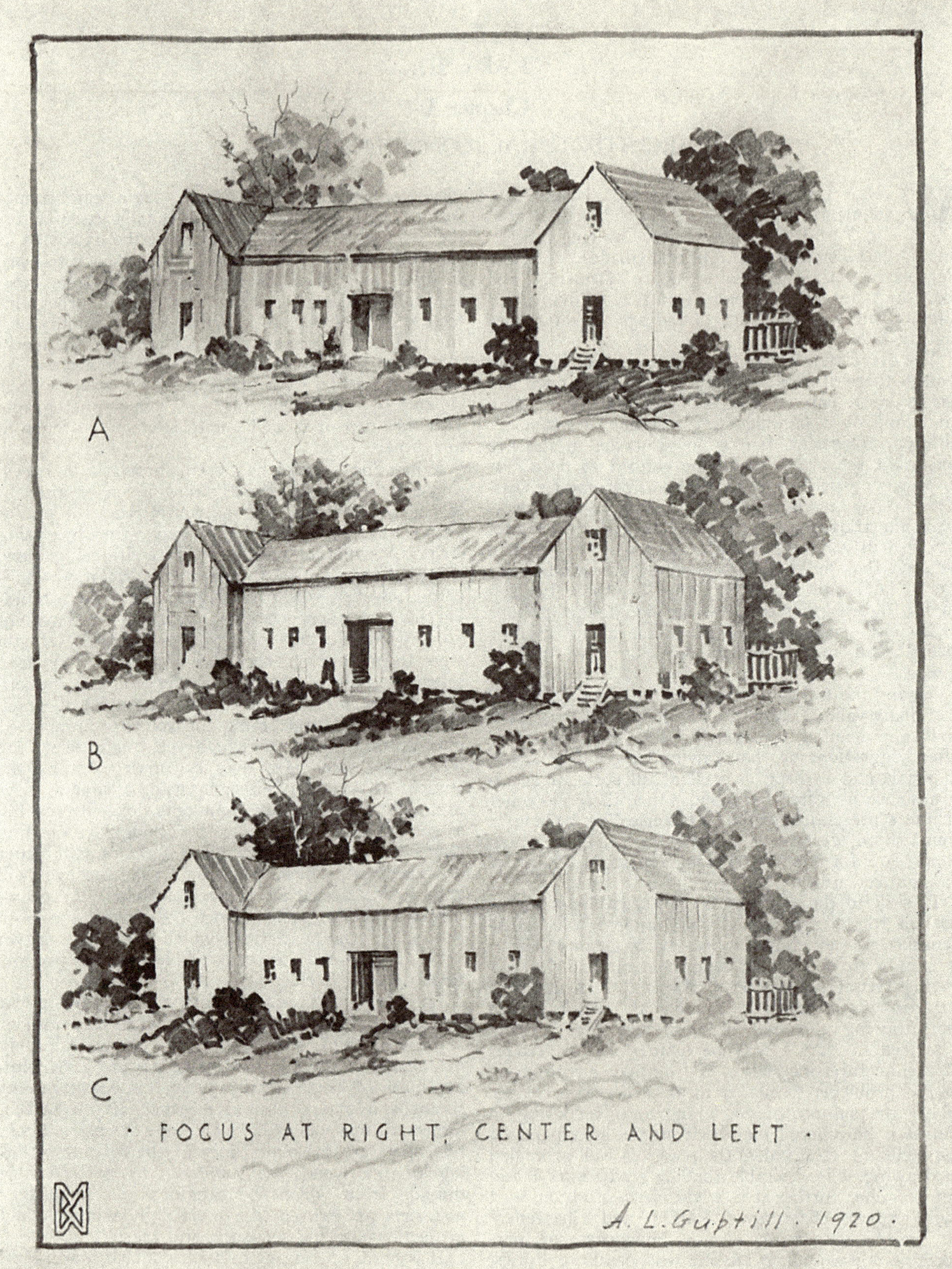

Figure 12. Illustrating a Method of Focusing Attention on Different Parts of a Building.

effect of the mass as a whole, the effect that we get not when we hunt for such details, but when we enter a room and look around in the usual way. If we do look directly at some object such as a chair in a room corner we see little detail with the exception of that in the chair itself and in those objects adjacent to it. Even in these objects we are not conscious of each tiny spot, but instead notice only the broad general tone and effect. The chair, being directly in the range of vision, is the center of interest and the other objects become more and more indistinct and blurred the farther they are from this center. It really is a surprising thing what a small area we are able to see plainly when looking in one direction only. We are so accustomed to shifting our eyes constantly from one object to another that we fail to notice this limitation. Stand within ten feet of a door and gaze intently at the knob. Without shifting the eyes, are you able to see the top of the door distinctly? If you raise the eyes and look at the top of the door, do you see the bottom plainly? Go to the window and look at some building across the street. Fix your attention on an upper window or chimney or some part of the roof. Are not the lower portions of the building blurred and indistinct unless you shift your gaze to them? When you look at the foundation you do not see the roof distinctly.

Now in making a drawing it is assumed that the artist is looking in some one fixed direction. He gazes at some interesting object or, if the entire object is too large to come within his range of vision, he selects some prominent feature which then becomes the center of interest or focal point. In making the drawing more detail is shown near this center of interest than in the other parts, which are allowed to become more and more indistinct towards the edges of the picture, just as they appear in nature. Every drawing should have this center of interest or focal point and all else should be subordinated to it.

Now turn to the illustration, Figure 12. Cover the lower two drawings and study the upper drawing "A." In this sketch the spectator was looking towards that part of the old farm buildings nearest to him, so this becomes the center of interest or focal point; all else is subordinated.

Look at sketch "B," first covering up sketches "A" and "C." Here the spectator's eye has turned towards the center of the building and interest centers in the large doorway and adjacent walls—here the details show most plainly and here are the strongest accents of light and shade. The two ends of the building become rather blurred and indistinct; they are subordinated.

Now uncover "C" and cover "B." In "C" the spectator is looking still farther to the left and even though that portion of the building is some distance from the eye, it is the portion on which the eye is focused, hence the strongest contrasts and accents are there and the rest of the building is subordinate.

Turn to Figure 13, the street scene. In the drawing at the left the spectator is looking at the upper part of the tower; that becomes the subject of the sketch, the focal point or center of interest. The street is blurred, the detail is softened. In the second drawing the spectator is looking down the street; the archway becomes the center of interest and the tower is almost lost against the sky. Now in drawing such a subject as this street scene from nature the student is likely to get into difficulty. He looks first, perhaps, at the tower and draws that. If he stops there all well and good; the tower becomes the subject of the sketch. But if he lowers his gaze to the street and adds the archway to his drawing it is quite possible that this will form a second focal point which will compete with the tower. Then the drawing will be a failure for the eye will jump back and forth between the tower and the archway and the balance will be destroyed. In such a composition as this, where there are two possible centers of interest, be sure that one is subordinated to the other.

Now turn to Figure 14, the little interior. Where is the center of interest represented in the drawing at the top of the sheet? Where does the eye see the most detail and the strongest contrasts of light and dark? The window with its seat is outside the focus and it is only when the eye turns towards it as it does in the lower picture that it becomes the center of vision or focal point. In this latter case the mantel is out of focus and might be omitted from the drawing; in fact, this room could be made the subject of two interesting sketches, one of the fireplace and one of the window and seat. In such a room as this we can well imagine that in the evening the fireplace with the family drawn up enjoying a cheerful blaze would be in all ways the center of interest in the room, while in the daytime the window with its seat would doubtless gain greater attention.

Now turn to the delightful sketch by Mr. Watson on page 66;—notice that he has built up his center of interest very effectively yet without forcing it upon the attention unpleasantly, and observe, too, that the drawing is allowed to soften or fade away gradually from those parts which come most directly within the range of vision.

Let it be plain, then, that in starting a drawing it is important to first of all select something of interest to draw; next, it is necessary to find the best point from which the drawing can be made; then we must analyze our subject to determine the center of interest or focal point, and having done this we must use every care to subordinate all those parts which have little or nothing to do with our subject, and which might detract from the center of interest.

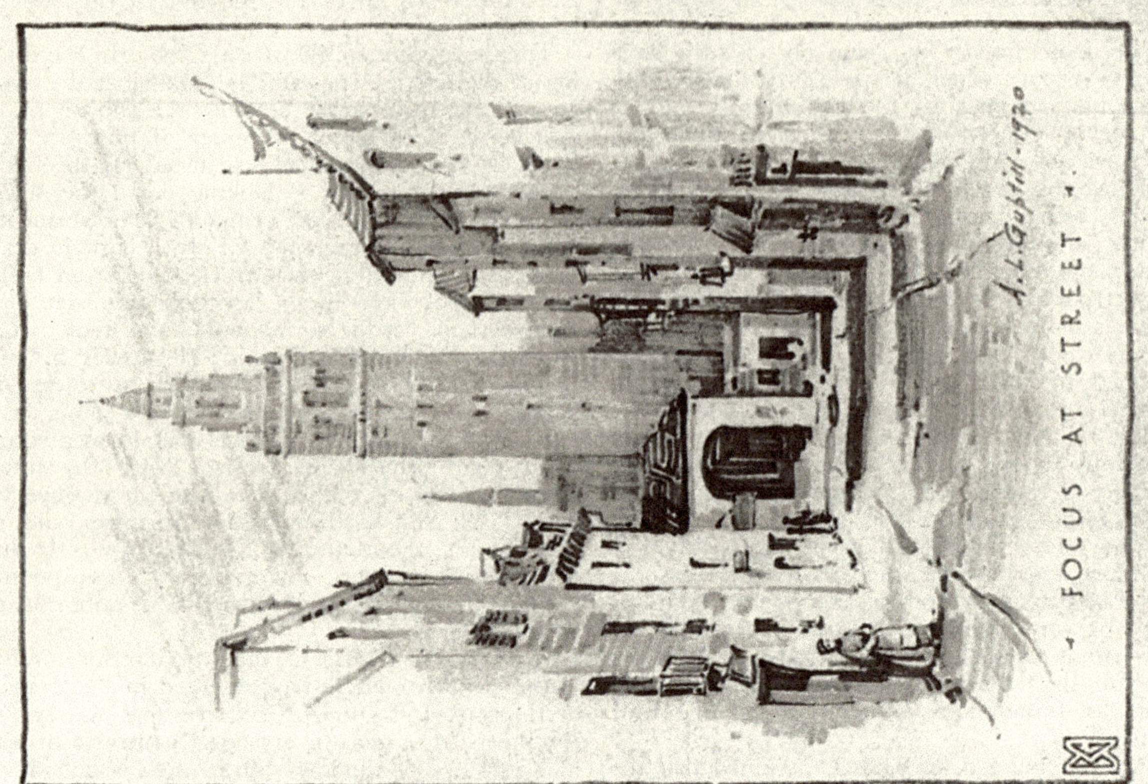

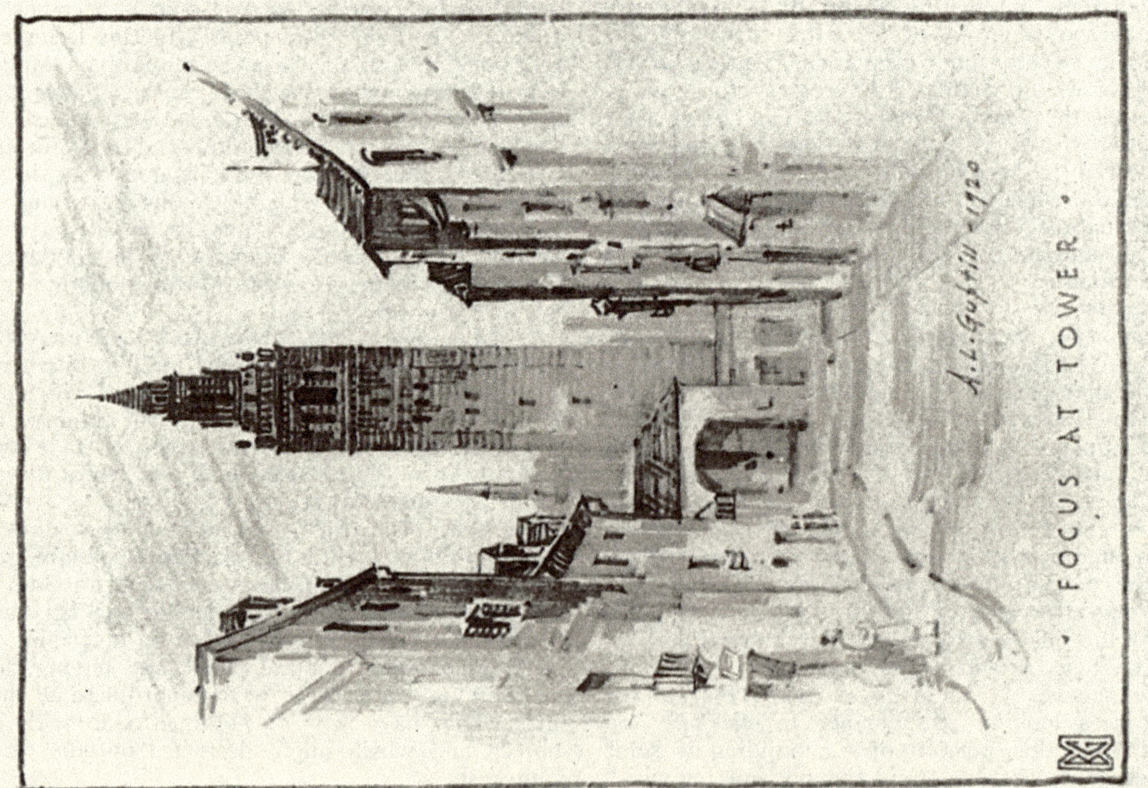

Figure 13. Illustrating Methods of Accenting Different Parts of a Street Scene.

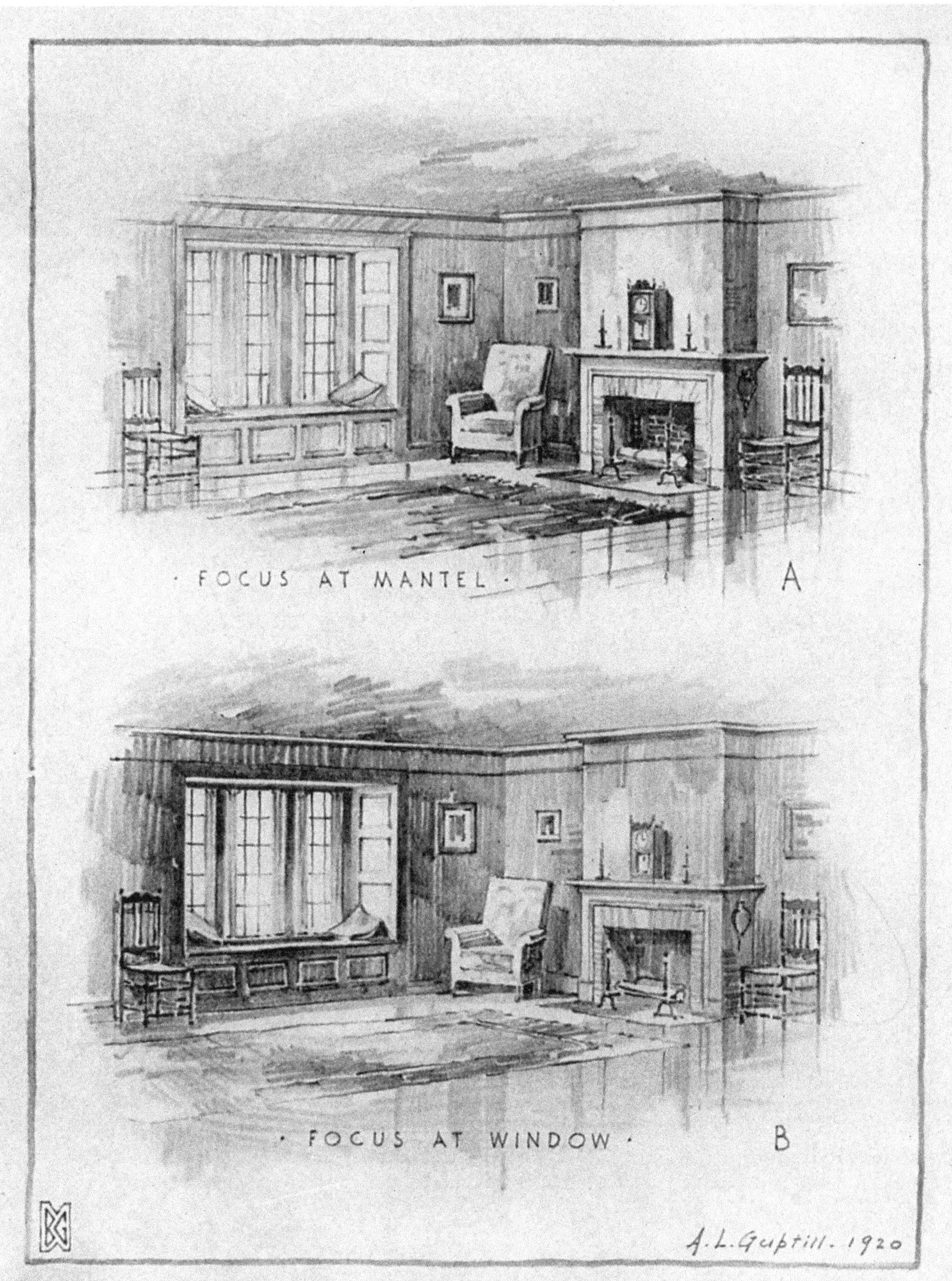

Figure 14. Illustrating Method of Accenting or Subordinating Parts of a Room.

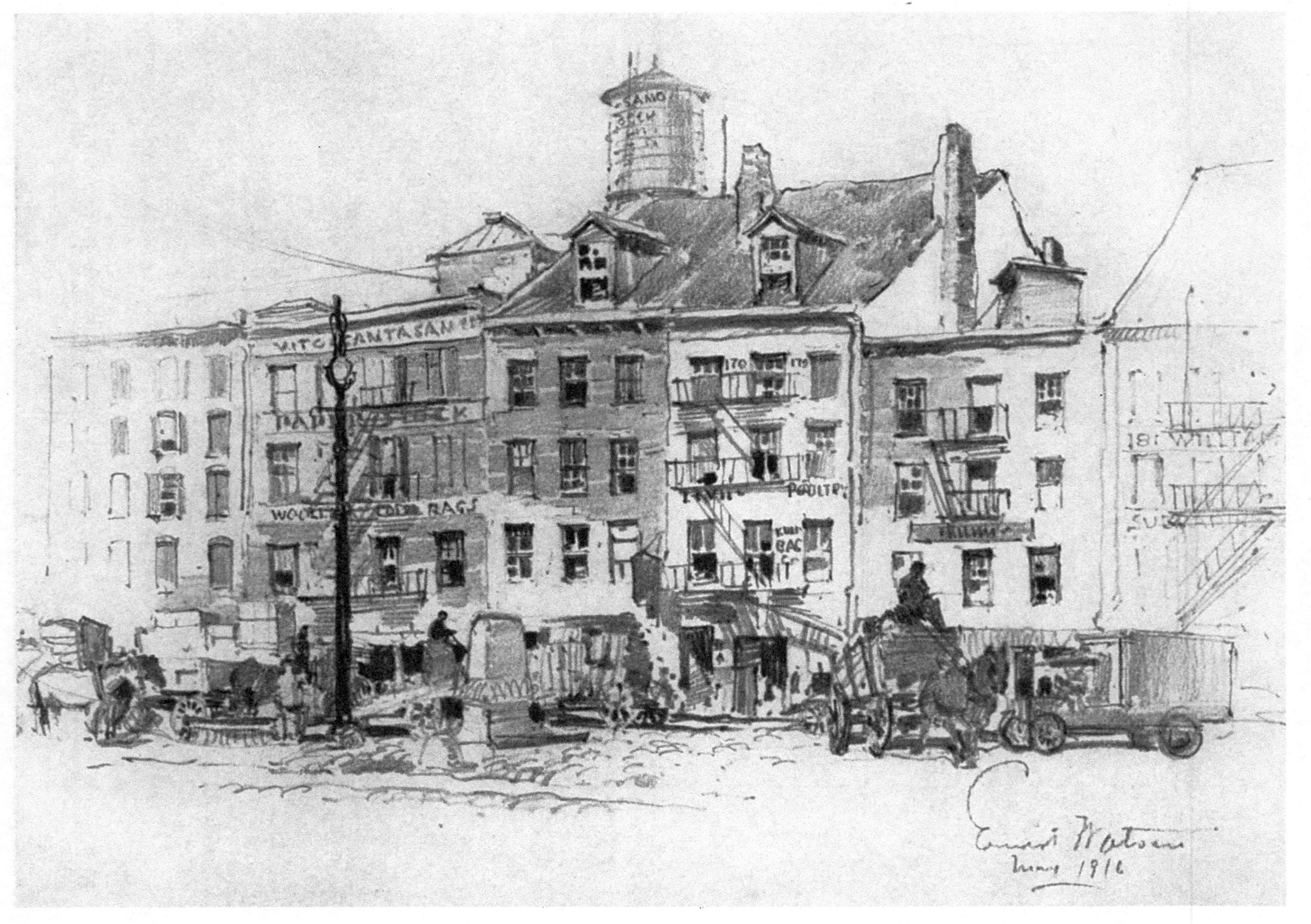

SKETCH BY ERNEST WATSON

Chapter II.

STARTING THE WORK

THE student should determine before sharpening his pencils just what they are to be required to do, and should point them accordingly. Sharply-pointed pencils will answer very well if a drawing is to be small or if much fine detail is to be shown, but if it is to be large, broad pointed pencils will usually produce an effect equally satisfactory in a much shorter space of time. Many drawings combine both fine lines and wide lines with excellent results.

No special directions for forming a sharp point seem necessary, but a broad point is not so commonly used, so the following suggestions are offered. First of all, cut away the wood in the usual manner just as for a sharp point, but leave one-quarter or three-eighths of an inch of the full-sized lead exposed. (If this lead is left too long, however, especially in the softer pencils, it will quickly break under pressure.) Next, wear the point down on fine sandpaper holding the pencil at an angle of about 45 degrees with the paper, until the lead has the appearance shown at "A," Figure 15. The end of the lead should next be smoothed by rubbing it on rough paper until each stroke gives a firm, even tone when the pencil is held as at "B." Occasional fine lines or accents in a drawing can be made with this broad point if it is held on its sharp edge as at "C," but if many fine lines are needed a sharply-pointed pencil will prove more satisfactory. The type of broad point just mentioned is used by many artists but others go still further, and by slightly squaring the whole of the exposed lead, after it has been sharpened as described above, obtain a very crisp, clean-cut line. The illustrations made by the author for this text were for the most part drawn with this latter type of point.

Regardless of how the pencil is sharpened care should be taken that the point is wiped with a cloth in order to remove all dust, for otherwise it is difficult to get a clean, firm line and next to impossible to keep the paper from becoming soiled by the loose grit from the pencil. Another point for the beginner to remember is that in sharpening the pencil the letters or numbers indicating the degree of hardness or softness of the lead should never be removed.

Having pointed and dusted the pencils, they are ready for use, though it will be convenient to so mark each one that its grade can be told at a glance. There are several ways of doing this. One is by cutting or painting the letters indicating the grade of the lead on several sides of the pencil where they can be seen easily, and another is by notching the pencils, increasing the number of notches as the pencils become harder in grade. Such letters or notches are perhaps most convenient if placed about one and one-half inches from the unsharpened end of the pencil where they will remain in view. If near the point they will soon be cut away and if at the other extremity they will be hidden if a pencil holder or lengthener is used. Some artists, instead of marking their pencils, always lay them on the drawing board according to grade. By this arrangement they can tell the degree of hardness of a pencil at a glance by its position on the board and when it has been used it can be returned to its proper place and another taken up. A still different way of marking pencils for identification is by dipping them into various colors, each color representing a definite grade of lead.

The question may arise as to the number of pencils necessary for one sketch. This number will vary all the way from one, for a quick sketch, to seven or eight as used by some draftsmen for carefully finished work. Some very well-known men never use more than one grade of pencil for an entire drawing but the student can as a rule get better results by the use of three or four. The two little sketches on Figure 20 were made with a 2B, HB, F, H and 3H.

Practice Strokes—When the pencils have been properly sharpened the student can do nothing of greater benefit than to draw many individual lines with each point before attempting complete drawings. Try to make every stroke a thing of beauty, for it is only by combining many beautiful strokes that a pleasing final result can be obtained. Draw lines of all kinds and in all directions; some straight and others curved; some uniform in tone from end to end and others grading from light to dark or from dark to light. Allow some to fade out so gradually that the ends are lost in the tones of the paper and accent others at the ends by using extra pressure as the pencil touches or leaves the drawing surface. Keep some straight and sharp, drawing them very quickly with much freedom, and form others rather slowly, allowing them to quaver or tremble. Use considerable pressure on some, thus smoothing or "ironing out" the paper, and in others barely touch the pencil to the surface. Make lines with both broad and fine points, with various grades of pencils, and on all sorts of paper until you feel a certain confidence in your knowledge of your mediums.

Tone Building—When this feeling of assurance is acquired, attempt building up even tones by massing the strokes together, either touching or with slight spaces between. Think clearly what you wish to do before you begin and then draw with directness and vigor, remembering that sharp "snappy" work is the kind most popular for architectural purposes.

There are no definite rules regarding tone building but perhaps the simplest method is to draw parallel straight or slightly curved lines just touching one another or with slight spaces between.

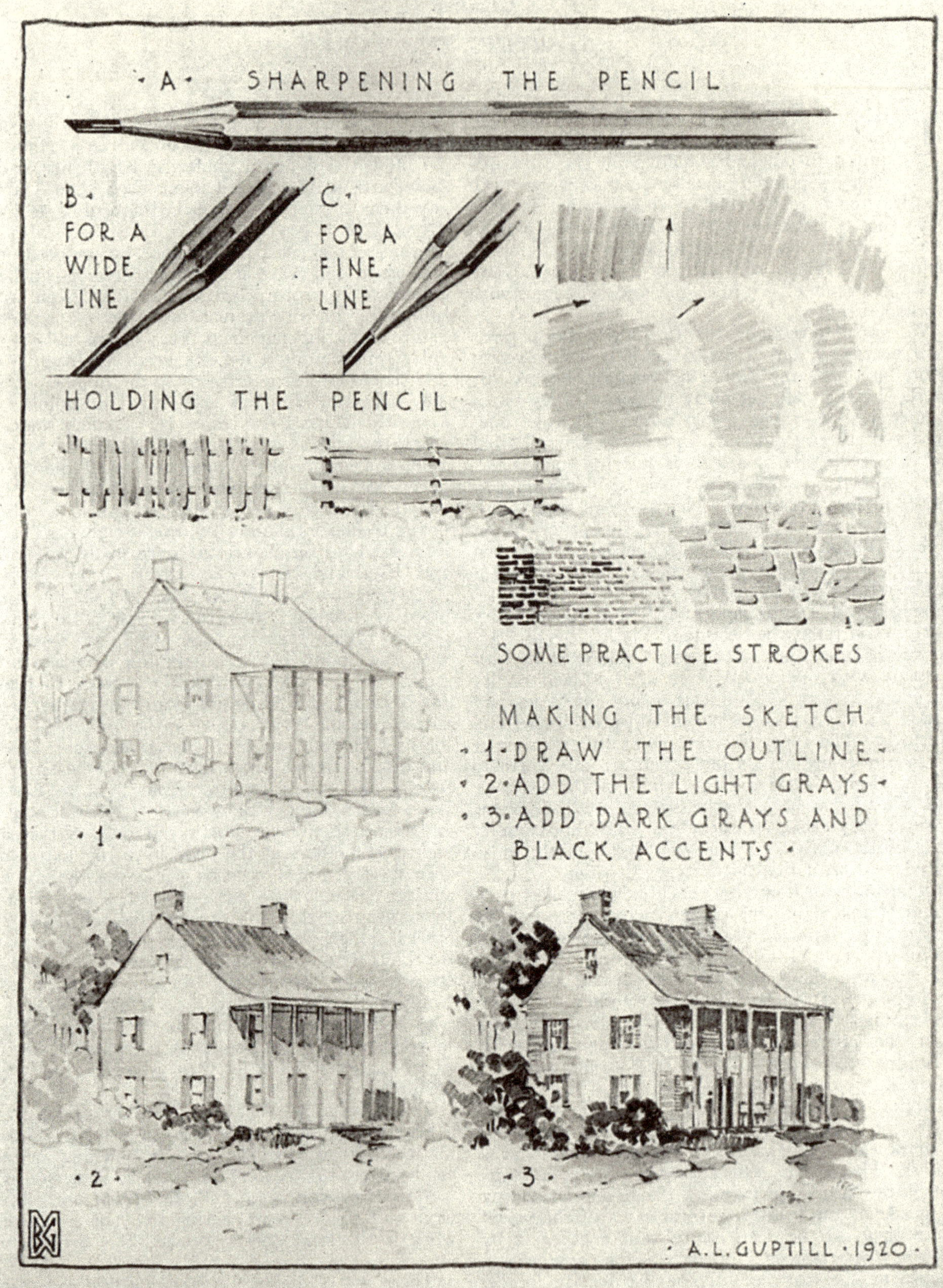

Figure 15. Illustrating Methods of Sharpening and Holding Pencil, Practice Strokes, and Steps in Sketching.

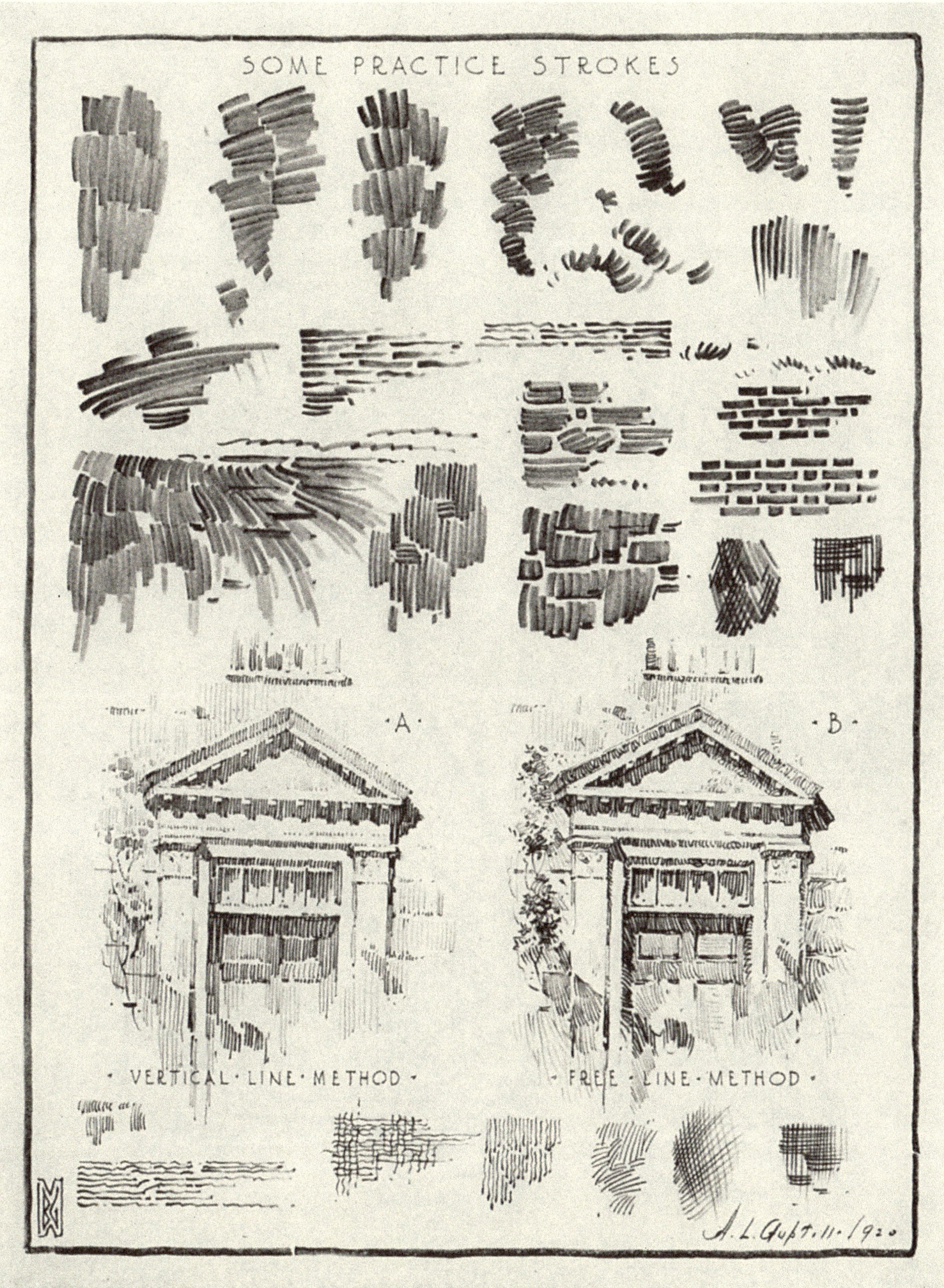

Figure 16. Illustrating Methods of Tone Building, and Two Ways of Making Sketches.

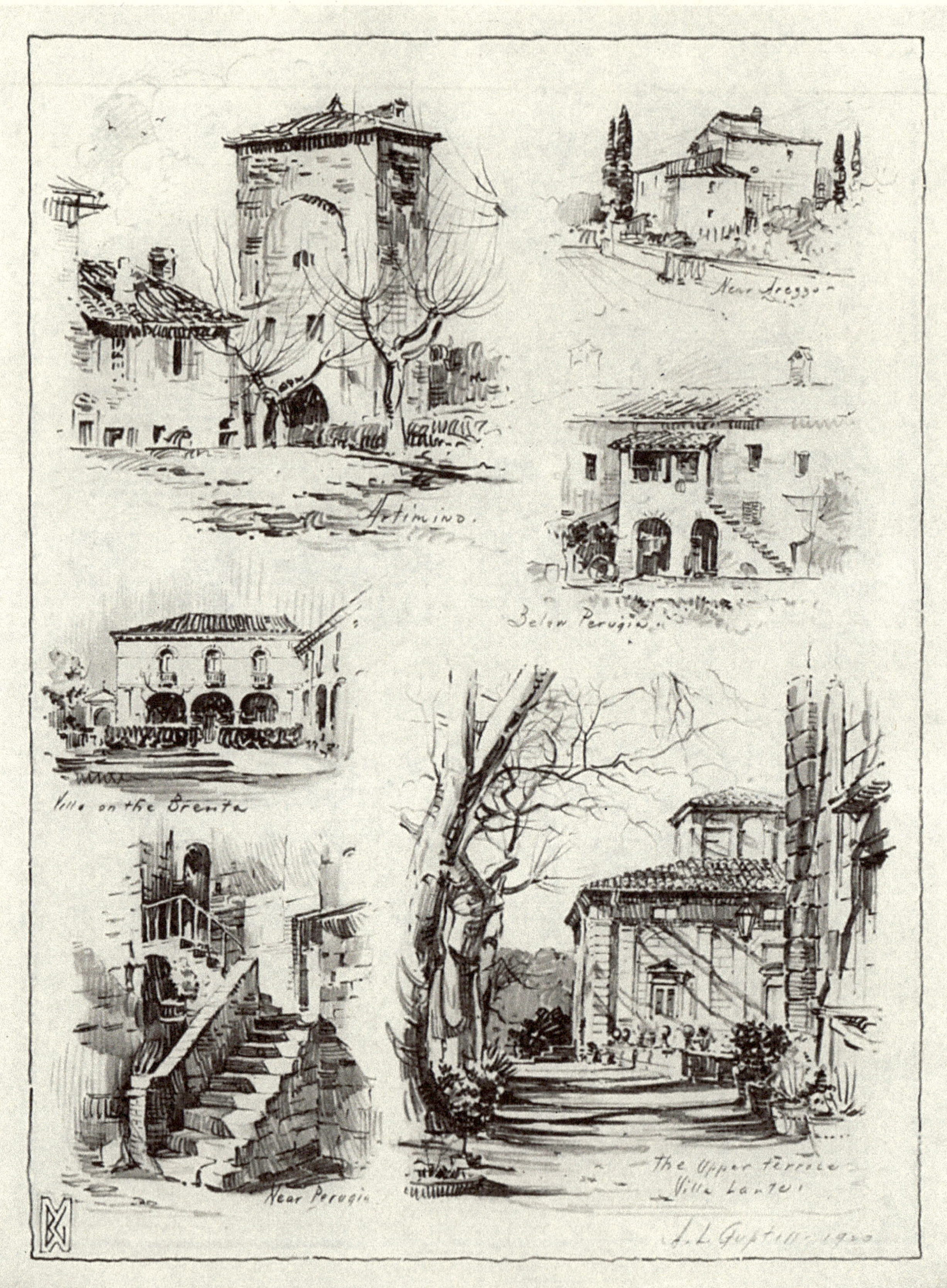

Figure 17. Illustrating Quick Sketching; a Means by Which Much Knowledge of Architecture Can be Obtained.

Sometimes these lines are horizontal but more often vertical. Occasionally entire drawings are made by using tones composed of vertical strokes only. The drawing of the doorway "A" at the bottom of Figure 16 is done by this method. There is danger, however, of such lines becoming too rigid or mechanical, or in some cases too conspicuous, so the method shown at "B," in which the lines are allowed to go in any and all directions, is a much more popular one, and one adaptable to all types of subjects. This method is sometimes referred to as the "Free Line Method."

In building tones there are several points concerning which the beginner should be cautioned. First, beware the use of too many small lines. If twenty lines will do, it is ordinarily folly to use forty. There is danger especially in the use of many short, broken lines, as they often produce a spotty effect,—the more so if the white spaces between the ends of the lines are too conspicuous. Long, unbroken lines, on the other hand, sometimes appear too mechanical. It is best as a rule to so vary the length of lines as to produce an interesting variety, avoiding too many lines of equal length and similar direction. Tones are occasionally built up by "cross hatching" but it is usually best to avoid this expedient. Figure 16 shows, however, several examples of cross hatching, and sometimes such tones are highly desirable, especially for shadows and background purposes. Frequently in drawing shadows, especially under cornices, the lines forming the shadow tones are so slanted as to suggest the direction of the light. A sparkling, sunny effect is obtained, too, if the shadow tone is sharpened or darkened along the lower edge, thus forming a strong contrast against the light surfaces below.

Needless to say, it is most important to so vary the lines and tones as to express the textures of the materials represented by the sketch. Observation and practice will teach the student the best way to indicate wood, masonry, glass, metal, cloth, water, and the like.

Do not erase unless absolutely necessary, as results are never entirely satisfactory over an erased surface. If mistakes are made, use a soft eraser with extreme care and be sure to dust the paper thoroughly afterwards with a soft brush or cloth. Always keep an extra piece of paper under the hand as you work to protect the surface of the sheet. Figure 15 and Figure 16 show a number of practice strokes and tones done partly with a broad and partly with a fine point.

Small Drawings and Quick Sketches.—When the student has practiced tone building for some time he is ready to try simple drawings. Often more benefit can be gained from making a number of small sketches than from attempting one large rendering. As has been before suggested, the architectural student will be wise if, when selecting subjects for his sketches, he chooses objects of architectural value and interest. The sheet of sketches, Figure 17, is shown for two reasons. First, it illustrates a quick method of sketching, the drawings being very freely and rapidly made; and second, it suggests to the student a means by which much knowledge of architecture can be obtained. One cannot fail, when making such sketches, to learn a great deal of value concerning the objects which he represents. Figure 18 is also published here for two reasons. First, it shows in a comparative manner two types of line, the broad and the fine, used side by side for representing the same building; and second, it is a typical presentation drawing such as is submitted to a client as a means of securing a commission. This sort of drawing often brings new work into the office, and is, for that reason, of the greatest value to the architect. This particular drawing was laid out instrumentally. The original sheet measures about 10½"x14½" to the margin lines. Figures 15 and 17 were originally drawn about 9"x12½", so the student should allow for this reduction when studying these sheets.

It may be of service to mention that, once a subject is selected for a sketch or rendering, whether large or small, it may be drawn in outline in either of two ways; the outline may be roughly blocked in with sketchy lines, which are to be erased when the final rendering is started, or it may be more carefully drawn directly with final lines, keeping them as a rule very light by using a hard pencil, and leaving them to become a part of the finished work. When the outline has been completed there are several methods of procedure before the student; he can put in the darkest tones of the whole drawing, later adding enough gray tones to complete the picture, or he can put in the gray tones first, as has been done in making the little sketch at the bottom of Figure 15, later adding the dark tones and sharp accents to finish the drawing.

Many artists complete their work as they proceed, beginning at the center of interest and working out, or beginning at the top and working gradually down towards the bottom. This latter method has one great advantage in that the drawing can be kept clean more easily than by the other methods, but unless the student is able to think very clearly before drawing or unless he makes first a preliminary sketch for the purpose of studying the values of light and dark, it is a difficult one. As a rule it is far safer to start at the center of interest, making sure that the strongest contrasts of light and shade and the sharpest details are there, keeping the rest of the drawing properly subordinated.

Contrasts.—There are various ways of obtaining contrasts and two of the most common are illustrated by Figure 19. A white spot against a black background always shows so plainly that the eye goes to it very quickly. Likewise a black spot against white attracts immediate attention. Now, many objects in nature are similar to these spots. For instance, a white house in strong sunlight against a background of dark trees is similar to the white spot mentioned above and the eye sees it quickly because of the contrast. A dark building silhouetted against the sky illustrates the idea of the dark spot against the light background. Now, a white spot against a dark tone appears even whiter if the dark tone grades gradually to white so as to have no sharp edges to lead the eye from the spot itself, and in the same way a dark spot against a

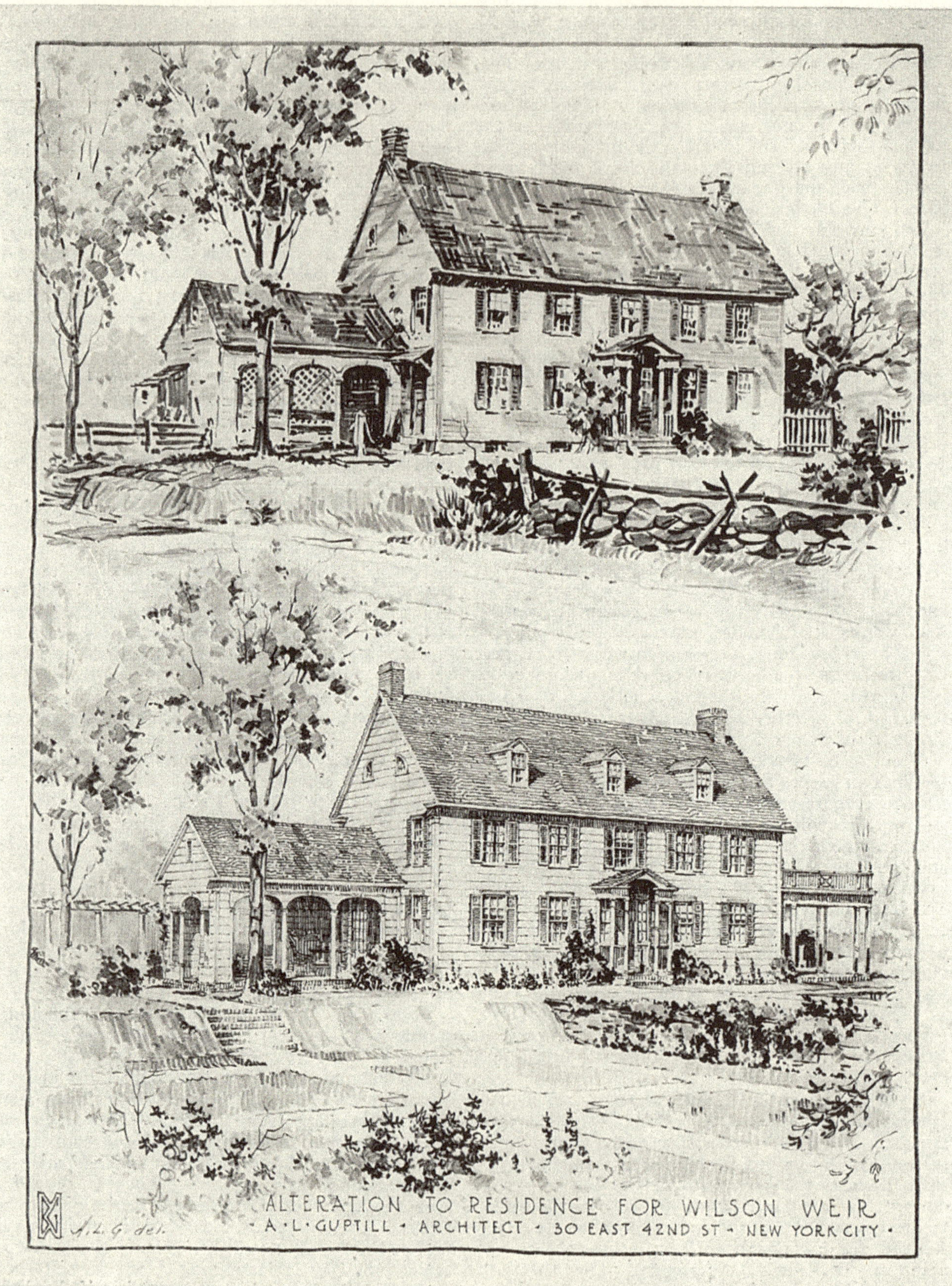

Figure 18. The Same Subject Drawn with Broad Lines and with Fine Lines. A Type of Sketch to be Submitted by the Architect to His Client to Show Proposed Alterations.

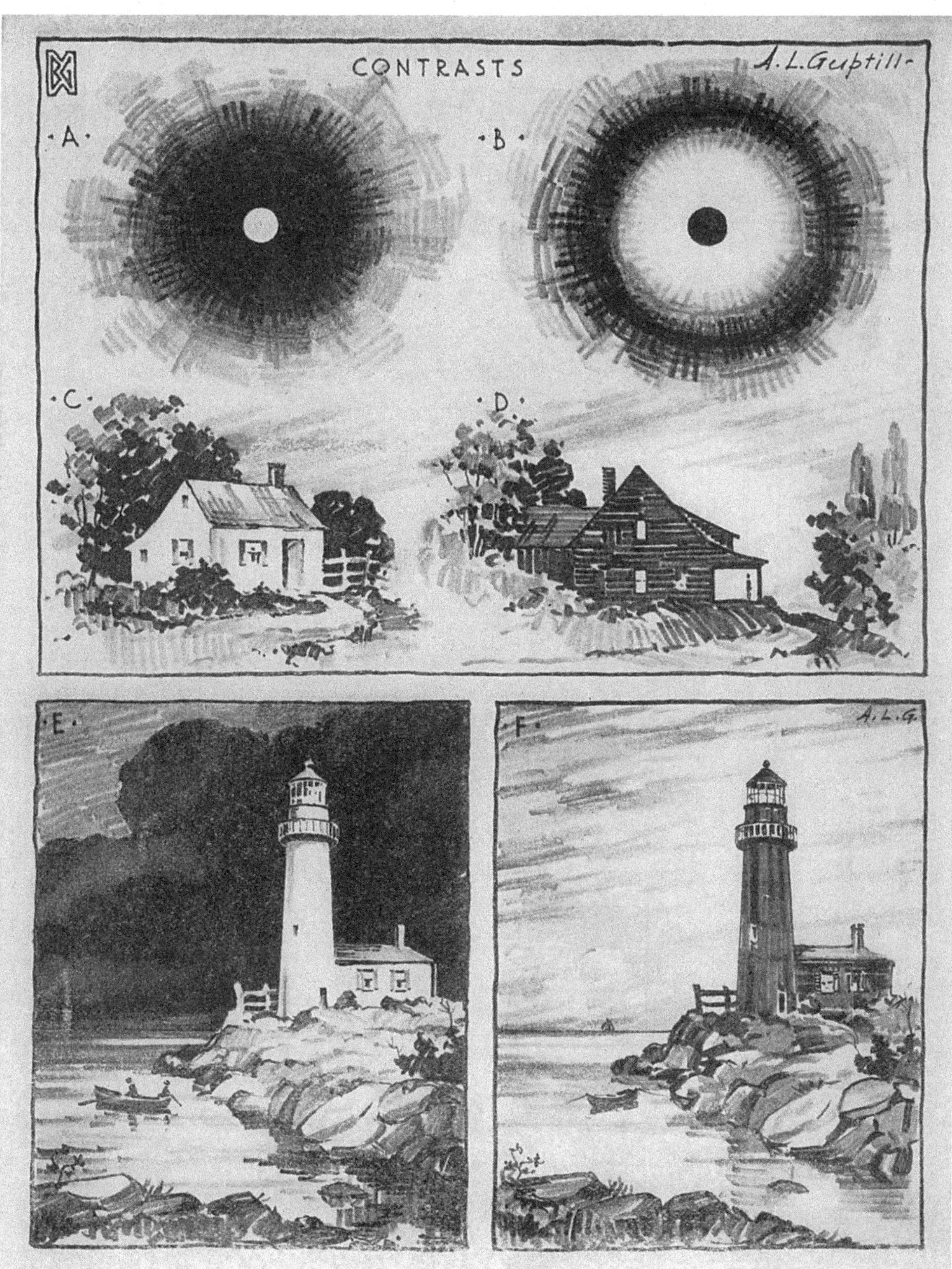

Figure 19. Illustrating Method of Focusing Attention by Means of Strong Contrasts of Light and Dark.

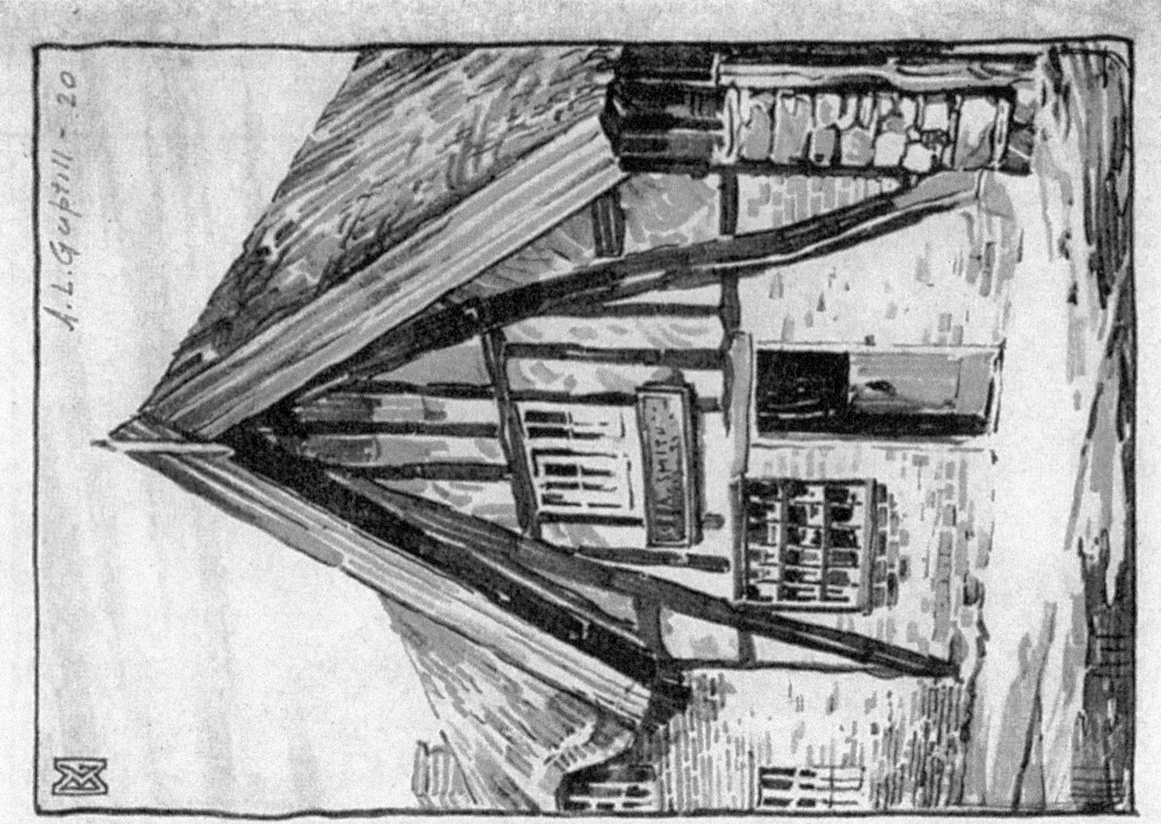

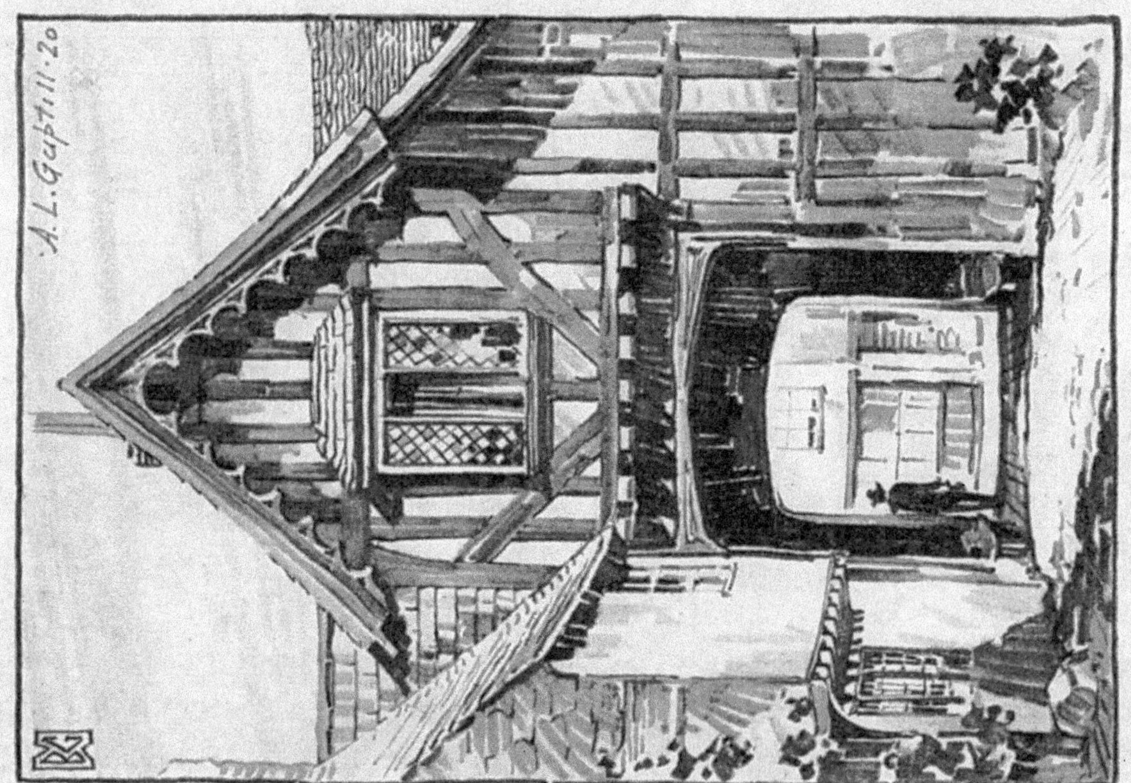

Figure 20. Illustrating the Focusing of Attention at the Center of Interest by Means of Strong Contrasts of Light and Dark.

white background will appear even blacker if the white background grades out gradually to gray or black, for this will cause the white background to appear even whiter by contrast. The spots "A" and "B" at the top of Figure 19 illustrate this point as do also the small sketches of houses "C" and "D."

It must be remembered, too, that the light conditions in nature vary constantly, so it is possible for an object to appear light against dark during certain times of the day and dark against light at others. For example an office building in bright sunlight might appear light against a deep blue sky until evening when it might change to a dark silhouette against a brilliant sunset sky. The drawings of the lighthouse, "E" and "F" at the bottom of Figure 19 still further illustrate this point. This example is rather extreme but serves to make clear that two sketches of a building made at different hours might vary greatly from each other. Therefore, when working from nature it is necessary to draw very quickly as the light is constantly changing.

In order to prevent a sketch being broken up into too many equal areas of light and shade, thus causing confusion, it is often well to look for some one leading light area and some one leading dark area in the objects to be drawn. If a sketch is to be made of a dark stone building, that perhaps becomes the leading dark area and the light area may be found in the foreground or sky or both. On the other hand, if a building is light in tone it becomes in itself the leading light area and the background of trees or sky or the foreground masses become the dark area. Having decided on these leading light and dark areas, look for subordinate areas, such as doors, roofs or similar details and give each just its proper amount of accent to make a satisfactory composition of the whole. It is usually true that we find in the same subject many contrasts of light against dark and dark against light, but in making a sketch remember that the eye would see the strongest contrasts near the focal point, or center of interest. Look for the sharpest accents here and in the drawing subordinate all others, for unless this is done the eye will jump from one point to another, which will cause the picture to lack unity and repose. It is easy to hold the eye at the center of interest as has been shown above if strong contrasts of light against dark or dark against light are shown there. The two sketches on Figure 20 still further illustrate this principle of contrast. The center of interest in the first is around the arched entrance and here the contrasts have been kept sharp and strong. First there is the light spot of the opening to the street. Then in sharp contrast to this is the dark tone of the archway itself. This in turn is strong in its contrast with the lighter tones of adjacent walls, and these light tones on walls and street are emphasized further by the fact that they are graded to dark at the edges of the sketch. In the second sketch, showing one of the earliest forms of timber construction, there are similar contrasts to hold the eye to the center of interest. First the dark doorway becomes the focal point. This is strong in its contrast with the surrounding light walls of the building and with the street, while these light tones are in turn surrounded by the large dark area of roof tones, verge board shadows and the like, which are graded outward to the edges of the sketch.

In starting a pencil drawing the student is urged to make a preliminary study of the values of light and dark as soon as the outline has been completed. This study can be made to good advantage on tracing paper directly over the outline drawing, and when completed will serve as a guide for the actual rendering. Once the values have been determined in this way, the student is free to give his attention to the technique. At this point it might be well to offer a few suggestions. First of all we must work for variety of line, for it is impossible to express all materials and surfaces with one type of line. Smooth, straight strokes suggest smooth surfaces, while irregular strokes are best for representing rough, uneven surfaces. As a rule it is well for the strokes to follow the structural lines of the objects to be represented. This means that the strokes used on vertical walls will usually be vertical or perspectively horizontal. The roof lines will follow the slope of the roof or vanish towards a point with the other parallel lines. Curved surfaces can as a rule be best represented by the use of curved lines.

It is suggested that the student try a few practice sketches to further fix in his mind some of the ideas suggested in this text. Do not be discouraged if the first results are not entirely satisfactory; it is only by making mistakes and profiting by them that one can learn to draw.

Chapter III.

INDIVIDUAL STYLE

STUDENTS of drawing often foolishly handicap themselves right at the start by attempting to produce sketches that show marked originality or individuality. Such students seem to be of the erroneous opinion that unless their work is so unusual in presentation as to appear almost freakish, it is not good. They therefore sacrifice truth in order to create drawings with a technique so peculiar and predominant as to detract from the subject of the sketch itself. In some types of decorative drawing a conspicuous method of technique is not wholly bad, but for architectural purposes anything that lessens the interest in the architecture itself is unsatisfactory.

It is not to be understood by this that work should not show a certain individuality; it should and will, for it is impossible for one to practice drawing for any length of time without developing certain original mannerisms. This is most desirable, for it would be unfortunate indeed if all pencil artists were to draw in exactly the same way, producing work of monotonous similarity. But there is no danger of this. Just as most of us acquire a certain characteristic style of penmanship which our friends are able to distinguish as ours at a glance, we are also sure to attain a style of drawing having a character exclusively its own.

To be sure many draftsmen do draw in very much the same way and this is perfectly natural and proper, for we are all influenced by the work which we see others do, and we all share, also, the definite limitations which our medium imposes upon us. It will be found, however, that drawings which seem very similar in technique at first glance, reveal individual differences on closer inspection, even though done by men with similar training and experience. Have no fear then of losing your own individuality, even though you frequently study or copy the work of master draftsmen.

In order to profit to the greatest extent by the experience of others, collect as many reproductions of excellent pencil drawings as possible. By carefully analyzing and comparing these, studying the composition, the values of light and dark, the methods of technique, the representation of details and the like, you will obtain many ideas applicable to your own work. Do not, however, attempt to imitate the style of any one man, as this will deaden your initiative and be unfair to him as well. Select, instead, from the drawings of many individuals the suggestions that appeal to you personally, and apply these, with any changes that may suggest themselves, to your own work.

It is surprising what a variety of ideas such an analysis and comparison of many drawings will reveal. If we consider the width of line used we shall find that some drawings are entirely made up of very fine lines, others of broad lines, and still others of solid mass shading. In some, two or more of these types of lines will be found combined. If we look at the kinds of lines we shall learn that some sketches consist wholly of sharp, crisp strokes; others of soft "woolly" lines; some show strokes almost mechanically perfect in contrast with others having lines made with the greatest freedom. If we consider the values of light and dark we shall see that certain drawings are left almost white, others rather gray, and some quite black. Most drawings, however, combine the white, gray and black, as all of these are usually necessary to properly represent the values existing in the object to be drawn.

Considering the great variety of work to be found, it is no small wonder that the student should be in doubt often as to the best way of treating a given subject. In such an emergency our good friend Common Sense is perhaps the best teacher. Decide first of all just what the purpose of the drawing is to be. Some drawings best meet the requirements if left in outline only. Others demand careful shading of every part. For a quick sketch the roughest sort of line is often just the thing, whereas a fully rendered drawing sometimes requires that every stroke be painstakingly made. For most architectural purposes firm, sharp strokes are better than rough, "woolly" ones, for firm strokes seem to best represent solid or smooth materials. Soft, yielding materials might perhaps be better suggested by rough, soft lines or tones.

Architectural pencil sketches are often shown to the client in conjunction with the instrumentally drawn plans and naturally harmonize better with these plans if sharp and clean-cut. The student should not take this to mean that such sketches should appear too mechanical, for the fact is that the average draftsman uses far too little freedom in his freehand work. It is sometimes difficult for him to remember that he should not draw every brick and stone, every modillion and dentil, but that he should learn rather to suggest and indicate these things in a clear, "snappy" way.

It is in learning how to thus suggest detail that perhaps the greatest benefit can be gained through the study of good pencil reproductions. It should be remembered, however, that such reproductions have as a rule been reduced in size considerably from the original drawings, and the student should take this into account. Many reproductions show drawings apparently made with very fine lines, while in reality the lines were several times as large as the reproductions suggest. Needless to say it is a foolish waste of time to attempt to cover large areas of paper with fine lines when broad ones answer as well, yet many draftsmen get the habit, possibly because they are accustomed to working with a sharp point, of making more tiny lines than

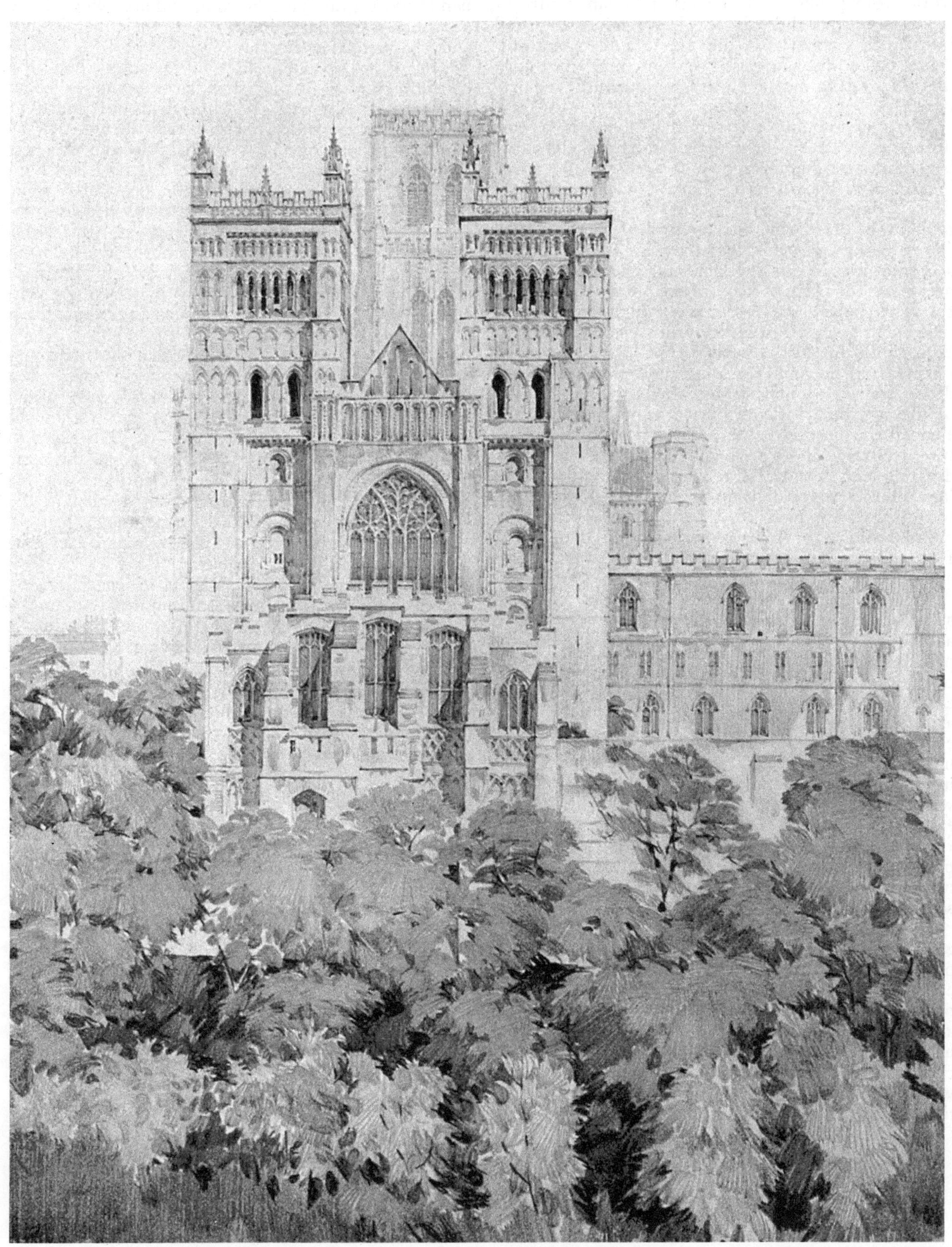

PENCIL SKETCH OF DURHAM CATHEDRAL BY KENNETH CONANT

are necessary. Partly for this reason it is unwise for the student to devote too much time to copy work from plates. When working from nature or the photograph there is far less tendency to fall into finicky ways. On the other hand, some students make drawings so sketchily and carelessly that they fail to meet the usual architectural requirements.

Warning should be given that there is a vast difference between the rough, scratchy sketches of beginners and the apparently carelessly made drawings by well known men. Some students feel, evidently, that the road to success lies through imitating this extremely sketchy sort of work. They fail to realize, perhaps, that these men have learned accurate drawing in the past, and that it is equally necessary for them to acquire the ability to do careful work before they can make rough sketches intelligently. An art student, visiting a collection of lithographs by Mr. Joseph Pennell, was heard to remark that he could "take a chunk o' charcoal and do as well." Doubtless this student was ignorant of the fact that during a period of many years Mr. Pennell made hundreds of illustrations of architecture, almost photographically accurate in their drawing and wonderfully delicate in their rendering. These years of training make it possible for Mr. Pennell to produce his lithographs in a very broad, bold way, with remarkable directness and freedom, but his earlier work offers more of assistance to the beginner.

This brings us to another fact: that a man's style of rendering usually changes with the years, as the best of men are constantly striving to improve, with the result that they gradually alter their manner of work. This fact should help to make clear the folly of the beginner attempting to at once arbitrarily make a "style" of his own. If he is content, instead, to do his work as well as he knows how, searching for truth in drawing and an honest interpretation of nature's values, studying all the while other drawings in order to benefit by the experience gained by other men, and seeking always for the best way to meet the requirements of the problem at hand, he will unconsciously develop a method or style expressive of his own individual self.

It is impossible to over-emphasize the need for constant practice if one is to acquire more than ordinary skill in drawing. Many students with considerable innate ability fail to make the best use of it because of their lack of interest or perseverance, whereas others, who show at first far less natural talent, but who are endowed with an aspiration to achieve dexterity and with a willingness to work for it, often gain such skill as to far outshine those students with greater inborn aptitude. It is deplorable that so many persons fail to make the most of their natural abilities, but it is, on the other hand, most gratifying to find others who force themselves to the front through their persistency and commendable effort.

The drawings illustrating this chapter should be carefully studied as they show a variety of excellent individual treatments. The originals of most of these were done entirely with pencil, though that by Mr. Eggers on page 79 (which is, by the way, reproduced at the exact size of the original) had light washes of water color added to the pencilling, while that by Mr. Long on page 87 is really a color rendering rather than a pencil drawing. In this latter example, however, the preparation for the coloring was done in pencil, so the reproduction is shown as an illustration of a style of work in which the pencil plays a by no means unimportant, although a rather inconspicuous part.

It is of interest to mention that the charming drawing by Mr. Eggers, to which we referred a moment ago, was made from his window in Milan in 1912, when he was studying as the first holder of the LeBrun Travelling Scholarship. His sketches on pages 80 and 82 were also done at about the same time, and are reproduced here directly from his sketch book, and with the exception of that at the top of page 80, showing Notre Dame, they are at the exact size of the originals so as to convey the technique as faithfully as possible.

The drawings by Mr. Conant on pages 77, 81 and 83, show a keen sense of appreciation and a sound knowledge of architecture, as well as remarkable skill and sensitiveness in drawing, and they are worthy of the most careful study.

On page 84 is a sketch by André Smith, which is notable for the direct method of drawing and the production of a wide range of values by skillful use of a very delicate line. The freshness of the drawing is due to the artist's habit of working rapidly and making a drawing at a single sitting.

The sketch by Mr. Maginnis on page 84 is handled in a masterly manner, conveying very delightfully the character and detail of an interesting architectural subject.

In the drawing on page 86 Mr. Watson has been very successful in rendering the structural strength and comparative lightness of one of New York's great modern bridges, and the activity along the water front, and in suggesting the shipping by means of smoke clouds, wisps of steam, a stack and a spar or two.

Compare these drawings with those of a similar nature in other parts of the volume or with examples which you may have at hand, noting the differences in individual style that such a comparison reveals.

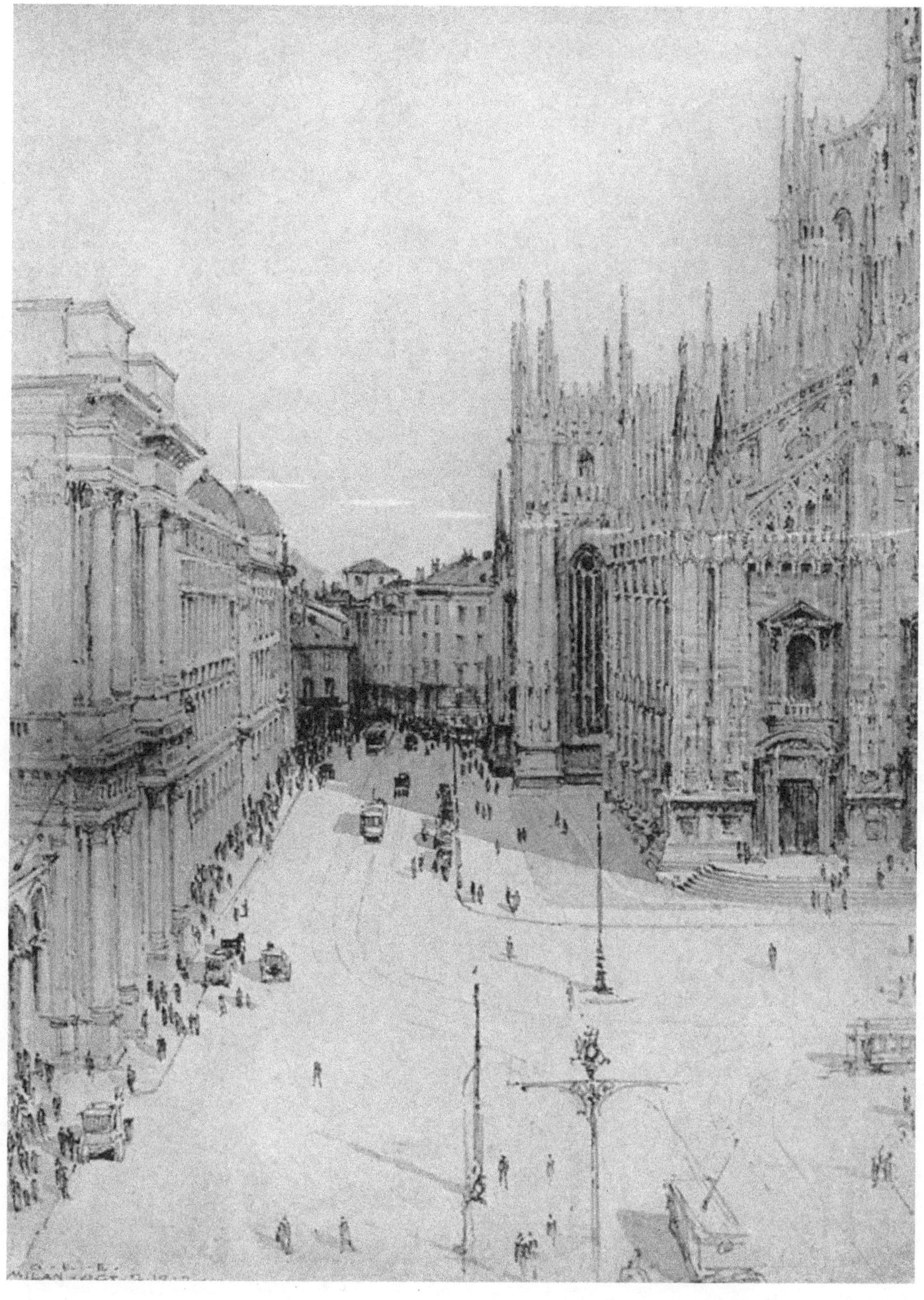

VIEW FROM A WINDOW IN MILAN. FROM A DRAWING BY OTTO R. EGGERS

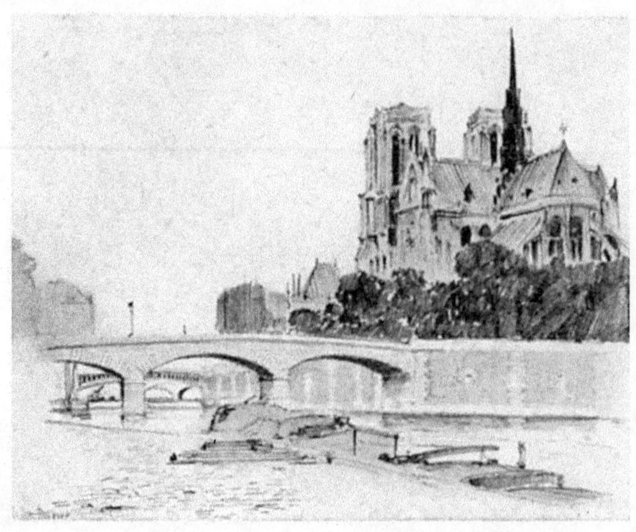

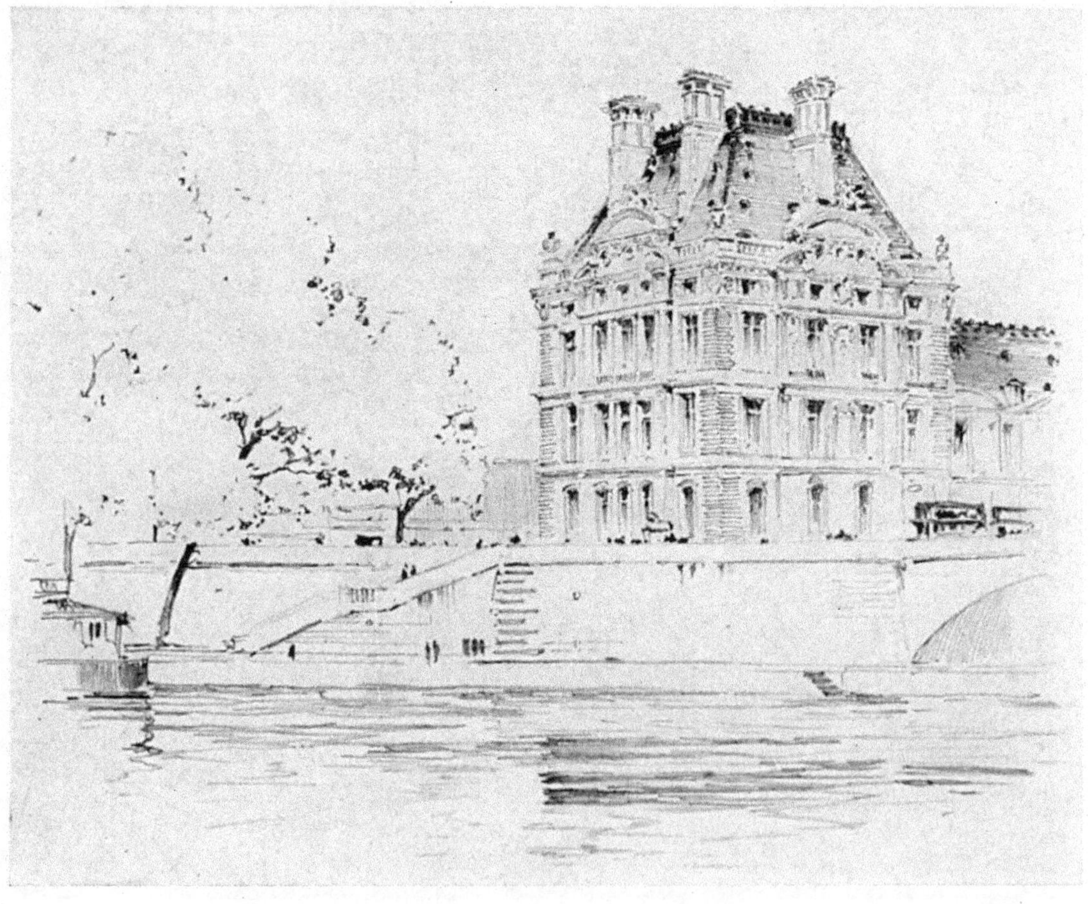

PENCIL SKETCHES BY OTTO R. EGGERS

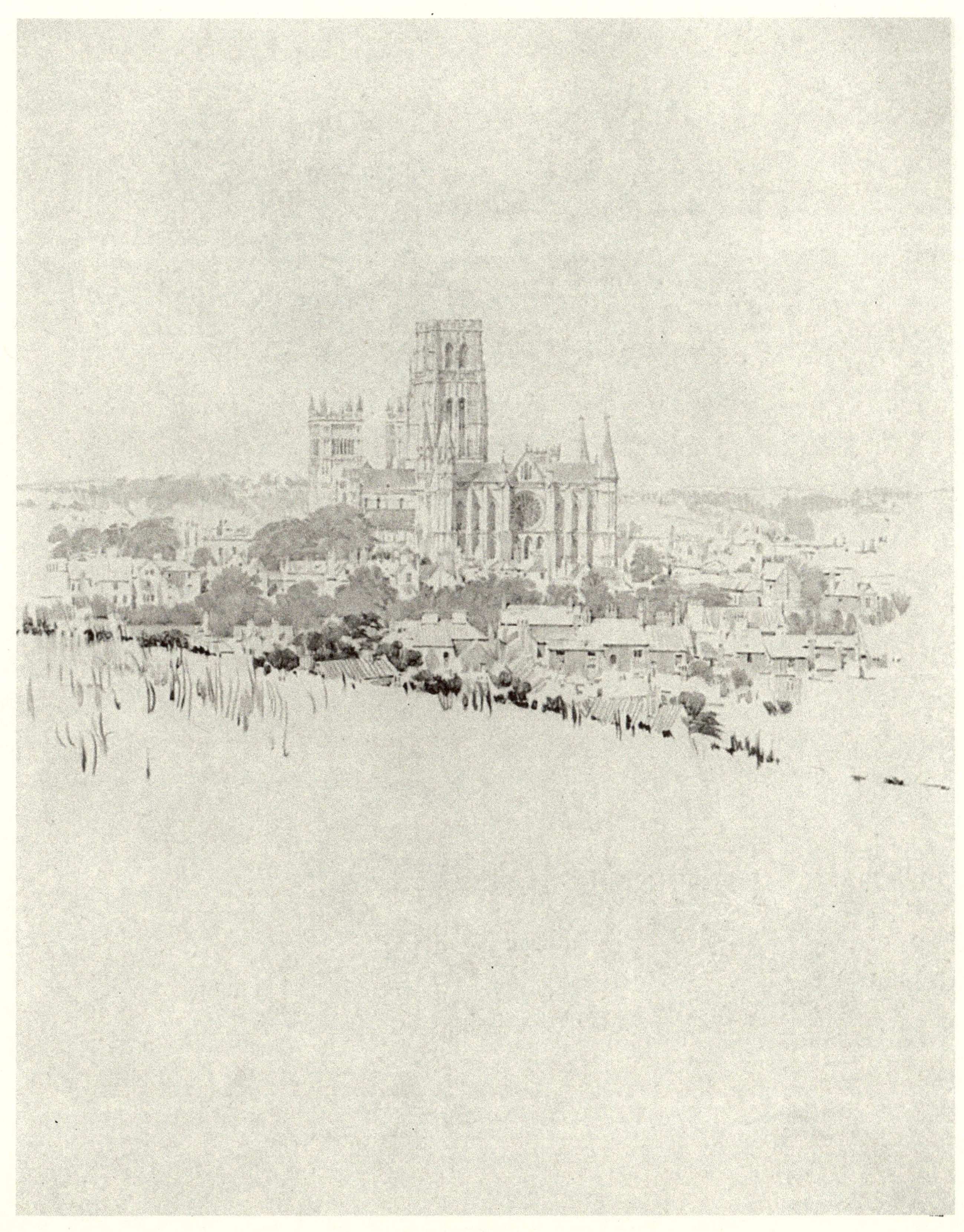

PENCIL SKETCH OF DURHAM CATHEDRAL BY KENNETH CONANT

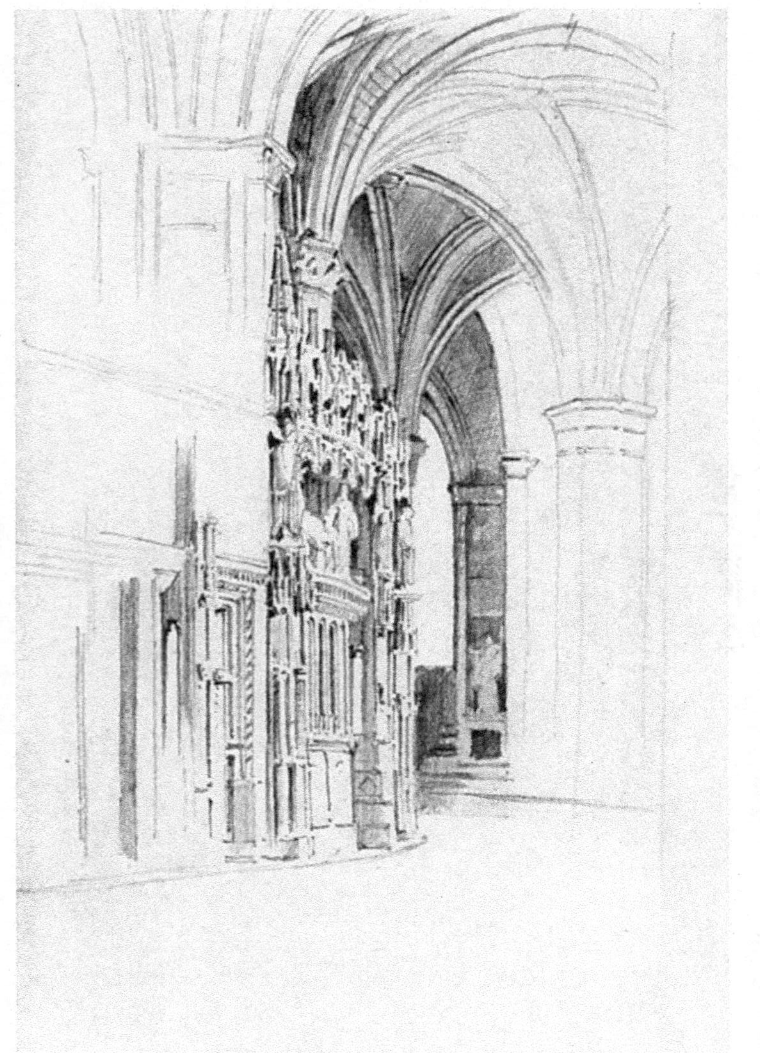

CHOIR SCREEN AT CHARTRES

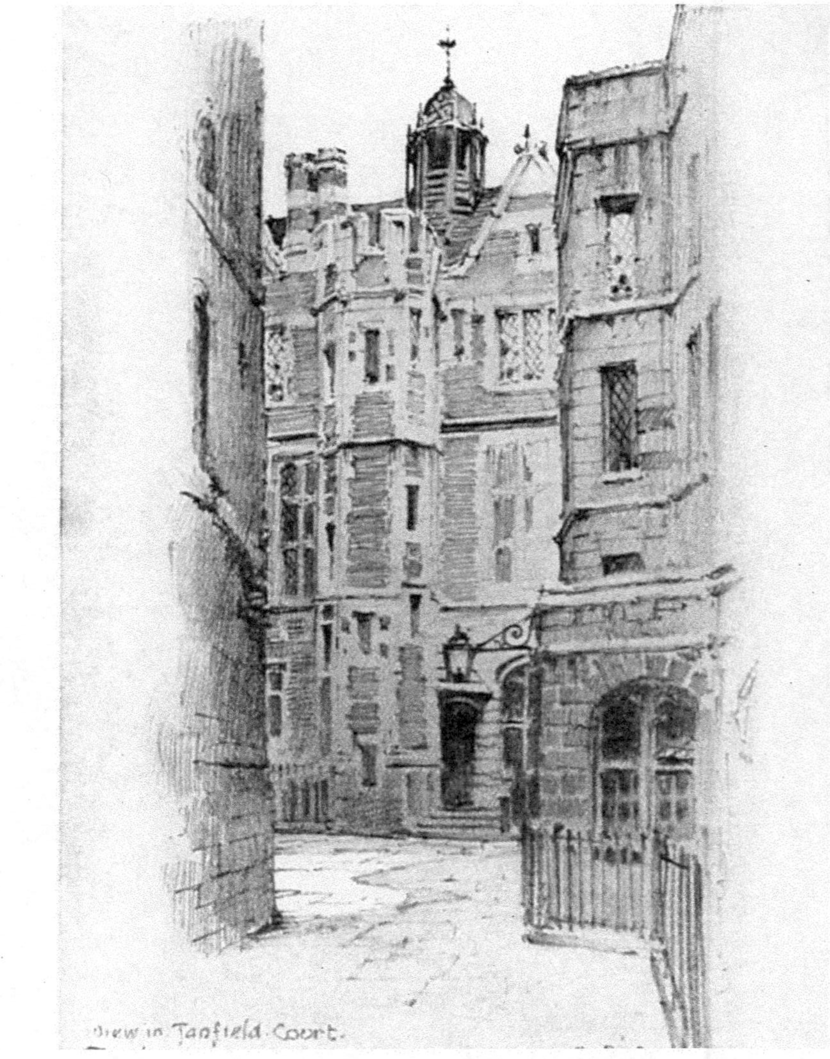

VIEW IN TANFIELD COURT

PENCIL SKETCHES BY OTTO R. EGGERS

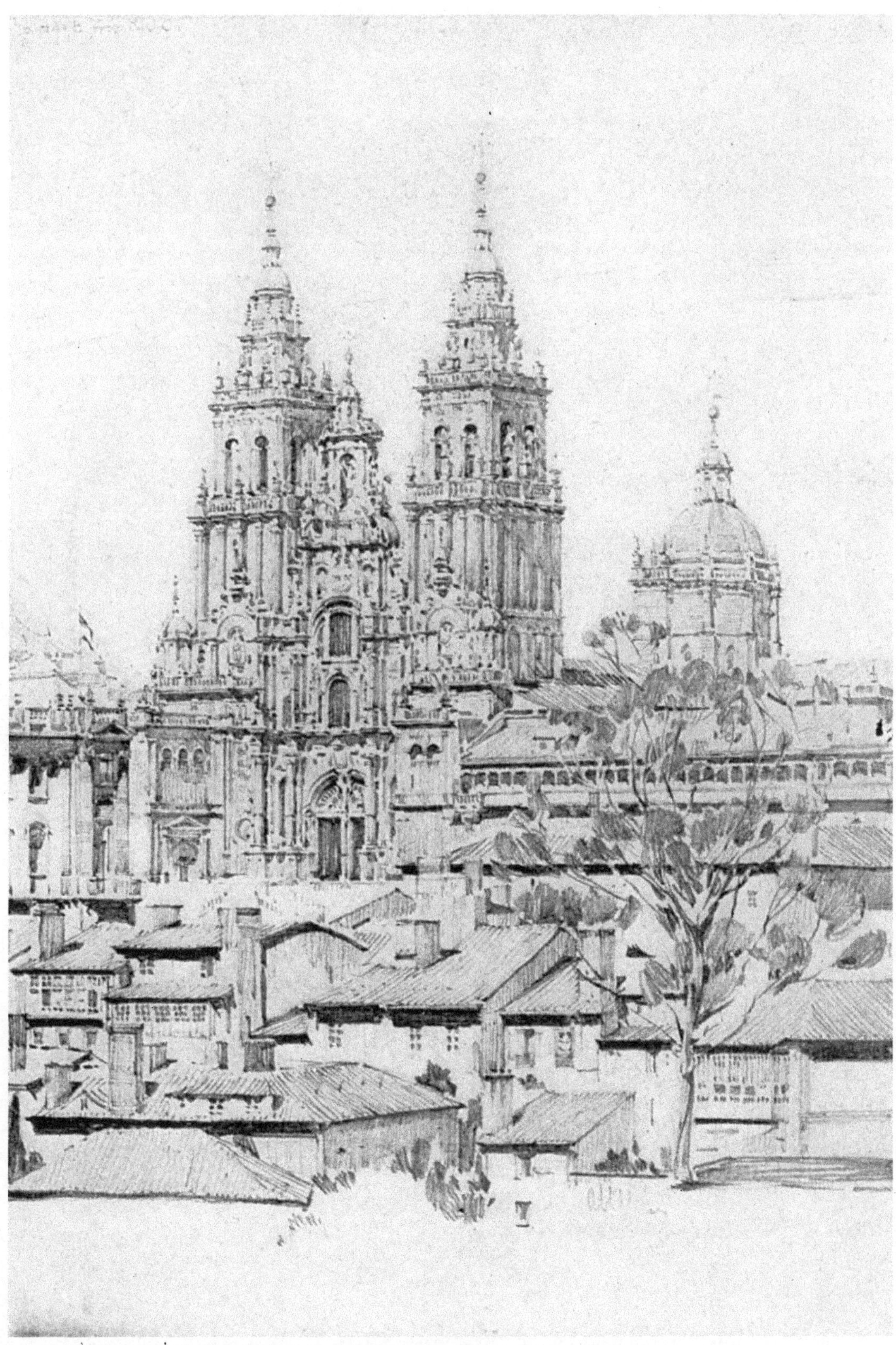

Courtesy of Arthur H. Harlow & Co.

CATHEDRAL, SANTIAGO DE COMPOSTELLA, BY KENNETH CONANT

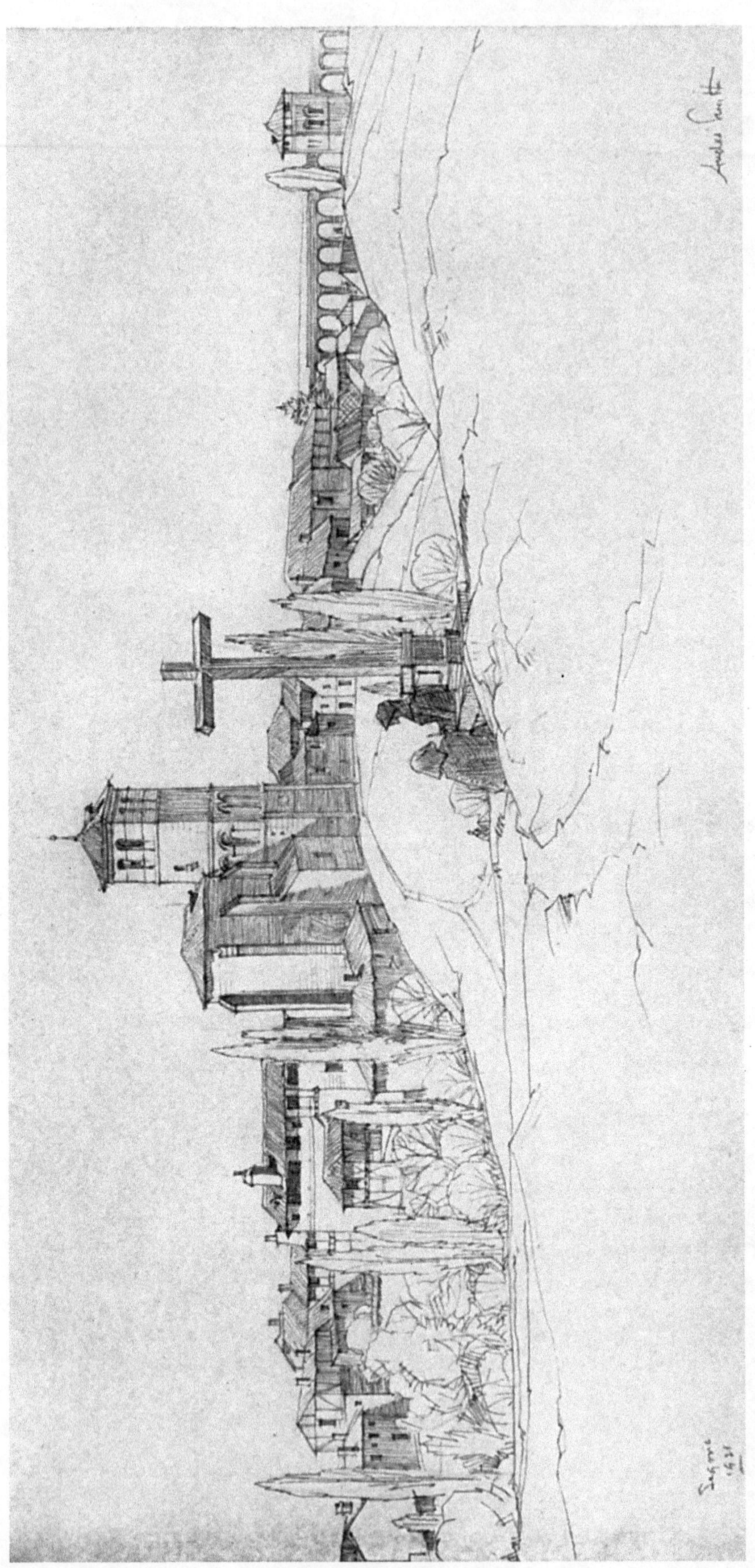

PENCIL SKETCH, SEGOVIA. BY ANDRE SMITH

Courtesy of Arthur H. Harlow & Co.

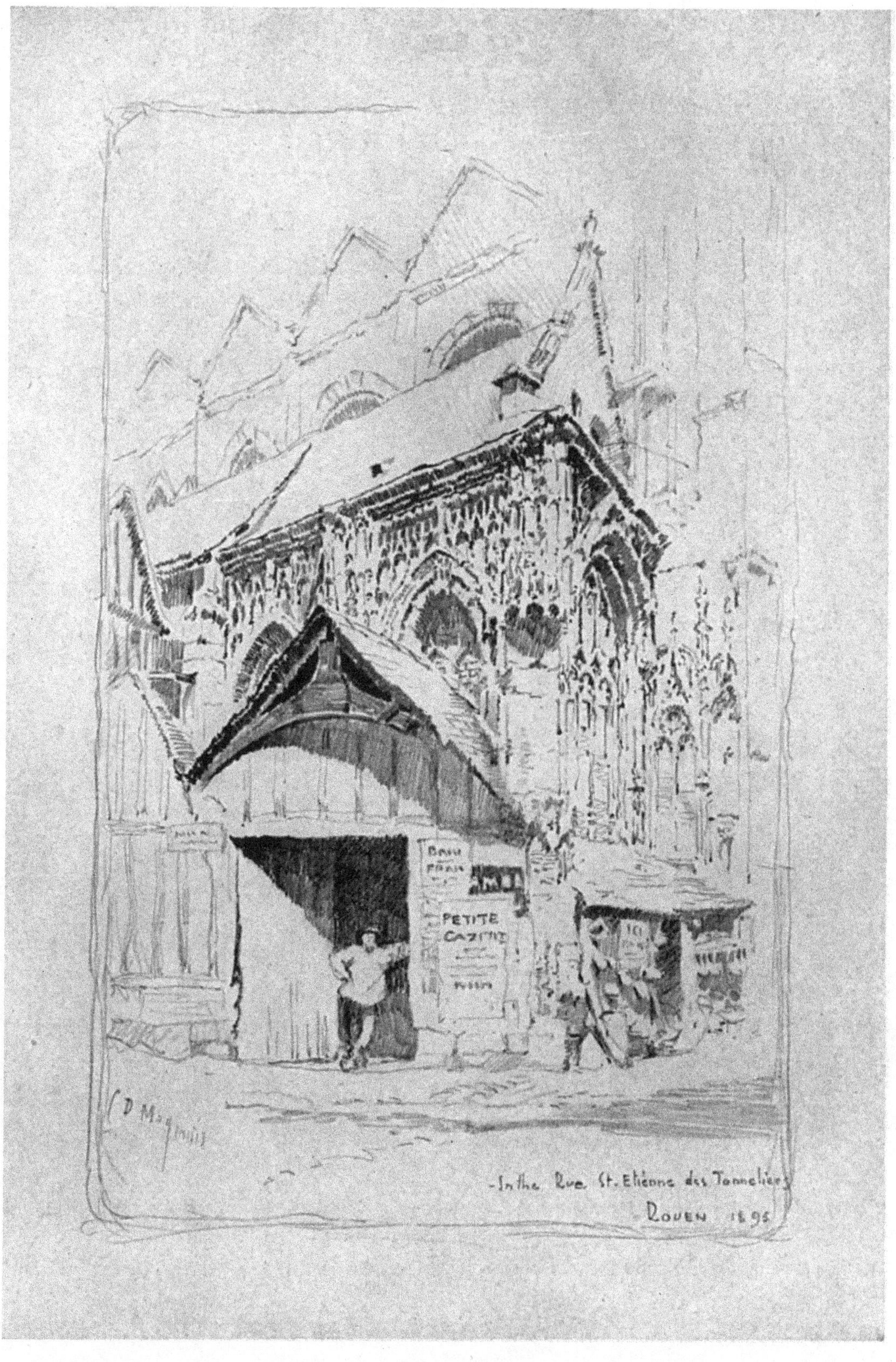

PENCIL SKETCH IN THE RUE ST. ETIENNE DES TONNELIERS, ROUEN, BY C. D. MAGINNIS

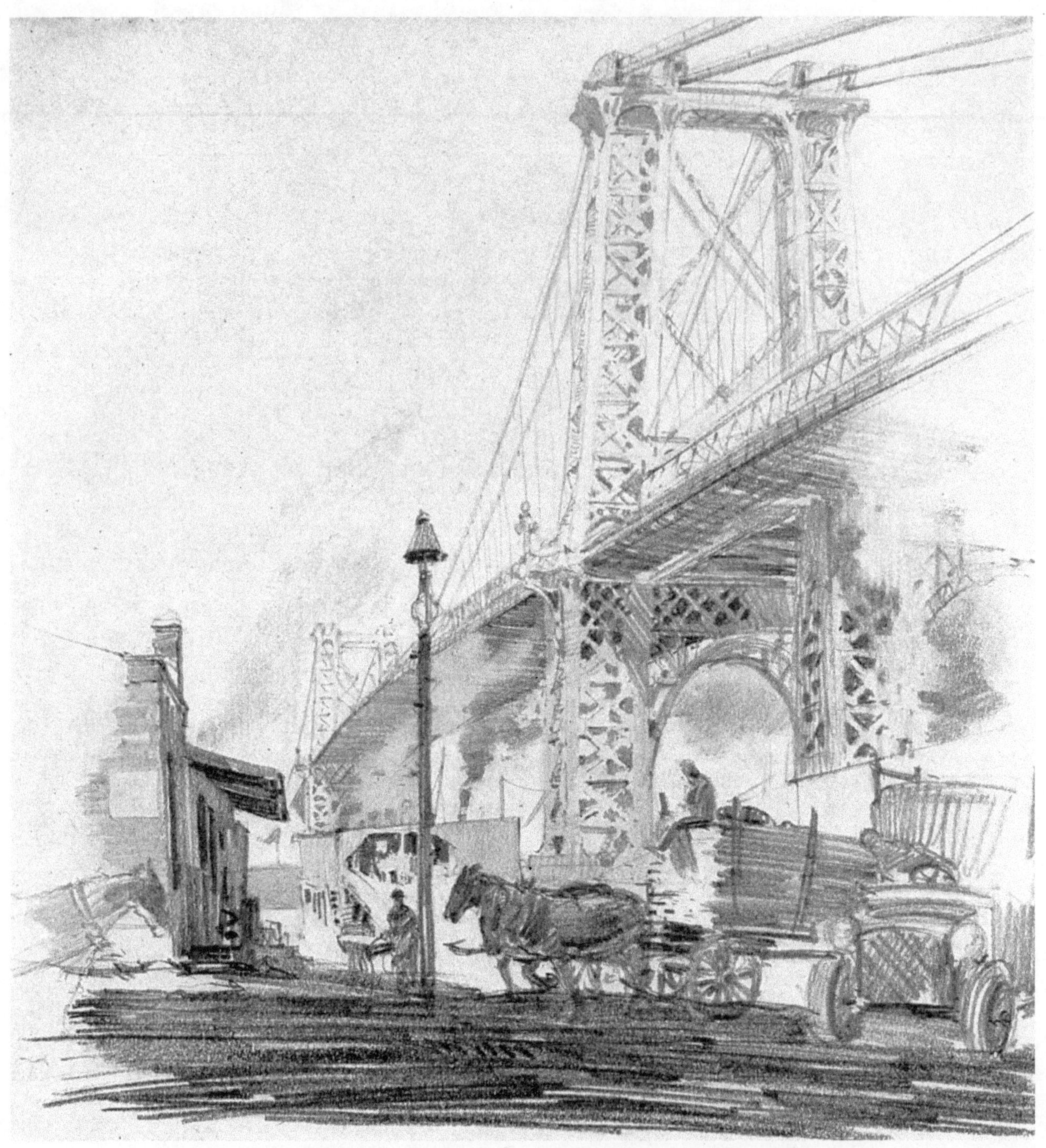

PENCIL SKETCH OF WILLIAMSBURGH BRIDGE. NEW YORK CITY. BY ERNEST WATSON

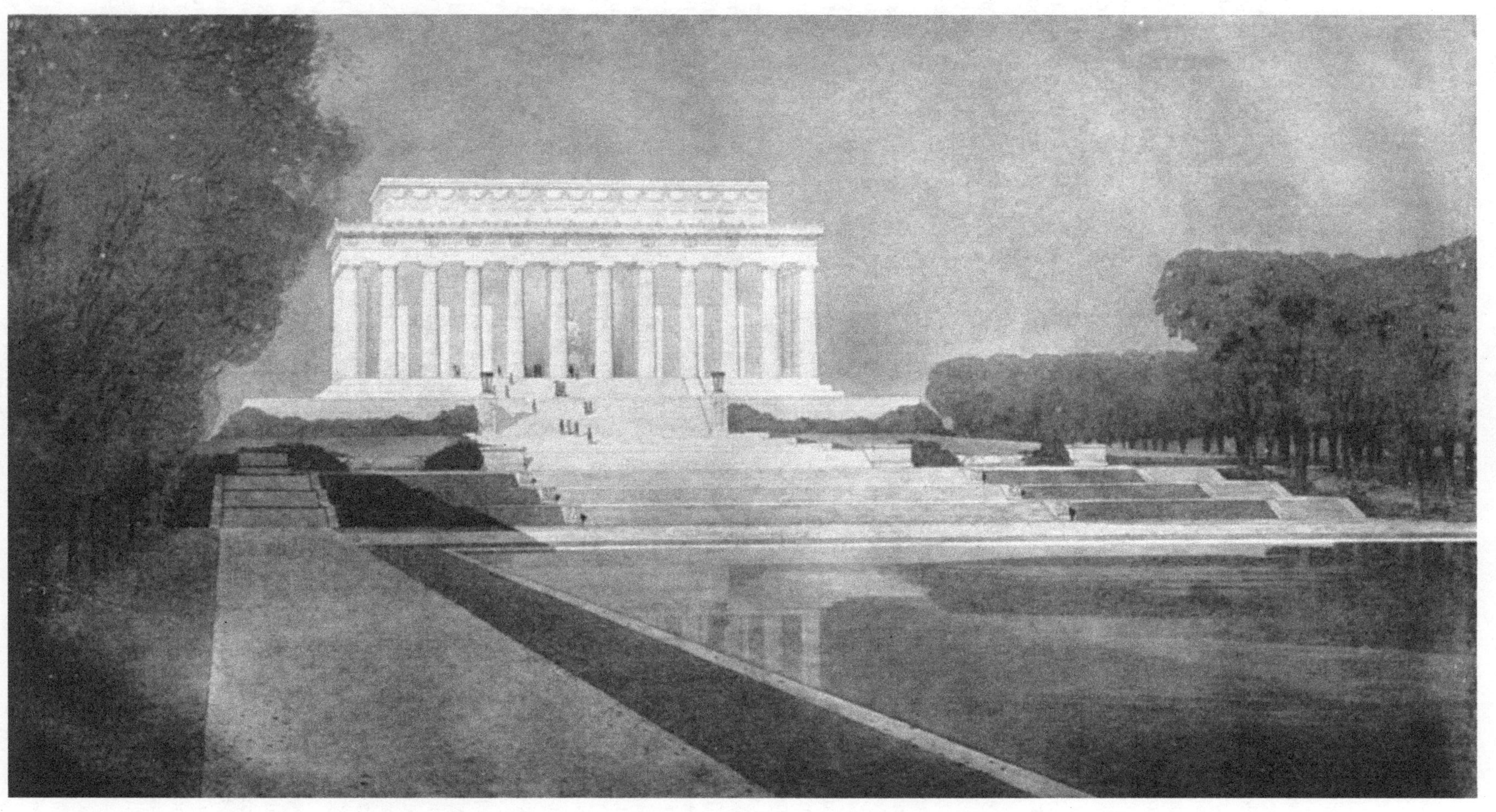

RENDERING BY BIRCH BURDETTE LONG, THE LINCOLN MEMORIAL, WASHINGTON, D. C., HENRY BACON, ARCHITECT

An Example of Water Color Rendering on Preparatory Drawing in Pencil.

Chapter IV.

METHODS AND LIGHTING

AS WE are unable to fully and exactly reproduce by means of pencil drawings, all of nature's intricate form, her complicated light and shade, and her varied coloring, we are forced to adopt certain conventional methods for their suggestion and indication.

Of the numerous conventions thus employed outline is perhaps the one most commonly used. Natural forms, it should be understood, have no definite outlines. We are able to distinguish objects one from the other only because of their contrasts of light or shade or shadow or color. To demonstrate the truth of this, study the objects about you, and you will see that each is visible only because it is light against dark or dark against light or because one color is contrasted with a different one, but never because it has an outline. It may by chance have a border of some strong color or tone which at first glance seems to be an outline, but closer inspection will prove it to be merely a narrow tone of light or dark or of color, so small as to appear as a line. Cracks between floorboards, for instance, often seem to be the outlines of the boards themselves, but in reality we see these cracks only because they form shadows or because they are filled with dirt or other materials of a color or tone different from that of the wood itself. Streaks of highlight along the edges of objects frequently appear to be outlines, too, unless the source of light causing them is hidden or moved, when they either disappear or change their positions.

Granting, then, that nature employs no real outline, it is remarkable that her forms can be so quickly and accurately suggested by its use. Even a child, as a rule, is able to so indicate objects by a few simple profiles that we can recognize them easily, and primitive peoples, ages ago, made outline drawings which we are able to read and understand with little effort. Because such drawings do indicate form simply and directly, it is important for the student to learn to make them well and he should frequently practice this form of work. By varying the lines used, the textures and materials represented can be more accurately and artistically suggested than at first seems possible. Shadow, too, can be indicated by darkening such edges as are turned away from the light. Outline drawing has, at the same time, so many limitations that for architectural purposes it is mainly valuable for the suggestion of form. Therefore whenever we wish to do more than simply indicate the light and shade or color we are forced to either supplement the outline by the addition of tones of gray or black, or to do away with it entirely, representing the object wholly by values of light and shade, approximating as closely as is possible those tones found in nature itself.

At "A," Figure 21, is a sketch of an old chimney done in outline only, but this outline is so accented as to suggest the textures of the various surfaces and a few tiny lines are added also as an indication of the shade and shadow. At "B" the same chimney is shown in full tone of light and shade but with the outline omitted. This drawing is much like a photograph of the same subject, in that the stone and brick and other materials have been given tones as similar as is possible to those appearing in nature. Though this type of drawing is used to some extent, it is not as popular as that shown at "C" in which much of the white of the paper is left. Drawing "C" not only has more character than "B" but the method used is a more economical one. In this particular instance the outline was drawn exactly as at "A" and then enough tone added to suggest the values of light and shade as found at "B." For architectural work this method is quite satisfactory, for much of the form can be represented by the accented outline; the white of the paper answers for the lighter values and the darker tones can be drawn with the gray and black of the pencil. Color cannot, of course, be more than suggested in any pencil drawing. A dark red brick wall can be shown dark, and light green shutters can be shown light, but unless explanatory notes are added or some color employed there is no way of making it clear that the brickwork is red and the shutters are green. Because of these limitations, tints of water color are frequently washed over a pencil drawing and the results obtained in this way are often very effective, especially if the tints are light and delicate. Colored pencils are sometimes used, too, with considerable success.

Figure 22 is one sketch in which the effect is gained by the use of values representing the color and tone of the various building materials and accessories, little attempt being made to show the shadows. It is sometimes possible to obtain a very pleasing result by this means and it would be well for the student to try a few such drawings, but the average subject demands some suggestion of the shadow tones as well. Many drawings can, in fact, be entirely made by the use of the shade and shadow tones only, the color of the building materials being largely disregarded, and the lower sketch, Figure 22, is shown to illustrate this point. This method proves especially useful when drawing objects made of light colored materials such as carved white marble, ornamental terra-cotta, white clapboarded or stucco walls, etc.

Although the natural tone and color of materials in buildings and their surroundings is of great importance, so much of the effect of a structure, both as a whole and in detail, depends on its

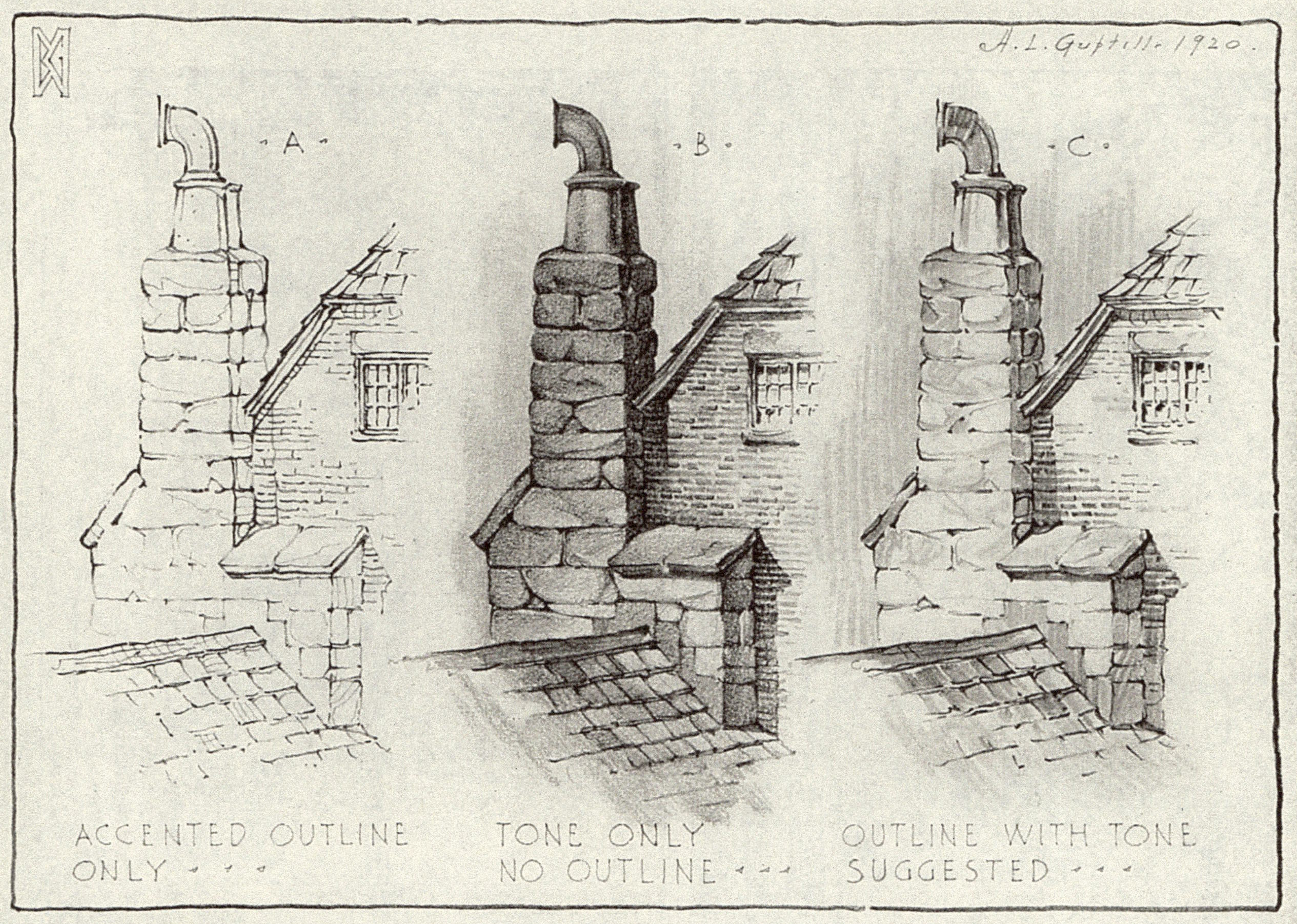

Figure 21. Illustrating Different Methods of Indicating the Same Subject.

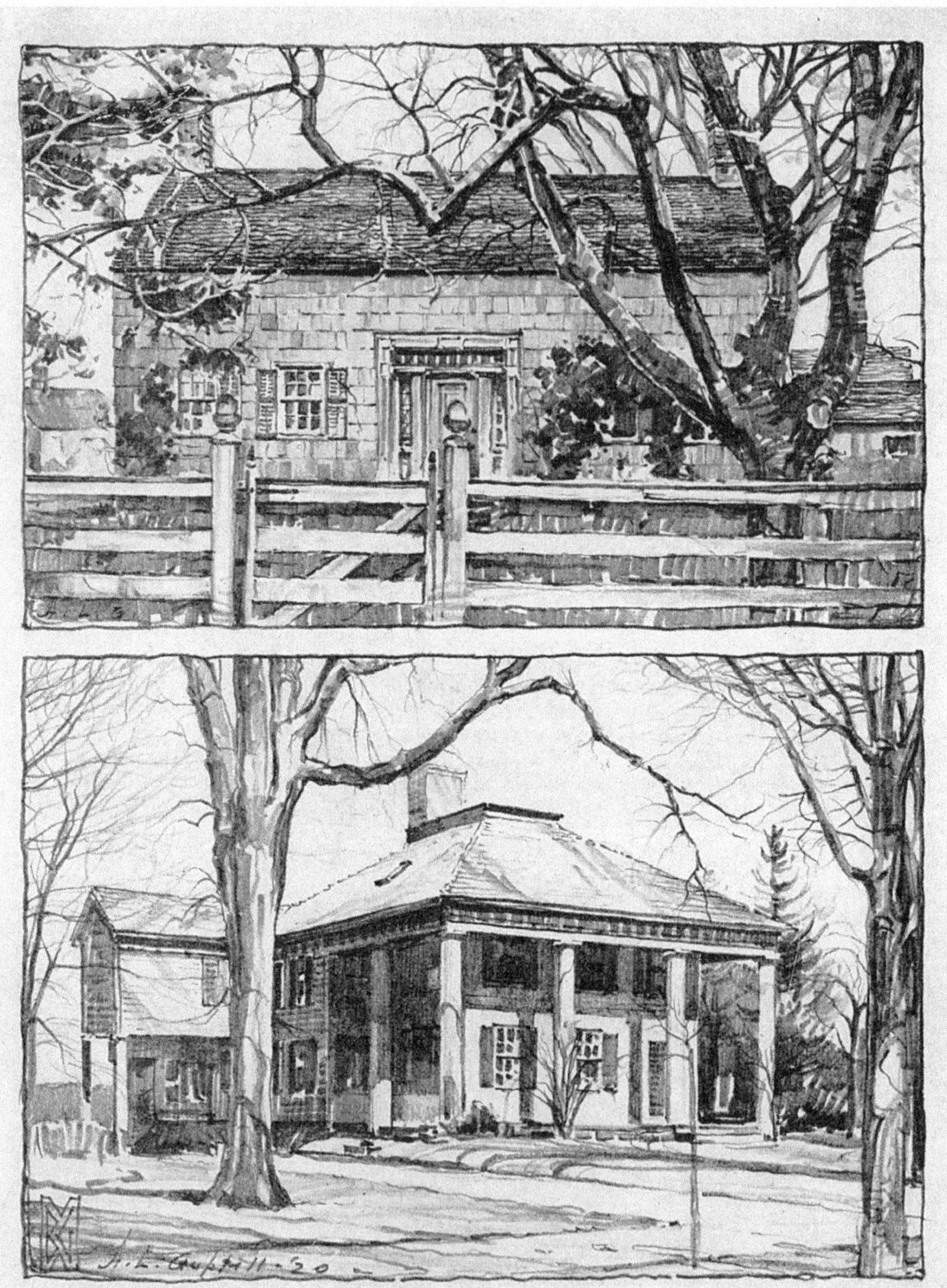

Figure 22. The Upper Sketch Shows an Effect Mainly Gained by the Use of Values Representing the Tone of Various Building Materials and Accessories. In the Lower Sketch the Effect Depends More on the Indication of Shade and Shadow.

shadows that the study of light and shade deserves special attention. When a sketch is in outline only, the light is either indicated in a simple manner or entirely disregarded, but when a drawing is to be done in full values it is especially important to determine both the source of the light and the direction in which it is coming before starting to render. Students have been known to cast the shadows on a building in one direction and to indicate the shade on the trees as though the light were coming at a different angle. Such inconsistencies are amusing, but warning should be given that they are almost sure to occur when students attempt to copy and combine parts of several drawings by other men or even make original drawings of their own unless the matter of lighting is carefully thought out before the pencil rendering is begun. Such mistakes show that the student cannot give too much study to this subject if he is to avoid many similar errors. There are, however, so many separate influences affecting the lighting of all objects, such as the condition of the atmosphere, the reflective or absorbing powers of different surfaces and materials, the constant shifting and moving of clouds and foliage, that it seems unwise to attempt here to give the student more than a few hints to point the way for his further individual study. Even in interiors the light often comes from so many sources and is reflected from so many surfaces that nothing but constant observation and sketching will teach the student what he should know of such conditions. The opening or closing of a door may be sufficient to entirely change the appearance of an interior and in the same way the shifting of a cloud may cause windows viewed from without to appear very light one minute and almost black the next. Sometimes the lighting varies to such an extent that an entire building may appear dark against light at one time and light against dark at another, as was illustrated in the example of the lighthouse in Figure 19. Such an extreme change as this, though by no means unusual, generally takes place at morning or in the evening or under exceptional lighting conditions, but even the average building under normal conditions will vary greatly in appearance from hour to hour. Because of these constant changes most buildings appear to better advantage at certain time of day than at others, and so if drawings of them are to be made it is naturally best to make them during these favorable moments. Buildings and foliage usually get the most satisfactory light during the late afternoon when the sun's rays are so slanted as to cause an interesting variety of shade and shadow, but there are of course exceptions to this, a great deal depending on the location of the building in relation to the points of the compass. Many architects fail when designing buildings to give sufficient attention to the fact that a design which will appear well when turned at a certain angle with the sun or other source of illumination, may be much less effective placed in some other position. It is not enough to make instrumental studies of buildings, with shadows cast in the usual 45 degree manner, but in addition the designer should consider how the structure will appear under the vertical rays of the sun at midday or the slanting rays of early morning or late afternoon, and should, in many cases, make special studies with the shadows shown as they would exist in the completed building. The author has in mind one particular public building which was most attractive in the preliminary drawings, with its shadows cast in the conventional manner. Unfortunately the building is so situated that for months at a time the sun seldom shines on the main façade and in the evening this façade is especially uninteresting when the bright light from the street lamps entirely eliminates the cornice shadows. Obviously it is impossible to foresee and prevent all such unpleasant appearances, but the student who has learned to study and observe light effects and has drawn much from nature will find the knowledge gained from this work of great assistance to him if he is called upon to do original work in design, both in avoiding such unpleasant results as we have mentioned and in making the greatest use of the lighting conditions as they exist. Such knowledge is of great importance, too, when one is called upon to make renderings of proposed buildings or sketches from memory or the imagination.

Do not for a moment think that it is our intention to condemn the practice of casting shadows on elevations in the conventional 45-degree manner, for that is not the case, as even the student of freehand drawing can gain considerable knowledge useful in sketching through a course in shades and shadows. What we do wish to make clear is that the draftsman or designer who studies light and shade directly from nature does not allow himself to be handicapped by the man-made rules governing shades and shadows, but supplements these with his knowledge of nature's own laws, and so applies them all with far greater intelligence. We are told, for example, when studying the architectural subject of shades and shadows, that those surfaces in a building which are turned most directly towards the source of light will usually appear, all other things being equal, the brightest. From this one might judge that a shingled roof receiving direct rays of light from the sun would appear very bright, and in fact it often does. Not infrequently, however, such a roof seems very dark under these conditions, even though the wood of the shingles be light in color, this appearance being largely due to the fact that the horizontal lines of the butts of the shingles, which are so turned as to receive little light and are also, because of the nature of their grain, often dark, show so black and are so conspicuous as to deepen and darken the effect of the otherwise light tone. The rule is worth remembering, however, in spite of such exceptions, as is also the rule that the darkest, sharpest shadows are cast by the edges of the surfaces receiving the most direct light. It naturally follows that surfaces so turned as to receive the light rays in a slantwise direction will be less bright than those receiving the direct rays. It is true, too, that a shiny surface generally appears brighter than a dull surface of the same actual value and sometimes even a black shiny surface will reflect some light tone and so

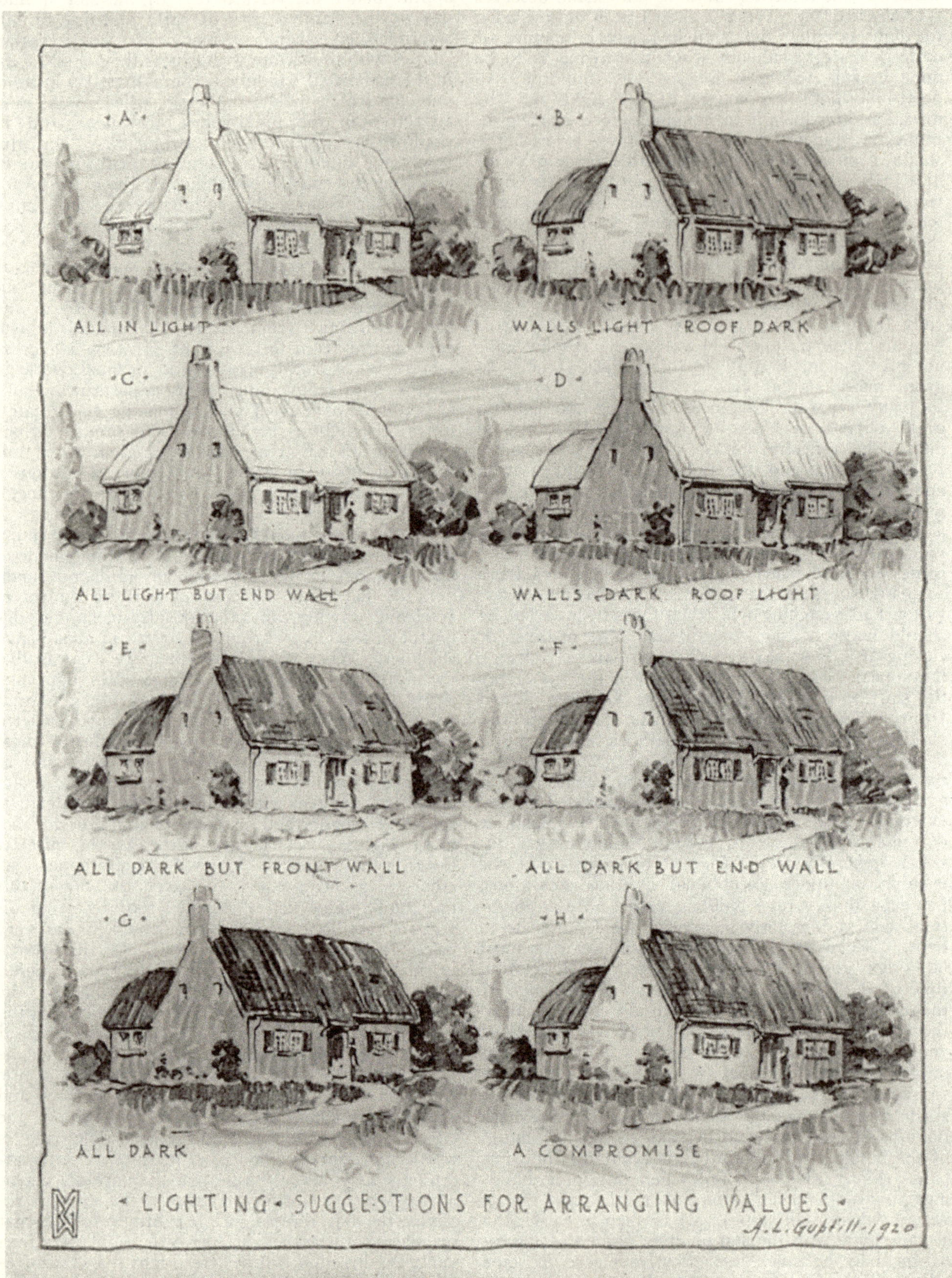

Figure 23. Illustrating Different Value Schemes for the Same Subject.

appear practically white. There are exceptions to this for a shiny, light surface may reflect some very dark tone and thus appear nearly black, and likewise a smooth gray surface may appear either lighter or darker than it really is. In other words glossy surfaces change in appearance with changes of light to a much greater extent than dull surfaces. Even light, dull surfaces, however, often throw much brilliancy onto other objects and white concrete walks or terraces or driveways sometimes reflect enough light upon adjacent buildings to materially affect their appearance, as such lights soften the shadow tone or even cast shadows themselves.

While we might go on with such general hints as these it is hardly worth while, for it is only by observing nature at first hand that the student can gain much knowledge of real value. One excellent way of studying constantly changing effects of light on a building is by making a series of snapshots from some one fixed point at intervals during a clear day and comparing them with care. Such photographs reveal much of interest and value to the observing student, especially if the building chosen be rather small. It might be well to make sketches from these photographs as this would help to fix the ideas in the mind, or, if the student has sufficient ability or training to sketch rapidly directly from the building, he can possibly learn more by making a series of sketches instead of the snapshots.

We have spoken of the fact that it is sometimes possible to make an effective drawing by the use of shadows only and sometimes by suggesting the building materials alone, but it is more often necessary to represent both the material and the shadows in order to obtain a satisfactory drawing. It is not always easy, though, to decide just how much of each should be shown, especially when working from the imagination as the architect is often called upon to do. This can, perhaps, best be determined by making several rough studies on tracing paper directly over the outline drawing or by making two or three small sketches similar to those shown in Figure 23. These eight sketches illustrate the fact that it is often possible to get many fairly satisfactory compositions of the same subject, but there are usually one or two which are better than the others, and one of these should be selected as a guide for the final larger renderings. It is suggested that the student make several similar small sketches of some object from memory or the imagination as practice in composition, and it is well to remember too, that in making drawings from the photograph it is often helpful to try similar studies on tracing paper directly over the photograph, to determine how much to omit and how best to compose that which it seems essential to show.

It may be well to repeat here that the only way to learn to draw is by constant practice. Reading a dozen books on drawing might give the student many ideas, but unless such suggestions are carried out they are useless. If you lack the inspiration to draw by yourself, it would be well to join some sketching class or engage a critic to help you with your work.

Chapter V.

COMPOSITION AND DRAWING FROM PHOTOGRAPHS

MANY draftsmen and students easily acquire the ability to satisfactorily represent small details of buildings like bricks and shingles and even such larger parts as doors and windows, but the skill to compose these lesser units into a complete and well-balanced whole is not so easily gained. And yet the student who is unable to pleasingly arrange all the smaller parts into a fine composition is seriously handicapped, regardless of his cleverness in sketching each single detail, so though it may prove a difficult task it will pay him well to earnestly attempt to master the art of composition. Even though it is only through serious study and faithful practice that the necessary principles can be acquired, once they are understood it will be found that they apply equally well whether a drawing be large or small and whether it is hastily sketched or executed with painstaking care. The principles are valuable also when using other mediums than pencil, such as pen and ink or wash or color.

It seems hardly necessary to give here more than a brief outline of the most important of these principles, and a few hints as to what to do and what not to do, but these suggestions should be supplemented by reading books on the subject such as "Pictorial Composition," by H. R. Poore, A. N. A., "Composition," by Arthur Wesley Dow, and the chapter on composition in John Ruskin's "The Elements of Drawing." A study of such books will show a difference in opinion on some points, for composition is an art rather than a science, and it is impossible to lay down exact rules as to what should or should not be done. Perhaps the greatest value of such works is that they point out many pitfalls which lie in the path of the artist, and by analysis of the pictures of acknowledged masters, give the student a certain standard by which he is able to judge and criticise his own work. Though the study of books is very desirable, one should never forget that drawing cannot be taught by rule, and a hundred lengthy volumes could do no more than start one in the right direction and offer suggestions to assist him in his progress.

As the word "composition" means the putting together of things and the arranging of them in order, so as to make one unit out of them all, it is evident that we must first have good things to put together if the final composition is to be good. This means that in starting work we should use extreme care in the selection of our subject, not only as a whole but in each of its parts. Students, more especially the beginners, seem to be of the opinion that any object found in nature is a satisfactory subject to draw, and they are led into this belief, perhaps, by hearing statements to the effect that all nature is beautiful. It is not for us to deny this but it should be made clear that good pictures are not to be obtained ready-made by simply copying bits of nature at random. Amateur photographers are well acquainted with the fact that a successful photograph is not often secured by simply pointing the camera in any direction and making an exposure; it is necessary to give some thought to the selection and composition of the subject. Experienced artists often do produce good drawings by re-composing poor material, but the student will avoid difficulties if he chooses either something which is well composed in itself or which can be made so with few changes.

We have previously spoken of the advantage of using a view-finder when selecting compositions and wish to call attention again to its value. Of the several types in general use one which we have already described as consisting simply of a rectangular opening two inches or so in length cut in a piece of heavy paper or cardboard, is especially helpful when working directly from nature. By holding it in an upright position and looking through it at the objects beyond, it is very easy to select interesting subjects and to determine, too, how large an area or how much of an object or objects it is best to show to give the finest composition. Again it has another use, for if the student is in doubt as to just what slope should be given to a roof line or slanting tree trunk, a comparison of these inclined lines in the objects with the vertical or horizontal lines of the opening of the finder will be of great assistance in determining the correct slope or angle. The finder will help the student, also, to judge correctly the values of light and dark as seen in nature, for each tone of the objects can be compared in turn with the value of the cardboard itself.

The other commonly used finder or frame consists of two "L" shaped pieces of paper or card, which will give, when lapped as shown at 1, Figure 24, an endless variety of shapes and sizes, and it is, for this reason, much better than the other finder when working from photographs. As soon as a pleasing composition has been selected this frame can be clipped or pinned in position on the photograph and left in place until the drawing is finished. It thus serves to hide those parts which have no relation to the sketch and permits the eye to rest on the selected composition without distraction.

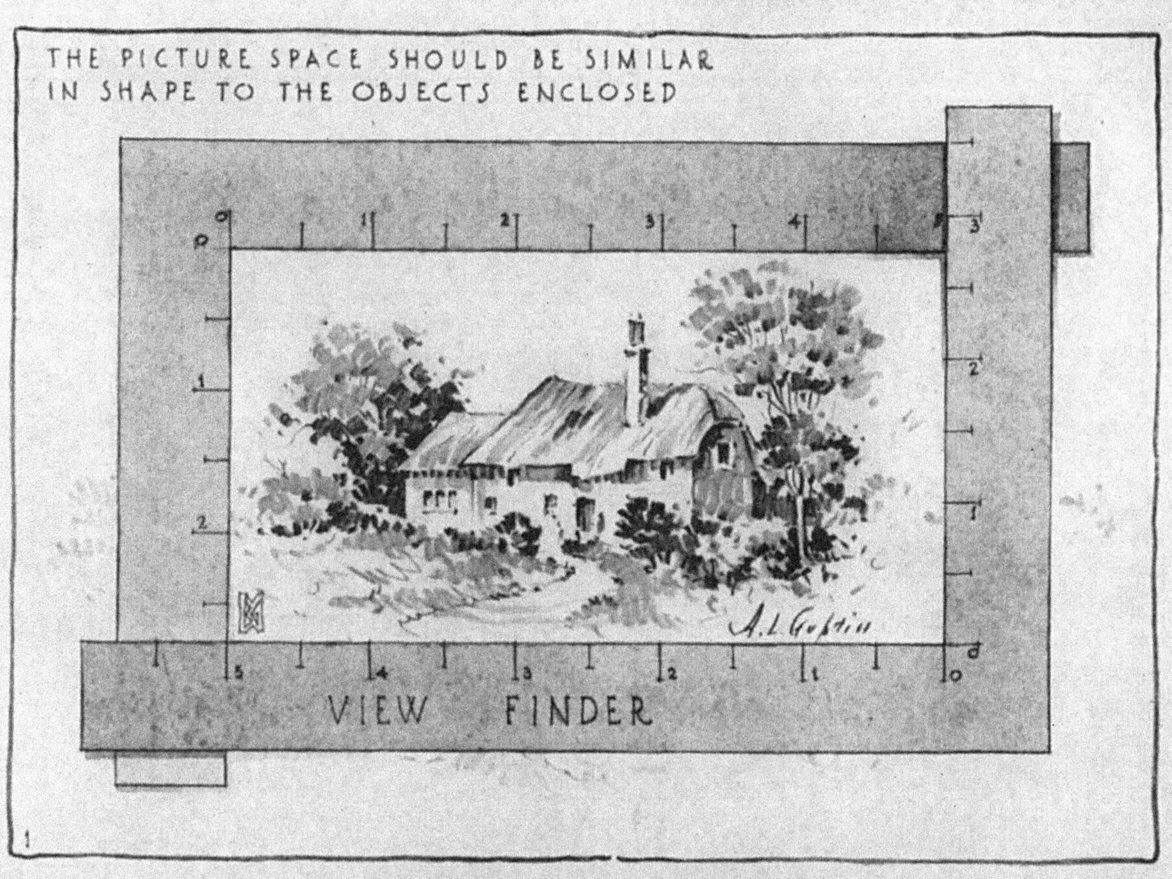

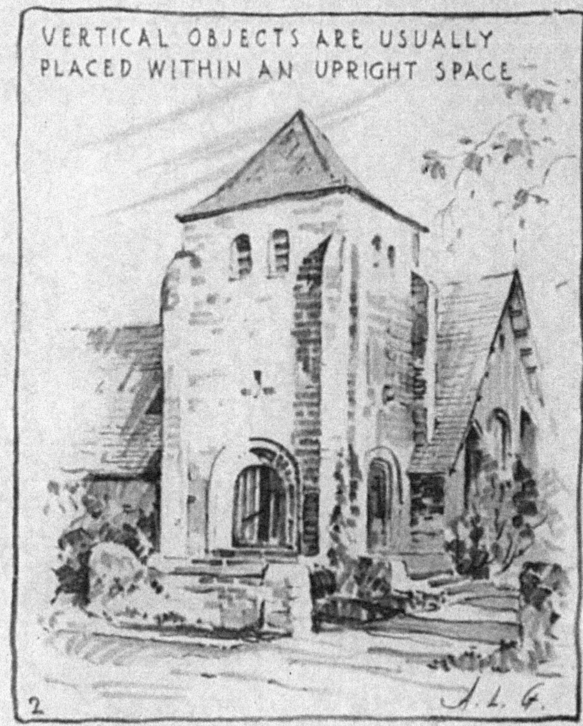

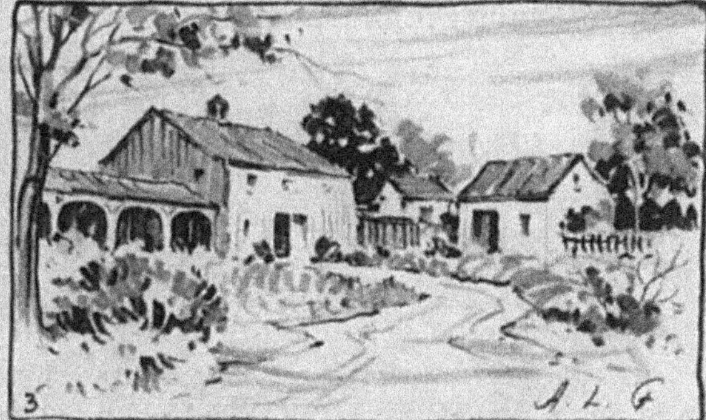

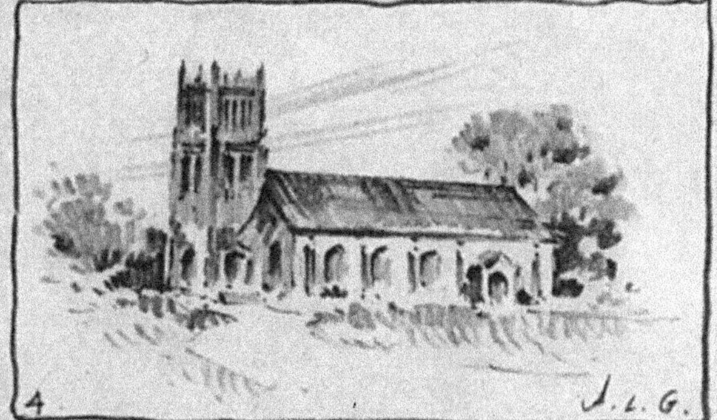

Figure 24. Illustrating the Use of the View-finder, and the Proportioning of the Picture Space to the Subject Drawn.

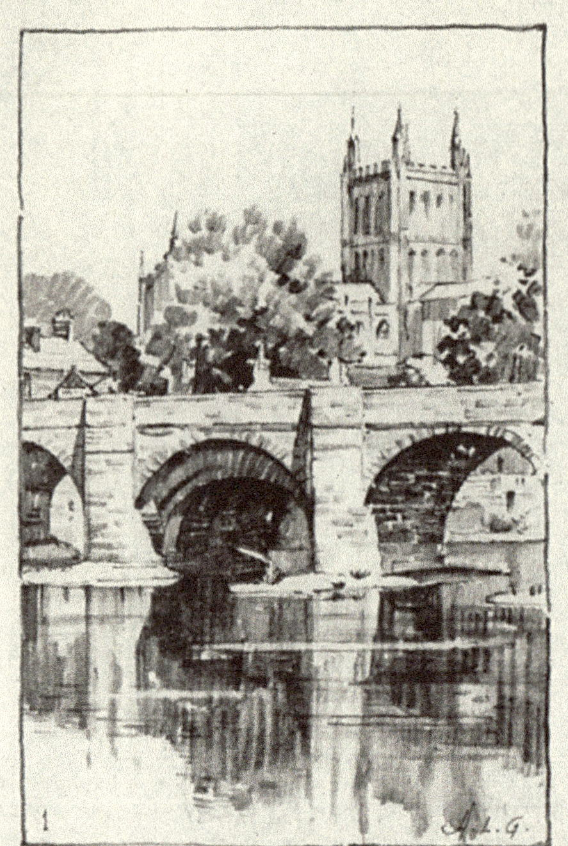

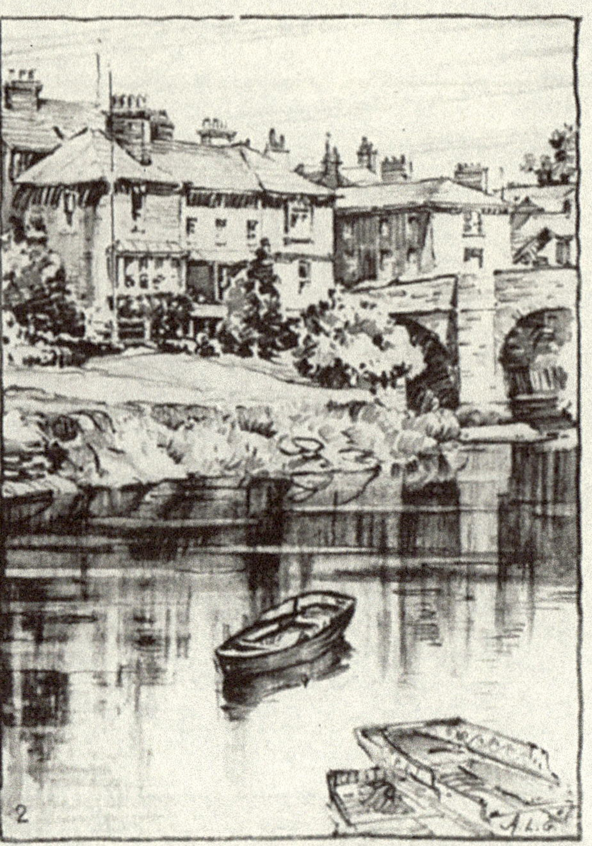

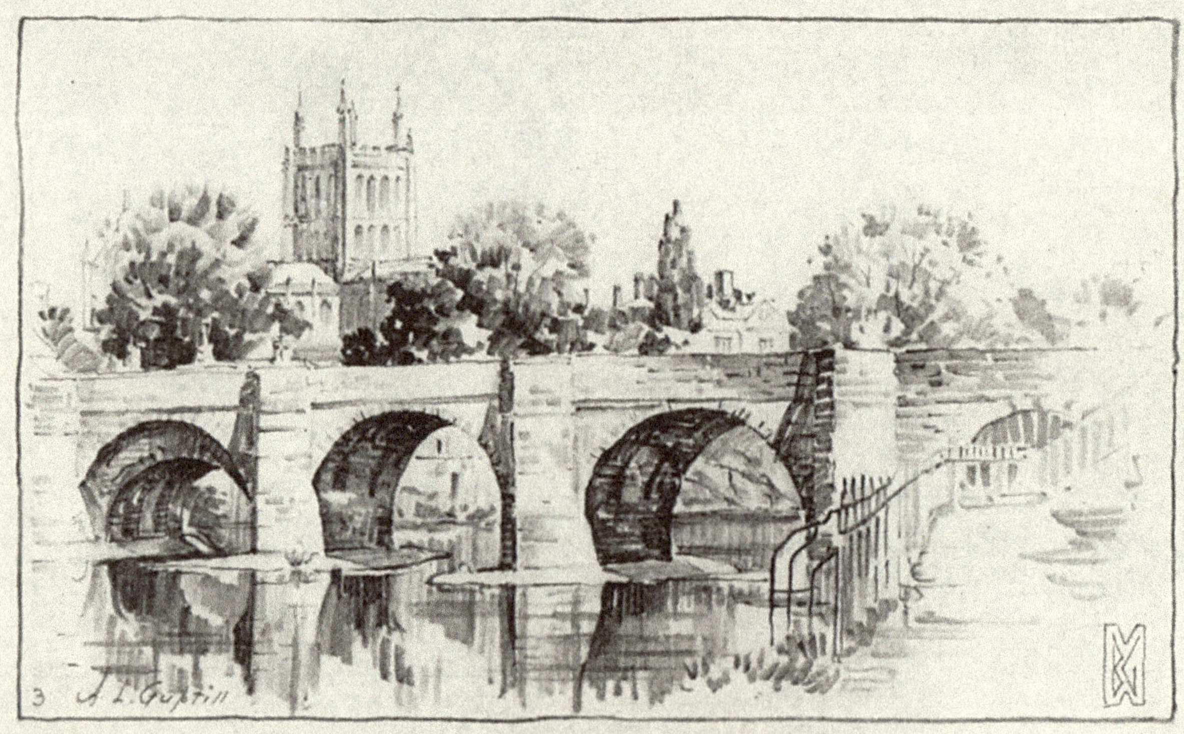

Figure 25. Illustrating Possibilities of Deriving Inspiration from Photographs. These Sketches Were All Based on the Photograph Shown on the Opposite Page.

Some art students carry a view-finder of the kind first described with them constantly and gain a great deal of pleasure and useful knowledge of composition by studying different objects through its opening. In making one, cut several spaces through your card instead of one, if you prefer, of various shapes and sizes. They need not be large as the card can be held near the eye; in fact two or three small openings or a single large one can be made in a finder of postal card size. Sometimes threads are fastened across the openings from side to side and from top to bottom in such a way as to divide them into a number of smaller rectangles or squares. Those who have preference for this finder feel that it lessens the difficulty of laying out correct proportions when drawing from nature, just as in copying a photograph or enlarging a sketch the work is simplified when the print or sketch is marked off into squares or rectangles.

Several excellent compositions can often be found for the same object or objects when viewed from one point, by showing more or less of the surroundings, just as a number of satisfactory photographs can be secured. Naturally, too, an infinite variety of compositions of any architectural object can be discovered by studying it from various positions and under different lighting conditions. When working from the photograph several excellent sketches can sometimes be made from different portions of one print, especially if the picture is a street scene or a general view similar to that of the Wye Bridge and Cathedral, published below on this page. It is easy to frame a number of attractive compositions on this photograph and it would be to the student's advantage to do so. Figure 25 shows three sketches drawn from this very picture.

It will be noticed that no attempt has been made to slavishly copy the values and details exactly as they appear on the print, for it is seldom wise to do this, but the general effect is indicated in a broad, simple way. There is perhaps no better manner of learning composition than by making such selections with the finder and also such sketches as we have shown here. For this reason the following exercises are offered to fix in the memory the ideas which we are considering.

First of all, obtain several photographs such as street scenes or general views, each showing a number of objects which might make pleasing sketches, and with the finder frame on one of your prints some selection which seems to compose well, remembering that each composition should have a center of interest. Remember, too, that there should always be a pleasing relation between the shape of the picture space or margin line and the subject itself. If, for example, a very tall building such as a skyscraper or church spire has been chosen, it is as a rule best to draw it on paper placed vertically or to frame it in a vertical picture space, whereas a long horizontal building or mass of buildings can usually be represented to the best advantage when enclosed in a horizontal manner. This has been illus-

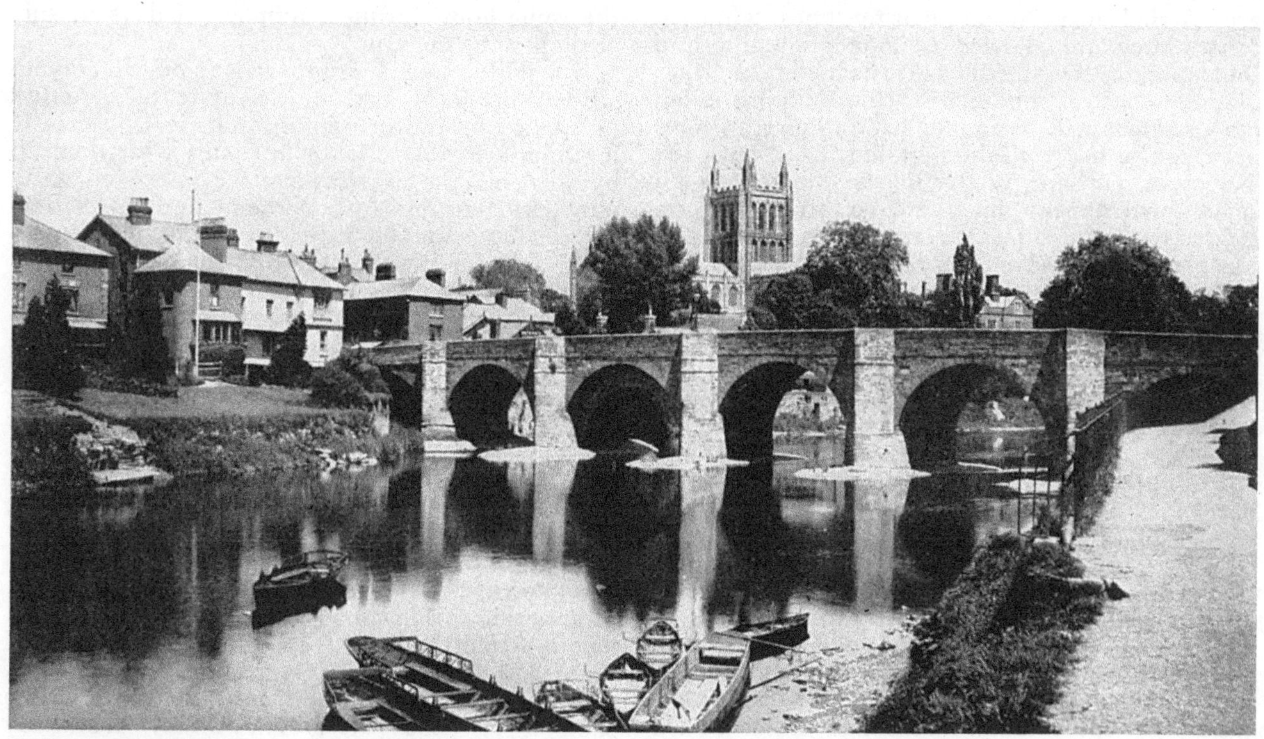

Courtesy of Pratt Institute

Photograph of the Wye Bridge and Cathedral. Three Sketches Drawn from this Photograph are Shown in Figure 25.

trated in Figure 24. The English cottage shown at "1" at the top of the sheet, seemed, when viewed in connection with the nearby trees, to demand a horizontal treatment, while the church tower at "2" suggested at once a vertical handling. A group of buildings such as that shown at "3" usually calls for a horizontal space, for if the horizontal masses are more prominent than the vertical the fact must be recognized and expressed. Thus the church at "4" is given a long, low, frame, but if its tower alone was to be shown the contrary treatment would be more appropriate. As a general rule it is well not to use circular or oval or triangular frames or margin lines on architectural drawings as such shapes often have little or no relation to the form of the architecture itself. A square shape might be well related in this respect and therefore might sometimes do, but from an artistic standpoint a square is usually less interesting than any other rectangle. It is even true that certain rectangles are more pleasing than others. One with a length just twice its width is not as desirable, for instance, as another which is one and one-half times as long as it is wide, while even this proportion is less subtle and hence less satisfying to the eye than one about three parts wide and five long.

While discussing margin lines it might be well to mention that the line itself should never be so black as to draw the eye away from the subject. The width and tone of line should vary in different drawings so as to always be in harmony with the sketch. Again, attention should be called to the fact that sketches in some cases are carried way to the margin lines while in others they are allowed to fade gradually into the paper, or "vignetted" as it is called. In either of these cases if the exterior of a building is being drawn it will be found that the margin lines need not be far from the building itself, with the exception, perhaps, of the line at the top, as all spaces will appear much greater after they are rendered than before, for such surroundings as are generally used add a sense of distance. If too much space is left in such drawings the landscape and accessories may easily become too prominent in relation to the architecture.

When a selection has been decided upon and framed to a good proportion, fasten the finder to the photograph and then on very thin tracing paper with a soft pencil make a simple tracing, not in outline alone but in values, trying to give the effect of the whole in a direct and simple manner, with sufficient accent at the center of interest. Do not spend more than five minutes on the sketch and then frame the same object in a slightly different way and make a second tracing. Compare the two. If one is better than the other, why? Is it because you have shown more foreground or sky, or because the frame has been kept of a size or shape better suited to the leading objects? Ask yourself such questions and then make perhaps a third and even a fourth sketch, comparing them all with care, and if one seems better than the others, make a larger and more carefully finished drawing using this last sketch as the basis of your composition. Next try to find some entirely different composition in the same photograph, using a new subject, and make another series of quick sketches or tracings, and again compare them and analyse each, trying always to learn by this comparison why one composition is good and another not. Select a different photograph and repeat the process, or, if you feel that you have the ability to work in a similar way from nature, do so, choosing a comparatively simple subject so that each sketch can be done in a few minutes.

One will encounter more difficulty when working from nature, for whereas on the photographs the forms and values remain constant, in nature the values are always changing and the forms more difficult to represent. We have previously had occasion to mention that subjects which are full of interest and good in composition during some hours are entirely different under changed lighting conditions, and buildings which appear to good advantage at certain times of day are much less pleasing at others. This is largely because the areas of shade and shadow are never the same for long. Part of the time they nicely balance one another so that the lights and darks are all well related. At other times too much light or too much dark appears at one side or above or below, thus destroying the restful effect. At some hours, too, there may be patches of shade or shadow so odd in shape as to prove distracting. It is therefore well to do your sketching during favorable moments, if this is possible, returning, if necessary, to the same subject at the same hour during a number of days in succession until the study is completed.

If a subject which is otherwise good in composition exhibits a few unpleasant features, either in nature or in the photograph, it is perfectly legitimate to take certain liberties with them, if by so doing the drawing can be improved without sacrificing the truth of the main idea. Should a tree, for example, seem a bit too small in relation to a building, or too light or dark in value, or should some shadow be too dense and black or form a displeasing mass, it is permissible to make such changes as seem necessary to improve the composition providing the final result represents a condition which might be possible under slightly different circumstances, without the breaking of any of nature's laws.

In landscape painting and decorative drawing more such liberties are taken, however, than are permissible in most architectural sketching or rendering, for architecture must as a rule be truthfully portrayed, the changes to better the composition being made for the most part in foliage, shadows, and the like. To illustrate this matter of changes, we have shown in Figure 25, Sketch 2, the dark boat in exactly the same position as on the photograph. This spacing is not wholly satisfactory as the boat seems isolated in the center of the sheet, attracting by its placement more than its proper share of attention. In such a case as this it would be better to improve the composition by moving the boat to the right or the left or it might be tied into the scheme by the addition of extra lines or tones. Amendments like this are always advisable, and it is also wise to omit from a sketch such objects as have little or no relation to the subject itself, and which, for this reason, detract from the main idea which the drawing is intended to express. This means that we must observe the "Principle of Unity," which requires that a composition must be a homogeneous whole, all its parts related and so thoroughly merged and blended together that they become a single unit. In order to secure unity in a drawing only as much of the material before us is selected as relates directly to the subject of the sketch. Separate your subject from everything else that is visible, and think of it as a single harmonious whole. This rule applies whether your subject be an entire building, or some portion such as a dormer window or some still smaller detail,—a door knocker, for example. Once you have determined which of the ideas are to be rejected as irrelevant, you must decide on the relative importance of those which have been accepted as essential, for unity in a drawing depends not only on the selection or rejection of material but on its emphasis or subordination as well, for unless each detail is given just the amount of attention that is proportionate to its importance, the composition will not count as a complete and satisfactory unit. Failure to give sufficient emphasis or accent to the leading parts of a drawing causes a loss of force to the entire composition and in the same way neglect to properly subordinate the unimportant parts leads to confusion and complication.

To further illustrate this principle of unity let us consider some simple objects found in everyday use. An ink-bottle, a turnip and a vase of roses might be arranged into a pleasing composition so far as variety of form and size and value are concerned, but unity would always be lacking in such a group for these objects are not sufficiently well related by use to ever become a satisfying single whole. It would be equally difficult to compose a coal scuttle, a hair brush and a cut glass pitcher, but a comparatively simple matter to form an excellent composition of a loaf of bread partly sliced, with knife, plate, etc., or of a garden trowel, flower pot and package of seeds. Fortunately nearly all objects of an architectural nature are so closely related that little difficulty is experienced in finding things which go well together, so the delineator of architecture has much less trouble in this respect than does the painter of still life. Unity in architectural work is often injured, however, because certain accessories are too important in relation to the architecture itself. It is not inappropriate to show an automobile at the curb before a Colonial doorway, but if it is indicated so large in size or made so conspicuous in any manner that it detracts from the doorway it then prevents a perfect unity in the sketch. It is mainly for this reason that in rendering architectural drawings such accessories are often left in what sometimes seems to the beginner an unfinished state. Trees are shown in a conventional and inconspicuous manner, clouds are often either omitted or only lightly indicated and shadows are simplified. This brings us to a discussion of the "Principle of Balance" which is so closely related to the principle of unity as to be really a part of it; in fact without balance there can be no unity, for by balance we mean, as the name implies, the equilibrium or restfulness that results from having all the parts of a composition so arranged that each receives just its correct share of attention. Every part of a picture has a certain attractive force which acts upon the eye and in proportion to its own power to attract it detracts from every other part. If we find our interest in a drawing divided between several parts,—if certain tones or lines seem too insistent or prominent,—we know that the composition is lacking in balance and likewise lacking in unity as well. It is impossible to give concise and definite rules for obtaining balance in drawings, mainly for the reason that the attractive force of each portion of a drawing depends on an infinite number of circumstances which are variable. A short, straight line drawn near the center of a clean sheet of paper has a power to catch and hold the eye. Let a figure "6" or some other curved line be drawn near the straight one and even though they are of equal size the curved line will prove the more powerful attraction of the two. In the same way a star-shaped form or a triangle has more strength to attract than a square or rectangle of like area. This power depends not entirely on shape, however, but on the value of light and dark as well. Draw two squares on paper, side by side, the one dark and the other light and if the paper is white the dark square will exert the strongest force but if the paper is black the white square will jump into prominence. Again, the attractive power of an object varies in proportion to its proximity to other objects. If, for example, a man is shown at small scale in a standing or sitting position near the center of the sheet he will receive considerable attention if by himself, but if surrounded by other objects he will seem much less noticeable. Then, too, a moving object or one which suggests motion, will be more prominent than a similar object in repose. Let a man be shown running and he is seen far more quickly than if he is at rest. Objects near the edges of the sheet or in the corners usually arrest the eye more quickly, too, than they would if near the middle of the paper.

These examples are sufficient to show the difficulty of attempting to give definite directions for obtaining good balance. The best suggestion we can offer is that the student make first of all, as soon as a drawing has been blocked out in its main proportions, a preliminary sketch such as we have described. A painter is able to make many corrections in his work as he progresses, until excellent balance in every part is gained, but in pencil sketching, where the nature of the medium and the limitation of time demand that the work be done very directly and with few changes, it is difficult to make well balanced drawings unless the artist or student has had considerable practice or unless preliminary studies are made. Almost invariably such studies save time and give results in the end that more than justify the labor spent on their preparation. Then,

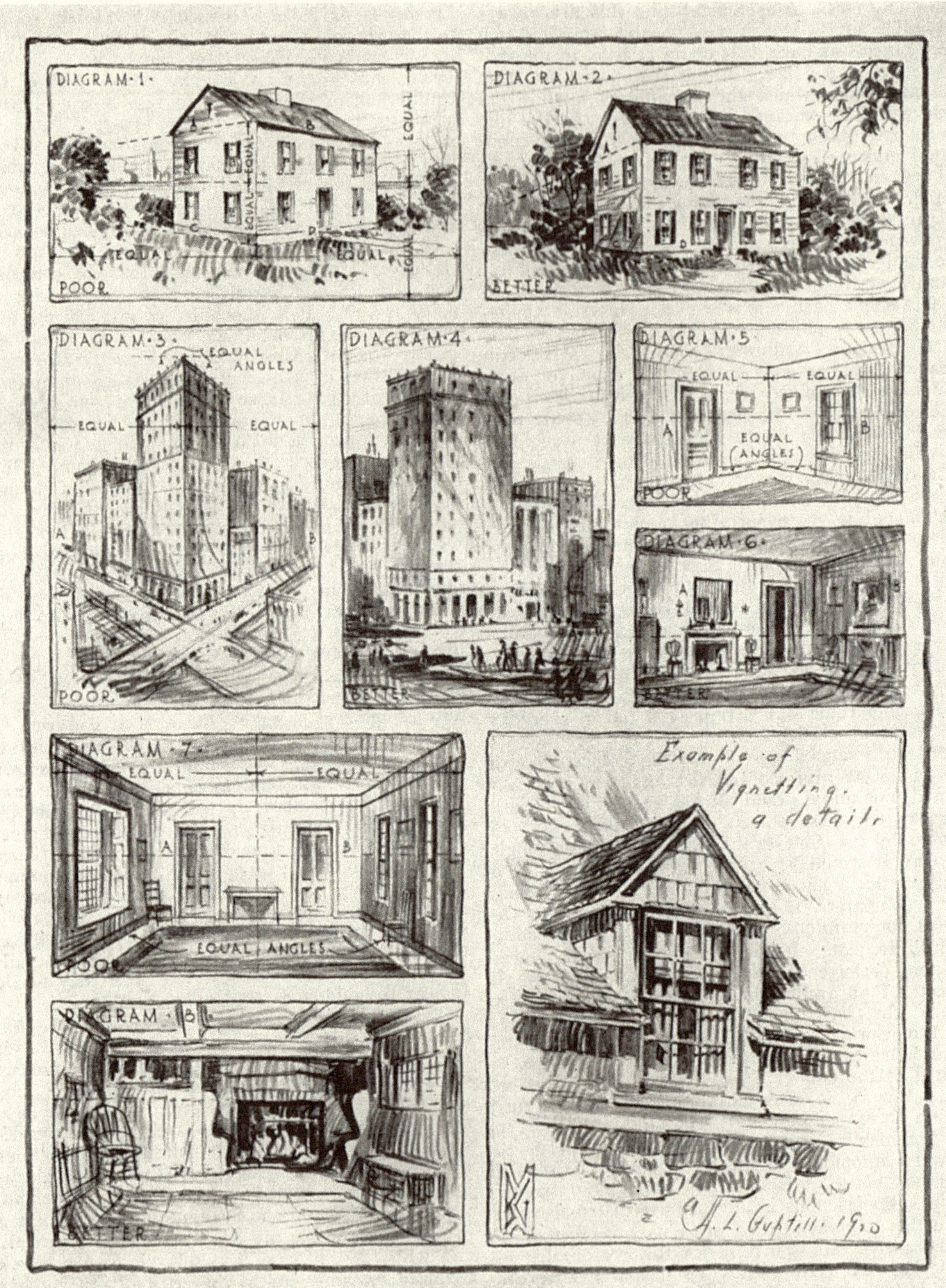

Figure 26. Illustrating Some of the Principles of Composition in Examples of Various Character.

by way of additional precaution, as the final sketch progresses set it away from you at intervals or turn it upside down or on end or even reflect it in a mirror so as to see it in a reversed or changed position. When so viewed the balance should still be good, and if not the necessary adjustments should be made. If some part seems too prominent either tone it down or accent other parts until balance is restored.

These principles of unity and balance which we have described all too briefly are most important as they apply to all forms of drawing and design, but we must leave them to offer a few suggestions which relate especially to architectural work.

First of all, in making drawings of architecture strive for an effect of restfulness and repose. A painter of birds and animals or of marine views often desires an appearance of motion, but care must be taken not to suggest much movement when drawing architecture, for each building should look permanent and solid and should appear to rest firmly on the ground. Avoid, therefore, any effect of violent wind or of speeding automobiles or hurrying people. If persons are indicated it is well to have them walking quietly into the picture or approaching the center of interest, for if they are shown walking away from the center towards the margin line the eye follows them and the balance is thus disturbed. There are, of course, exceptions to this. If many people are shown, as in a street scene, they may be represented as going in all directions, for the sense of motion in one direction will be offset by that in the other. Figures of any sort greatly injure a drawing, however, unless they are well drawn and naturally arranged into effective groups, and so should either be omitted entirely or represented well.

Figure 26 is designed to show certain displeasing effects often found in architectural drawings, which it is best to try to avoid. A reference to Diagram 1 will disclose that the foremost corner of the house is equi-distant from the two end margin lines. It is seldom advisable to place a building in this position, a possible exception being a tower which is absolutely symmetrical. Diagram 3 illustrates the same point, while Diagram 5 applies the idea to an interior, and in both of these the effect is somewhat unpleasant. Do not, then, divide the picture space into two equal parts by having some important line directly in the center. Look again at Diagrams 1, 3 and 5 and you will find that the horizon line or eye level towards which all the receding horizontal lines seem to vanish is just one-half way from top to bottom of the picture space, and this division is unsatisfactory, too, and better results are obtained when the horizon or eye level is either above or below the center of the sheet. In the same way the sketch of the bridge at 3, Figure 25, would be better if the top line of the bridge was not so near the center, for here the picture space is also divided into two nearly equal parts by this line. Again, it is usually well to avoid many opposing lines of the same slant or angle, for variety is always desirable. In Diagram 1 the lines at A, B, C and D are all of equal pitch. This leads to monotony. The same fault is found in 3 and 5. It is better to so place the building on the sheet as to avoid these difficulties and Diagrams 2, 4 and 6 are better in placing than 1, 3 and 5. Diagram 3 has other faults. First the perspective is so violent that the building has the unstable effect of resting on its lower corner, and the crossed lines of the streets form too conspicuous a pattern with a tendency to draw the eye away from the building towards points A and B. Diagram 4 has a more pleasing variety of masses and the interest plainly centers in the main building. Diagram 5 shows a fault in that the two visible wall surfaces are equal in size and shape, as are also the ceiling and floor, and here, too, there is no real center of focus, for the eye jumps back and forth between A and B. Diagram 6 is better, for the interest undoubtedly centers at A, and even though there is an important mass at B it is toned down so as to seem unimportant. The floor, too, has been made larger in mass than the ceiling, but the advantage thus gained is largely lost, for the rug is unfortunately of the same size on the drawing as the visible portion of the ceiling, so that this sketch could be still further improved by adding either more rug or more ceiling. Diagram 7 shows that when a room is so turned that we are looking directly at one of its walls or is placed in "parallel perspective" as this is called, similar faults may develop. Here the main surfaces are all monotonous, the interest is divided and the drawing made still more unpleasant because the receding lines exactly meet the margin lines at the corners. At 8 an attempt has been made to avoid some of the difficulties of Diagram 7.

The little sketch of the dormer is shown to illustrate an important matter of composition. When drawing small details care must always be taken that they do not seem to be merely suspended in the air. They should appear instead to be attached to a solid background or support, and one of the best means of giving this impression is by allowing each sketch to fade out gradually into the sheet, showing enough of the adjacent surroundings to give the whole a sense of stability and strength.

If at all essential, we might go on with many suggestions on composition similar to these which we have given, but if the student is interested and really serious he will take the time to obtain additional ideas from such books as we have recommended. The student is urged to make drawings of his own to illustrate and make clear in his mind any of the principles he acquires, for unless he does so it is probable that many of them will be soon forgotten.

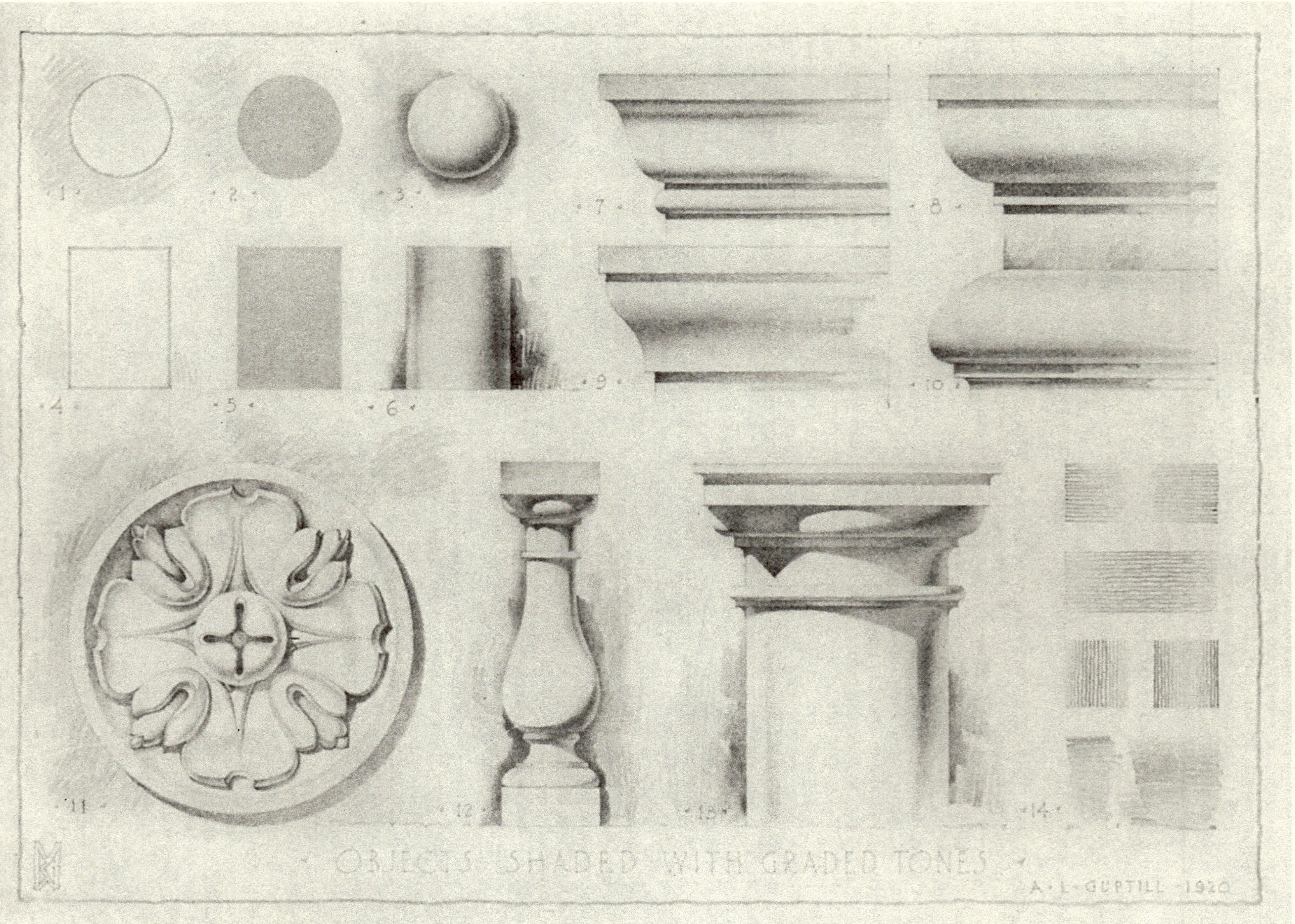

Figure 27. Illustrating Uses of Graded Tones on Details of Architecture.

Chapter VI.
GRADED TONES

CAREFUL observation and study of objects in nature, as well as those contrived by man, will reveal one fact of the greatest value to the student of drawing, and this is that although not a little of the beauty of such objects depends on color, on profile and on the proportions of the various parts into which they are divided, more of it than we usually suppose is caused by the varying light and shade and especially by the gradation of tones from light to dark or from dark to light.

There are, to be sure, some objects which seem to have no gradation of tone, each surface being apparently of one value throughout, but in spite of such exceptions there are far more "graded" tones in nature than "flat" tones of uniform appearance, and it is certainly true that a graded tone has more interest and variety than one of exactly the same value in every part.

It naturally follows that in representing nature by drawings, graded tones usually prove of greater value to the artist than do those which are flat. Almost any object can be represented satisfactorily by graded tones, whereas many objects, especially those which are rounded or curved, cannot be made to appear correct if flat tones alone are used. We can, for example, make a pleasing drawing of a square box, and, if we wish, have every tone graded. It is impossible, on the other hand, to nicely represent a sphere or an object of spherical form by the use of flat tones only, unless we resort to a succession of small adjacent flat tones, each slightly different in value from its neighbor, and such a combination really is, after all, a graded tone. If we try to portray a sphere by drawing its outline as at "1," Figure 27, we fail to give our picture any effect of convexity of form, and shading the entire circle with a flat tone as at "2" gives no better result. It is only when we copy as well as we can the gradations found on such surfaces in nature, as we have done at "3," that we approach the desired effect. In fact we would not even recognize a sphere when placed before us were it not for this subtle grading of its surface tones, for without these gradations it would appear simply as a flat circular disk. In the case of the cylinder and cone and similar rounded forms it is perhaps a bit less difficult to suggest their shapes on paper without recourse to graded tones providing they are drawn in perspective, for when so drawn their forms can be fairly well indicated even in outline. If a real feeling of solidity and roundness is desired, however, it can best be obtained by the use of graded tones. If such objects are shown in elevation, instead of perspective, it will be found that these tones are absolutely essential for their successful representation. Take for example the cylinder which is shown in elevation at "4," Figure 27, drawn in outline only. In this form it appears as a rectangle and seems flat. A smooth tone added as at "5" is of no help, and it is only when we use the grades as at "6" that we get the real appearance of roundness.

Now just as the surfaces of cylinders and spheres and such geometric forms depend largely on gradation of tone for a pleasing effect, so, in architecture too, much of the beauty of the mouldings and ornament depends on similar gradations. After all, the mouldings are mainly combinations of curved surfaces, and if these curves are pleasingly designed the light and dark will be graded in a satisfactory manner. In fact these gradations on mouldings so nicely express the profiles which cause them that we are often able to judge the curve of each moulding at a glance even though its profile is not visible. If the light is favorable we are usually able to name every member composing a cornice and tell its exact form without once seeing its true profile. One of the main reasons why a designer works so hard to produce a good profile for a cornice or similar group of mouldings is that he is seeking the most pleasing arrangement of light and shade and shadow possible, and knows that an excellent profile is important, not as a thing in itself, for it is seen in its true form only at the corners or breaks in a building, but as a means of obtaining the most satisfactory results in light and shade. A poor profile usually means a poor cornice.

At "7," "8," "9" and "10," Figure 27, are four sketches of typical architectural mouldings, drawn in elevation, and with their tones graded. For convenience their profiles have been shown but even if these had been omitted it would not be difficult to visualize the correct curves. It should be borne in mind, however, that without the use of graded tones it would be impossible to produce such effects of curvature.

Now just as it is necessary to use graded tones for a truthful expression of the curved surfaces of mouldings, they are obviously needed also in the representation of other rounded surfaces such as those which we so often find in ornamental work. Most ornament, in fact, consists so largely of curved surfaces of every possible shape that it would be very difficult to represent it on paper without the use of some graded tones. At "11," Figure 27, is a drawing of a rosette, nearly every surface of which is curved, and therefore represented by grades of light and dark. Certainly an object of such gradual curvature as this can be successfully portrayed only by equally subtle gradations of its values.

Balusters, columns, archways, round towers and all sorts of similar architectural objects and details require a certain amount of graded shading. At "12" and "13," Figure 27, a baluster and a capital are shown. Even though drawn in elevation the rounded effect is very evident. Had they been done in perspective less care would have been needed in the shading to express roundness, but for architectural purposes it is often necessary to work in elevation and therefore these sketches have been done in that manner to prove that it is not essential to show objects in perspective when a feeling of projection and curvature is required.

In order to illustrate the points under discussion in the clearest possible manner the drawings on Figure 27 have been done with very evenly graded tones, for by this means the values as found on the objects themselves could be more accurately represented than by the use of tones built up of separate lines. As a general rule, however, such smooth tones are not needed, for much the same effect can be arrived at by forming them of lines just touching, in the usual manner, and the result is less mechanical or photographical and hence more desirable. At "14" a few suggestions are offered for the formation of graded tones by individual strokes. (It is suggested that the student make a few drawings similar to these on this plate, trying some with the smooth tone and others with a more sketchy handling.)

It should be remembered that although the exact form which the gradation of a tone takes depends largely on the curve of the surface, it really owes its effect to the light which causes it to be visible. If we had no light the most perfect mouldings would be lost in darkness — if we have too much light their beauty is often destroyed. The author has in mind a certain coffered ceiling of unusual beauty. After this ceiling had been in existence a number of years and had been much admired, it was decided to install a new indirect lighting system in the room, and this was done. The system was so arranged that the light was uniformly distributed over the ceiling in such a way that nearly all of the shade and shadow was destroyed. The lighting engineers pronounced the job a perfect one, but from an artistic standpoint the effect of the ceiling was ruined; the mouldings and detail were barely visible while the few shadows that remained took weird and grotesque shapes of a most bewildering nature. In this case too much light, or rather light distributed in too uniform a manner, destroyed the effect. This all goes to prove that even a beautiful curve may lose much of its value through unfavorable lighting, and it shows also that the gradation of tone on any given moulding or curve varies with changes in light. Spheres and cylinders, for example, do not appear the same at all times and hence cannot always be represented in the same way. It should be remembered, too, that the gradation of tone on any given form, take a cylinder for example, depends not a little on the nature of the material of which the object is made. A study of a number of cylinders of equal size and of various materials such as wood, plaster, polished white marble, sandstone, red granite, brass, silver, etc., will reveal, even under the same conditions, a surprising difference in the values and the method of gradation of the tones. Those cylinders with highly polished surfaces will show a greater complication of values and much sharper and more sudden contrasts, as a rule, mainly because their surfaces serve as curved mirrors to reflect distorted images of other objects. Such surfaces usually have brilliant highlights in spots while those of the wood or plaster or other dull appearing objects will not only lack these highlights but will show throughout a more simple and gradual change in tone. It is because of such conditions as these that there can be no definite rules given as to just how such objects should be represented. Observation and study will give the student the desired knowledge.

We have, up to this point, spoken mainly of graded tones as found on curved surfaces, yet it should be realized that smooth flat surfaces often appear to grade from one part to another. Prove this to yourself by observing objects around you. It is especially true that on surfaces indoors, where the light is frequently coming from a number of sources and is all more or less diffused, we find many tones which are graded. A ceiling, for instance, often appears light at one side and dark at the other, but it is in the shadow-tones especially that we find a great amount of gradation. As a rule the shadows of objects indoors seem the darkest and have the sharpest edges near the object casting them. A chair leg, for example, usually casts a dark shadow where it touches the floor, but this shadow softens as it gets farther from the leg and soon disappears. The little sketch of the pencil touching the paper at "1," Figure 28, was made to illustrate this point, the shadow being the darkest at "A," softening as the light becomes more diffused towards "B." In brilliant light, such as bright sunshine, the opposite effect is often found. Let an object project from the wall like the little cornice shown at "4" and the lower edge of the shadow as at "B" frequently seems sharper and darker than the edge nearer the object as at "A." Such an effect is as a rule only an optical illusion for unless there is something to cause a strong reflection of light into the upper portion of the shadow the tone is usually of equal value throughout. The effect of darkness towards the lower edge is due to the fact that sunlight is so extremely brilliant that when it falls on a light wall or similar surface it produces a value so bright that it is impossible for us to correctly represent it on paper, and so when a shadow tone cast by some object similar to the cornice at "4" falls on this bright surface the tone appears,

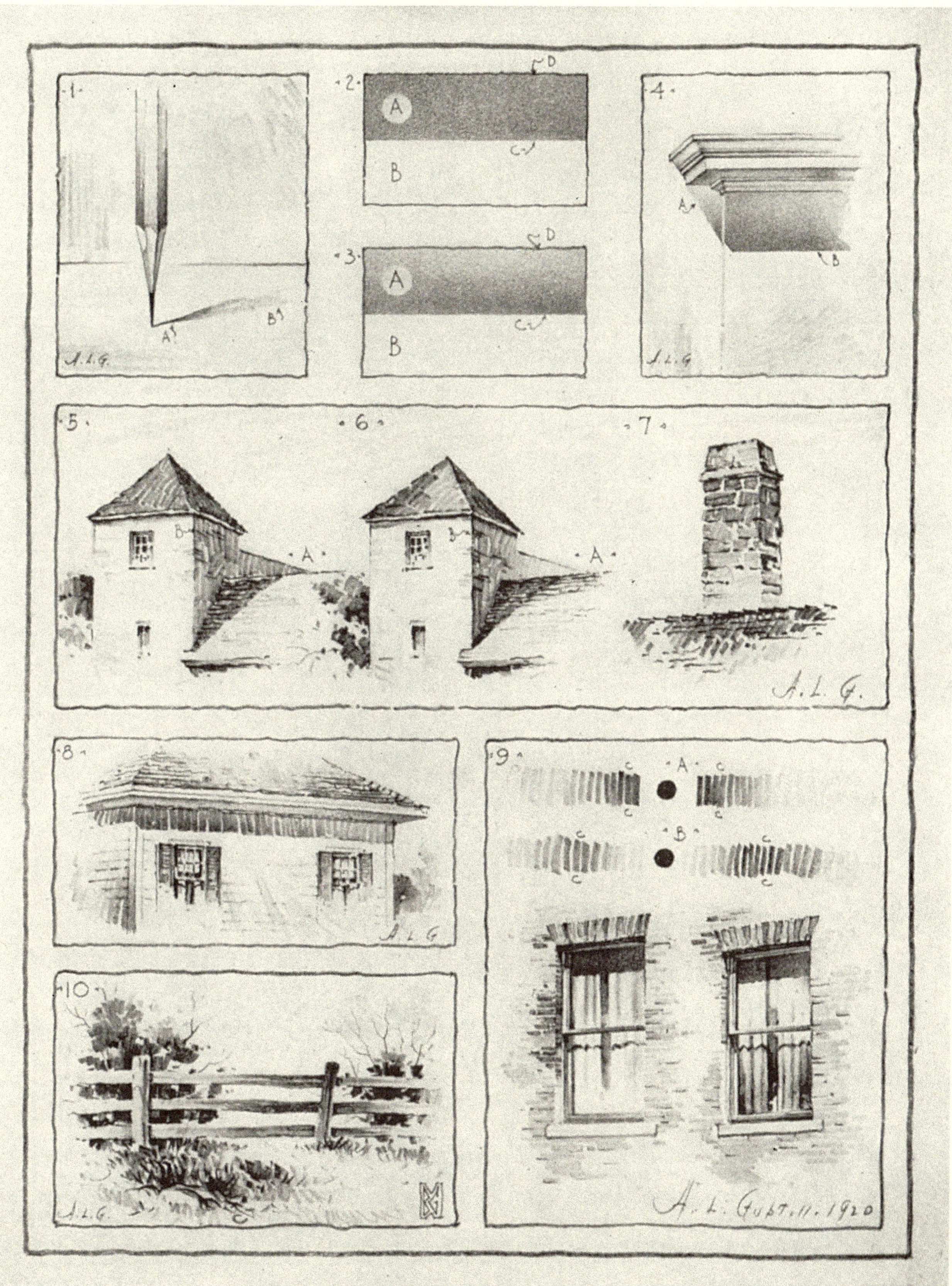

Figure 28. Some Applications of Graded Tones.

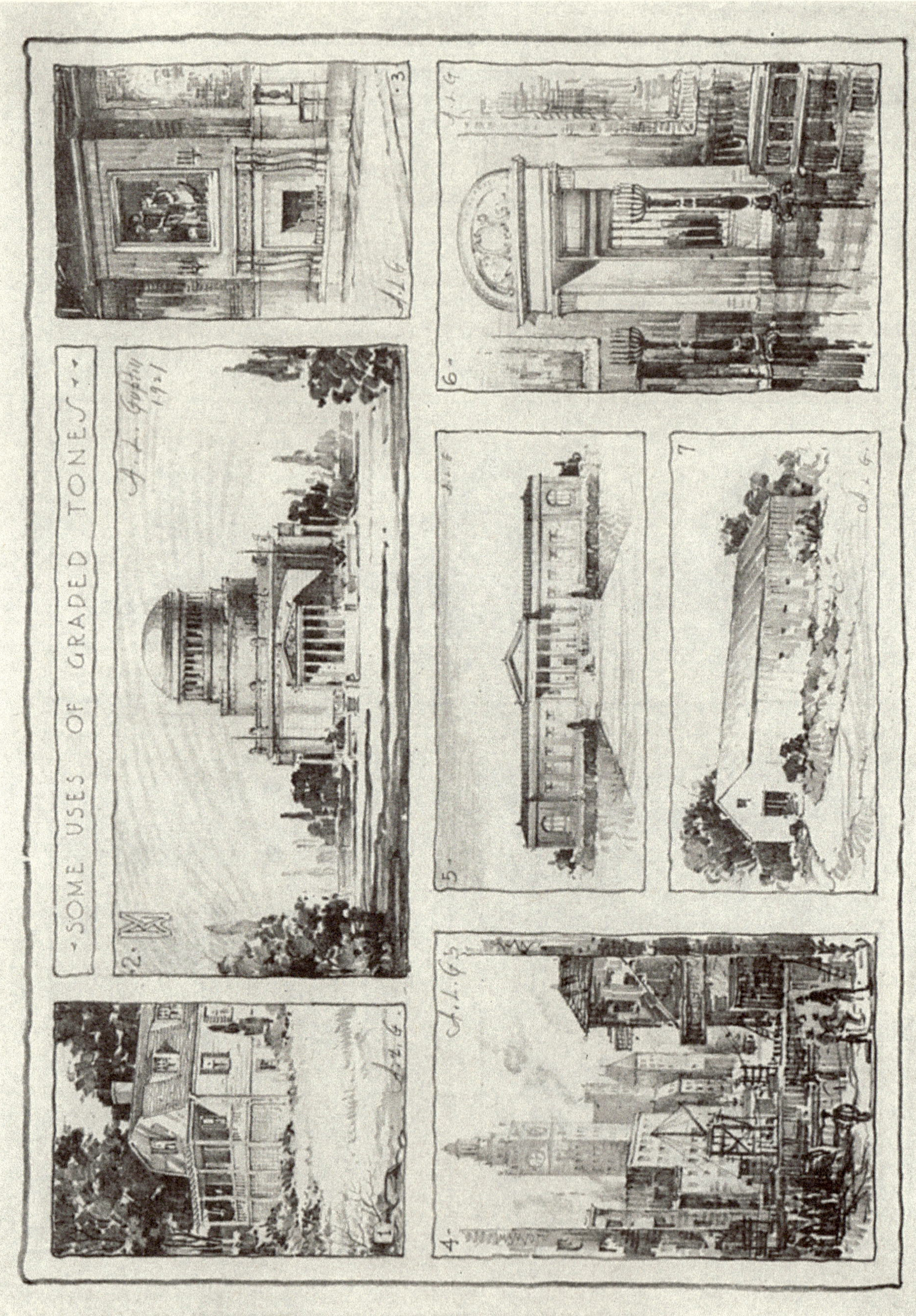

Figure 29. Graded Tones Applied to Larger Compositions.

in its relation to the bright surface, darker than it really is. A shadow may be a medium gray if compared with black but if its lower edge is thrown into sudden and sharp contrast with extremely brilliant light it often seems actually black. In drawing shadows, therefore, there is a legitimate reason for such a gradation as we have shown in the sketch "4," as this method causes the white of the paper to appear brighter than it otherwise would, and therefore to more correctly represent the sunlit surface. The lighter shadow tone above also gains, by this gradation, a quality of depth and transparency.

There is another use for graded tones which is of the greatest importance and this is to so employ them as to give a sense of distance and of detachment or separation of one object from another. We can perhaps best explain this by reference to sketches "5," "6" and "7," Figure 28. Objects in nature, even when they are of the same value, can usually be easily distinguished one from another because of differences of color or by their motion or in a number of other ways. In photographs, such objects, if the values of light and shade are the same or nearly the same, often seem lost or indistinct. Sketch "5," made from a photograph, shows at "A" just the condition which we describe; the roof tone and wall tone lack detachment — it is hard to distinguish one from the other. In sketch "6" this same wall tone has been graded back to light from dark and at "A" the roof has been darkened. The result gives us a much greater feeling of separation — the roof seems to come nearer to us and the wall tends to recede — as it should. The edge at "B" still appears just as sharp as it did before the wall was lightened towards "A," in just the same way that edge "C" in diagram "3" seems as sharp or even sharper than the same edge in diagram "2" (because in "2" the edge "D" detracts from "C" to a greater extent than it does in "3"). We therefore have about the same relative contrast in sketches "5" and "6" between the wall in light and the wall in shade, so that sketch "6" is not injured in any way because of the changed values at "A." Sketch "7" is another and very emphatic illustration of the use of graded tones in securing detachment, the chimney being lightened towards the bottom and the roof darkened towards the top in order to gain a sharp contrast. This method brings the roof forward and carries the chimney back, and so gives an effect of distance. The idea is, therefore, a useful one to remember as it can be applied in many different places in nearly every drawing. In sketch "1," for instance, the horizontal line is softened as it goes behind the pencil, thereby bringing the pencil forward.

Sketch "8" shows a similar application of a graded tone, for by darkening the cornice shadow towards the nearest corner of the house, that corner actually seems to come nearer. This method is of even more value when the wall is turned at a sharper angle, making the foreshortening more acute.

Graded tones are of the greatest assistance in forcing the eye to any given portion of a drawing, and the little diagrams "A" and "B," sketch "9," show two methods of bringing attention to a desired spot, in this case the dark circle. The sketches really explain themselves. Method "B" is perhaps the stronger one for the dark tone at "C" in sketch "A" detracts from the spot itself. Of the two little window sketches below, the second carries out the same idea represented by method "B," the dark shadow taking the place of the dark spot in the diagram. The eye here is forced to the bright upper portion of the window. The first window sketch shows in place of such strong contrast a more gradual grading from dark at the top down to light.

Occasionally it is necessary to apply the idea of separation or detachment to such accessories as fences and tree trunks. In sketch 10 the fence is so graded as to bring it light against the two dark masses of foliage and dark against the light background. When this same idea is applied to trees the trunks and branches often appear dark against the sky, then are graded to a lighter tone against the background of hedge or other foliage, and sometimes reappear dark in contrast with the grass of the lawn.

Just as graded tones prove of value in innumerable ways when representing small details, they are of use, too, in composing entire drawings. Occasionally compositions grade from dark at the top to light at the bottom as do "1" and "3," Figure 29; sometimes they are light at the top and dark below like "4" and "6" on the same sheet. These are all rather extreme examples, however, though it is frequently the case that drawings combine grades in two or more directions. Sketch "2" in Figure 29, for example, shows dark masses of foliage behind the building which grade away to light. At the end margins there are opposing dark masses causing a sharp contrast which seems to set the building back into the middle-distance. Sketch "5" also shows two sets of grades, the one on the building itself, going from light at the center to dark at the ends; the other on the hedge, which, by grading in just the contrary direction, gives contrasts which carry the eye towards the center of the composition. Sketch "7" is a further illustration of forcing the attention to a given point, in this case the near end of the building, by so grading the walls that they are left light at the end to form a strong contrast with the trees. Drawings are sometimes graded off into distance in just the opposite way — that is, they are carried from dark in the foreground to light in the background.

In fact there are so many places in which graded tones are found and so many uses to which they may be put, it has been our main purpose simply to call attention to their beauty and enough of their uses to give the student a realization of their importance. It is not our intention to give the impression that flat tones should never be used, for there are instances in which drawings have been wholly done with flat tones with a remarkable degree of success.

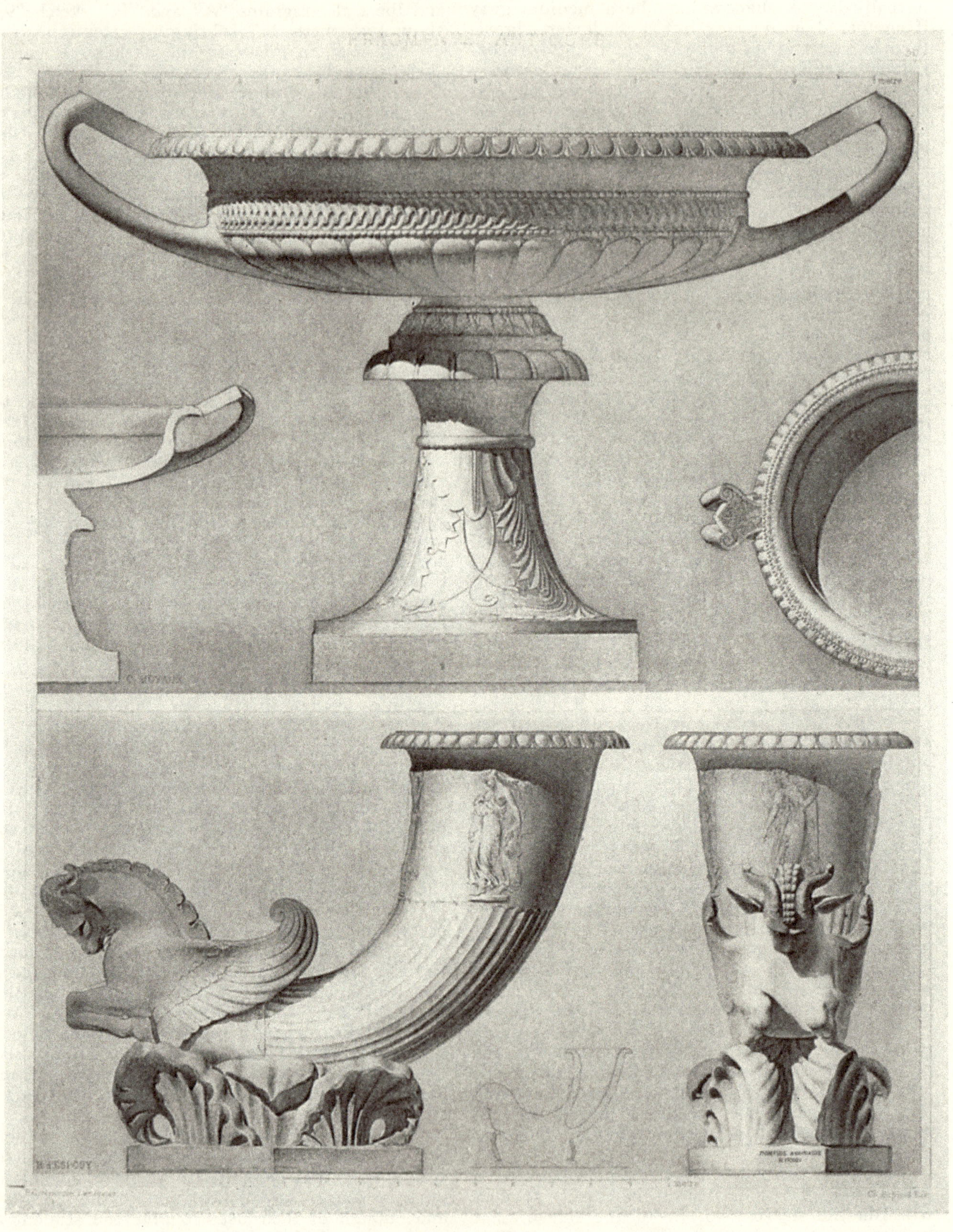

Wash Drawing from H. D'Espouy's "Fragments D'Architecture Antique" to Illustrate Uses of Graded Tones in Suggesting Roundness of Objects Which Show no Perspective.

Chapter VII.

THE REPRESENTATION OF SMALL BUILDINGS

WE HAVE already pointed out a few of the many advantages to be gained through practice in pencil sketching and rendering. It is our present purpose to further explain some of the reasons why a knowledge of such work is of value, especially to the draftsman anxious either to better his position or to build up a practice of his own, and to offer as well some practical suggestions as a help towards this end, these suggestions relating especially to the representation of the simpler sort of building such as the small house.

It should be remembered that the average client who comes to an architect's office builds but once or twice in a lifetime, and for this reason is, as a rule, entirely unfamiliar with the drawings employed in carrying on such work. The instrumental plans mean little to him, though he can read them, perhaps, so far as the general layout of the rooms is concerned, and can understand the elevation drawings if the building is simple in form, but let it be broken up into an irregular mass with numerous projections and varying roof pitches and he finds it impossible to visualize its finished appearance. This is not to be wondered at for even experienced designers and architects are sometimes surprised when they see one of their own buildings taking definite form on the site;—with all their training they are not always able to judge beforehand just how the completed work will appear in relation to its surroundings. Doubtless one of the main reasons why clients are sometimes disappointed with their buildings when finished is that they prove entirely different from what they expected them to be, for they have not really understood the architectural drawings and so have been unable to judge until too late whether or not the submitted designs were satisfactory. Unwilling to admit this inability or overconfident because of the architect's words of assurance that everything would come out all right, they have approved the designs and given word to go ahead with the work, when they actually had very little idea as to how the completed structure would appear. When such a building is finished it is only natural, then, that the client may be displeased, but if so he is much more likely to condemn the architect than to admit any error or lack of understanding on his own part.

It is largely because of this difficulty of expressing a building adequately by the plans and elevations alone, in such a way that the client will fully understand the scheme, that the practice has grown of preparing rendered perspective drawings which show in a very clear manner exactly how the completed structure will appear. Such perspectives are of value to the architect in many ways, for they not only serve as a convincing expression of the problem to the client but are of equal use in his own drafting room as a means of studying the design. In addition to this, new jobs are often brought to the office because of such renderings, submitted to some possible client frequently in competition with work from other architects. Again, when an attempt is being made to raise money to finance the erection of a new building, such a perspective, submitted along with the plans and specifications, may prove of the greatest service in obtaining the necessary loan.

These are only a few of the uses of perspective drawings, but enough to show that they are of immense value to the architect, and this being true it is only natural that there is a constant demand for draftsmen who are able, in addition to doing the usual instrumental work on plans and details, to make such renderings. Men with the skill to sketch and render well are almost certain to advance rapidly, as they soon come to the notice of their employer and are able to serve him in many important ways. First of all, when a new project is conceived many little sketches are needed as a means of study. These are usually done freehand, in pencil. Then as the design takes more definite form, accurate but simple instrumental perspectives are sometimes laid out and over these, on tracing paper, the designs are given further study, a few of the main lines being perhaps drawn instrumentally and the rest free-hand. With these designs quite definitely settled, a carefully finished drawing is often made to show the client, done instrumentally and rendered in any desired medium. After this perspective, with its accompanying plans, elevations, sections and the like has been approved and the final contract drawings started, free-hand studies are frequently made of such details as chimneys and dormers. Then, after the contract is let, another accurate rendered perspective is sometimes worked up, showing all the corrections and changes. Even while the building is being erected sketches are occasionally needed — perhaps to explain matters to the client — often to make some detail clear to a contractor or workman, or again simply as a means of giving further study to a doubtful point. It should not be supposed that so many renderings and sketches are needed for every job, for naturally everything depends on the cost and nature of the work. Often no finished perspectives are made and few sketches, on the other hand there are buildings of complex design which require, in addition to several perspectives both of the interior and exterior, many ornament drawings, including such details as carved stone or wood, wrought iron, leaded glass, etc., as well as carefully lettered inscriptions. All of these offer work for the man who can sketch and render. There are, to be sure, many professional delineators who are sometimes called upon to render the drawings of large or unusually important buildings, but there are many smaller jobs, such as suburban houses, in which the architect's fee is not sufficient to warrant the expenditure of any great sum for renderings. It is such jobs as these which usually fall to someone in the office and the man who is capable of doing them is often advanced to a position of greater responsibility with its corresponding increase in salary.

There is another important advantage which often comes from having skill in making sketches or renderings of small buildings, for it is true that such drawings are frequently the principal means by which a draftsman is able to obtain his first commissions as an architect. Many a draftsman has learned to his sorrow that it is much easier to open an office calling himself an architect and with his name on the door, than it is to induce clients to enter. When we consider that even the cheapest of buildings usually costs a number of thousands of dollars, we can hardly blame the public for failing to patronize young and comparatively inexperienced men when older and better known architects with many buildings to their credit are willing to accept the work for the same fee. But the young architect must get his start in some way and unless he is so fortunate as to have wealthy and influential friends to shower him with their favors he is often wise to remain associated, perhaps as draftsman or designer, with some fairly well-known firm, and to gradually build up a clientele of his own. This may be done in a number of ways, one of which especially concerns us. Some of the larger firms do not care to bother with small houses and the like and so frequently turn any clients that desire this sort of work over to some draftsman or designer. If such a draftsman is able to impress the client favorably he is quite likely to get the work, for even though his experience as an architect may be limited his connection with the well-known firm will give him a certain standing. There is perhaps no surer way of creating such a favorable impression than by submitting attractive rendered drawings showing just how the proposed building will

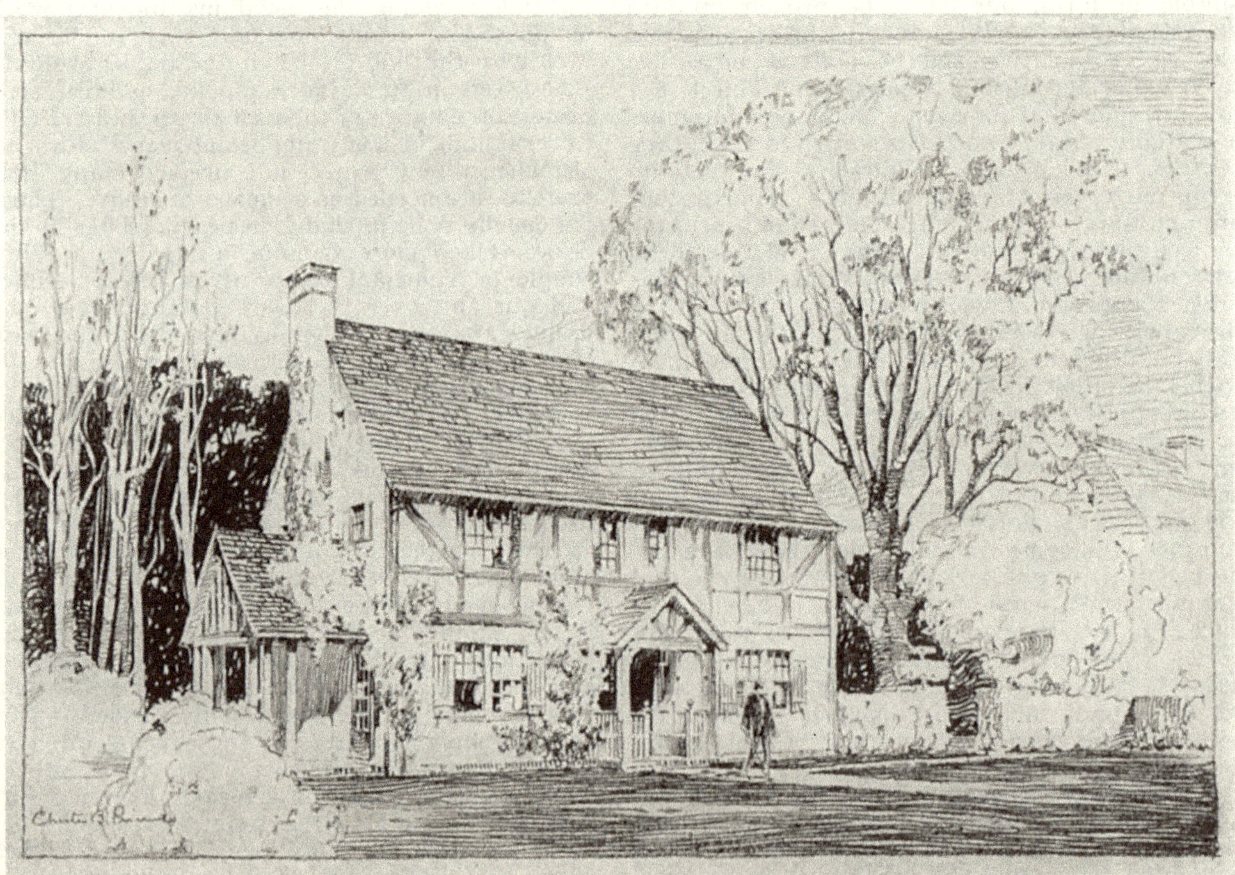

Rendering by Chester B. Price, Portion of a Proposed Housing Development Near Stamford, Conn. McKim, Mead & White, Architects.

look when completed. Somehow people seem to feel that if sketches are nicely done the job itself will be executed as well, and many times the man submitting a pleasingly rendered drawing done in perspective will be given work, when blueprint plans and elevations from other architects, showing a scheme of equal merit, will be ignored.

Perhaps you are one of those draftsmen with a desire to learn to make renderings of a quality suitable for the average job but with the feeling that it will never be possible for you to do so. If this is the case you should be offered encouragement, especially in regard to pencil rendering. It is not easy, of course, to become an artist in the true sense of the word, and a half dozen lessons or a bit of study will not make one an expert, but on the other hand it is not difficult to master the few principles of composition and tricks of rendering which are needed to enable one to do a creditable sketch for the ordinary building. The writer has seen many students of only fair ability turn out excellent drawings of simple buildings after a comparatively brief period of training, though they often lacked at first the confidence which is necessary for success in this work.

Pencil rendering of architectural subjects really is, after all, comparatively simple. One does not encounter the same difficulties as when working in color for there are only the values of light and dark to consider; neither is it difficult to make changes as in work with the pen. Originality is not looked for as it is in some forms of art work, nor is it necessary to strive for a decorative effect. As the small drawing does not often need figures or animals it is not absolutely necessary to be able to draw them; even if figures are to be shown they are usually so small in scale as to need little detail.

The most convincing sort of pencil technique for the usual architectural subjects is the conventional type such as is employed in most of the offices, published examples of which appear from time to time in all of our architectural magazines. The student should collect such reproductions as seem excellent and study them with care. Better yet, if opportunity offers to see originals of this work in the offices or the architectural exhibitions, analyze them thoroughly. Notice the way in which the various details such as the doors and windows are indicated. Study the methods of suggesting different materials — shingles, clapboards, brickwork, stone, stucco, etc. Look at the way the foliage is shown. Copy either the whole or portions of some of these, trying at the same time to memorize the methods of expression. It is valuable also to compare the drawings with photographs of similar subjects or even with buildings themselves, and sketch directly from the buildings, too, trying small drawings of doors and windows or other similar portions first. Photographs of small houses will offer many suggestions for surroundings which can be copied to advantage. As a help to the student we have introduced in the following chapters a number of drawings showing certain methods of representing details of various sorts, but it should be remembered that it is always well to study the work of a great many different people in order to adapt those ideas which appeal most strongly to you.

After considerable practice has been given to the drawing of details, a real rendering of some small house may be undertaken. It is perhaps well to remind the student that a rendering is a more carefully finished production than a sketch; that whereas a sketch is usually made rather hastily, a rendering is more in the nature of a study — this in spite of the fact that many such drawings appear at first glance to be hastily done. In order to gain an accurate result the subject to be rendered is first laid out instrumentally directly from the plans and elevations. This work of course demands some knowledge of the science of instrumental perspective. The few facts necessary for drawing the usual type of building can be acquired easily, however, even though one does not go deeply into the theory of the subject, and many men learn simply a few "rule of thumb" methods which really answer all general requirements. It is not within the scope of this volume to give instruction in instrumental perspective but there are a few points which it seems essential to cover as they relate to both instrumental and free-hand work, and concern especially the composition of the entire sheet.

First of all, it is wise when starting a perspective to decide where to stand in order to obtain the best view. Though this position varies with different buildings it is usually well to show much of the main façade and if the plot be flat to take the eye level or horizon line about five feet above the ground, as the eye is actually approximately this distance from the plane on which the building rests. If, instead, it is to be on a hill so it would be natural to look up at it, that is the way it should be drawn, and in this case the horizon would be way below the house as it is always level with the spectator's eye. Contrarily if we are to look down on the building from above, as in a bird's eye view, the eye level or horizon will be towards the top of the picture. Now it is seldom that we do see houses from above, and even if we should, as from a mountain or airplane it would not generally be wise to show them that way, but there are cases where the building is very irregular in plan or where we have a complex group of buildings to picture and under these conditions there is sometimes no other means of expressing the entire subject adequately. Another point worth remembering is that it is best not to stand too close to a building when making the perspective, as this causes the receding lines to become so acute as to seem unpleasant. A little experience will teach the correct distances for various types of buildings. Again, if you are to make a perspective and the plot has already been purchased, obtain either photographs or sketches of the site to help you in drawing the surroundings. A plot plan or survey showing the contours of the land, location of rocks, trees, etc., is always of immense help, too, in

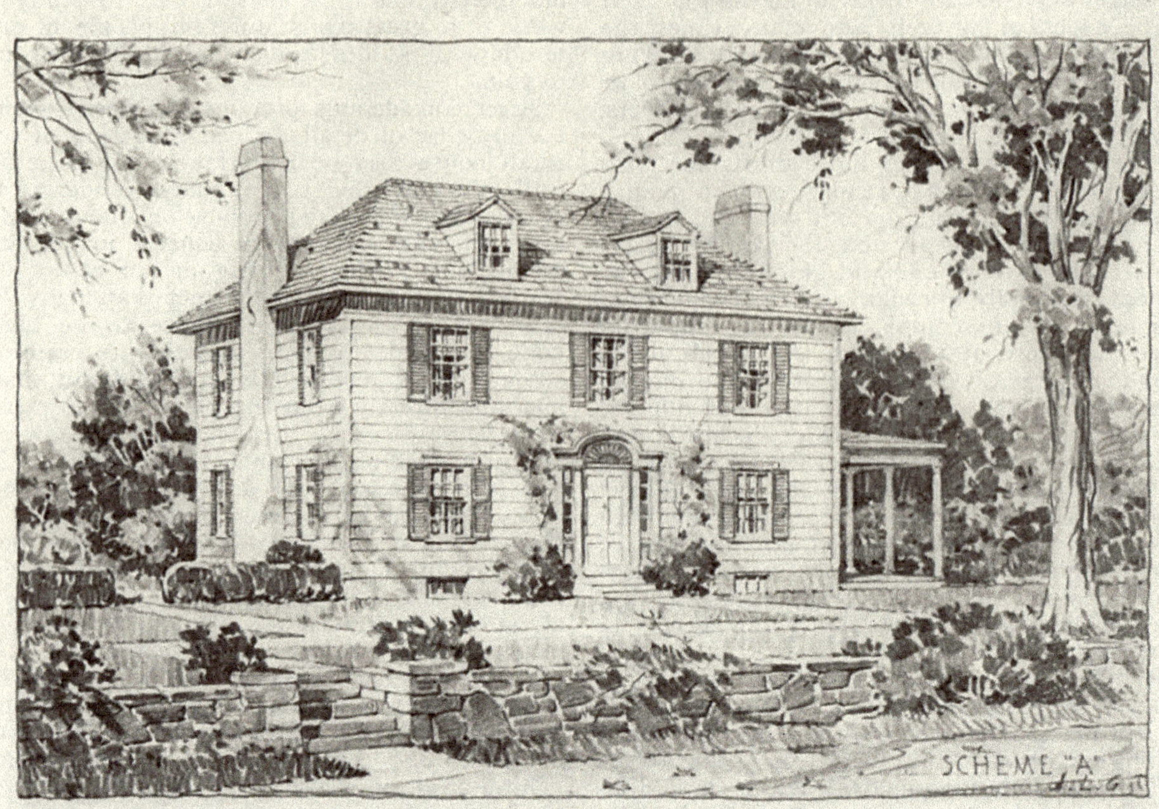

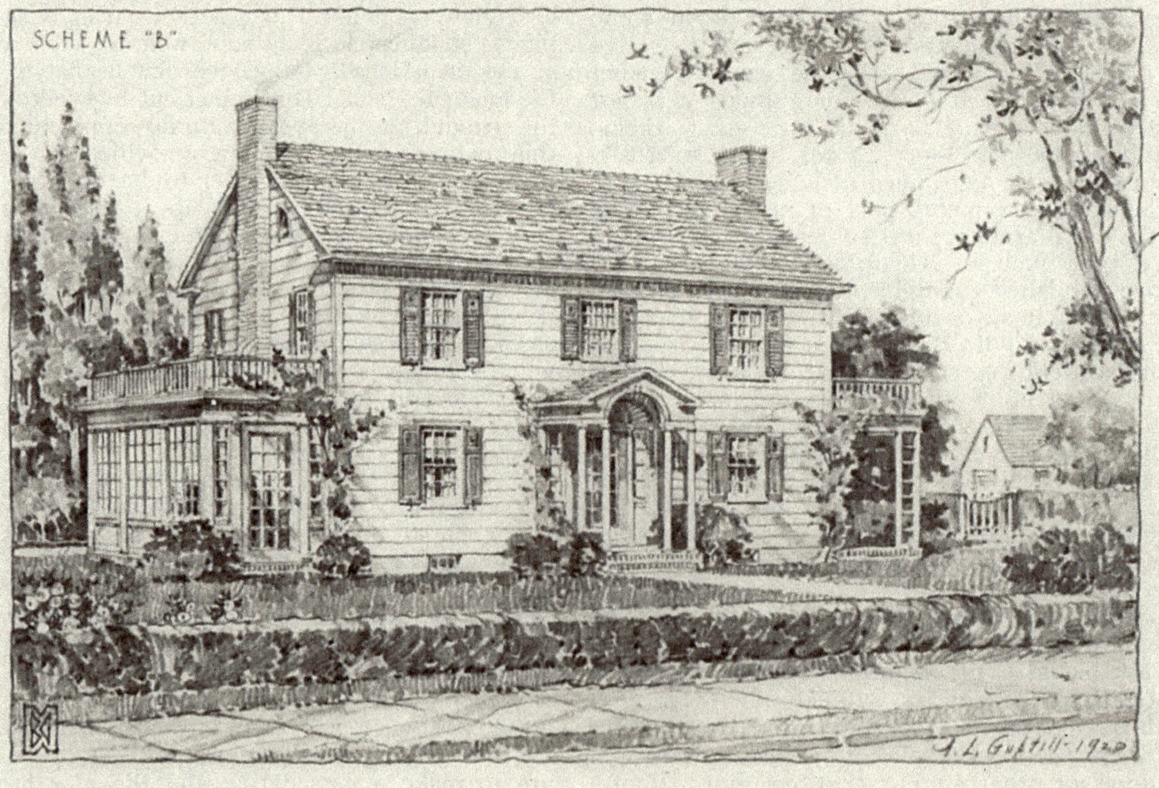

Figure 30. Two Schemes for a Small House; Typical Renderings of the Type Often Submitted to the Client for the Purpose of Showing How a Proposed Building Will Look When Completed. These Were Drawn Directly from Blueprint Plans and Elevations.

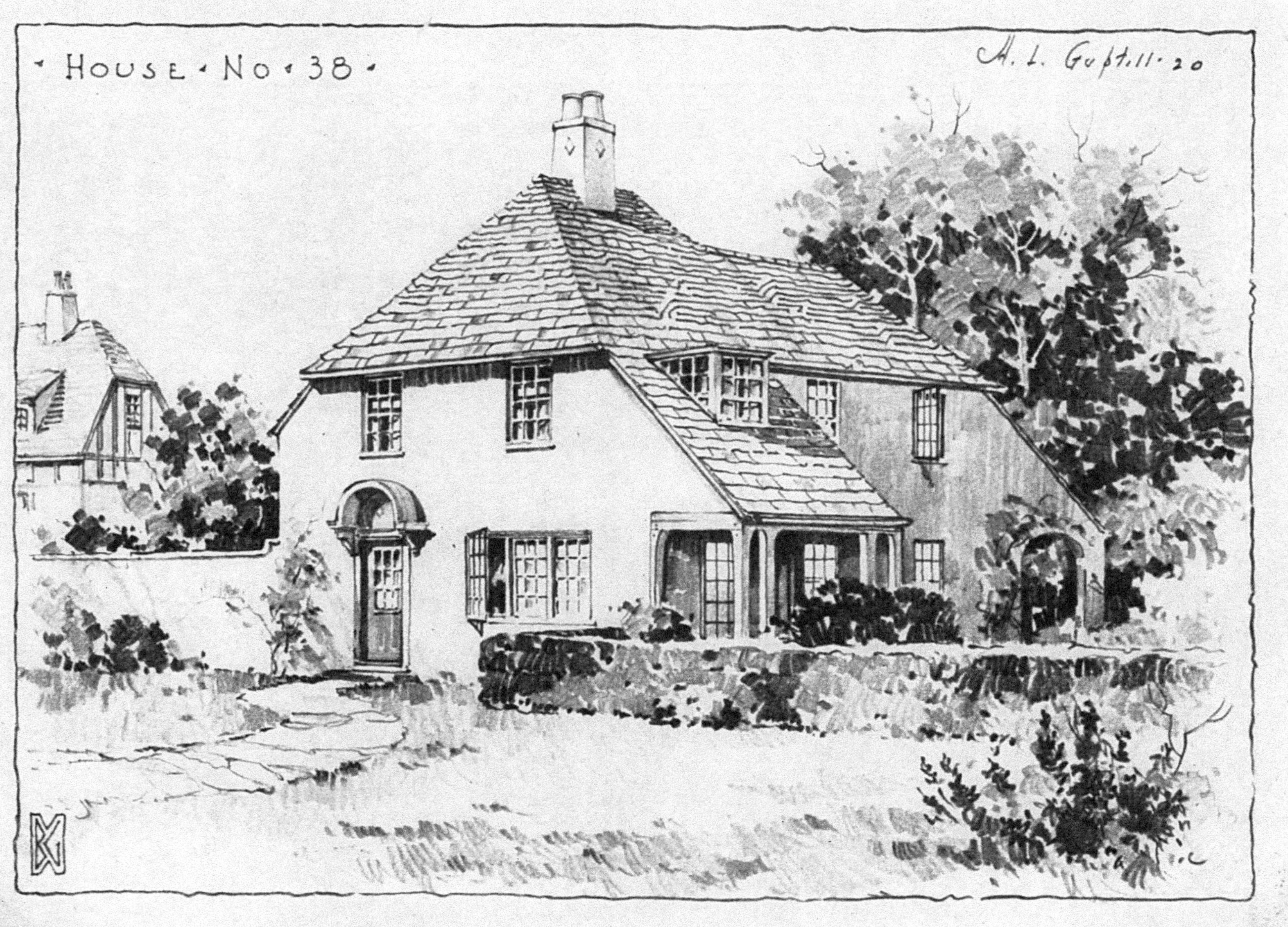

Figure 31. A Quickly Made Sketch for a Proposed House, Done with a Broad Point.

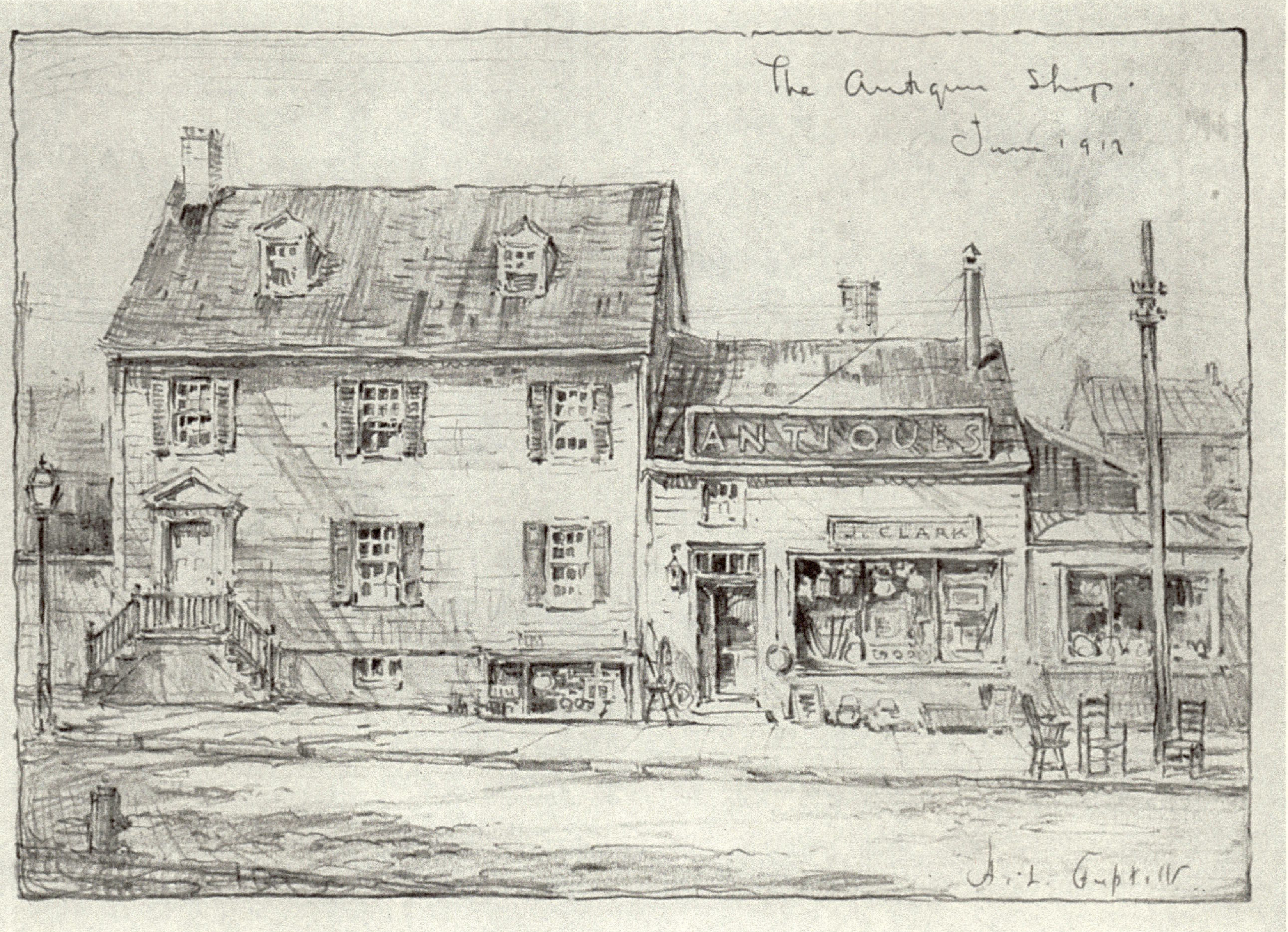

Figure 32. A Quick Sketch Done Directly From a Building, Picturing the Main Characteristics in a Direct and Simple Way, the Detail Being Only Suggested.

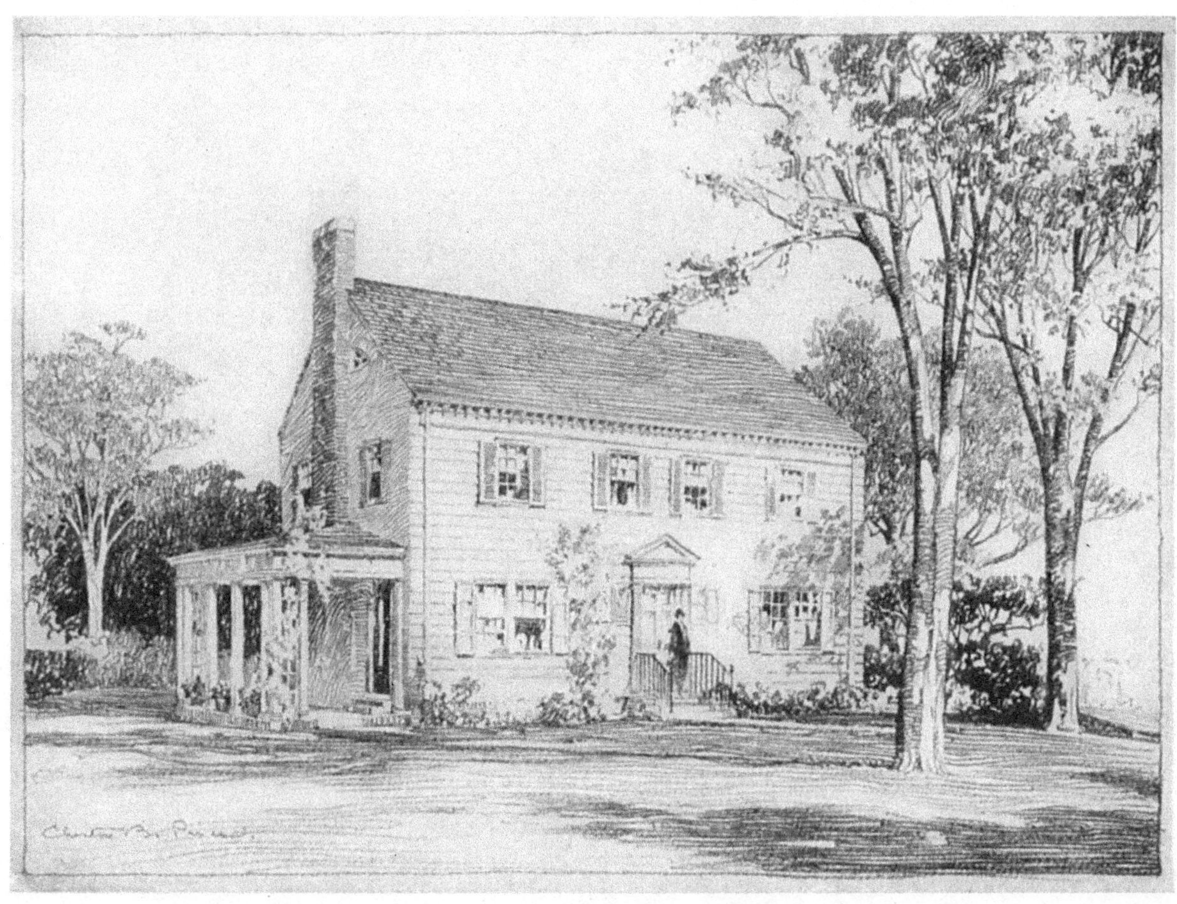

Rendering by Chester B. Price, Portion of a Proposed Housing Development near Stamford, Conn. McKim, Mead & White, Architects.

getting a layout correct. If no plot has been selected, photographs showing houses of a similar nature to that which you are drawing may offer valuable suggestions, especially for the entourage. It should be remembered that a pleasing relation should exist between a building and its environment — the house should seem to belong to the spot. If, for instance, you are drawing a little English cottage of informal nature, do not arrange your landscape in too formal a manner. Have some curved walks, irregular hedges, a quaint garden, etc. A Colonial house of dignified proportions demands, on the other hand, a more symmetrical treatment with formality extended throughout the scheme. A rustic camp in the forest should show a real forest character and not look like a suburban cottage, and if a house is to be in Florida do not use trees found only in the North, and likewise avoid hills and mountains if the location is in a level country. These are of course only matters of common sense and may seem too simple to mention, but they are, nevertheless, extremely important. There is something else, too, which helps a composition immensely and this is to have some line or group of lines such as a path or drive or shadows on the lawn or perhaps a succession of bushes, which will serve to lead the eye into the picture. In Figure 24, Chapter V, Part II, it will be noticed that all four of the sketches have paths which cause the attention to be directed gradually to the center of interest. It helps a drawing, too, if there are little vistas to draw the eye out of the picture again. A glimpse of some distant lake or down a pathway to the garage or of a neighboring building seen through the trees will add value to the picture, though naturally care must be taken not to make these incidentals too prominent, otherwise they will take interest from the house itself. In this connection we refer the reader to Figures 30 and 31 in this chapter. The end of the distant house in 31 and the garage in 30 add to the effect. When a definite plot has been chosen such buildings as may be visible should of course be correctly represented if shown at all.

Leaving the subject of composition for the present, let us return to the consideration of practical points relating to the laying out of the drawing. Now after the station point at which the spectator is to stand has been decided upon and the eye level or horizon determined, the various vanishing points are correctly located and the work is under way. As most perspectives are drawn directly from the working drawings and as these are often at the scale of one quarter inch to the foot this same scale is frequently used for the perspective. There is no

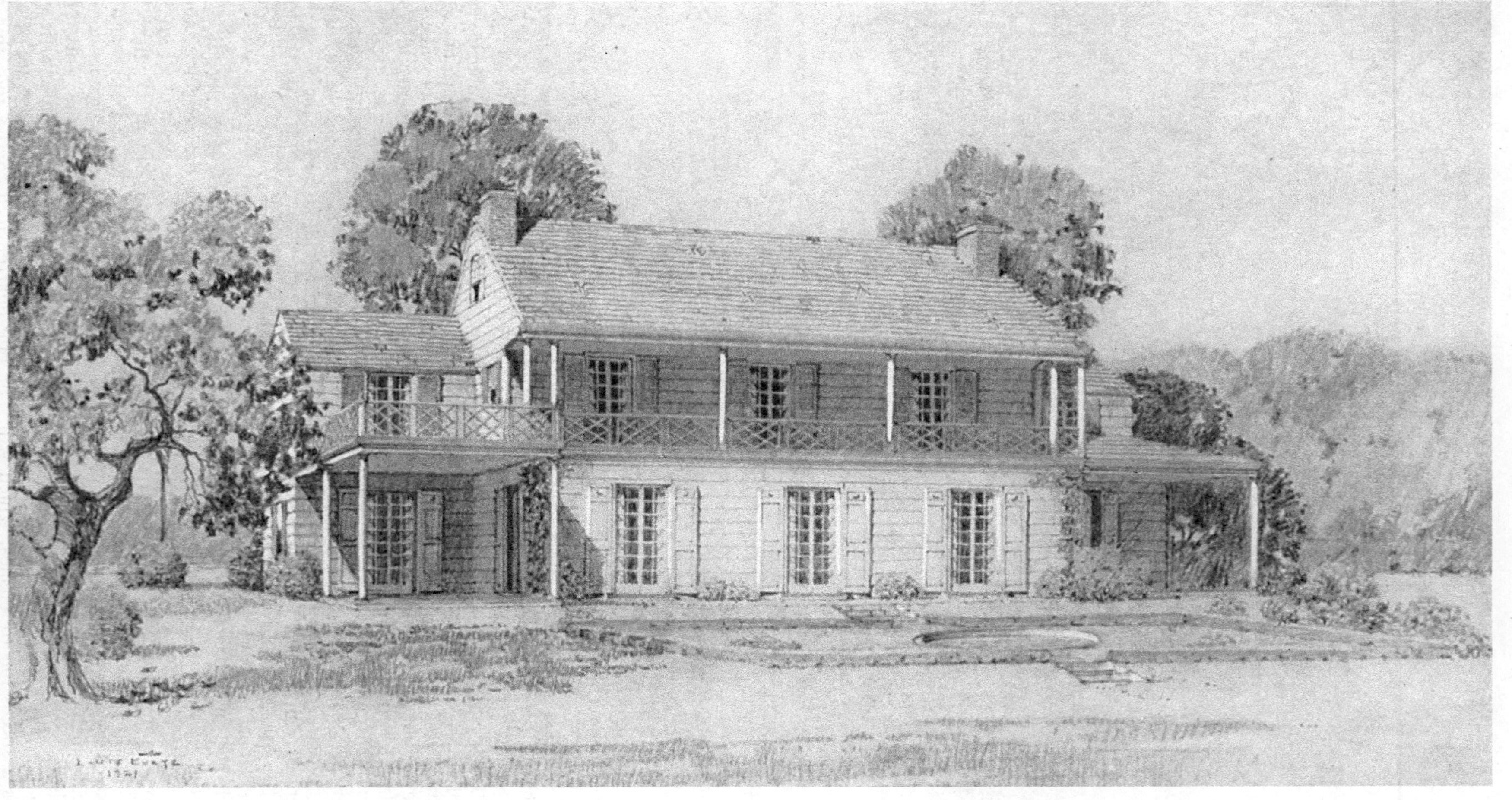

SKETCH BY LOUIS KURTZ FOR HOUSE AT KINGSPORT, TENN. ELECTUS D. LITCHFIELD & ROGERS, ARCHITECTS

rule about this, however, but it is sometimes difficult to show enough detail if a smaller scale is chosen. The English house in Figure 31 was done at the scale of one eighth inch to the foot and is reproduced here at the exact size of the original, so this gives a fair idea of about what can be easily done at that scale. The two houses in Figure 30 were also made at one eighth inch but are reproduced at about one-half that size. Once the scale is decided, the work of the layout can be pushed right ahead and as soon as this is completed we are ready for the rendering. There are several customary methods of proceeding with this. Sometimes the layout is on common paper and then the rendering done on tracing paper placed over the other. One advantage of this system lies in the fact that there is no special need to keep the paper clean when drawing the layout—again there are no hard mechanical lines to show in the final result, and if the rendering is spoiled in the making for any reason it is easy to begin once more. When the drawing is completed the tracing paper can be smoothly mounted on heavy cardboard. Another method, and the more common one, is to make the layout right on the final paper, using a fairly hard pencil such as a 3H, and drawing not only the outline of the large portions, but also all the window mouldings, clapboard lines and other such details as well. When this is completed go over the whole with a soft eraser until the lines are just visible as a guide for the freehand work. This final rendering may vary in style somewhat, according to the subject to be drawn. An English cottage of hewn timbers and rough brick or stucco, roofed with thatch or uneven slate, can be done with a rather sketchy line, as this will satisfactorily express the irregular surfaces. If a formal house of cut stone is to be pictured, smoother tones and straighter lines are often better. This does not mean that it is impossible to nicely represent such a house by a very sketchy sort of line, but it is certainly wiser for the beginner to render a building of this character in a painstaking way. With these facts in mind you are ready to start work, considering carefully the direction of the light, casting the shadows with care. A knowledge of the subject of shades and shadows is of course of great help here, while photographs of similar buildings offer many suggestions. Then a preliminary sketch is often made on tracing paper and the values carefully worked out on that. If this is done it often seems best, when making the final drawing, to render from the top down, for it is possible by this means to keep the paper clean quite easily. In theory it is better to work from the center of interest out towards the edges, as we have stated in a previous chapter, or to put in the darkest tones first, all over the drawing, later adding the half tones. If no preliminary is made, one of these methods should be followed unless the student has had a great amount of experience. In any case there is no excuse for untidy work and if reason-

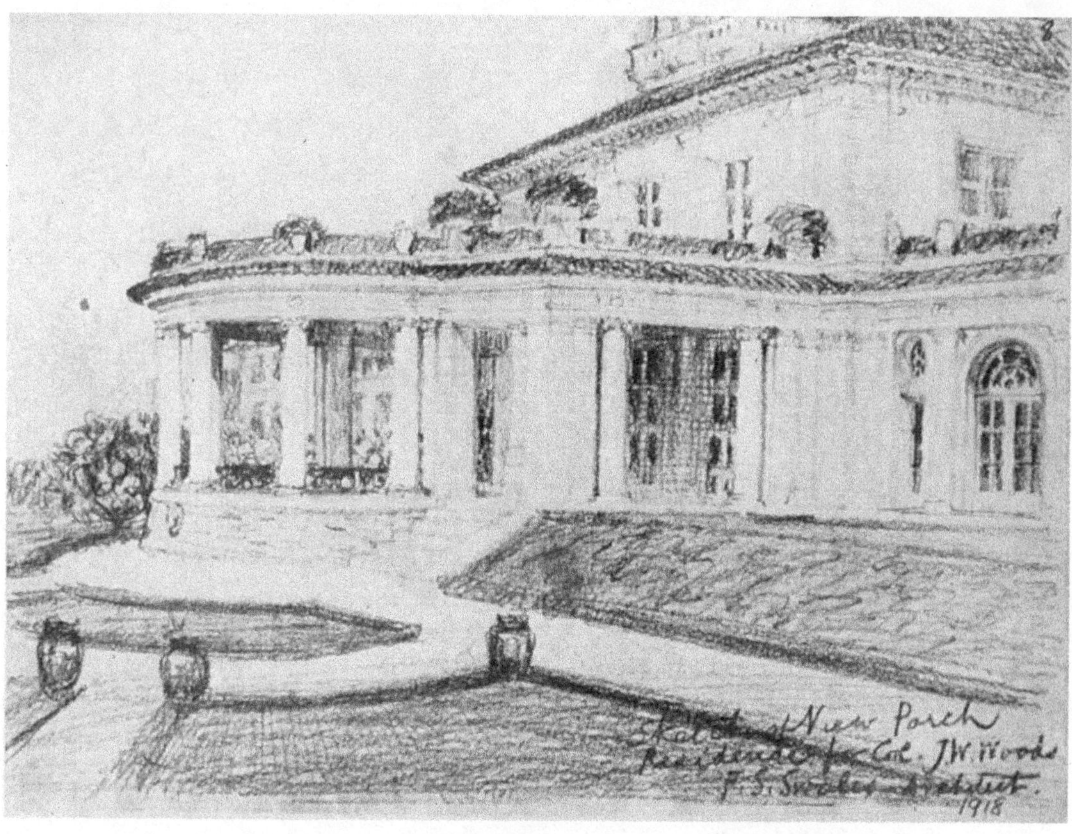

Rapid Pencil Sketch to Show to Client. New Porch for Residence of Col. J. W. Woods. Designed and Drawn by Francis S. Swales, Architect.

able care is used to keep the drawing brushed off and the pencil wiped clean, with a paper always under the hand to protect the surface, there should be no difficulty from that source.

Finish the drawing to the best of your ability and if you are not satisfied with it, and you are not likely to be, try another of the same or a similar subject. It is only by such practice, and by learning to look for your own mistakes and to profit by them, that success will be gained, but have in mind always that it is well worth the effort.

The illustrations, Figures 30 and 31, are given simply as typical of the sort of renderings which can be quite easily and quickly done. These drawings show little individuality or originality, in fact they are very similar to dozens of drawings which we see from time to time. In both instances they were drawn to accompany sketch plans before any definite site had been chosen. Figure 30 may have some additional interest to the student as it shows two different compositions for the same house, for Schemes "A" and "B" are both developments of the one plan. Figure 32 is a sketch done directly from nature and by comparing this with Figure 30 the difference between a sketch and a rendering of a similar building should be very evident, for the old antique shop is drawn very hastily and in a free manner, no use being made of instruments, and with no attempt to more than express the general character of the building.

The supplementary illustrations accompanying this chapter, and Figure 50 on page 170, offer additional suggestions for the treatment of small buildings. Study these and as many others as you can find.

Chapter VIII.

THE REPRESENTATION OF DETAILS

WE HAVE now reached a point in our discussion of sketching and rendering where it seems advisable for us to give additional attention to methods of indicating brickwork, stonework, clapboarded and shingled walls, slate and tile roofs, etc., and such details as chimneys, dormers, cornices and doorways, for it is plain that unless the student learns to nicely suggest these various component parts he cannot hope to make an excellent drawing of a building as a whole, any more than a portrait painter can obtain a satisfactory likeness of a person without a knowledge of how to draw the ear and the eye and the mouth. These representations of chimneys and dormers and the like, are, in other words, the draftsman's alphabet,—the A B C's that he should learn before attempting difficult compositions.

In previous chapters a few instructions of a general nature for the drawing of such portions of buildings have already been given, so the present text with its accompanying illustrations is mainly an amplification of these earlier suggestions. If repetition is found it is because certain points seem worth repeating, for the importance of the subject is such that it deserves elaboration.

Unfortunately for the beginner there are few definite rules to help him in such sketching, for each artist develops methods of his own which he varies from time to time as he feels inclined, choosing always the one which seems appropriate to his particular problem. Naturally his manner of working differs, too, according to the size at which the details are to be drawn, for it is obvious that a window, for example, shown at one-quarter inch to the foot, requires treatment decidedly different from that demanded by the same object presented at a much larger scale.

Because there are so many methods of indication in common use it is not strange that students feel uncertainty as to just how to approach a problem of this nature. Of course in theory it is best to turn to actual buildings and to landscape for inspiration and practice, observing and sketching the desired details directly from the buildings and their surroundings. The average student finds it rather difficult, however, to work in this way without considerable preliminary preparation, and therefore, valuable as such practice undeniably is, the beginner can perhaps learn more at first (as we have explained in a previous chapter) by studying good drawings, copying portions of them over and over again, later applying the ideas thus acquired to similar original problems.

The plates which accompany this text show certain methods of indicating such details as we mention and it might be well to make copies of some of these, not, however, blindly imitating the manner of handling. Give, instead, serious thought as to why they were done in this way, for each line and tone should be made with a definite purpose. As these sketches offer only a few of many possible methods do not rest content with copying parts of them, but study other similar drawings and copy some of them, too, in order to learn additional tricks of indication. In all of this work if you feel that you can obtain equally good results by a slightly different process, do so, for it is by no means necessary to reproduce the original from which you are drawing line for line, so long as the same general effect is gained. If you supplement this copy work with sketching from the photograph and from nature, using both broad and fine lines, on all sorts of paper and with pencils of various kinds and grades, your efforts will surely bring increased skill and a natural individual style will be gradually acquired.

It is usually best to adopt some standard size sketching paper, the notebook proportion of 8″ by 10½″ being convenient for the smaller sketches. A cover for preserving sheets of this size can be secured easily. It seems advisable to retain all such sketches or at least the best of them, for this gives you the opportunity to note your progress from time to time, and the drawings themselves may prove of great help when making finished renderings. Group a number of sketches of similar subjects on one sheet, so arranged that they permit easy comparison,—have, for instance, sketches of chimneys drawn with a fine line on one, others done with a broad line on another, dormer windows on a third, details of stonework on a fourth, and so on.

Before proceeding with our discussion of the plates it may perhaps be well to once more warn the student, especially the architectural draftsman, never to attempt to draw every tiny detail that he knows to exist. It is not strange that one so familiar as he is with all the variety of small units which go to make up a building finds it difficult to remain free from the desire to overemphasize the importance of some of them. The mere fact that one has been trained to accurately draw each detail, whether large or small, when making an instrumental elevation of a portion of a building, acts as a hindrance when it comes to pictorial representation, where we are striving to gain the effect of the whole in a broad, direct manner in a comparatively short space of time. As an illustration of the fact that an accurate instrumental elevation gives less of

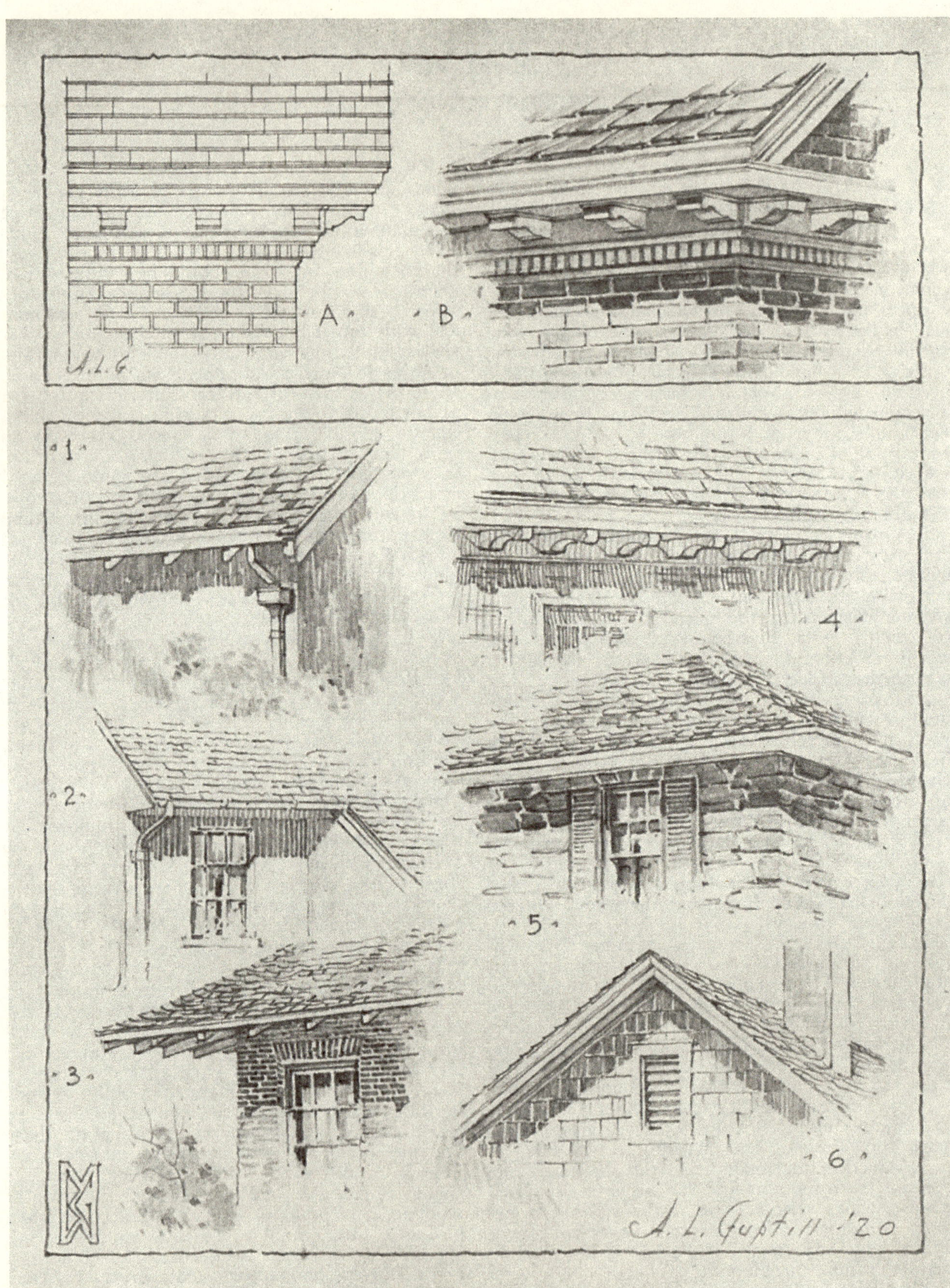

Figure 33. The Representation of Cornices and Cornice Shadows.

the true appearance than does a sketch of the right sort with the nonessential lines omitted or subordinated we have made two drawings at A and B, Figure 33, of a typical cornice such as we might find at the eaves of a Colonial residence. The one at A is done instrumentally at the scale of 1/2″=1′-0″ and is a copy of an actual working drawing. Such a mechanical representation as this, offers, of course, an accurate statement of certain facts of form, but it stops there. It gives us a wrong sense of the values, for the numerous lines necessary to bound the various members form a dark mass on parts which in the executed work might appear rather light, and there is nothing to show the difference in tone between the brick and wood. In a sketch or rendering, on the other hand, we usually work for an effect of reality, and even though certain details are of necessity slighted, by means of a free handling we are able to suggest in addition to facts of form, the light and the shade and the tone and texture of the materials. In the sketch at B we have attempted such an indication of the cornice shown at A, striving to gain approximately the same relative values as might be found in nature. The brickwork is shown darker in the shadow than in the light, as is the white woodwork, too, while the shingles are given a tone which quite accurately suggests the color that they might appear in the direct rays of the sun. As this particular sketch is at a fairly large scale it has been possible to retain most of the fine detail shown at A, but if a smaller rendered drawing of the same cornice were to be made it would probably prove necessary to further simplify the subject.

This one illustration is doubtless sufficient to show that the draftsman must work for a wholly different result in a sketch from that required in an elevation, forgetting or merely suggesting many of the tiny members, in obtaining the broad effect. As a further example we might add that in drawing a window he must not allow his knowledge of the blind-stop, the pulley-style and the parting-strip to interfere with the simplicity of the result;—in fact whatever the detail may be, the same care should be taken not to overemphasize relatively unimportant portions of the subject.

Let us return for a moment to our discussion of cornices, for they contribute so much to the effect of a building that extreme care must always be used in their representation. First of all do not overdarken the projecting portions, for it is the contrast of the light corona against the shadow below which gives the desired sense of projection. We might also speak again of the advantage which may sometimes be gained by using a graded shadow below a cornice, allowing the tone to gradually darken towards the bottom, thus giving transparency at the top and a clean-cut contrast at the lower edge. (See Chapter VI and illustration 4 at the top of Figure 28.) Remember, too, that the cornice shadow is usually made darkest at the corner of the building nearest the spectator, lightening gradually as the walls recede, thus adding to the effect of distance. There is sometimes a question as to how much detail should be shown in a cornice shadow, and the answer to this is not easy, for all depends on the size and purpose of the drawing. If it is large and made as a means of studying the proportions and detail it may prove necessary to draw every modillion and dentil, but if it is small or made simply to give the general effect, the less important parts can be omitted. Sometimes mutules or brackets or rafter ends or any details with considerable projection are left white or nearly so, for if the sketch is small and such parts are drawn in their true values they may be lost in the darkness of the shadow. This point is illustrated by Sketch 1, Figure 33, in which the rafter ends are shown lighter than they would probably be in the executed work. In some drawings such details are made quite distinct in a few places, especially in those parts of the building nearest the eye, and then made less definite or omitted in others. If well done this treatment gives an excellent impression with a minimum expenditure of time and effort.

Of the various ways of building up a shadow there are three which are in general use. The first is illustrated at "B," Figure 33, where the lines composing the shadow are so merged together as to make it difficult to tell their direction,—in fact in a shadow where the lines themselves are so indefinite this direction is unimportant and the tone may be formed in the most convenient way. In the second method, illustrated at "1" and "2," Figure 33, the shadow value is "built up" by a succession of adjacent strokes, either touching or nearly so, the strokes being often drawn in a vertical position, as our illustrations show, but sometimes taking the same general slope as the rays of light which cause the shadow. This method is frequently employed when the sketch is made at small scale. If a drawing is of such a size or character as to demand much detail, however, a still different method is popular. In place of the mass shading of the first and the parallel strokes of the second, the lines run in the direction or directions which best suggest the bricks or the clapboards or whatever the materials in shadow may be. Sketches "3," "5" and "6" illustrate this third method and it is not difficult to tell, even by the shadow tone, which sketch represents brick, which one stone, and which shingle. In using this method the student must be careful not to get too "spotty" a character to the value for it is essential to preserve a restful breadth of effect throughout the tone.

We should not leave the subject of cornices without some reference to reflected light and reversed shadows. It is frequently the case that bright light is reflected from some brilliant object into dark tones such as those beneath a cornice. This not only means that the shadow value itself is neutralized and so made lighter, but a reflection of this sort is often the cause, also, of what are termed "reversed shadows," which really are shadows within a shadow, caused by modillions or any such projections which prevent the reflected light from penetrating some of the deeper corners. These reversed shadows are of especial value in rendering elevations in wash such as that shown on page 134. In this sort of drawing where the shadows are cast in the conventional 45-degree method, the reversed tones are usually reflected in just the opposite way, as is the case in the rendering to which we have just referred. (Note particularly the reversed shadows cast by the dentils.) In nature, however, the location and the form of the reversed shadows will of course depend on the direction of the rays of reflected light, and this direction may vary from hour to hour as the sun or other source of direct illumination changes in position. So far as cornices are concerned, however, it is true that reflected light often causes the soffit to appear quite brilliant, so in many drawings the soffit value is represented no darker than in Sketch "5," Figure 33, and in tiny drawings such horizontal planes as this are sometimes left actually white.

Though we have so far spoken of reflected light mainly as it influences cornice tones, it should not be supposed that it has no effect on other values, for it has, though as a rule the horizontal planes seem to catch more such light than do the vertical. A window soffit, for instance, is often quite brilliant as is the intrados of an arch, while even as large a surface as a porch ceiling is often visibly brightened.

Before we drop our discussion of Figure 33, attention is called to the variety of methods of suggesting roof shingles which it shows. Too much care cannot be given to such representations, for in a drawing of the average residence so large an area is taken up by the roof planes that unless they are well handled the effect of the whole drawing may be ruined. First of all the values of the different parts of the roof must be decided upon, as some portions can perhaps be left white or nearly so while others will appear quite dark. Next, the method of indicating the roof material must be chosen, and it is here that the sketches on Figure 33 may prove useful, or, if the roof is of some other material, Figure 34 offers some suggestions. Sketch "A" on the latter plate represents shingles, flat tiles or slate—Sketch "B" indicates a rough textured slate in graduated courses—Sketch "C" shows shingle thatch, "D" straw thatch, "E" suggests tile, while "F" again shows slate, though a similar indication would answer for shingle. It may be well to mention here that good pen renderings are sometimes of great assistance when drawing roof or wall surfaces as they offer much in the way of material indication which can be adapted to pencil rendering.

There are several faults frequently found in representations of roof surfaces, concerning which the student should be warned. First of all, if a drawing is small in scale one should seldom attempt to show every course of slate or shingles, for if this is done the value is almost sure to become either too complex or too dark. It is better to space the lines separating the courses somewhat further apart than they would be in the actual building. In larger drawings this criticism does not hold unless the roof pitch is very low or the roof planes greatly foreshortened, in which case a small number of lines may prove sufficient to suggest many courses. When graduated courses of slate are shown as at "B" Figure 34, decreasing in size from the bottom to the top, an unpleasant effect of curvature of the roof sometimes appears. Such an effect, if conspicuous, can usually be overcome by throwing a shadow bounded by approximately straight lines onto the roof, as from a tree or some neighboring building. In fact, the addition of any straight lines following the pitch of the roof will help to correct such distortion. Whatever material is used as a roof covering, avoid breaking the tone into too many conspicuous spots, for one of the most common defects of the drawings of beginners is the spottiness of surfaces which in actual buildings would be either "flat" throughout or gradually graded.

Just as roofs deserve careful attention, wall surfaces also need to be represented with the greatest care. Here again it is seldom advisable to try to show every brick course or each stone but the materials should be so indicated as to leave no doubt as to their nature. Figures 33, 34, 35 and 36 all give suggestions for the treatment of such surfaces, the larger drawings on Figure 35 being of sufficient size to show the detail very clearly.

Window Representation—There is no great difficulty in acquiring the skill to render a wall of brick or stone, or a roof of slate or shingle, but when it comes to successfully representing windows or glazed doors or any objects containing large areas of glass, our task proves less simple, for glazed surfaces are so complex and changeable in their appearance as to demand special care and skill in their indication. It is not hard, to be sure, to learn to draw a typical window or two, especially if shown at small scale, but if the scale is so large as to make any considerable amount of detail necessary it is no easy task for the beginner to do even this much well, while it is still more difficult to so render a number of adjacent windows as to give them the best effect in relation to one another and to the remainder of the building. If they are made too dark or too light they may, even though good in themselves, attract more than their proper share of attention, and if all are drawn in the same way the result will probably prove monotonous, while if, instead, too much variety is shown, the breadth of effect of the whole drawing is almost sure to be destroyed. Before attempting finished renderings of windows the student should, therefore, acquaint himself through observation and study with the appearance of glass under different circumstances and conditions, for it is only by so doing that he can represent it to the best advantage in any given problem. Walk along a street and study the windows that you see, —not only those near at hand but those in the distance as well. Compare those on the sunny side with those in the shade, and those in the upper stories with those in the lower. As you make these comparisons ask yourself such questions as the following: What is the difference in the appearance of glass in sunlight and in shade? Do windows in the upper stories have the same general effect as those in the lower? How do windows in the distance compare with those near at hand? Can you see the curtains or shades distinctly in

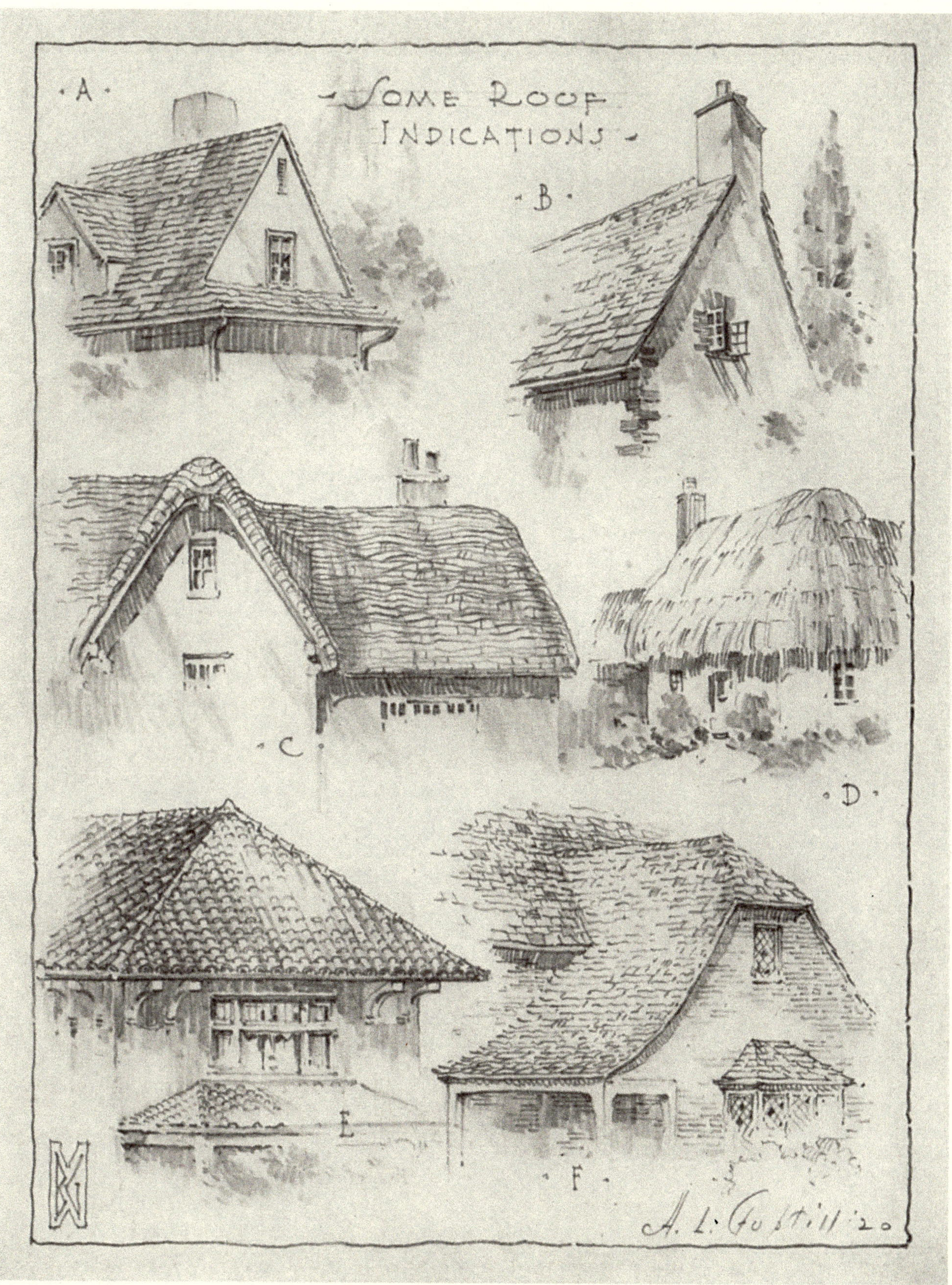

Figure 34. Some Roof Treatments, Suggesting Shingles, Slate, Thatch and Tile.

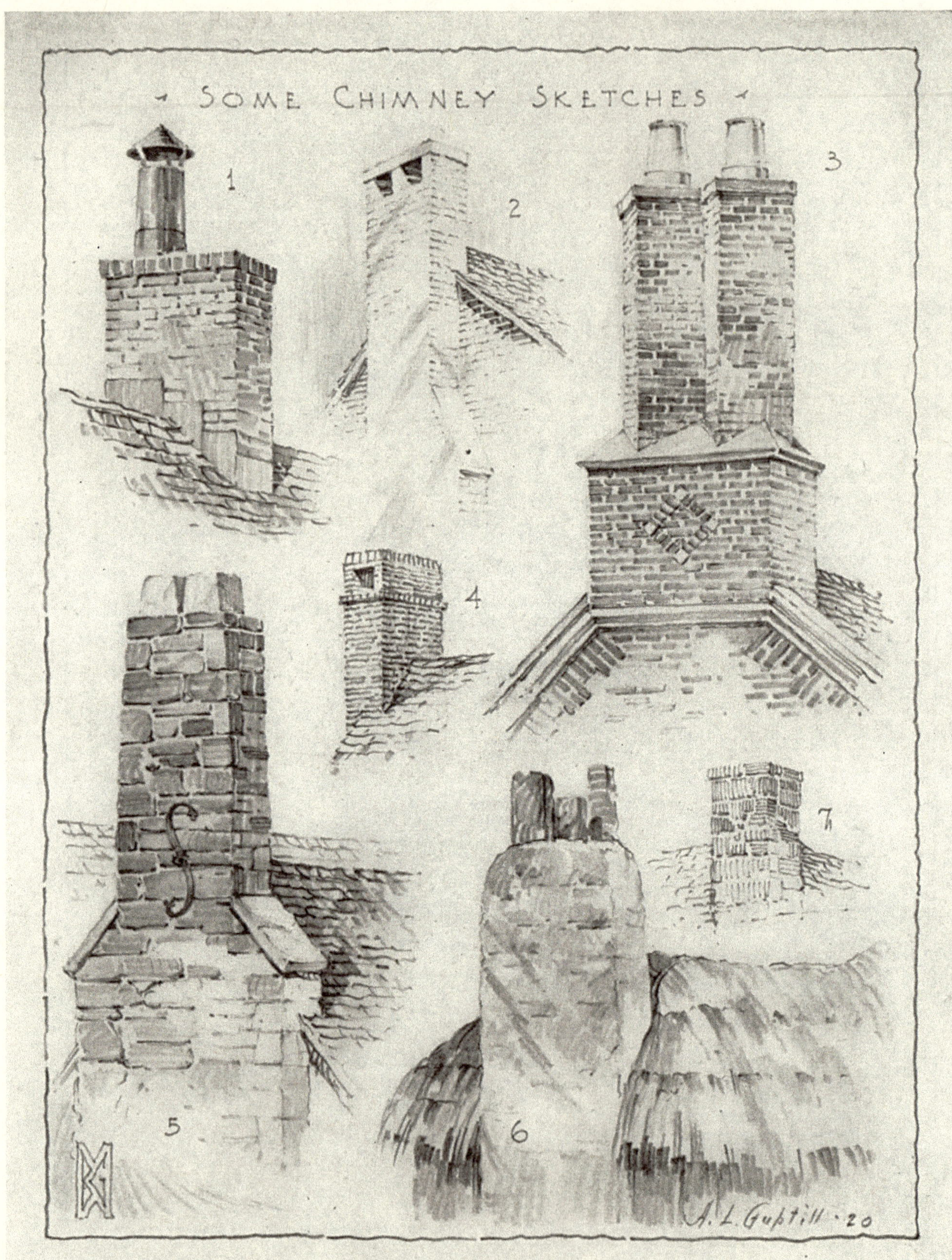

Figure 35. Various Indications of Brickwork and Stonework.

all the windows? How much of the interiors of the rooms do you see as you pass? Is the glass always plainly visible? Is it hard to tell if panes have been broken from a sash? Is it easy to distinguish plate glass when you see it? If so, why? Do all the lights of glass in one window look the same? Does the glass usually seem lighter or darker than the sash itself? Do you see images reflected in the glass? If so, are they sufficiently definite to permit you to tell trees from buildings? Does your own image appear in the windows? Are images more distinct in glass in shade than in glass in the sunlight? Are reflections as clear on a rainy day as they are when the sun is shining?

A little observation will answer such questions as these and make it evident that ordinary window glass has two leading characteristics which relate especially to its appearance, and which are, therefore, of the greatest importance to the student. First comes its transparency. Under certain conditions glass seems practically invisible. This is especially true of clean plate glass favorably lighted. We are sometimes able, then, in our representation of windows, to neglect the glazing and treat the sashes just as though the panes were non-existent, showing distinctly the shades and hangings within, or, if the drawing is made from an interior, looking out, the foliage and sky beyond. The other characteristic, and the one which causes much of the trouble of the beginner, is the power that glass has to act as a reflector or mirror, giving, very often, a shiny effect to the window, and usually images of objects as well, which in some cases are almost as clear as those obtained in the usual "looking glass." One of the difficulties confronting the student who tries sketching directly from buildings is the complication in the effect of glass resulting from these reflections, for often trees and buildings and skies and clouds and people are all pictured in the windows, showing so plainly as to prove confusing, for the images are not only somewhat distorted, as a rule, because of imperfections in the glass, but are crisscrossed by the sash bars and mingled and blended with the curtains in a most bewildering manner. It is not easy, therefore, to know just what to put in and what to leave out, so considerable experience will be necessary to teach what really is essential and what should be subordinated or omitted. It is worth remembering that as a rule the two characteristics of glass which we have mentioned appear in combination;—the glass seems sufficiently transparent to enable us to see through it quite easily yet has enough reflection to give it a shiny appearance. Sometimes, however, this power to reflect neutralizes the effect of transparency to such an extent that we find it impossible to look through the panes at all. This is especially true in windows near the top of a building where the reflection of sunlight or bright sky is frequently so strong as to make the curtains within either invisible or very indistinct. Such windows, and particularly those of the upper stories of very tall buildings, often take on much the same color and tone as the sky, and if the sun itself is reflected, the windows become dazzling in their brilliancy. A reflected light cloud may make the glass almost white, while a blue sky may cause a blue reflection of a value similar to that of the sky itself. If we observe the windows nearer the street level we find as a rule that most of them seem darker, for in place of the sky reflections we have those of nearby buildings and trees. It is useful to bear in mind, then, that when rendering tall buildings the general tone of the glass, taken as a whole, may often be correctly shown lighter in the upper than in the lower stories. Even in the ordinary suburban home or country house the windows of the lower floors frequently seem darker when viewed from without than do those above, especially if the nearby foliage is comparatively low, so as to reflect in the downstairs windows only. It is true, too, that glass within shadow, or on the shady side of a building, usually seems much lighter than we would expect, so it is by no means necessary to represent it by a dark tone simply because it is within shade or shadow. Its light appearance is generally due to the fact that it mirrors the brightness of the sky or some nearby building in sunlight. This power which glass has to reflect varies under different circumstances. If glass has black or darkness as a background, or is in shadow as we have just mentioned, it usually proves a stronger reflector than it does when in light or with light shining through from behind, or with a light background. Paint glass black on the back and it becomes a good mirror, reflecting objects very distinctly. When we look at a window from without, in the daytime, and it has no shades or curtains, its glazing may be likened to the painted glass just mentioned, the darkness of the interior being relatively of a deeper value than the outdoor tones and therefore taking the place of the black paint, and such a window shows reflections more distinctly than one with light curtains behind. If a window by chance shows portions of a black, or any very dark window shade and of a light one as well, the reflections will be more distinct on that portion of the glass which has the dark shade behind it, and contrarily if a similar window has a light shade lowered to the sill so as to fill the whole opening the reflections will be comparatively indistinct. As a further proof that glass is a good mirror when backed up with black, stand facing a window in a lighted room at night, with the shade raised, and if it is dark out-of-doors your own image can be easily seen. In the daytime, however, if you stand in the same place and look out into the sunlight you will find your reflection to be quite indistinct or even invisible. When making a drawing of an interior as it appears in the daytime it is, therefore, seldom necessary to show any reflections in the glass of the windows or doors of the outside walls, as the brighter light without renders them impotent. In fact in architectural drawing it is only occasionally that definite reflections of objects are shown, for unless extreme care is used to keep them inconspicuous they may become so noticeable as to seriously detract from the result. It is not often advisable, for instance, to show the reflections of tree trunks or nearby buildings, and if such images are indicated they should be drawn correctly and kept subordinated. There are times, however, when a reflection of a window reveal or an arch intrados or some similar adjacent part of a building may prove interesting, and in the sketch at "5," Figure 36, a dark reflection of the shaded intrados is shown. Even though comparatively little use is made of definite images of objects, when representing glass, the effect of most windows is, nevertheless, modified to such an extent in general tone by the indefinite reflections of the sky and distant objects as to demand some expression of this modification, but as the spectator, when viewing a drawing, seldom has an exact knowledge of what these objects influencing the appearance may be, the artist is usually at liberty to assume such conditions as best suit his requirements and convenience. This means that if it pleases him to draw his windows light, on the assumption that they are reflecting a bright sky, or dark for some similar reason, he is at liberty to do so, and as windows often change in effect completely and suddenly, it is hard to dispute his authority.

Now to get down to a few practical facts of value to the beginner. First of all, decide whether the glass is to be shown light or dark. This depends largely on the surrounding material. If the walls are of light plaster, and strong contrast seems desirable, keep the glass dark; if, instead, the walls are of dark material, light windows will attract more attention. There are many cases, however, where it seems wise to keep certain windows inconspicuous, as a matter of presentation, and under such conditions strong contrast is of course to be avoided. The best way to determine which windows should be dark and which light is by making a preliminary study on tracing paper before starting the final rendering. As a rule those windows nearest the spectator, or, in some instances, nearest the center of interest, should show, not only the sharpest contrasts but also the greatest amount of detail. This gives us an opportunity to get a certain variety of treatment in the different windows, which is essential, but at the same time care must be taken not to provoke unrest by overemphasizing the differences of representation. Once a general scheme for the values has been determined upon, it is necessary to reach a decision as to how much detail is to be shown through the glass. This will depend largely on the location of the windows and on the nature of the building. If a dignified façade is to be rendered, it is seldom wise to show much inside the glazing, as curtains and the like sometimes detract from the architectural character of a formal building unless rendered in a very conventional manner. An informal building, such as a suburban residence, permits greater freedom of expression, however, so in a building of this sort it is usually best to show the shades and curtains quite distinctly. Stiffness of effect is avoided if an occasional window is shown open, or with the shutters partly closed, while awnings and screens and such things sometimes add to the feeling of reality. In a formal building if shades are shown in the windows they are usually all lowered to the same point, generally about one-third to one-half way down from the top, or are arranged in some uniform manner, but greater variety of spacing is permissible in less formal structures. Inside draperies harmonize better with the structural lines of the building if shown hanging vertically or nearly so, and for this reason it is often well not to drape them in curves, as curved lines frequently attract too much attention. Neither is it necessary or desirable to show much detail or design in the hangings, though there is no harm in suggesting some simple pattern, as in "4," Figure 36, especially if a sash is unbroken by muntins or other objects. When it comes to the rendering of the sashes and the window frame, treat the woodwork very broadly, merely suggesting by one or two lines all the various members of which the whole is composed. The sash bars will usually be sufficiently well indicated if a single line, representing their shady side, and their shadow on the glass is used. Sashes are, as a rule, left white on renderings, but there are instances where the glass is shown so light as to cause dark sashes to seem essential as a means of producing proper contrast. In "5," Figure 36, it will be noticed that the woodwork of the door is left light at the bottom where the glass is dark, but graded to dark at the top so as to count strongly against the light reflection. In "9," Figure 37, the sashes are in shadow and consequently dark, but the glass here is catching a strong reflection of light, as in the previous example. It perhaps seems a bit extreme to leave the glass as white as it is in this sketch and in the doorway at "13" on the same sheet, but an effect of transparency is obtained in this way, and the light tone of the glass pleasingly breaks up the monotony of the shadow. Often, however, the glass in such windows is shown very dark, this being a matter of choice, as both conditions are found in actual buildings.

In most drawings of windows the shadows cast by the frame and by the sashes on the shades and curtains are made quite prominent, and this often adds greatly to the effect, and it is well as a rule to emphasize the shadows of the shutters also. There is another point worth considering and this is that if there is a large dark shadow near the top of a window it is best not to have a similar dark tone at the bottom, as such duplication may injure the result.

Figures 36 and 37 show a variety of suggestions for the treatment of windows. Figure 36 was drawn at exactly the same scale as here reproduced, but Figure 37 was reduced from a larger drawing measuring 8 inches by 11 inches. These sheets seem to call for no special comment in addition to that already made unless attention is directed to "6" and "12" in the latter plate. In "6" it should be noted that the open sash is shown transparent, the shadow cast by the sash itself on the wall behind being visible in its entirety. In "12," however, the sash appears as a reflector, the dark vine behind being invisible just as though the glass were opaque. These two sketches illustrate the two characteristics of glass already described.

In Figure 39 are shown several interior sketches in which windows are featured. These drawings explain themselves, though mention might be made of the fact that when facing a window or any

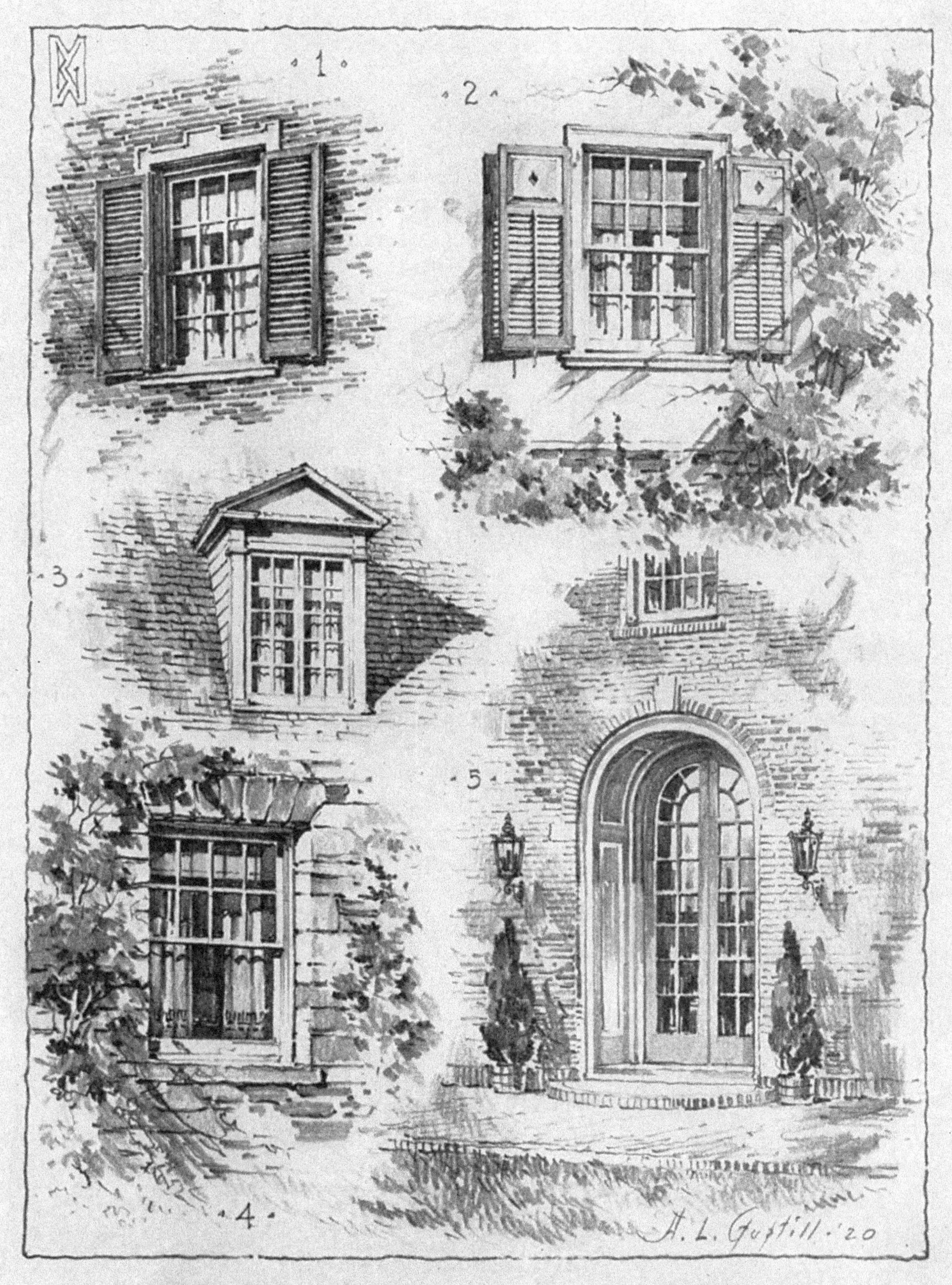

Figure 36. Some Door and Window Suggestions, with Considerable Attention to the Representation of the Smaller Architectural Details.

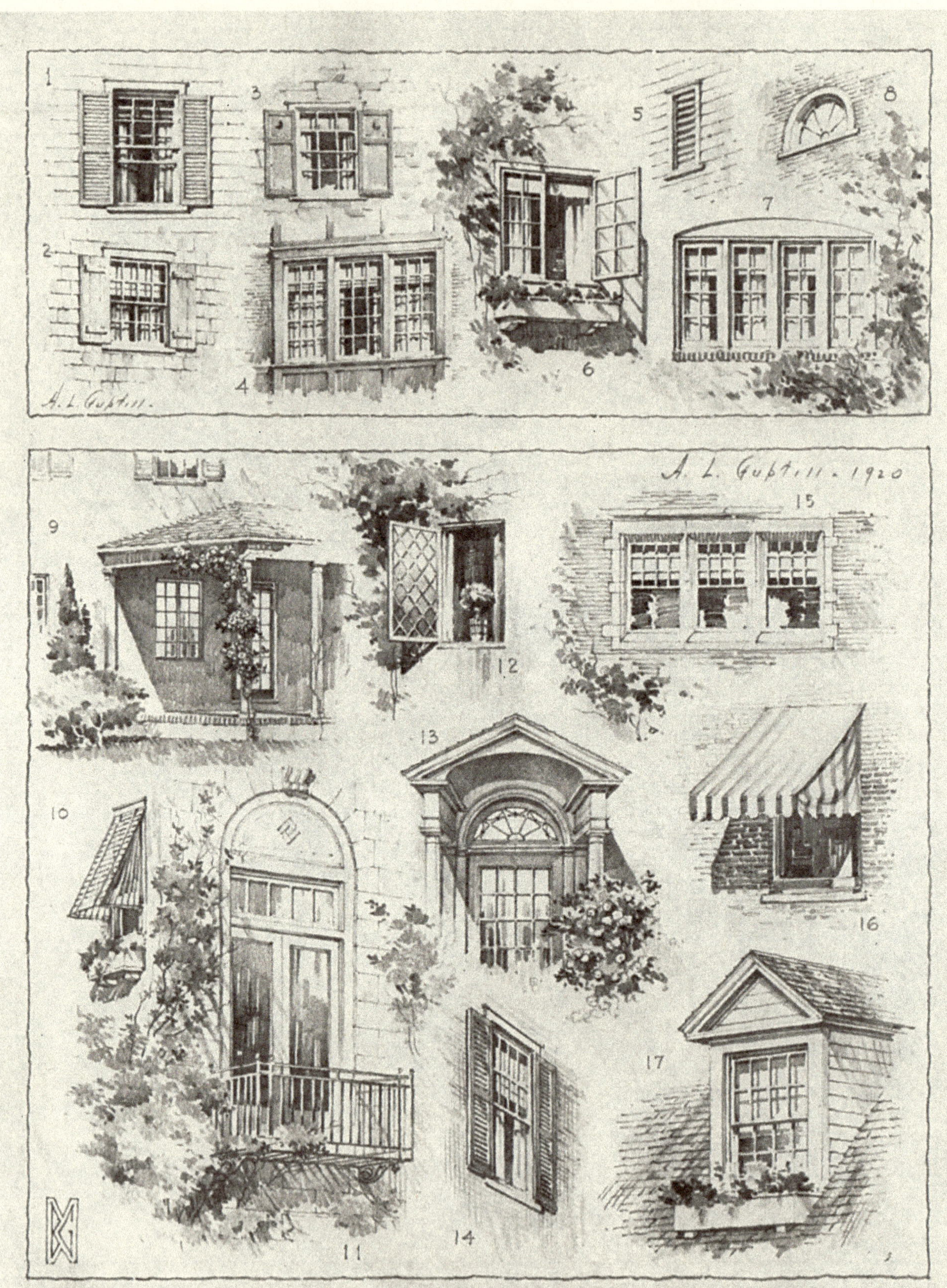

Figure 37. Additional Details Such as Are Common to Architectural Delineation.

glazed opening from the inside the sashes and frames usually appear dark in their relation to the outdoor light beyond. Because of this strong contrast even light woodwork often seems very dark if seen in silhouette.

When drawing an interior it is not wrong to show objects out of doors providing they are not made so prominent as to take too much interest from the interior itself. Unless such objects are quite near the glass, however, they should be drawn very simply and lightly.

Having studied the illustrations accompanying this text, as well as other reproductions that you may have at hand, and having demonstrated for yourself the truth of some of the facts mentioned here, try some studies of your own, attempting to get a glassy effect to each window, and crispness of drawing as well, remembering all the while that windows are too important to be slighted in representation.

The drawing by Schell Lewis on the following page is an unusually fine example of pencil rendering of a portion of a building drawn in elevation, and shows that even without the aid of perspective it is possible to obtain a very truthful and at the same time interesting effect. In this type of drawing a knowledge of shades and shadows is particularly desirable as the sense of relief and projection depends largely upon the form and value of the shade and shadow tones. Notice the manner in which the feeling of curvature in the goose necks above the leader boxes has been obtained, and give particular attention to the handling of the smaller detail within the shadow of the cornice of the doorway itself.

The sketches by Albert Kahn on pages 131, 132 and 133 are excellent representations of an entirely different sort of detail, for these are measured drawings made directly from examples of wrought iron and carved wood in the South Kensington Museum. Apparently a few of the main lines were laid out to scale instrumentally on a smooth coated paper and the rest of the work done free-hand. Obviously architectural students or draftsmen can profit greatly by making such measured drawings as these, as they offer not only a means of becoming acquainted with and preserving a record of the objects drawn, but train one also for the making of drawings from which original work is to be executed.

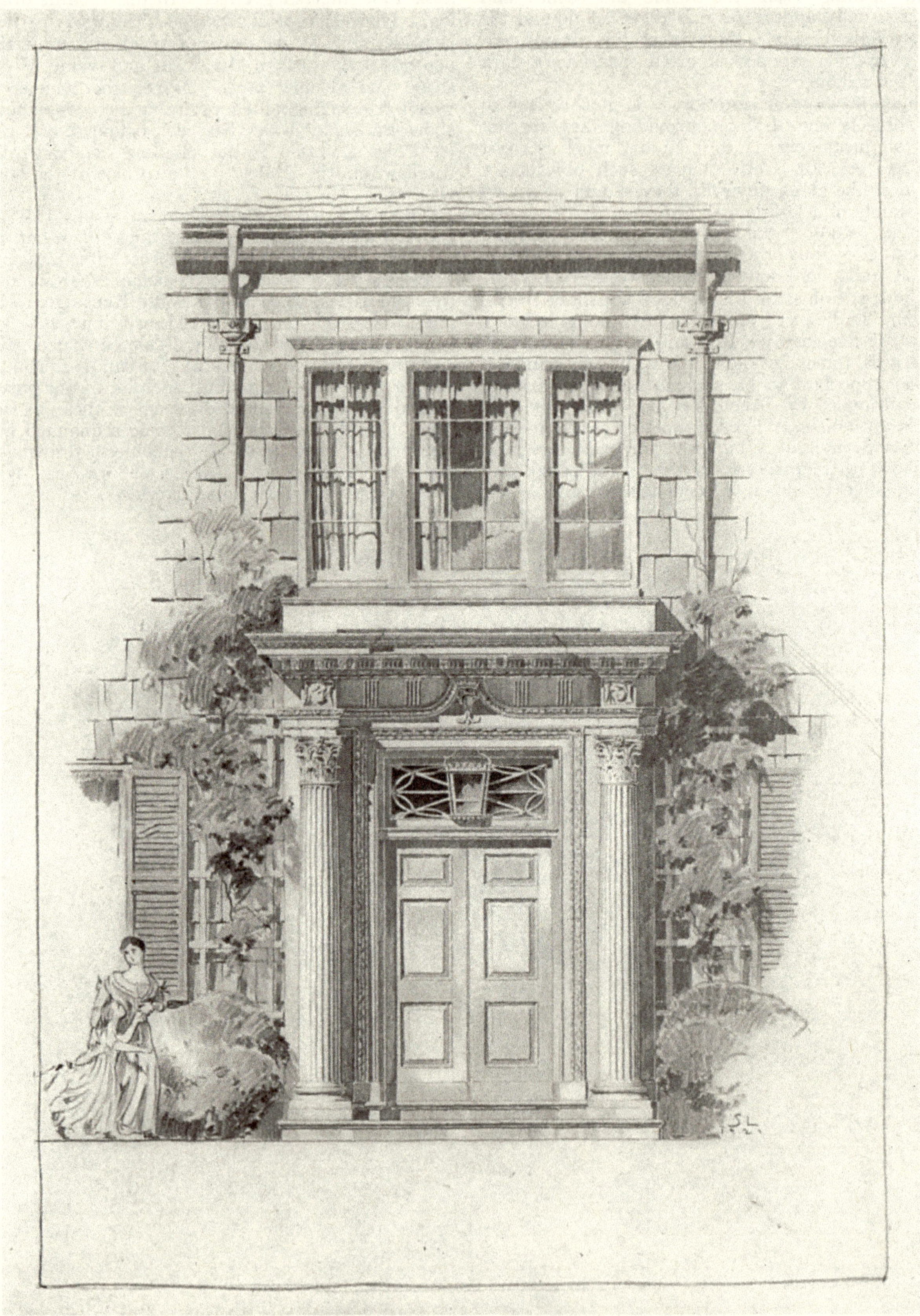

PENCIL DRAWING BY SCHELL LEWIS. DETAIL OF A COUNTRY RESIDENCE

CHARLES A. PLATT. ARCHITECT

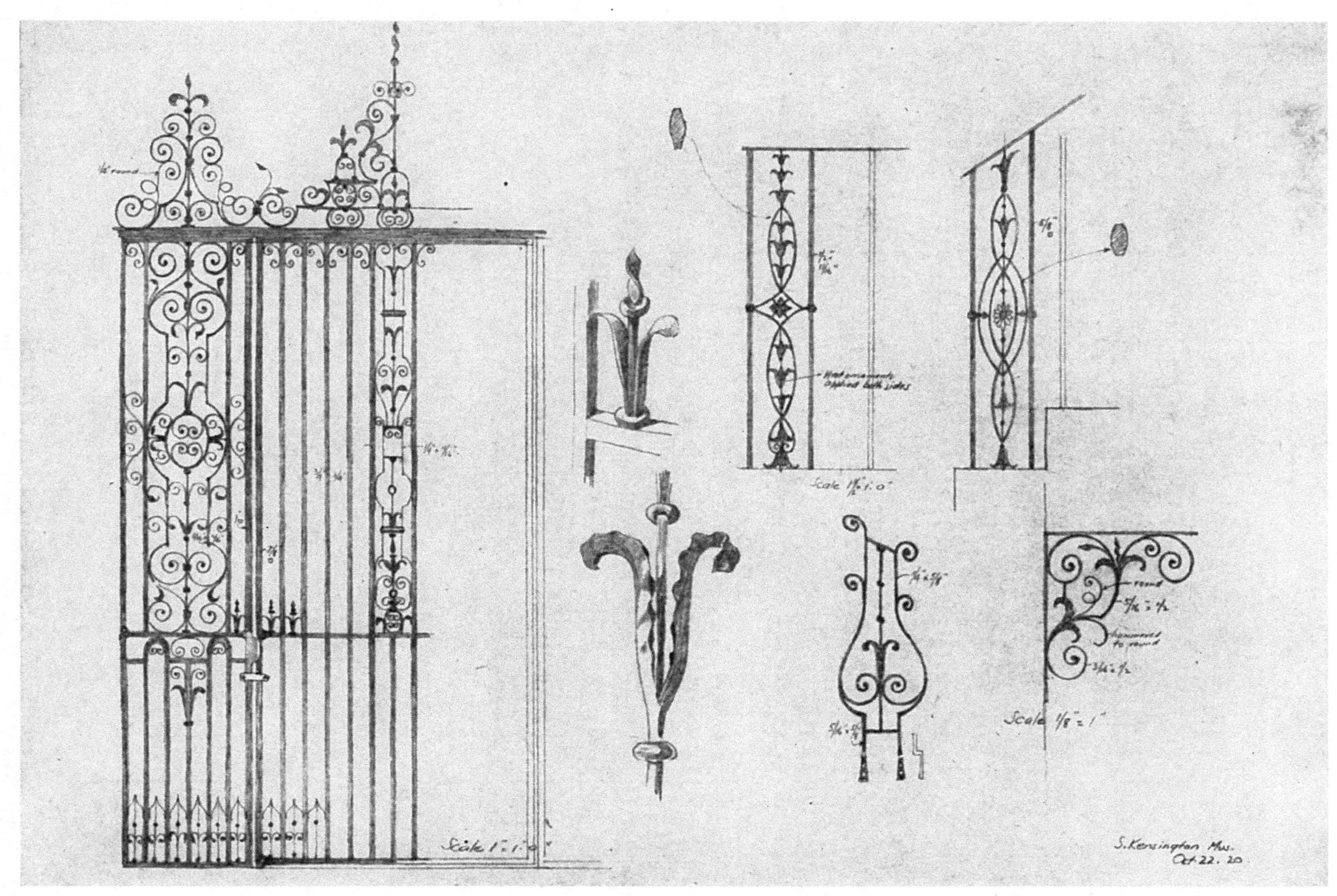

PENCIL SKETCH BY ALBERT KAHN. WROUGHT IRON WORK IN THE SOUTH KENSINGTON MUSEUM, LONDON, ENGLAND

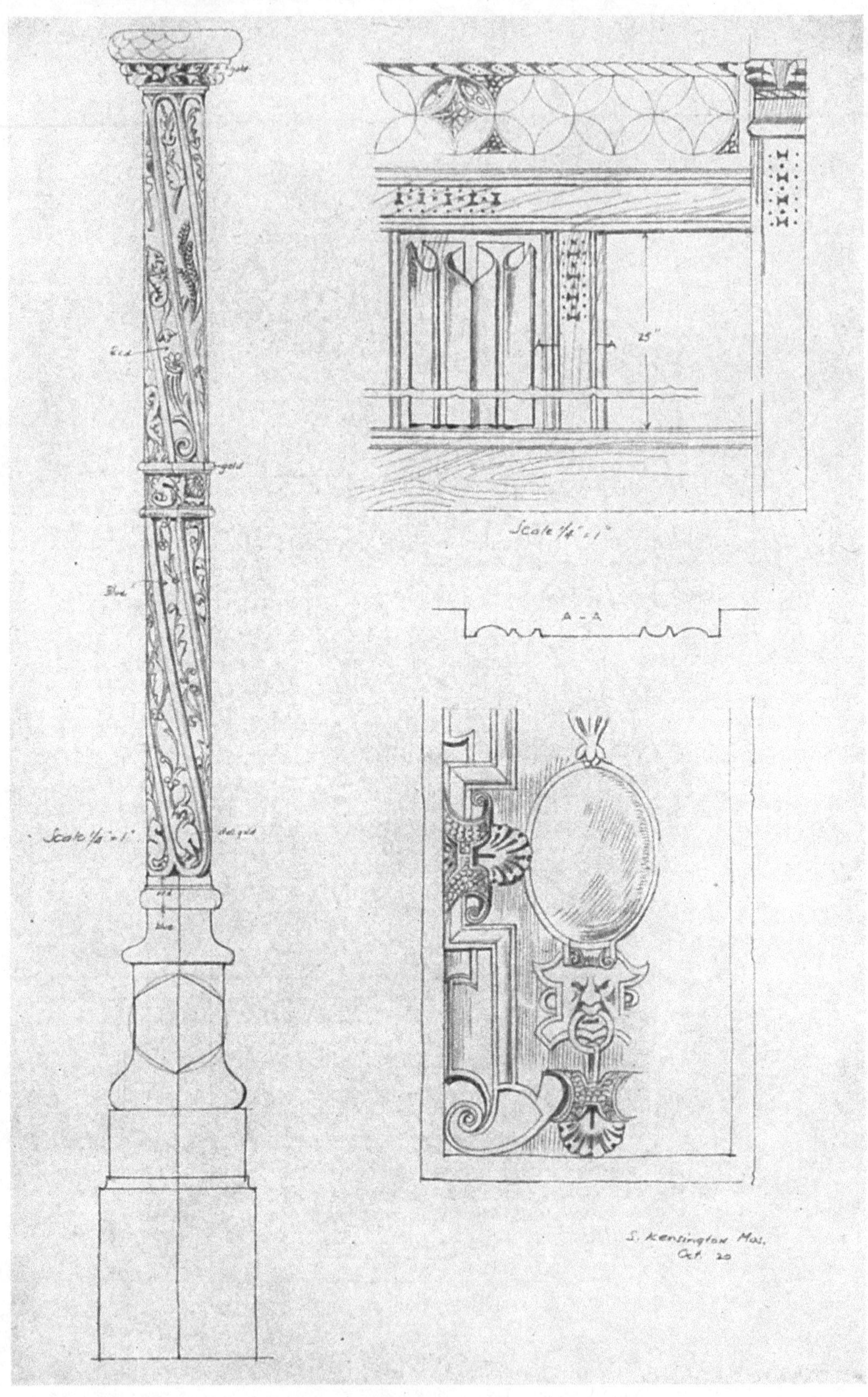

PENCIL SKETCH BY ALBERT KAHN. DETAIL OF WOOD CARVING IN THE SOUTH KENSINGTON MUSEUM. LONDON

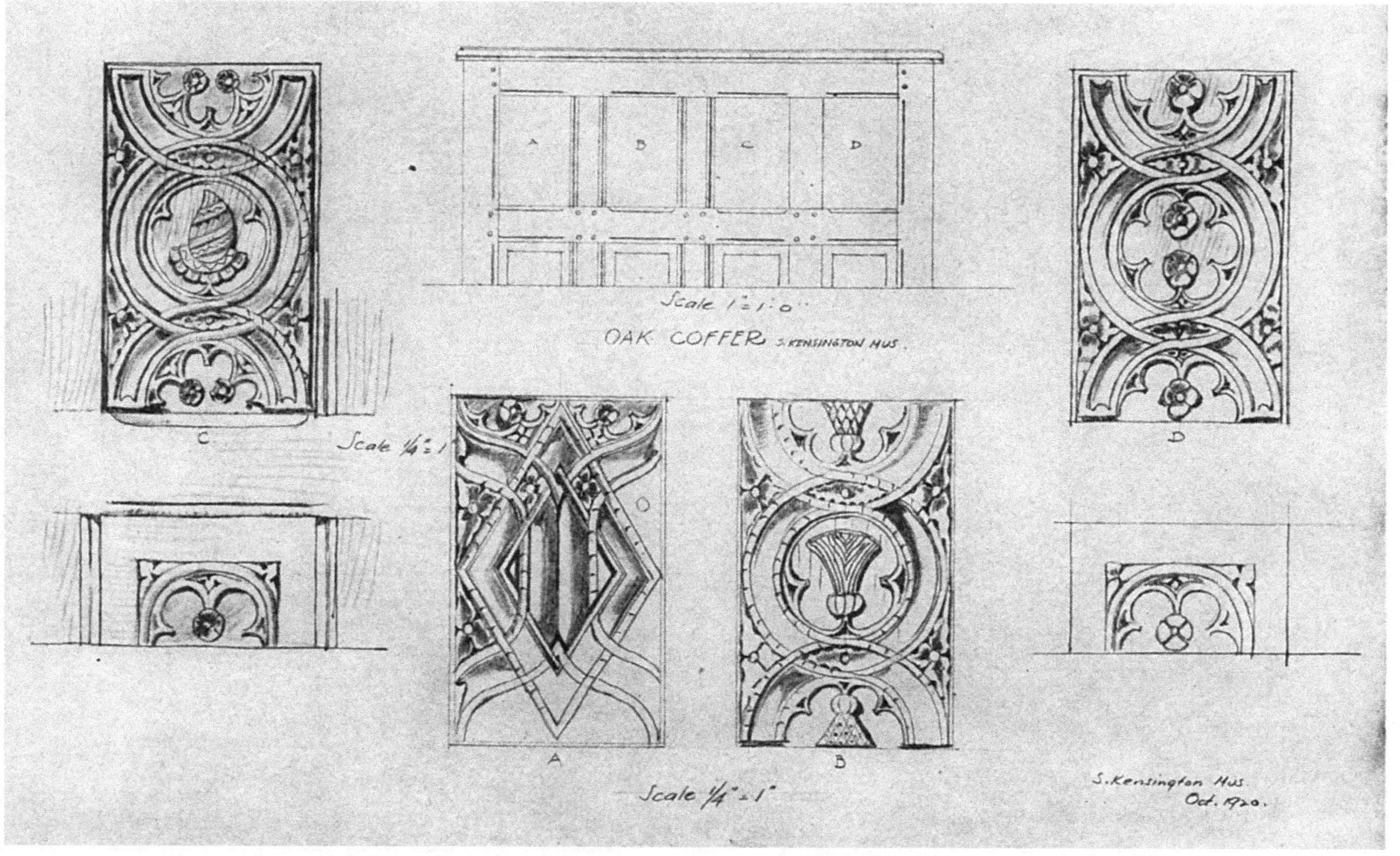

PENCIL SKETCHES BY ALBERT KAHN. DETAILS OF WOOD CARVING IN THE SOUTH KENSINGTON MUSEUM, LONDON, ENGLAND

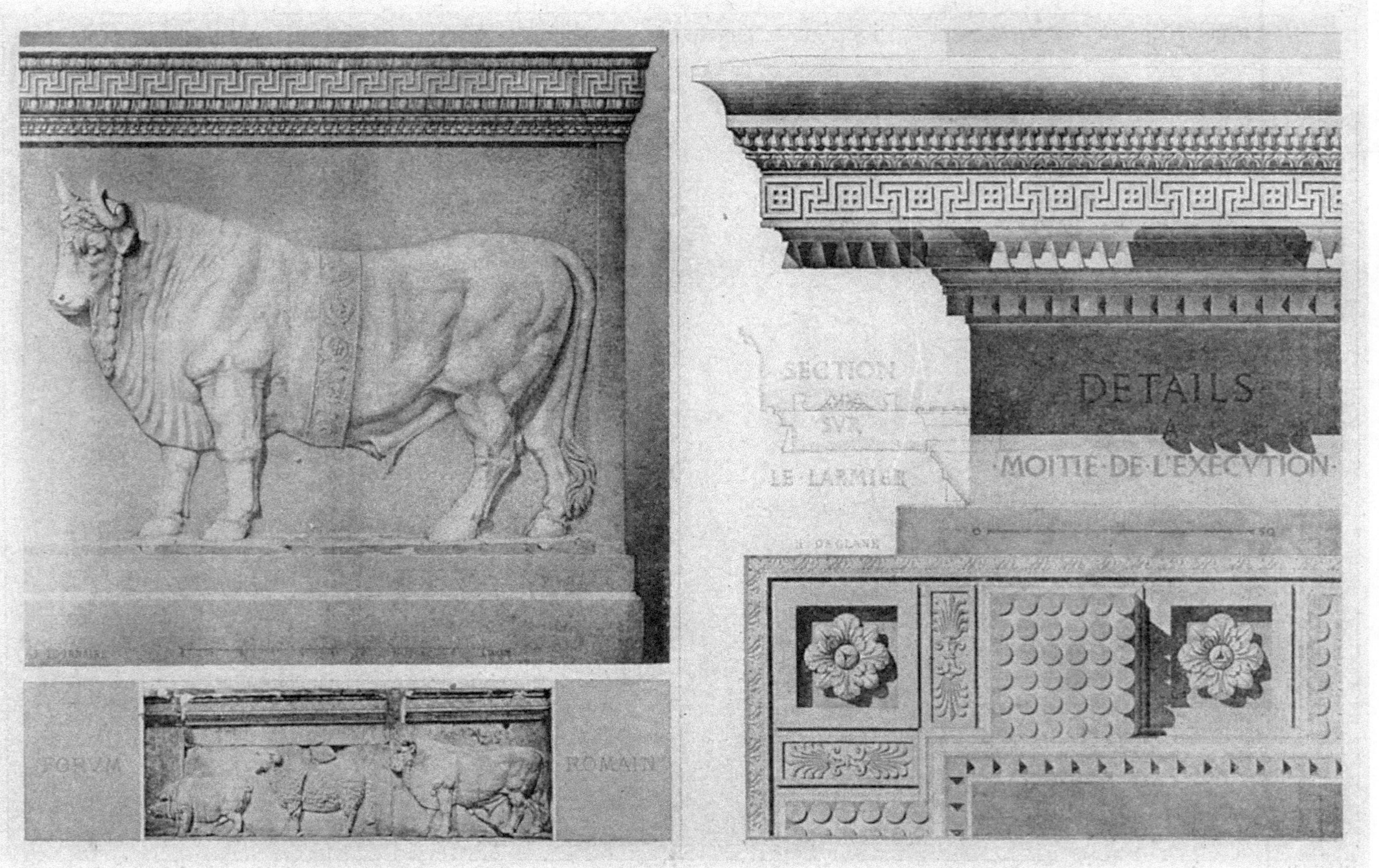

Rendering in Wash Illustrating Effect of Reflected Light in Shadows, Particularly in Those Cast by Dentils Shown in the Drawing at the Right. Fragments from the Roman Forum. From H. D'Espouy's "Fragments d'Architecture Antique."

Chapter IX.

INTERIORS AND FURNITURE

THOUGH a large percentage of all perspectives and renderings made for architectural purposes show exteriors of buildings, the draftsman is, nevertheless, sometimes called upon to make drawings of interiors, including such accessories as furniture and draperies, and, as interiors offer certain problems not usually encountered in exterior work, special practice and study are necessary to insure their satisfactory solution. Then, too, there are some draftsmen and designers, particularly those employed by decorators, or in furniture or upholstery houses, who devote the greater portion of their time to rendering interior subjects, and these men, even more than those doing the usual form of architectural work, need a knowledge of how interiors actually appear and how this appearance can be best represented.

A lengthy discussion of this interesting subject seems hardly necessary, for many of the suggestions already offered in previous chapters relate to interior as well as to exterior work, and, therefore, as some special comments have also been made which refer to interiors only, it is our present purpose merely to add a few ideas, bearing especially on methods of representing some of the many objects and materials which do not appear in exteriors, such as the furniture and draperies mentioned above. Before doing so, however, it will perhaps be well to first call attention to a few of the essential differences in the appearance of interiors and exteriors, for a comparison of these differences, and of their effect on the manner of indication should prove of value to the student.

First of all, interiors are considered by many artists to be more difficult to draw than exteriors, and for a number of reasons. To begin with, the actual mechanical process of laying out an interior, preparatory to the work in rendering, is usually more laborious than for an exterior. Exteriors are, to be sure, often far from simple, but when doing an office building or a hotel or some structure of similar general form, the mass of the whole is seldom complicated, so it is usually easy, once the main construction lines are instrumentally laid out, to project the various measurements of the windows and the like along the wall surfaces to the desired position. Interiors, however, though often as simple in mass, are only begun when the architectural shell of ceiling and floor and walls (with their accompanying doors and windows) is completed, for there remain such details as furniture and lighting fixtures, and these require considerable time, for it is, as a rule, rather a lengthy process to accurately obtain all of the different measurements in perspective, as many of these objects stand away from the walls, which adds to the difficulty of projection; and once the correct placing and general dimensions are obtained, it is frequently the case that the objects themselves are so irregular in form as to necessitate considerable labor, for often many curved or slanted lines are required;—in fact, such pieces as rocking chairs sometimes consist entirely of curved lines and lines sloping at various angles. Then, too, it is not uncommon to find furniture so turned that nearly every piece requires vanishing points of its own. It is, therefore, mainly because of such accessories that the mechanical layout of the typical interior proves laborious to make, though there are certain types of buildings where the block form itself is difficult. One of the hardest kinds of interiors to draw accurately is the theatre, where the bowled floor, the disposition of the seats in curved rows with radiating aisles, the rounded and sloping balconies, the tiers of boxes, the proscenium arch and the vaulted or domed ceiling, all offer labor enough to tax the patience of the most persevering.

In addition to this difficulty of instrumental construction, the draftsman of interiors is sometimes handicapped a bit by his inability to introduce accessories just where he wishes to have them for the purpose of obtaining the best composition. In drawing exteriors the artist can often make an otherwise ordinary composition interesting by arranging his trees and vines and clouds and automobiles,—in fact, all such accessories,—about where he wishes, and many of these can be made, also, of almost any desirable size and shape. Interiors sometimes permit the use of potted plants and vases of leaves or flowers to serve a like purpose, and of course in conservatories we find much of this sort of thing, but on the whole there is less opportunity for such freedom of arrangement, though the furniture and pictures and hangings do offer a similar means of relieving the bareness of the architectural background, so that this of course offsets to some extent the handicap just mentioned.

Another difference in appearance between interiors and exteriors is found in the effect of the light and shade, for in exteriors the sun usually affords a single direct means of illumination, so that the shadows can be laid out by an accurate mechanical method, if one knows the science of doing so, and the division between the light and the dark is generally clearly marked. Interiors, however, are usually far more complex in their lighting, the rays of light coming frequently from several sources, thereby causing complicated values, the shadows often falling in a number of directions at the same time, and the tones of these various shadows dif-

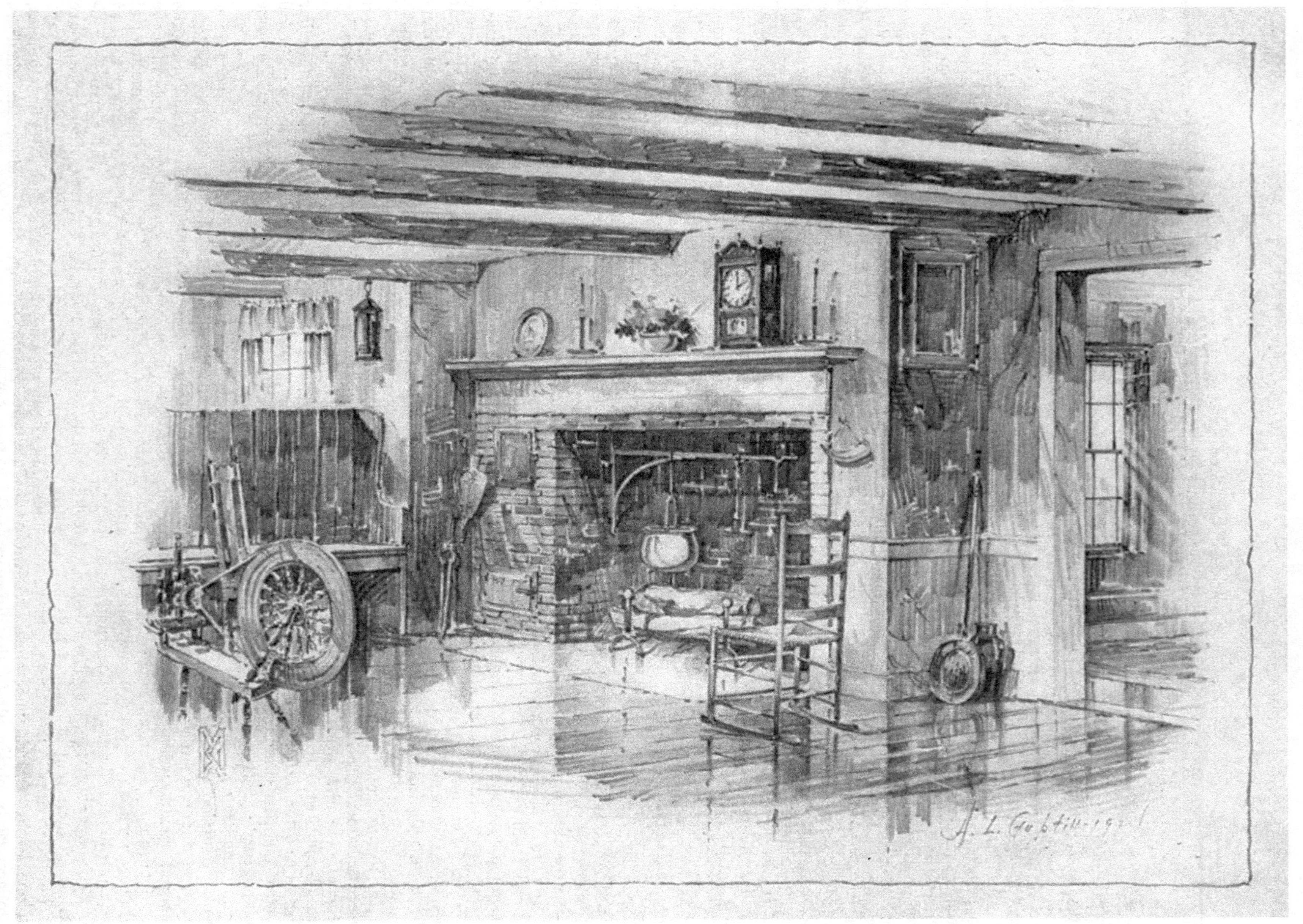

Figure 38. A Sketchy Handling Appropriate to the Informality of the Subject.

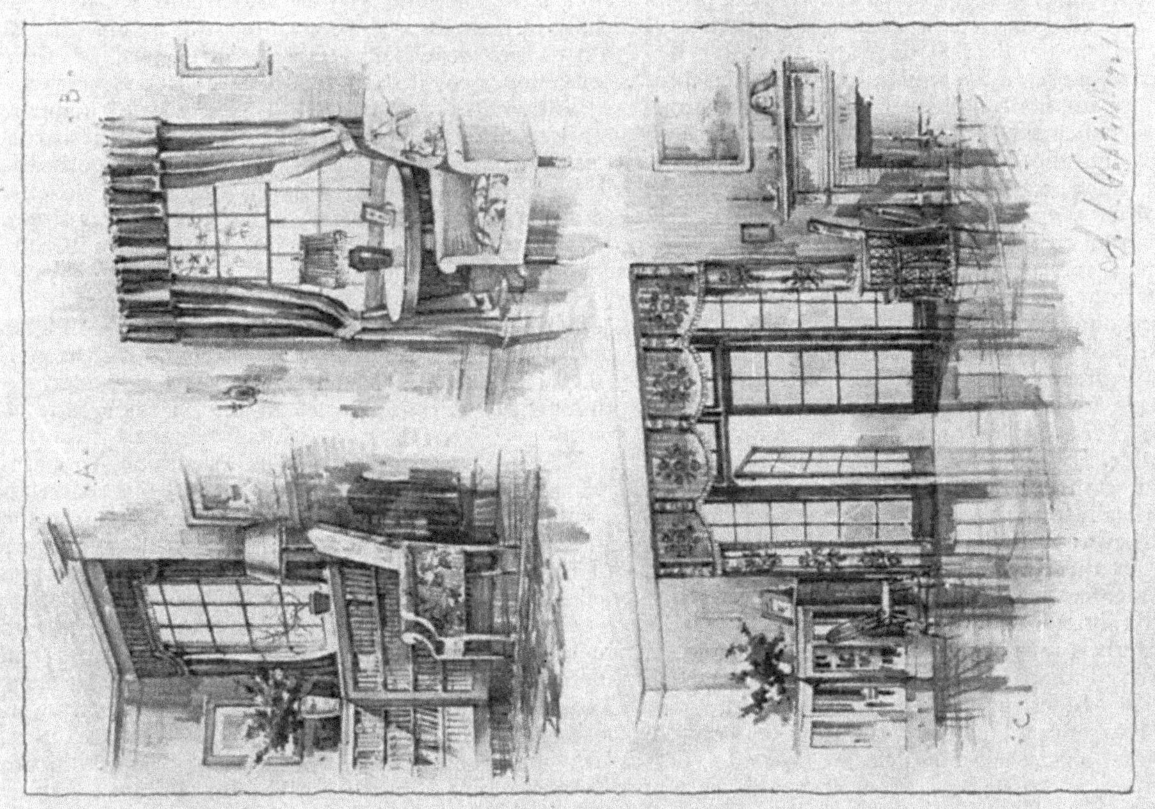

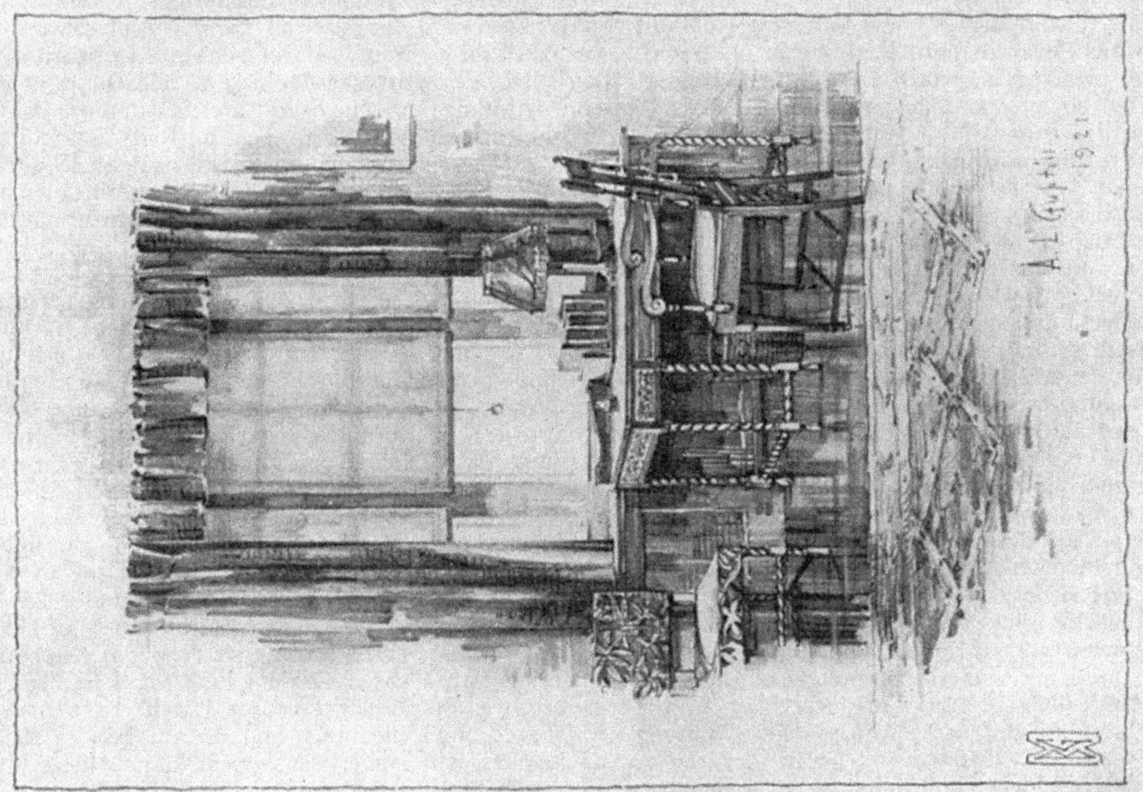

Figure 39. Interior Sketches Showing Doors and Windows.

fering greatly, some being light and others dark, with certain edges sharply defined and with others indistinct. A chair leg, for example, often casts several shadows on the floor at once and a lighting fixture as many more on the wall or ceiling. This complication is further augmented by the numerous reflections, concerning which we will say more in a moment, but notwithstanding all this, the mere fact that such a complex condition does exist, though often very confusing to the beginner, frequently works to the advantage of the more experienced man, for, as we are accustomed to this complexity of tone, the skilled artist is able to arrange his values almost as he chooses and we are unaware that any liberties have been taken so long as the natural effect has not been sacrificed.

As a rule it is best for the beginner not to draw every little change of tone that is seen, but he should, instead, simplify the whole, working for the general effect in a broad, direct manner, for when one enters a room he is not conscious of all this detail,—therefore it should not be forced on the attention in the drawing. There is another point worth remembering and this is that because much of the illumination of interiors is indirect and the light rays therefore diffused, the general effect is usually softer than is the case where we have an exterior in direct light,—the tones blending or merging into one another and the division between the light and shade being less clearly defined. This indefinite effect, though often desirable in certain types of drawing, can be easily carried to extremes, and the artist who strives for it sometimes obtains a result which, even though satisfying in one sense, may be displeasing in another, for such a rendering is often so gray and lacking in contrast as to prove hardly suitable for architectural purposes, where a drawing with clean-cut edges and sharp definition of tone is preferred as a rule to a soft and vague interpretation. The artist who is working for a crisp result will find a certain fact to his advantage, and this is that many objects found in interiors, being well polished and smooth, offer strong reflections and highlights which, if judiciously used, serve as a pleasing break in the grayness of the general effect. Out-of-doors we seldom find such shiny surfaces as we do inside, with the exception of a few like those of smooth water and glass. The building materials used outside are usually rather dull in finish, and even if polished when first put in place soon lose their gloss because of the action of the weather. Materials found in interiors, on the other hand, often exhibit the contrary characteristics. Floors are of highly polished wood or marble; the trim is frequently varnished or given some enamel finish, and glazed tiles or similar objects are sometimes introduced, particularly around mantels, but it is especially in the furniture and in such accessories as the lighting fixtures, vases, etc., that we find many surfaces of high reflective value. Table tops, for example, frequently act almost like mirrors, while the glass in the framed pictures on the walls has similar characteristics. Chair arms, door knobs, clocks, dishes, etc., all add little highlights, often of extreme brilliancy in relation to the surroundings, and the student is wise who learns to employ these sharply contrasting accents to give life to his work, especially in drawings of an architectural nature. Many otherwise "dead" drawings receive most of their character from just such accents as these.

So much of a general nature by way of comparing exteriors and interiors. The main points to be remembered are that interiors are usually more difficult to lay out,—that it is not, as a rule, so easy to arrange the accessories to assist the composition, —that the values are more complex, with the shadows made difficult because of light from various sources, and, last of all, that the general effect is sometimes rather vague and soft, but that highlights and accents are frequently to be found on the polished surfaces, which, if properly interpreted by the artist, will give a clean-cut character to his work.

Now, as we proceed to our discussion of methods of representing various objects and materials common to interiors, it is necessary to repeat the statement which we have already made a number of times, and this is that few definite rules exist to tell us how to do such work. Each student must learn to see and to interpret the things that he sees in his own way, and books and instructors can merely offer a few suggestions by way of assistance. Learning to draw is, in fact, so much a matter of learning to see, that it is impossible to overemphasize the importance of cultivating the ability to observe things intelligently. In order to draw draperies, for example, or upholstery materials, it is necessary to first of all carefully observe the various fabrics employed for such purposes, studying each one with care, looking at it close at hand and in the distance, in bright and in subdued light, laid out smoothly and draped in folds, searching always for its special characteristics under all such conditions, and endeavoring also to retain mental impressions of these peculiarities for future use. Then compare one fabric with another, or drape several in such a way that they can be easily seen at one time. It is surprising what differences can be discovered by an inspection and analysis of this sort. A piece of satin and a piece of cotton cloth of similar color and tone will vary greatly in appearance, and even a light piece of cotton and a dark piece of the same material will show marked dissimilarity of effect in addition to the contrast in color. It is impossible to describe such differences in a single chapter, but there are one or two suggestions worth offering: first of all, light colored cloth usually shows more contrast in its values than does darker material of a similar kind, as the dark color seems to absorb many of the lighter values of shade and shadow. A smooth material with a sheen will not look at all like some dull fabric of similar tone, as it will have many highlights and reflections, and certain fabrics such as velours will sometimes appear dark where we expect them to be light, and light where other materials would be dark, and by rubbing the nap the effect can be changed from light to dark or from dark to light instantly. Many materials of a shiny nature grow dull and soft with age, but there are exceptions, for some others,—leather, for example,

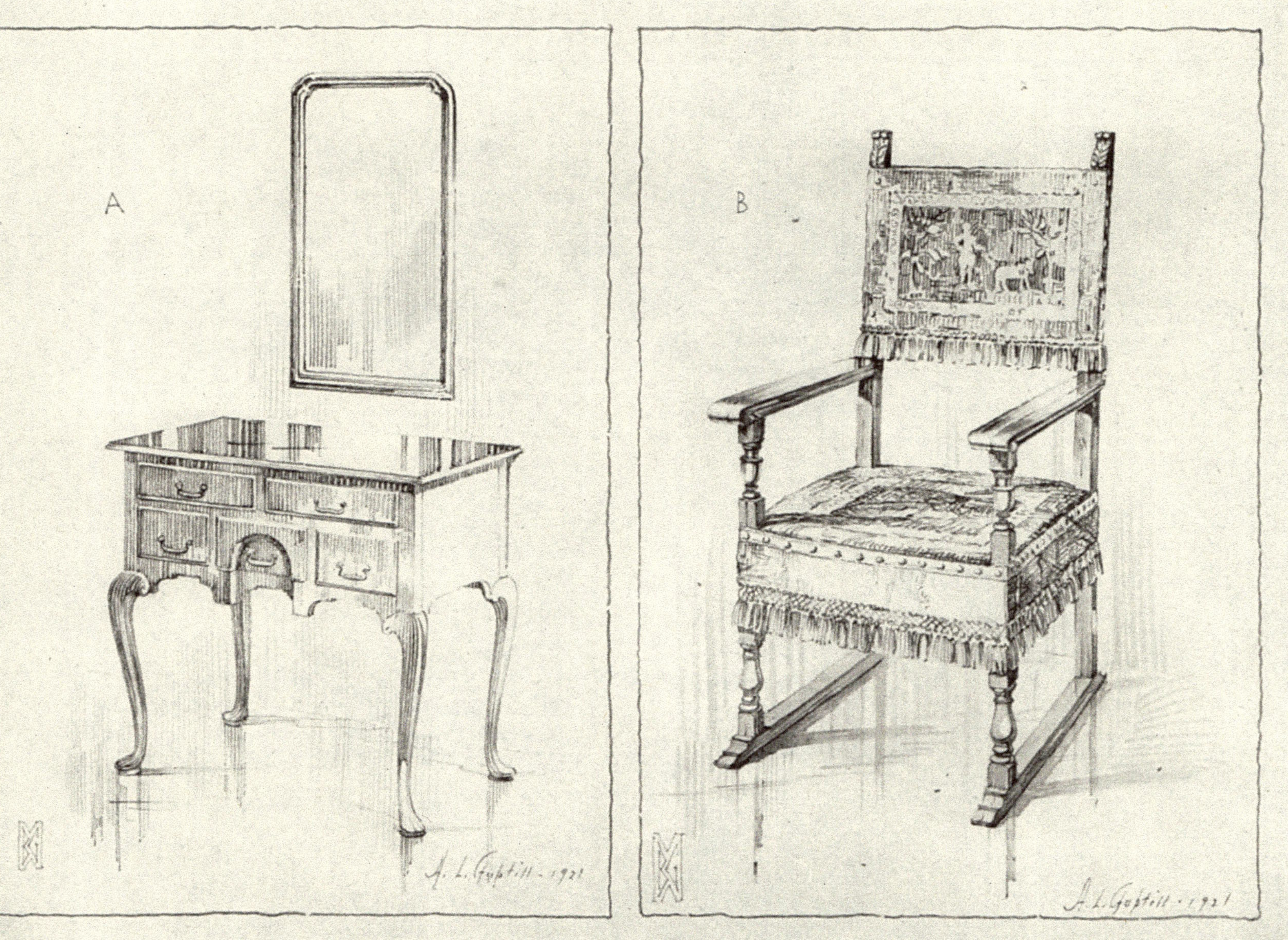

Figure 40. Furniture Sketches of the Kind Frequently Used for Commercial Purposes. Note the Large Amount of Paper Surface Left Untouched.

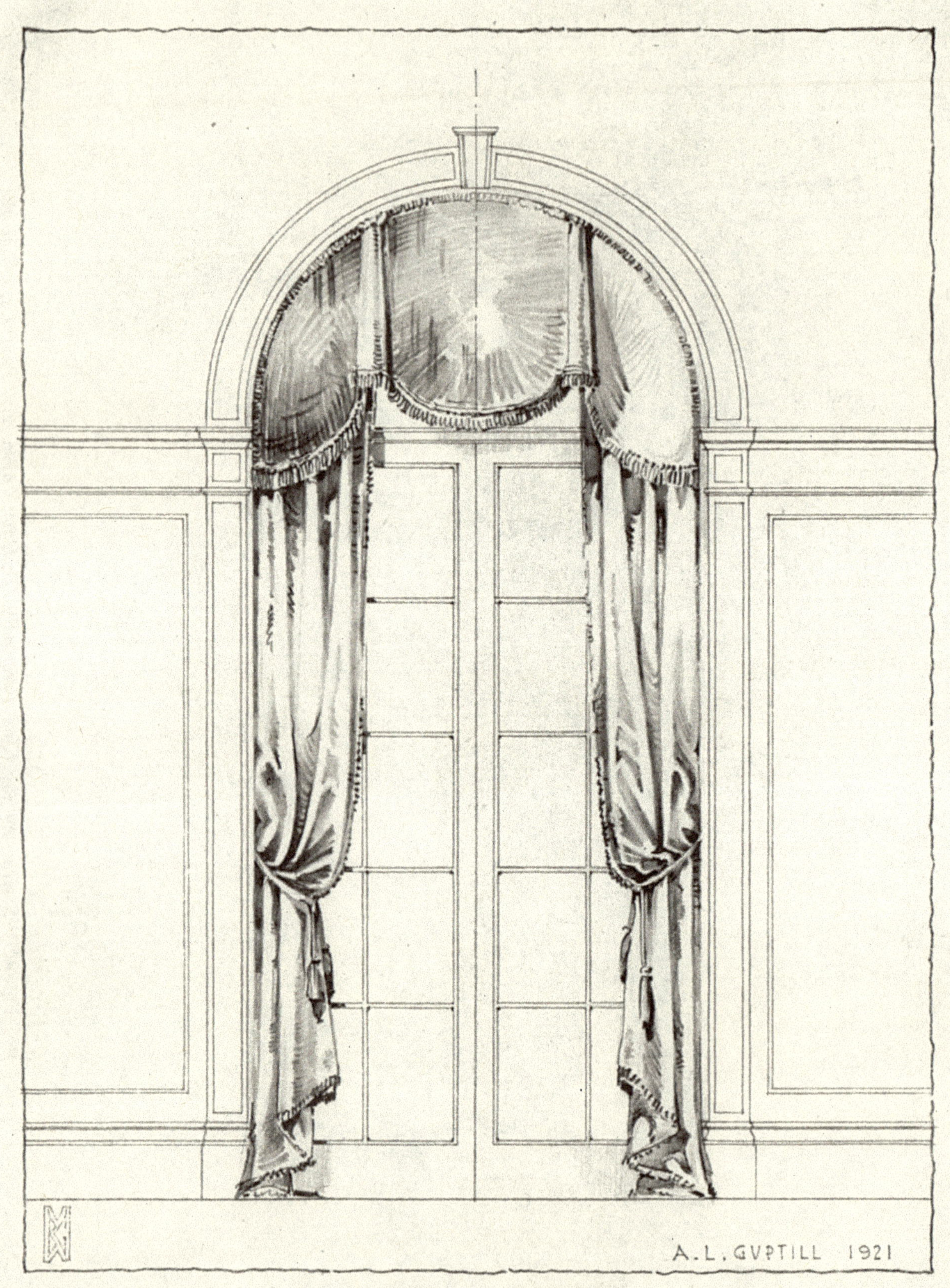

Figure 41. A Conventional Drapery Study Combining Free-Hand and Instrumental Lines. Note the Simplicity of Treatment.

—often become smooth and glossy with wear. The smoother the material, the more complicated and changeable are its values, as a rule, and the stronger its highlights. Now when it comes to draping fabrics there is great variety in the way they hang, for some are stiff and inflexible and others soft and yielding. Heavy materials usually hang quite straight and show fewer small folds and creases than do those which are light in weight. Heavy materials, too, are generally opaque and for this reason are sometimes less difficult to represent than are thin nets and scrims and similar fabrics which are so translucent or even transparent as to show light, or occasionally objects, through them.

As soon as the student has carefully studied the appearance of all these things he is ready to attempt some drawings, giving special attention to the representation of surfaces and textures. Whereas there is no harm in sketching one single object, like an upholstered chair, it is often of greater benefit to arrange compositions of several objects which are associated by use, and which offer, in addition, a variety of surfaces. Old objects such as are found in museums are especially good for practice of this sort as the textures of antiques are more varied and interesting than are those of most modern pieces. If it is not convenient to do museum work, however, things at home will answer very well. Arrange an easy chair and a table and reading lamp, for instance, in natural position to form a pleasing group, adding, perhaps, a book or magazine and such other accessories as will make the composition complete. Have the light coming from one direction if this is practical, so as to avoid complicated shadows. Then in making the drawing use the greatest care in suggesting such things as the shine of the table top and the floor, the numerous touches of highlight, and the texture of the rug and the table runner and the lamp shade. Try, as in any composition, to properly emphasize the center of interest, and give especial attention, also, to the treatment of the edges separating the light from the shade, having them clean-cut where they appear so in the objects and indefinite where such an effect seems called for. If a trial proves that it is too difficult to draw directly from objects, or if it is hard to secure suitable ones, work from photographs, instead, selecting those which show the detail quite clearly and have little effect of perspective distortion. It is sometimes advantageous to choose pictures of period furniture and furnishings for this work, for by so doing valuable knowledge of the periods may be obtained in addition to the drawing practice.

Figures 38, 39 and 40, accompanying this text, require little explanation. Figure 38 is shown mainly for the suggestions that it offers for the treatment of such textures as we find in the brickwork, the rough plaster, the hewn beams and the polished floor. It might be well to mention that when drawing such a surface as a shiny floor or table top it is well to show some lines representing the reflections of objects, and others, often in the opposite direction, indicating the surfaces of the boards themselves. A study of the floor shown here will reveal both these sets of lines and for additional examples see the top of the dressing table and the chair arms and the floors in Figure 40. Figure 40, by the way, is a more conventional type of rendering than Figure 38, for here the background is simply suggested, all of the attention being focused on the furniture itself. Such drawings as these are often used by furniture houses and for advertising work. Observe that in these particular examples comparatively little tone is used, the white of the paper counting quite strongly. Figure 41 is also a conventional rendering, the drapery itself receiving all of the attention, the architecture being merely suggested by the fewest possible lines, and here again much of the paper remains untouched. One advantage of this type of rendering is that after the student has had a reasonable amount of practice it can be done very quickly.

The supplementary illustrations on the following pages should prove of great interest and value as they are excellent examples of widely different types of work. Those by Otto R. Eggers on pages 142 and 143 were made to show the client how the rooms of his house, as designed, could be made to look,—how the comparatively low ceiling and the simple window treatment would produce a dignified and home-like effect if the rooms were furnished in a suitable manner. These interiors were sketched lightly in pencil without being laid out instrumentally. The washes of water-color were then applied roughly and when dry the sketches were completed with lithographic pencil, this procedure being necessary as water-color cannot be successfully flowed over lithographic pencil lines. The drawing by Mr. Pauli on page 144 shows an entirely different handling, the whole being carefully blocked out instrumentally and finished free-hand in pencil with infinite care, some of the instrumental lines being allowed to remain. Such drawings as this are often used for catalogue purposes where furniture or lighting fixtures or things of that sort are advertised. The ceiling drawing on page 145 also combines free-hand and instrumental work, being a typical vaulting development such as is frequently employed by interior decorators, this particular study being from the office of Theo. Hofstatter & Co. From the same office is the drawing of the side table on page 146, which was done in pencil with washes of color added, this presentation effectively showing the piece in a way to give the decorator's client a clear idea of it. Now compare these drawings with others in order to learn different methods of obtaining similar effects, and—what is still more important,—practice constantly.

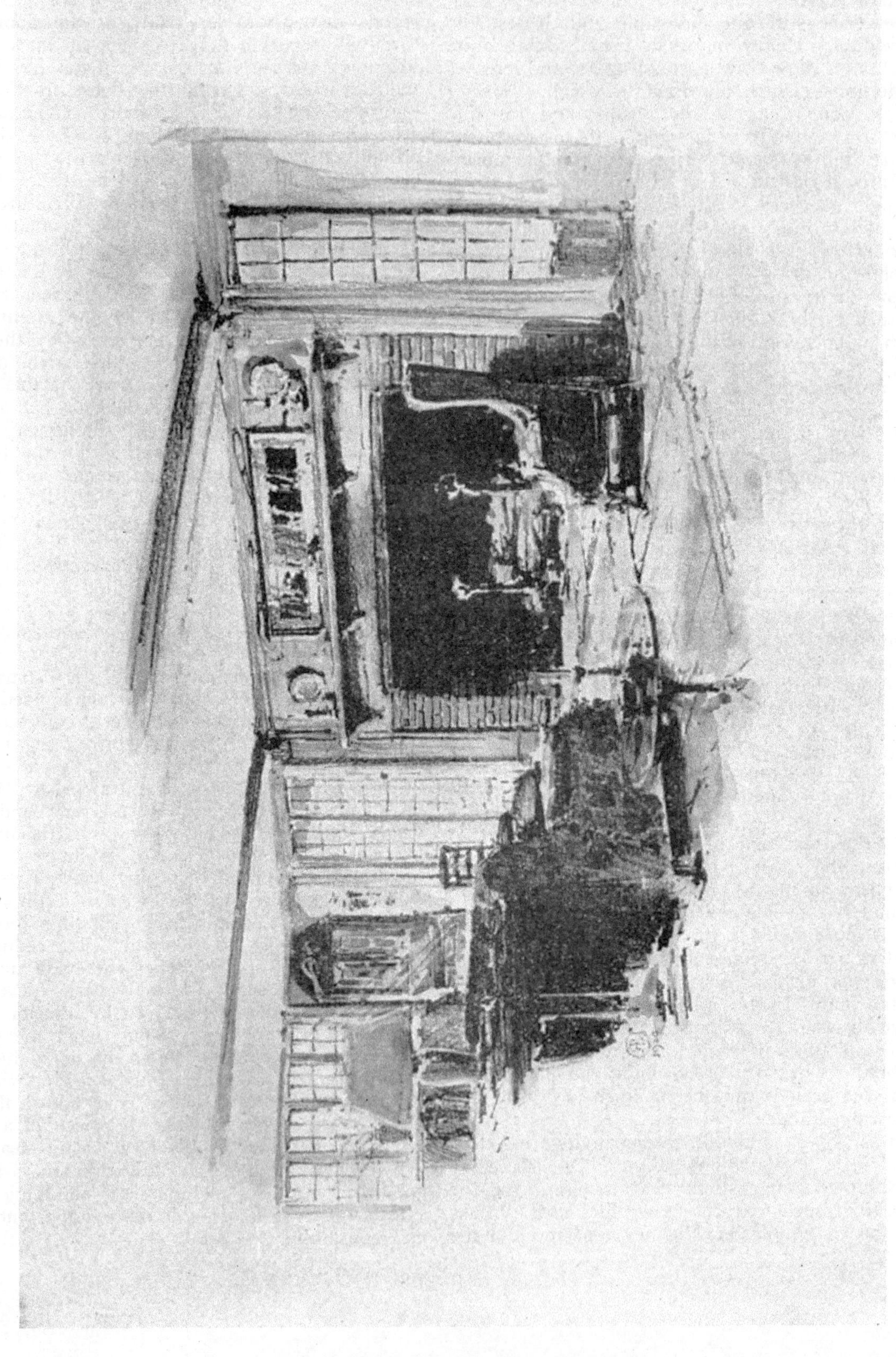

SKETCH BY OTTO R. EGGERS OF A PROPOSED TREATMENT FOR A LIVING ROOM

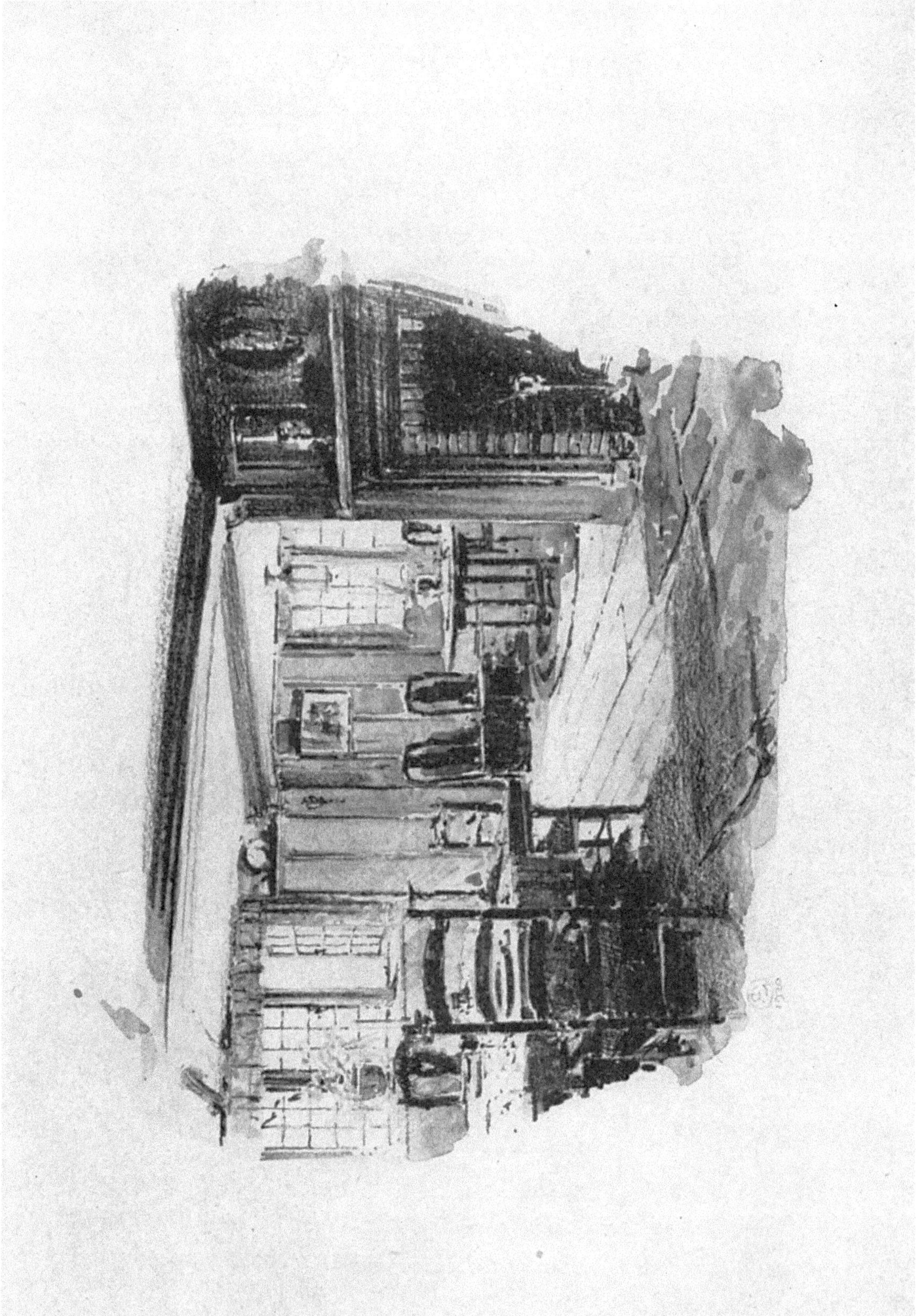

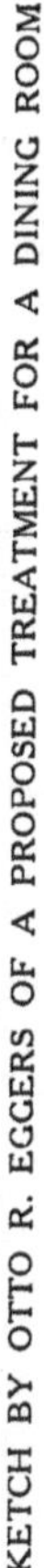

SKETCH BY OTTO R. EGGERS OF A PROPOSED TREATMENT FOR A DINING ROOM

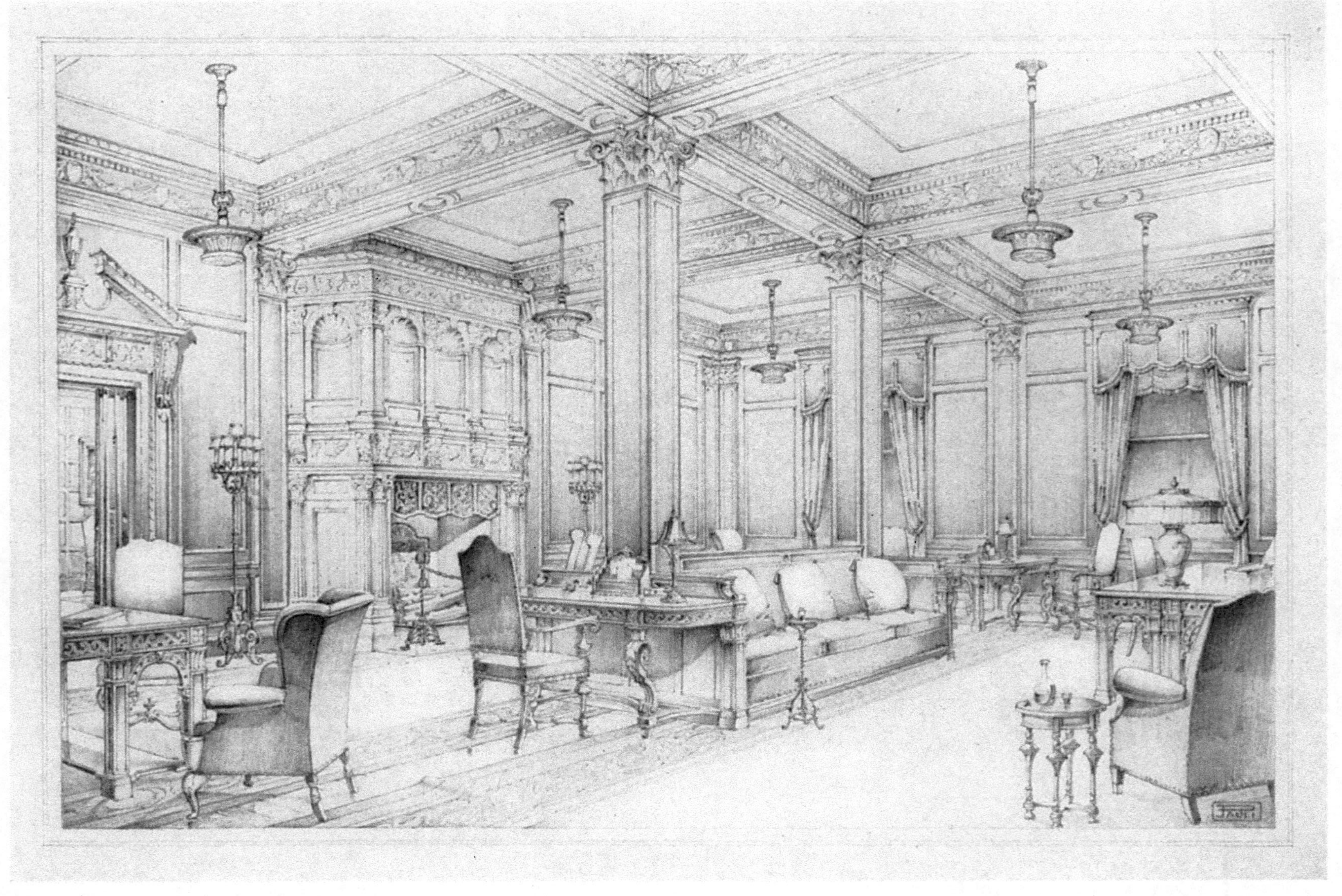

PENCIL RENDERING, BY ERWIN J. PAULI, OF A DESIGN FOR A CLUB ROOM

Example of Careful Drawing of Kind Required by Manufacturers to Illustrate Catalogues, Etc.

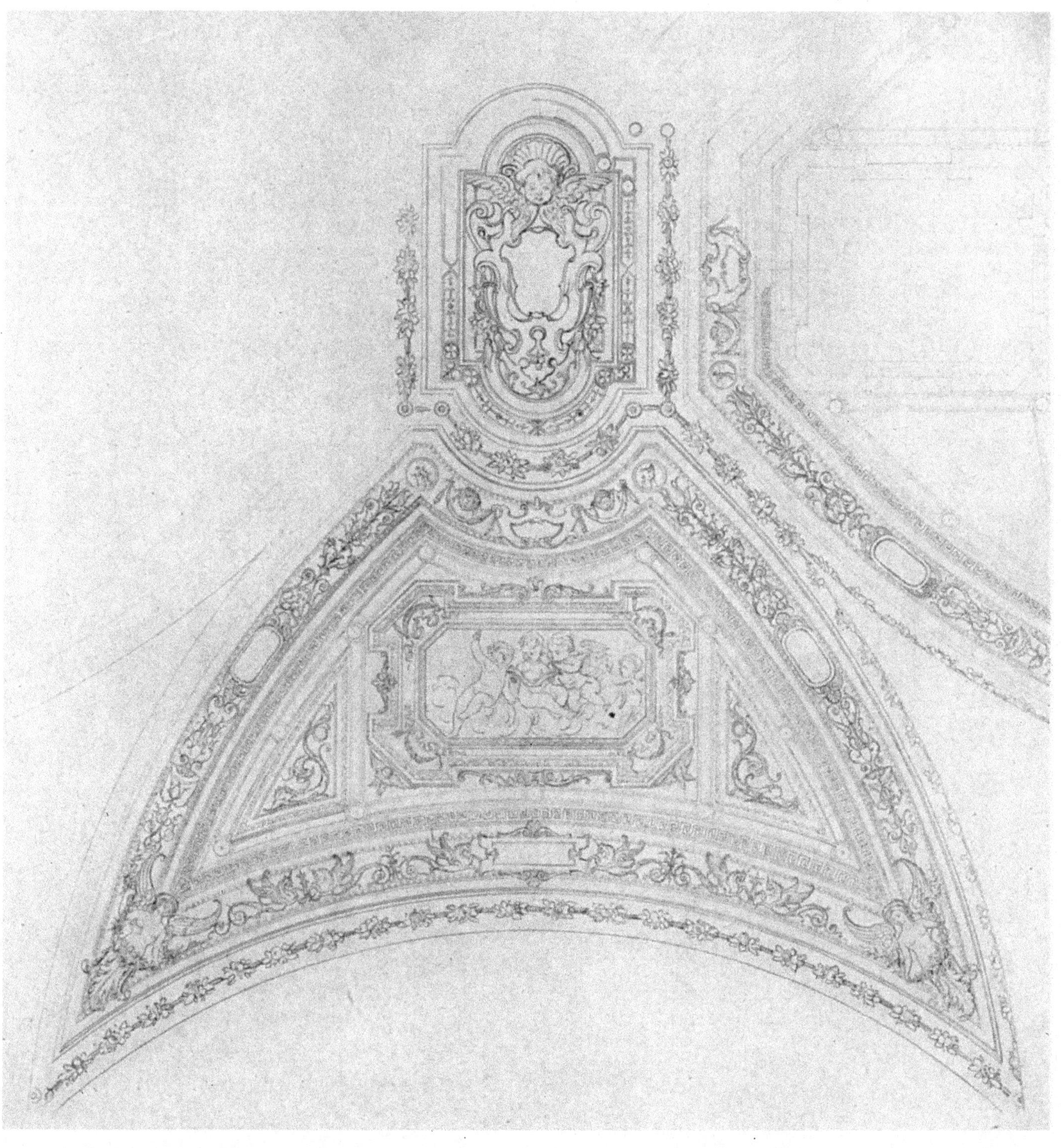

PENCIL DRAWING OF DESIGN FOR DECORATION OF VAULTED CEILING. THEO. HOFSTATTER & CO., DECORATORS

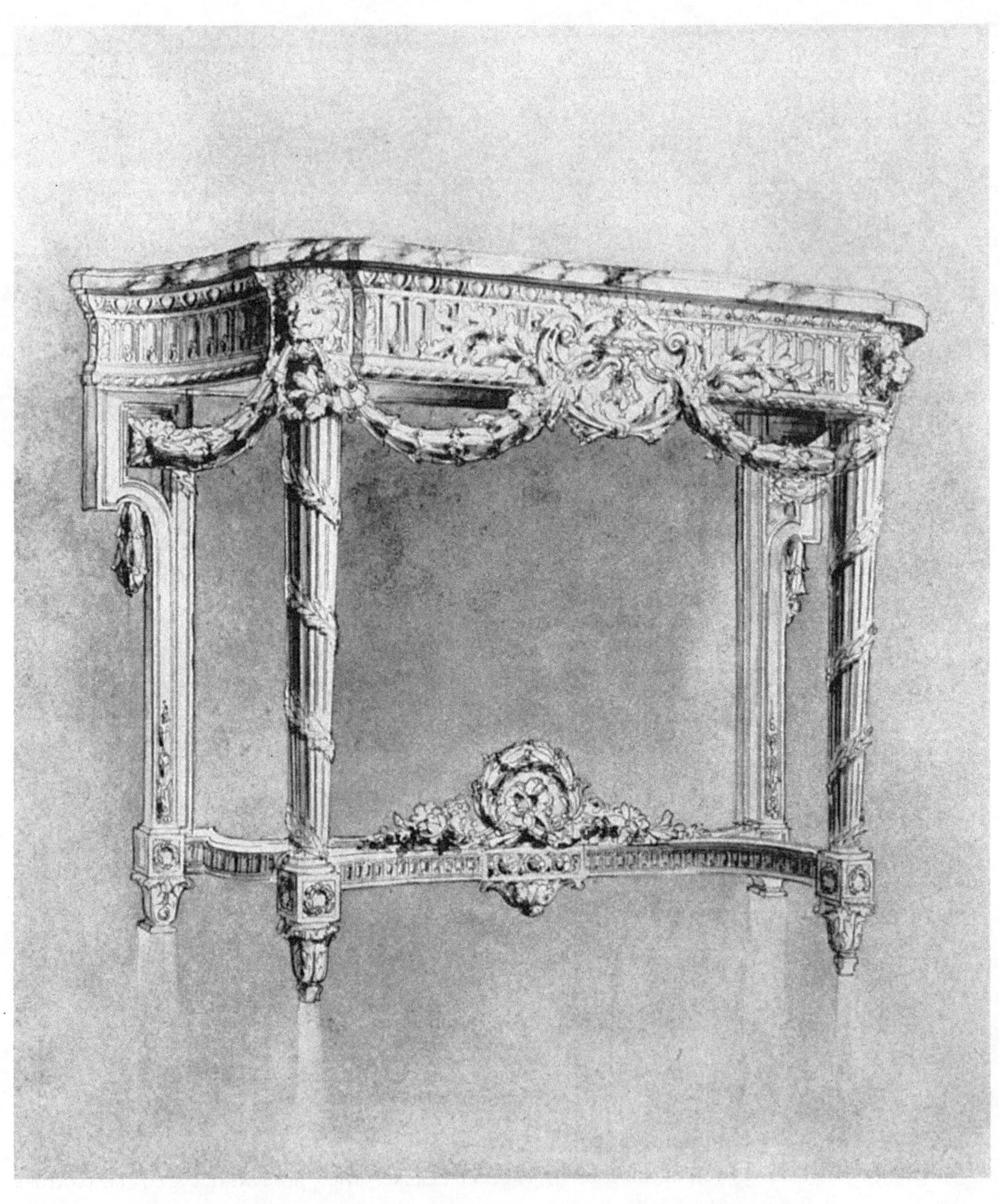

RENDERING IN PENCIL AND WATER COLOR. TABLE IN THE LOUIS XVI MANNER.

THEO. HOFSTATTER & CO., DECORATORS

Chapter X.

OUTDOOR SKETCHING

IN THE last few chapters special attention has been given to the representation of minor portions of both exteriors and interiors of buildings, and it has been pointed out that these small details really are the draftsman's A B C's, which he should learn before attempting large or important compositions.

His alphabet will not be complete, however, until he has added to his knowledge of how to draw these elements of a building itself a fund of information concerning the indication of such accessories as clouds, water, automobiles and other vehicles, also animals, people and foliage.

Foliage is especially important as there are comparatively few drawings of architecture which fail to show more or less of it, while in many renderings it occupies a very large and prominent place. (We use a broad meaning of the word here, including under the one general term "foliage" not only masses of leaves but all such forms of plant life as trees, bushes, vines, grass and flowers.) It is, in truth, almost as essential to be able to draw the natural setting for a building, as it is to draw the building itself, and the student should constantly bear this in mind; neither should he lose sight of the fact that when sketching foliage, especially trees, he is acquiring, in addition to a knowledge of drawing, certain principles of design directly applicable to architectural work, for there is a very definite analogy in several ways between trees and buildings. As an example of one such similarity, suppose we liken a tree to a tall tower. Just as the tree starts at the ground with a strong and sturdy trunk, and gradually, as it rises in height, becomes more complex and delicate in its parts, so, the tower, springing likewise from a solid base, becomes lighter, also, and its smaller parts more numerous, until, finally, as it meets the sky it terminates in some crowning feature, graceful in proportion and fine in detail. Nor should it be forgotten, when studying foliage, that the student is assimilating a knowledge of plant form which may be of value when designing or drawing ornament, for much architectural ornament is either copied more or less literally from nature or thoroughly conventionalized like the lotus of the Egyptians and the acanthus and anthemion of the Greeks. Again, aside from all æsthetic considerations, the architectural student should not overlook the fact that he can acquire from the study of trees much valuable knowledge of various building and finishing woods.

It is because of these numerous advantages to be gained from a study of trees and their foliage, and because there is, too, so much pleasure to be derived from such a pursuit and especially from the outdoor sketching which is so frequently a part of it, that we are devoting an entire chapter to its consideration.

First of all, before discussing actual means of representing foliage, it may be well to point out that its frequent employment in drawing is natural, not only because we are accustomed to see buildings in an environment of green, but also because compositions which are otherwise ordinary can be made interesting by its use, even "bad" architecture becoming sometimes so improved in effect as to seem attractive, if the surrounding planting is well designed and rendered, while the beauty of "good" architecture is correspondingly enhanced by a proper setting. Then, too, foliage can probably be put to the greatest variety of uses of any of the accessories, and in the most ways. Trees, for instance, can be shown of any kind and age, thus permitting a wide diversity of shapes and sizes. Bushes and shrubs can be drawn in almost any place and of any reasonable proportion desired by the artist, while vines can be given an equally free treatment without any feeling of their being inappropriate or inharmonious. Of course in some instances it becomes impossible or undesirable to exercise such complete freedom, for if a site for a building has already been selected, having existing foliage worth retaining, it is usually advisable to show with considerable accuracy that part which falls within the range of vision, but even under these or similar conditions many liberties are possible. It is within the artist's province, for example, to decide whether the trees are to be shown with or without leaves. Then if he feels that an improvement in the composition can be obtained by slightly shifting the position of a tree or two, or by adding a few bushes or flowers, the privilege is his. He can vary his effect, also, by his choice of the values used in their representation, employing either light or dark tones as he wishes.

With these facts in mind, consider for a moment the common methods of indicating people and animals and automobiles and note the contrast that such a comparison shows, for though such accessories as these last are undeniably important, especially in renderings of city buildings, it is easy to see that the artist finds greater restrictions when drawing them. To begin with, they must be shown with considerable accuracy of form and size. Whereas trees may vary a number of feet in any dimension, or somewhat in contour, without attracting attention to such variations, let a single figure be too large or small or poorly drawn, or an automobile out of scale, and the fact is usually appar-

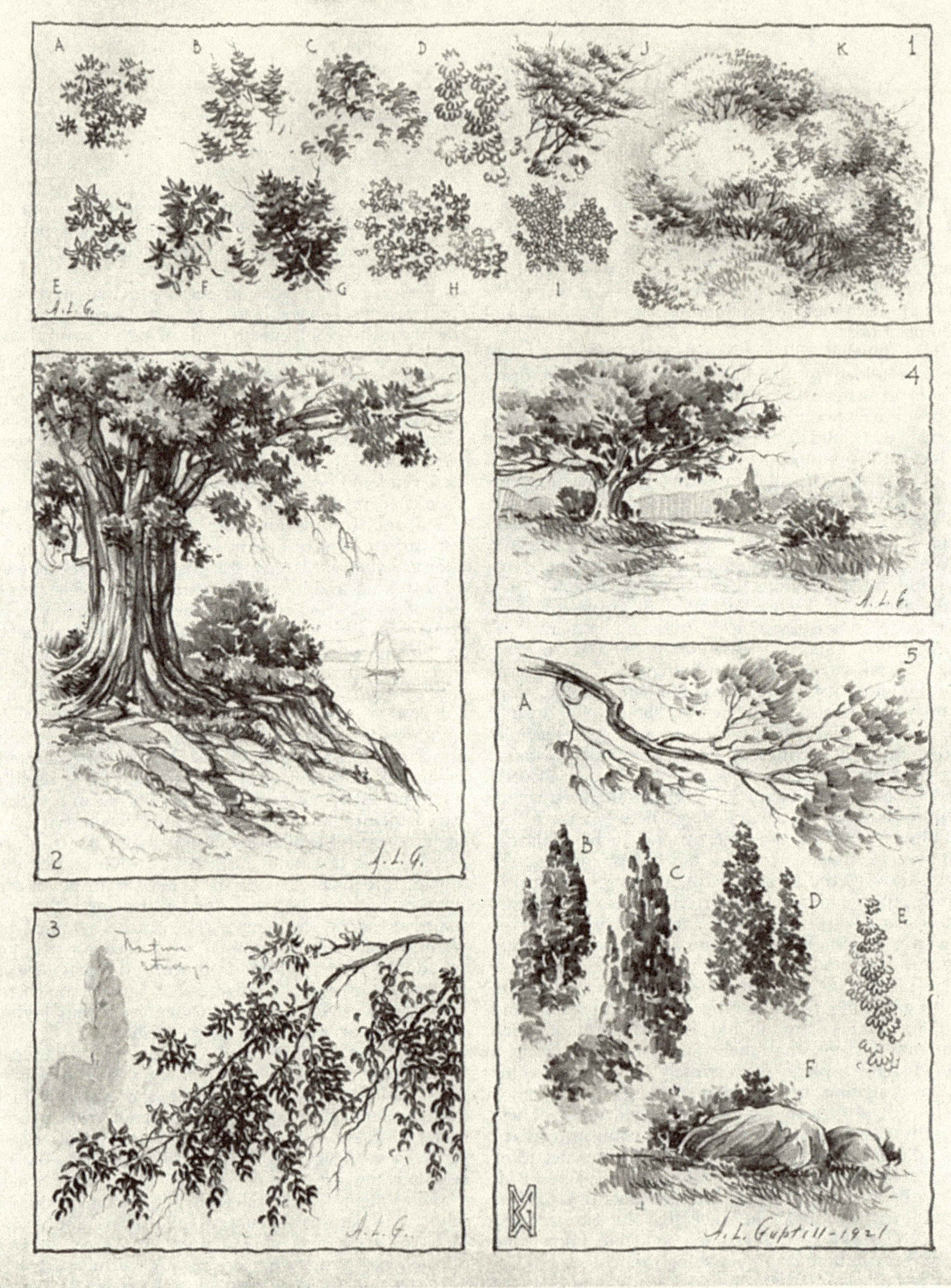

Figure 42. Some Methods of Suggesting Foliage.

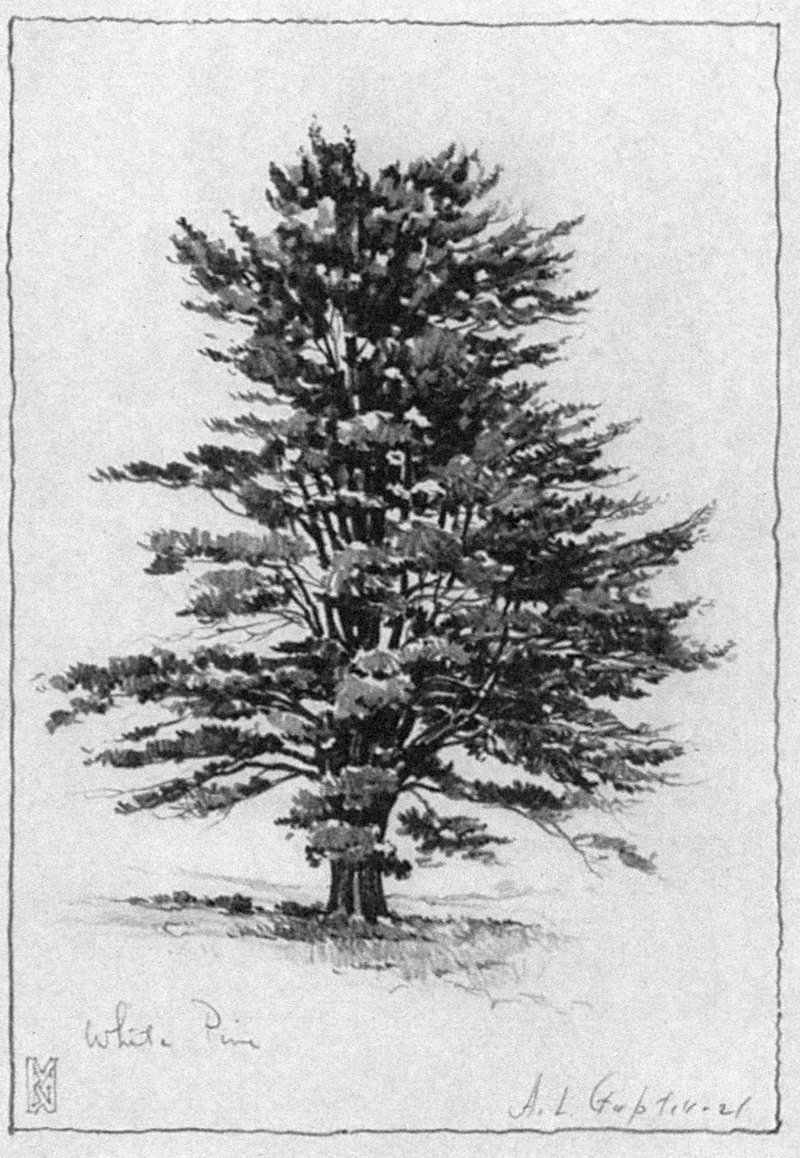

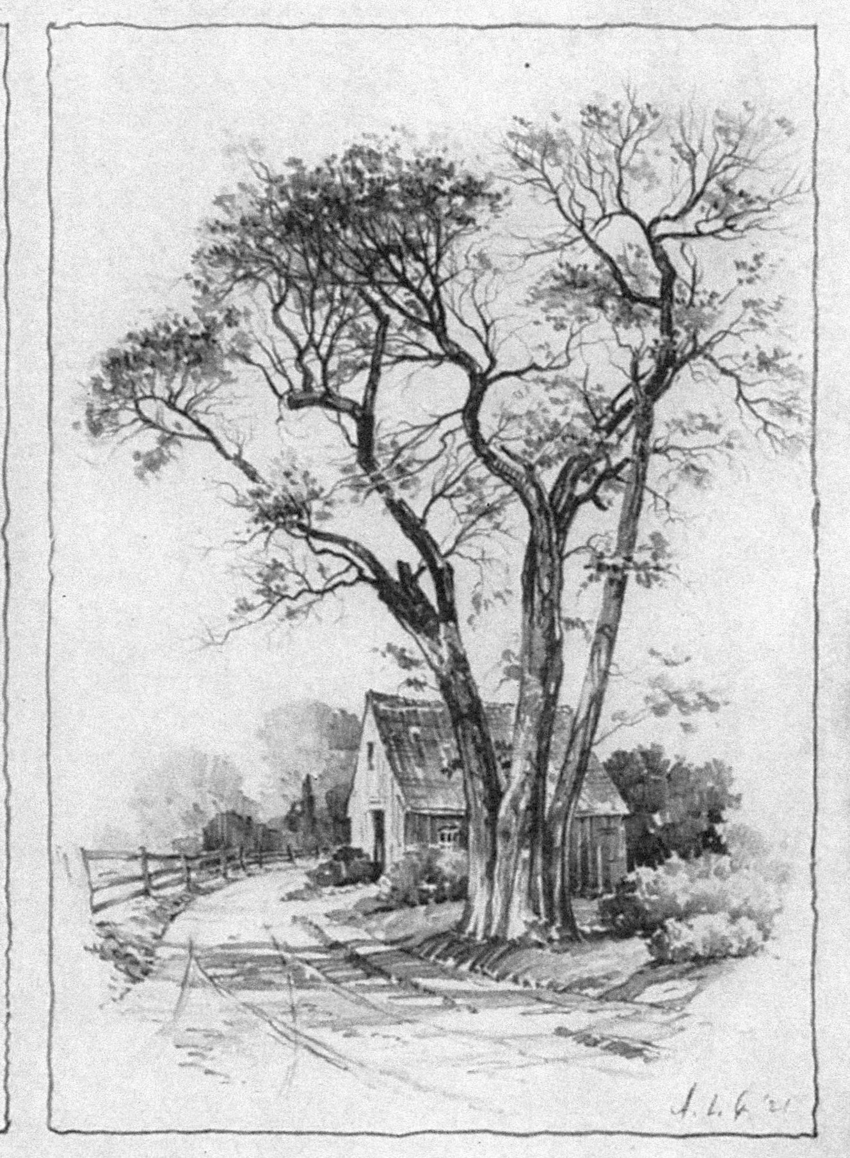

Figure 43. Typical Outdoor Sketches of Trees Portraying the Larger Characteristics in a Simple Way.

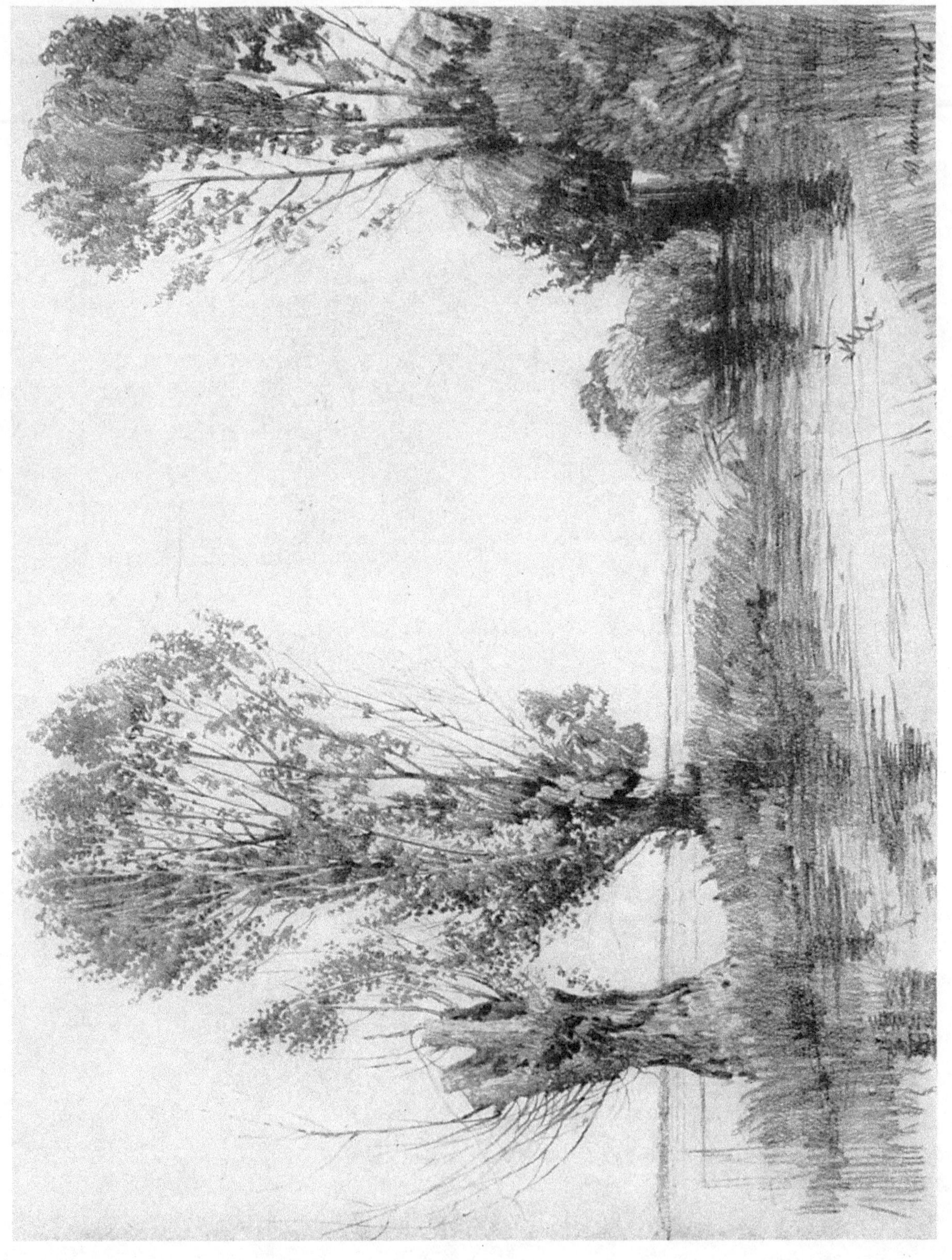

PENCIL SKETCH BY M. R. HERMANN

ent. Foliage is, therefore, often rather less difficult to represent than are these other accessories, yet mainly because of its varied uses it is frequently of greater value to the student, especially as a means of obtaining satisfactory composition. Warning should be given, however, that in architectural renderings one should never make the foliage so conspicuous that it detracts from the architecture.

It is not our intention to give the impression that the representation of foliage offers no problem, as this is not the case, for to draw it well is, indeed, far from being a simple matter,—in fact, many draughtsmen who have little trouble in rendering a building find foliage a stumbling block. To draw it well one should know it well. Too often beginners try to sketch from memory, forming masses of almost meaningless lines on their paper, trusting to chance that the result will be satisfactory. Perhaps it will, occasionally, but unless one has drawn a great deal from nature or at least from good photographs, his memory will probably play him false or lead him into the common error of drawing all foliage alike, for there are many men who have acquired the knack of indicating one or two typical forms fairly well and who use them over and over again regardless of conditions. Such repetition of course produces inexcusable monotony.

Whereas it is from such outdoor sketching and drawing from photographs as we have just mentioned that one is able to acquire most easily a knowledge of foliage representation, it is suggested that as a valuable preliminary preparation the student should study his botany, and read, also, some of the many excellent books devoted mainly to the consideration of trees. (There are plenty such, so it seems unnecessary to call attention to any particular ones here, though for a concise volume on the subject, F. Schuyler Mathews' "Field Book of American Trees and Shrubs" is excellent, especially from the draughtsman's standpoint, as it is fully illustrated with pen, crayon and color reproductions. Then there are some written entirely from the artist's standpoint, among which Rex Vicat Cole's "The Artistic Anatomy of Trees" is an excellent example, for although it is an English publication dealing mainly with trees native to England, it nevertheless offers many suggestions applicable to the representation of our own trees.) A perusal of such volumes will not only familiarize one with the names and leading characteristics of the more common varieties, and train him in the laws that govern their growth, but should, also, strengthen his love and appreciation of the beautiful in nature. It is by no means necessary to learn all the scientific terms employed by the botanist or to memorize more than a few of the essential facts, but it is advantageous to gain enough of a knowledge to enable one to answer such questions as the following,—What are "evergreen" trees? What are "deciduous" trees? Name some characteristics of the Pine family;—of the Maple family;—of the Birch;—of the Beech.

Do Elms grow in Ohio? Are Hemlocks found in Kentucky? Name five trees that are tall and pointed. Name five that are short and wide-spreading. Questions like these may seem unrelated to pencil sketching, but they really are not, for the architectural delineator may be called upon to make sketches for a building in Florida or Maine or California or in some part of the country which he has never visited, using trees of an appropriate kind and shape. Unless he acquires such a knowledge, therefore, or knows where he can easily secure the information when it is needed, he may make absurd errors.

It is, of course, especially important for the artist to be familiar with the foliage in his own vicinity, so as soon as he has gained a considerable amount of this "book" lore he is ready to visit a park or the country, sketchbook in hand, looking for actual examples to illustrate the things which he has read. Before starting to draw, it is well to take a walk among the trees, comparing one with another, observing the shape of the general mass of each, analyzing, also, its skeleton of trunk, limbs, branches and twigs. Search, meanwhile, for a suitable subject for the first sketch. This may be a whole tree, or simply some portion of one, or perhaps a pleasing group of several. In any case the view-finder will be of help in selecting an interesting composition.

At this point it may be well to offer a few practical hints, and one is that the best time of day for sketching is usually the late afternoon, for the rays of the sun are then so slanted as to produce an excellent contrast of light and shade and shadow. Needless to say, however, there is no time between dawn and dark when one cannot sketch to advantage. The student is wise to sit in the shade, if this is possible, or at least to keep the sunlight from falling directly on his paper, for a bright glare will not only prove trying to the eyes but may prevent a correct judgment of the values, especially if one is accustomed to spending the greater portion of his time indoors. In order to offset to some measure the brilliancy of the outdoor light, some artists use gray or straw-colored paper for sketching purposes, which, besides having less tendency to cause eye strain, also permits a pleasing use of white pencil or chalk for picking out some of the high lights. More will be said about such tinted paper in another chapter. As to the size of paper, anything will do, some of the pocket sketch-books being very convenient. The objection to the smaller ones is that they prohibit freedom of movement of the arm and wrist and thus force one into unnecessary difficulties. The notebook proportion of 8 in. by 10½ in., which we have previously recommended, seems practical, and some artists prefer still larger sheets. As the main object of outdoor sketching is to record facts in a direct and forceful manner, one should not use many grades of pencils, for this is no time to worry over technique. Have several pencils, however, of each selected grade for they wear down rather quickly, and be sure to carry a knife as they will need frequent pointing.

Now as soon as the subject for a sketch is selected and the materials prepared, make yourself as comfortable as circumstances permit, in order to have your attention free for the task at hand. In this connection another suggestion may prove worth mentioning and this is that a newspaper or magazine

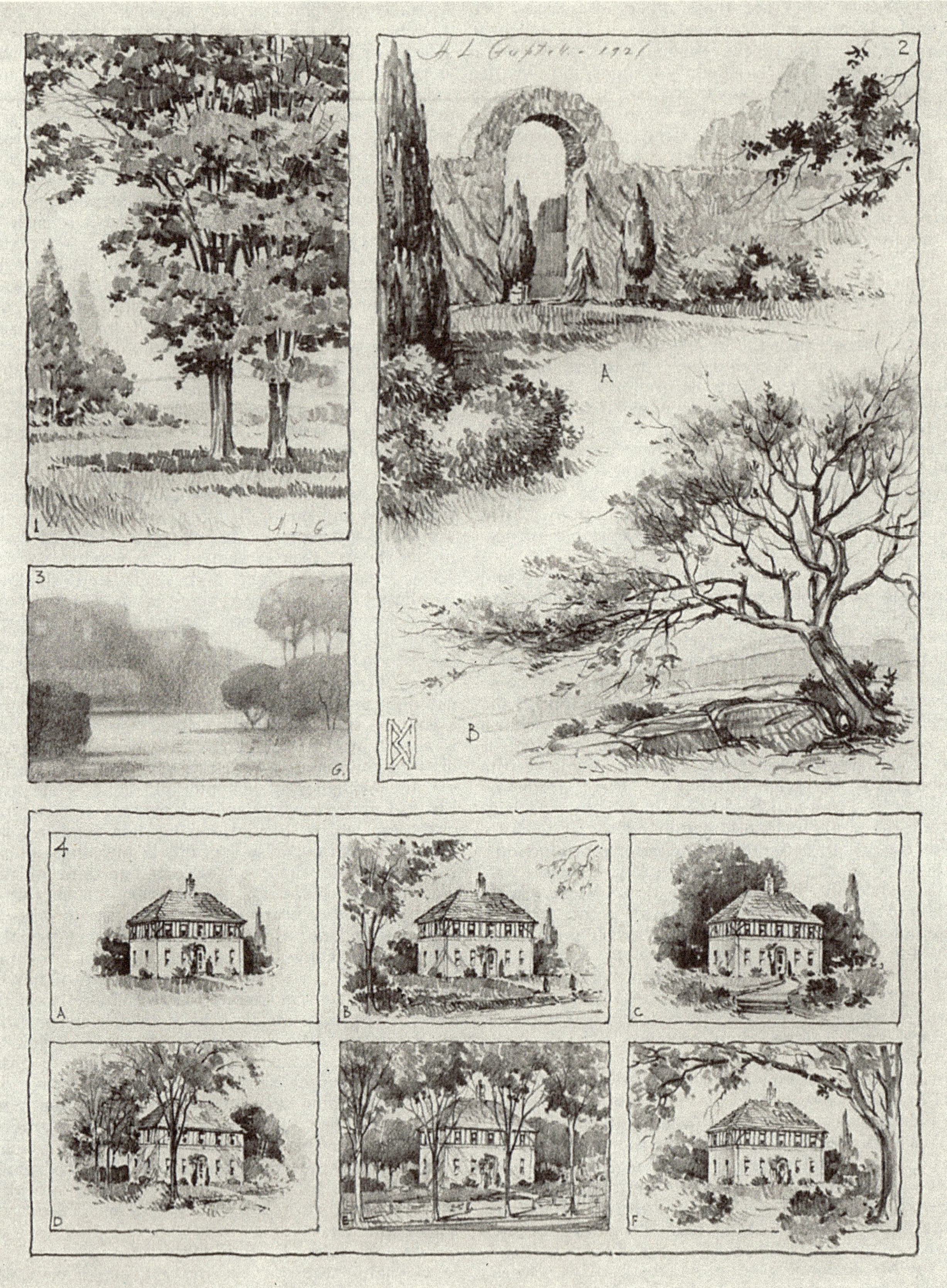

Figure 44. Additional Studies from Nature and Suggestions for the Uses of Trees in Conjunction with Architecture.

makes a fairly comfortable seat on the ground or on some stone or log or wall, if no better one is available.

When all is in readiness, proceed with your sketch, blocking in the main proportions lightly, indicating also the lines of the trunk and principal branches. Observation will prove that the contour of a tree is seldom as round as we sometimes imagine, in fact the general mass of most trees can be bounded by an outline made up largely or wholly of straight strokes. When starting a sketch remember this truth. Then, once this outline and the main subdivisions have been quite definitely established, begin the shading, considering carefully the direction of the light, studying the subject through partly closed eyes in order to eliminate the less essential values, remembering the impossibility of drawing every leaf and twig. Some foliage masses seem very sharp and clean-cut against the sky while others soften gradually into the surroundings, so it is necessary to choose the type of line best suited to the conditions at hand. This choice depends partly on the individuality of the artist and the time available but mainly on the characteristics of the foliage itself. The line which would nicely suggest the leafage of the willow might fail, for instance, to represent the individuality of the pine. The sketches at "1" at the top of Figure 42 show a number of ways of building up foliage tone, while at "5" sketches "B," "C," "D" and "E" show different methods of representing similar masses. This variety of strokes should make it plain to the student that there is no set manner of working. Consequently sketch the objects before you in what seems the most natural way, and if the results are not satisfactory try again using some other kind of strokes. The type of line employed is of less importance than are the values themselves, for if these are carefully worked out the tree will seem properly modelled to give a sense of depth and projection. Use care, too, in suggesting the roundness of the branches and trunk, noting the great difference in the tone of the bark in sunshine and in shade. The shadows cast by the various branches on one another are worthy of special attention as are also those cast by each tree on the ground and on surrounding trees or buildings, in fact, so far as architectural purposes are concerned, it is most essential to be familiar with tree shadows as they appear when falling on the walls or roofs of buildings and on the lawns and sidewalks.

Because of the many difficulties encountered when drawing entire trees it is often well to sketch first of all certain portions only, making studies somewhat similar to "2," "3" and "5A," Figure 42. After a number of these have been done it is time to attempt complete single trees such as those on Figure 43, adding a bit of the surroundings if you choose. Later try groups of two or more trees, as indicated at "1," Figure 44. This sort of work is most important, but neither should hedges and bushes and grass be neglected, so make some studies similar to "2A," Figure 44, and even some of rocks and ledges such as those at "2" and "5F," Figure 42, and "2B," Figure 44, for though these cannot be classified under the term "foliage" they can be studied to advantage at this time. It is not enough to sketch nearby trees, but those in the distance should be done as well, Sketch 3, Figure 44, showing the simplicity which is often found in far away foliage. It is sometimes advisable to draw the same tree from both near at hand and from the distance, and it is also beneficial to sketch it at different seasons of the year, for it is in the winter when the leaves are gone that the best opportunity is presented for studying the tree "skeleton." If the winter proves too cold for outdoor work several photographs might be taken to be sketched later,—the first when the limbs are bare and others in the spring, showing the leafage at various stages in its development. During all of this study and sketching try to memorize the leading characteristics, for by so doing you will build a firm foundation for future memory work. It might be well, in closing, to point out the desirability of preserving all such sketches, for no matter how incomplete or imperfect they may seem, when foliage is required in later renderings they will offer many suggestions of great value, for the only real difference between the work from nature and that done in architectural renderings is that in the case of the latter the foliage is made rather inconspicuous and is also in many cases given a more conventional handling.

At "4," Figure 44, are shown six "thumb nail" sketches of the same house done from the imagination, each with a distinctive foliage treatment. These show only a few of numerous possible schemes which could be devised by the student to meet similar conditions, but in order to successfully develop any of them at large scale the kind of knowledge gained from outdoor work would be of great help.

It is suggested that the reader study at this time the various drawings of trees which are found from place to place in this volume, and especially the masterly outdoor sketches by Mr. Hermann on pages 150, 154 and 155, which are excellent examples of studies made directly from nature.

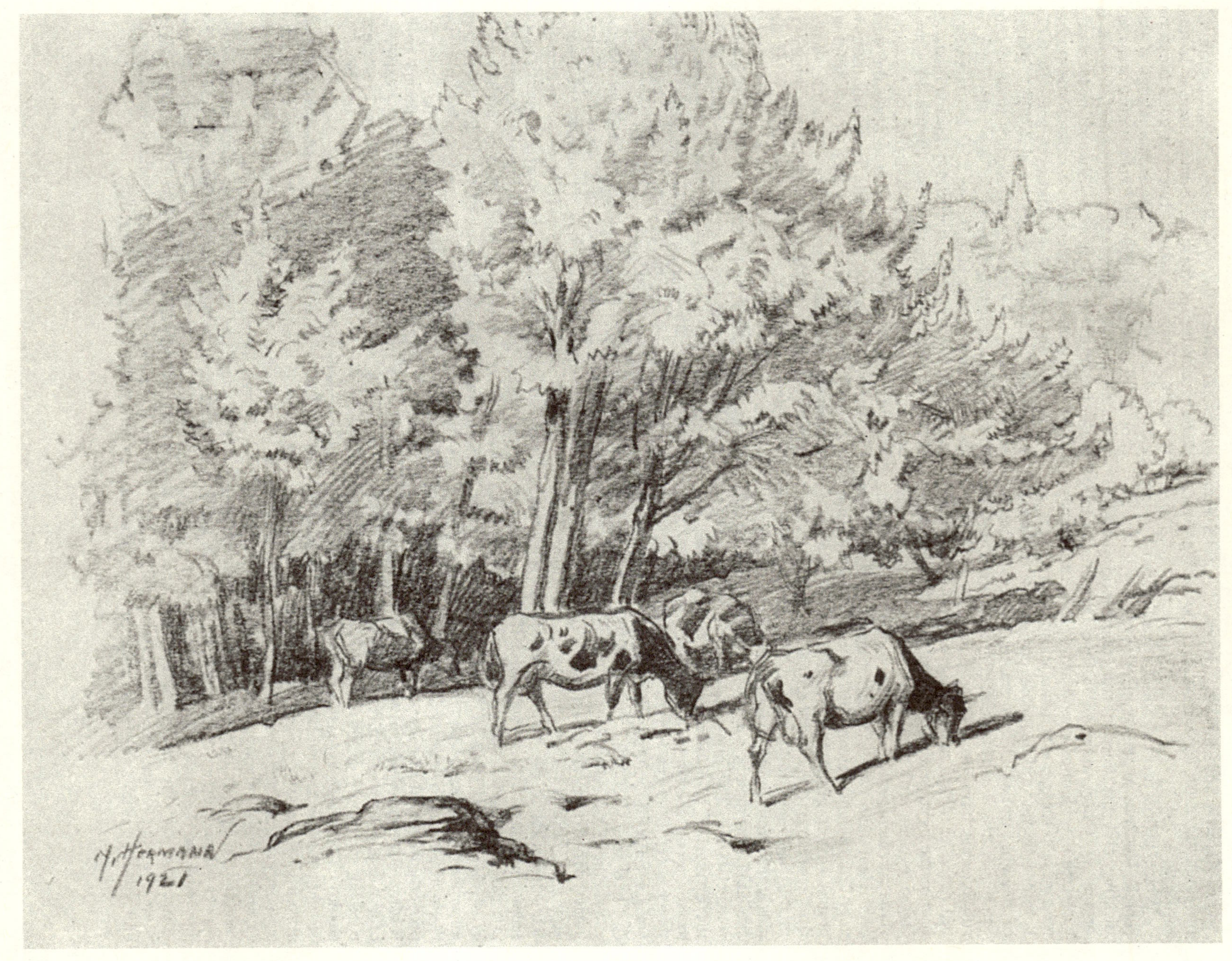

PENCIL SKETCH BY M. R. HERMANN

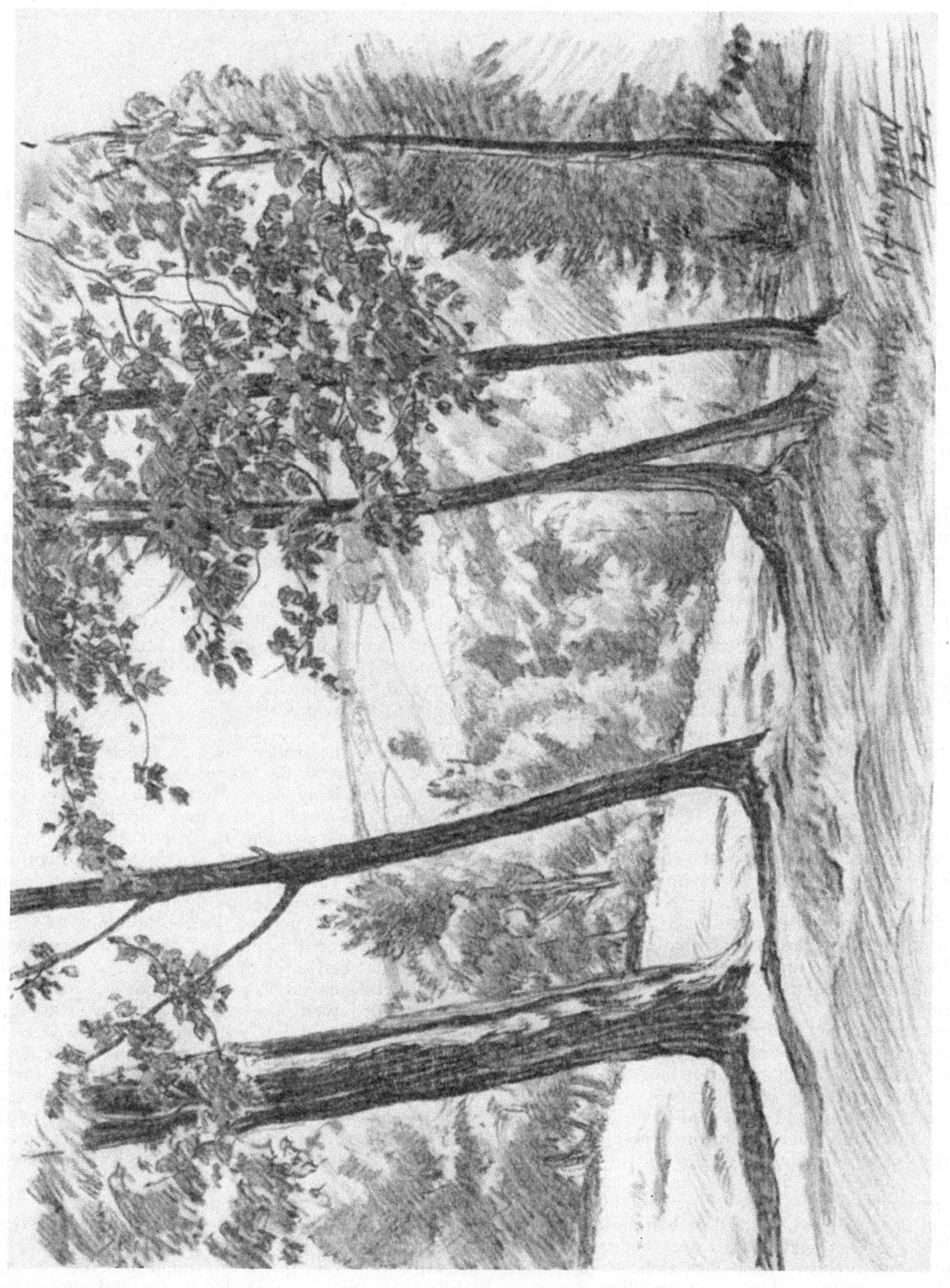

PENCIL SKETCH BY M. R. HERMANN

Chapter XI.

ACCESSORIES

IN LATER chapters we will consider the rendering of large buildings, the decorative handling of architectural subjects, and the uses of tinted paper, colored pencils, etc., but before doing so it seems advisable in this chapter and the next to round out our discussion of architectural accessories by touching upon the representation of water, skies, clouds, people and vehicles, repeating for the purpose of emphasis a few of the suggestions already given and adding such others as seem essential.

Needless to say these accessories are of sufficient importance to deserve a more exhaustive treatment than this, but the student who is interested in obtaining additional information can find many special treatises devoted entirely to these and similar subjects. There are various publications, for instance, describing the different kinds of clouds, and numerous books on figure drawing and anatomy; the recent book on figure drawing by Mr. Bridgeman, "The Human Figure" by John H. Vanderpoel, "Figure Drawing and Composition" by R. G. Hatton, as well as volumes on composition with chapters on the arrangement of groups of figures. The student is advised to consult books of this sort, and it seems hardly necessary to add that the knowledge thus acquired should be supplemented by sketching all these things directly from nature or from the object, taking a course in life drawing (if this is possible) as a means of acquiring not only an understanding of the human figure but excellent training in drawing as well.

Now let us turn to a brief consideration of the representation of water, and suppose we liken it in appearance, for a moment, to window glass.

We have mentioned in a former chapter the complicated effect of glass, but if that offers difficulties to the student, so indeed does water, in fact, the latter is even harder to draw well, for whereas the former has the two important characteristics of transparency and power to reflect images of objects, water not only has these but adds to them a new peculiarity in that its surface is constantly changing in form, being smooth one moment, rippled the next, and disturbed a little later, perhaps, into large waves. Smooth water often gives as perfect a reflection as does a mirror, yet under slightly altered conditions the images are distorted or destroyed or the surface becomes like a transparent pane of glass, the bed or bottom below being plainly visible. Again such water sometimes seems opaque and lifeless, the surface alone being visible. Such appearances and changes are due in part to three conditions: First, the depth, color and purity of the water; second, the point from which it is viewed, and lastly, the angle at which the rays of light reach its surface. Deep, pure water, for instance, is usually, if still, an almost perfect mirror, especially if we look along it rather than straight from above, but in a shallow or muddy stream or pool the reflected images are often merged or blended with the tone of the water itself and with that of the bottom showing through, distorted by refraction. If we look directly down upon water it seems far more transparent, as a rule, than when viewed in a more-nearly horizontal direction and this is true whether it is smooth or rather rough. It is true, too, that when the light rays reach the surface at some angles, reflections which otherwise exist wholly or partially disappear, and the effect of transparency is lost also, the surface becoming apparently opaque. This refers to calm water. Let the slightest breeze ruffle the surface and the complications are still greater. And each change in the force or direction of the wind causes a still different effect. These things all show the impossibility of giving definite rules as to how water should be rendered and make it plain that only personal observation and practice will bring any real proficiency in its treatment.

There are, however, a few suggestions that may be of help to the student, one of which is that the greatest care must be exercised to have the lines bounding any body of water correctly drawn, for unless this is done distortion may appear, the water seeming to slope or bend in an unnatural manner. It may be well to point out that in a large lake or sea where the farther shore is invisible because of distance the horizon line for the water will coincide with the eye level for any visible buildings. Occasionally, however, this line is "faked," up or down a bit, if a better composition can be obtained thereby. In smaller bodies the distant shore lines, unless viewed from a very high point, also appear practically horizontal. Once the outline is correct it is well to block in whatever definite reflections there may be, drawing them with the greatest care. If the water is smooth the reflection of an object will appear very much as the object itself would if suspended in an inverted position. If the water is rough the reflection will be more or less elongated and distorted, for the waves will act like a series of convex and concave mirrors, the amount of elongation depending on the size and shape of the waves. This is illustrated at "1," Figure 45, where at *A* the reflection practically duplicates the object, while at *B* the waves in the foreground show bits of reflection thus elongating the whole image. Such images are often slightly darker than the object

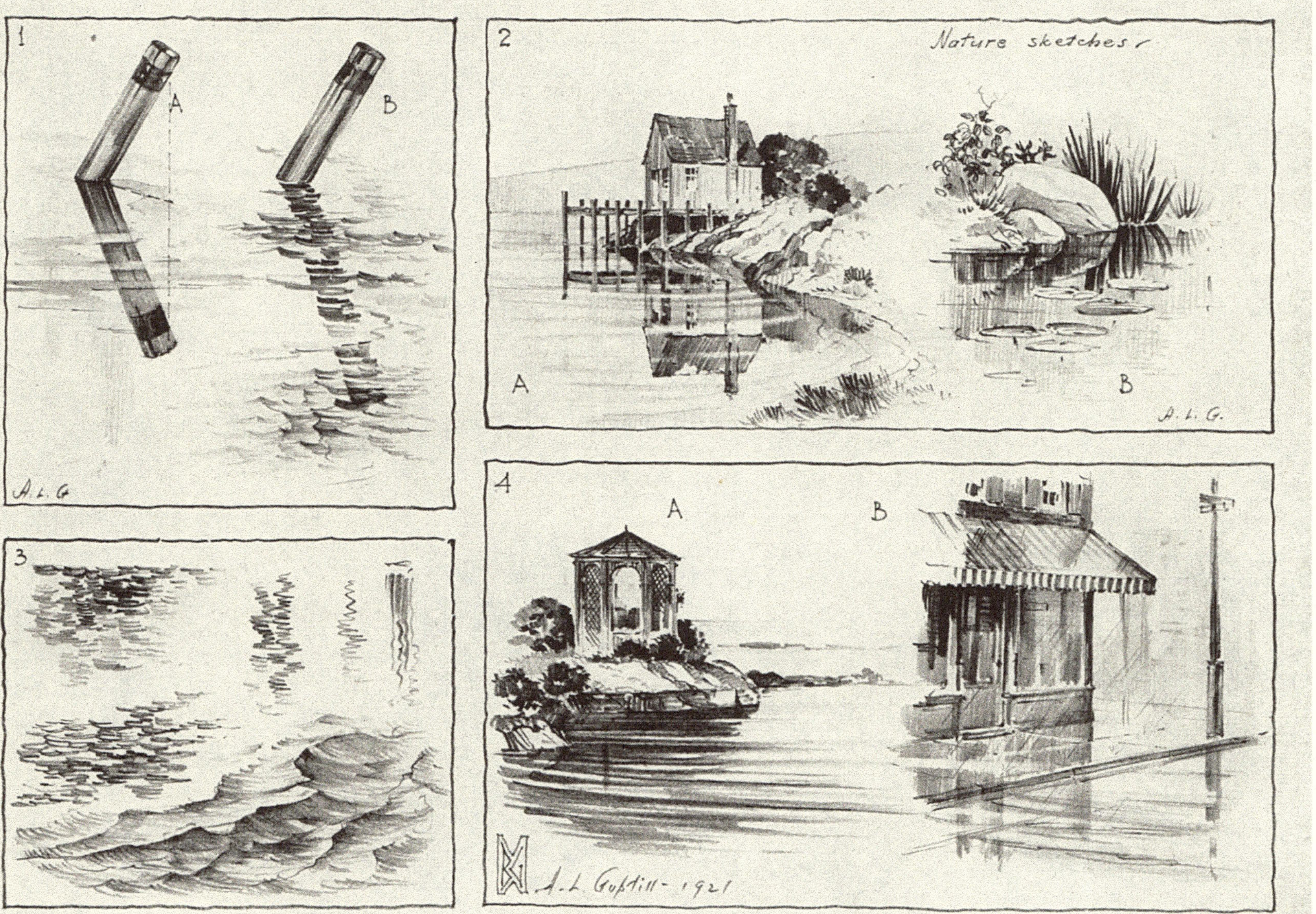

Figure 45. Some Typical Indications of Water.

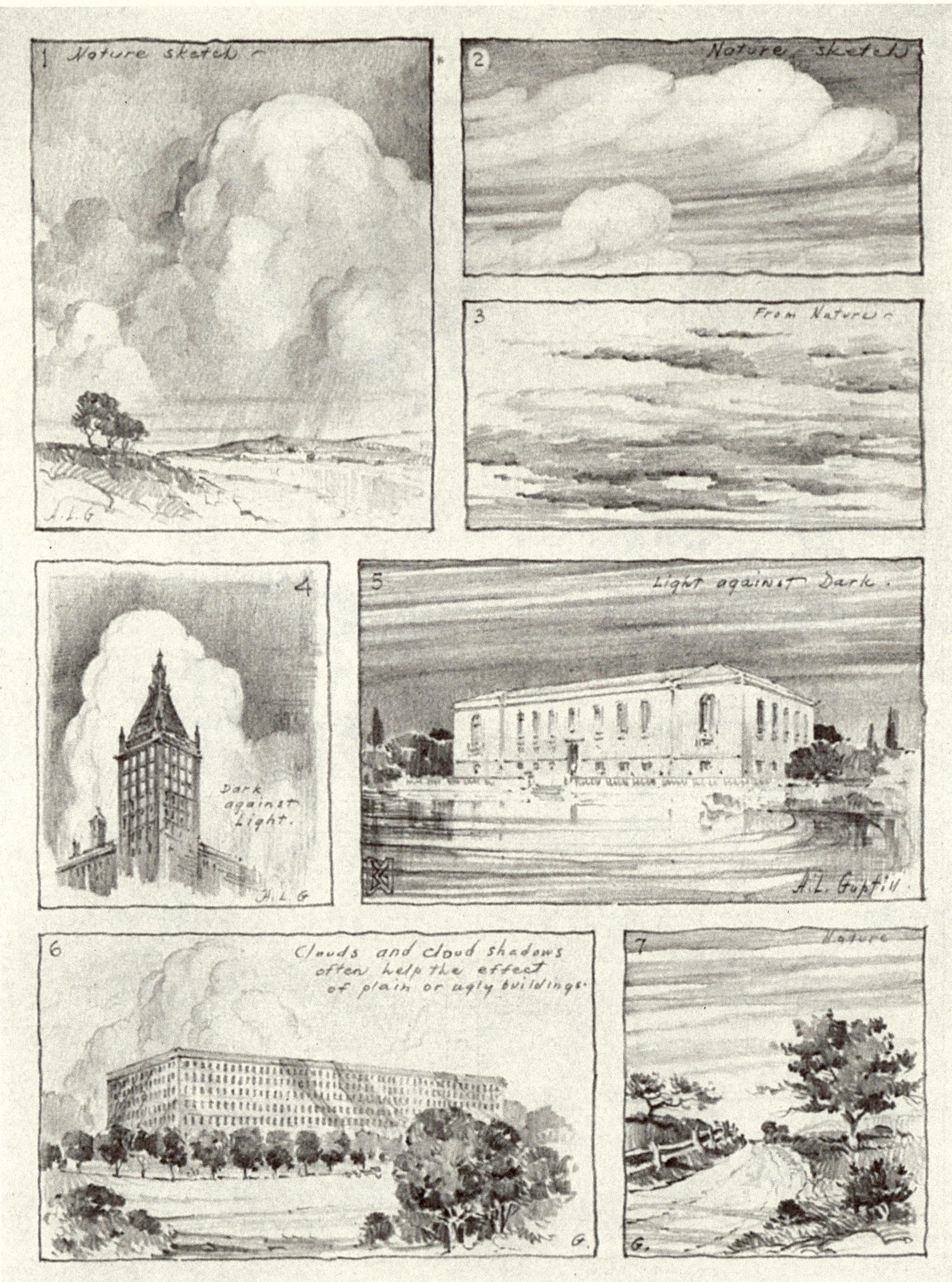

Figure 46. Clouds as Seen in Nature and as Used in Conjunction with Architecture.

reflected though the reverse is sometimes true, and they are usually quite definite near the object and more and more broken and interrupted by contrasting values as the distance from the object increases.

Another very important point is that in representing a large body of water account should be taken of the fact that nearby waves appear larger than those in the distance; consequently larger pencil strokes are often employed in their indication. Remember, too, that the distant shore is usually rather indistinct, therefore it should be shown so, with all detail subordinated.

The general tone of water often depends on its reflective power. If a sky is light, for instance, the water will be quite light also, as a rule, especially if smooth, and *vice versa,* though there are many exceptions to this.

So great is the variety in the effect of water that every sort of line is needed for its indication. Vertical strokes are often satisfactory when it is smooth, whereas those of a generally horizontal direction are sometimes better when it shows ripples or waves. The sketches in Figure 45 offer a number of suggestions for water, using different strokes. Perhaps the only one of these needing special comment is that at *B* sketch 4, showing the wet streets. This has been presented because delineators of architectural subjects sometimes show wet streets and sidewalks in their renderings, mainly for the purpose of introducing a little interest and preventing a hackneyed result, and such sketches as this offer suggestions for that kind of work. On wet sidewalks and streets as well as where water is of greater depth it is usually well to combine with the lines suggesting reflection, others, generally opposite in direction, indicating the surface itself.

Before leaving this subject it may be well to mention that shadows are often cast upon water by various objects, the dark tone having a tendency to cause the water to appear still darker; this is simply another of the many complications that make a thorough study of the whole matter essential.

Now let us give a few moments' thought to the indication of skies and clouds, which are, perhaps, as easy to handle in pencil as any of the accessories. A few suggestions on essential points should prove sufficient for it is by no means necessary to attempt more than a simple sky treatment in the average architectural drawing. It is, in fact, often possible to allow the white of the paper to remain untouched or to cover it with a uniform tone of gray or to grade it in the simplest manner from dark above to light at the horizon. The value selected usually depends on the tone of the building illustrated; when it is dark in color or has a dark roof the sky is left light, but if light it is sometimes shown against a dark sky in order to secure a satisfying contrast, as in sketch 5, Figure 46. These simple treatments are especially appropriate in renderings of formal buildings where many clouds might prove distracting. Picturesque buildings permit greater freedom, for the accessories should have a character similar to that of the building,—but even these informal structures may be left with white paper for the sky if there is foliage and the like to add interest to the whole. It is perhaps in the representation of very plain buildings with a rather monotonous setting that clouds serve the best purpose, for even though restrictions prevent the use of trees or other accessories, there is seldom an exterior drawing in which clouds cannot be employed if one wishes, and nature gives us so many kinds and arranges them in so many ways that there is always opportunity for an appropriate selection. A building of awkward proportion or displeasing contour can be so disguised by skilful sky treatment as to take on a far different aspect, and perspective distortion can likewise be hidden in many cases, or made less conspicuous, while the shadows cast by clouds can also be used to great advantage, thrown across a monotonous roof or wall surface or upon the ground. Clouds, like other accessories, should never be made too prominent, however. Some students draw the masses so round that the curves fail to harmonize with the straight lines of the architecture while others form such "wooly" strokes or such rough textures that no sense of distance is obtained, the clouds seeming nearer perhaps than the architecture itself. Each line and tone should quietly take its place. So unless a drawing is large or done with a very bold, vigorous technique, rather light but firm strokes would seem best, using a medium or hard pencil and striving for a silvery-gray line, for smoothness suggests distance. Again, as skies seem softer in effect and the individual clouds smaller in size and less definite as they recede towards the horizon, it is best, as a rule, to have the boldest strokes and the largest and most definite masses near the zenith. Storm clouds, especially those showing strongly contrasting forms and values, are seldom desirable in architectural work, and sunrise or sunset effects detract, unless skilfully handled, from the architecture itself.

In the actual representation of clouds two methods are common, one being the simple indication of the forms by outline alone; the other a naturalistic rendering of the full tone. As the former obviously requires less time it is often the more desirable one, though the choice really depends on what seems demanded by the remainder of the drawing. Avoid too mechanical an outline in any case, but work instead for a suggestion of the variety of mass and edge found in nature, giving special care to the suggestion of modelling, remembering that clouds are not the flat disks that students sometime represent them to be.

Figure 46 shows a number of sketches from nature such as the student should make for purposes of study, and several others showing sky treatments applied to architectural subjects. We should perhaps remind the reader, before going on, that clouds are possibly the one thing in nature least affected in appearance by man, for though he may destroy forests and alter shore lines, they continue to go their own way uninterrupted.

Now we turn to a consideration of the representation of what is perhaps the most difficult of all the architectural accessories, the human figure. It is not our purpose to discuss at any length the drawing of the individual figure, but rather to offer a few suggestions for the use of figures as

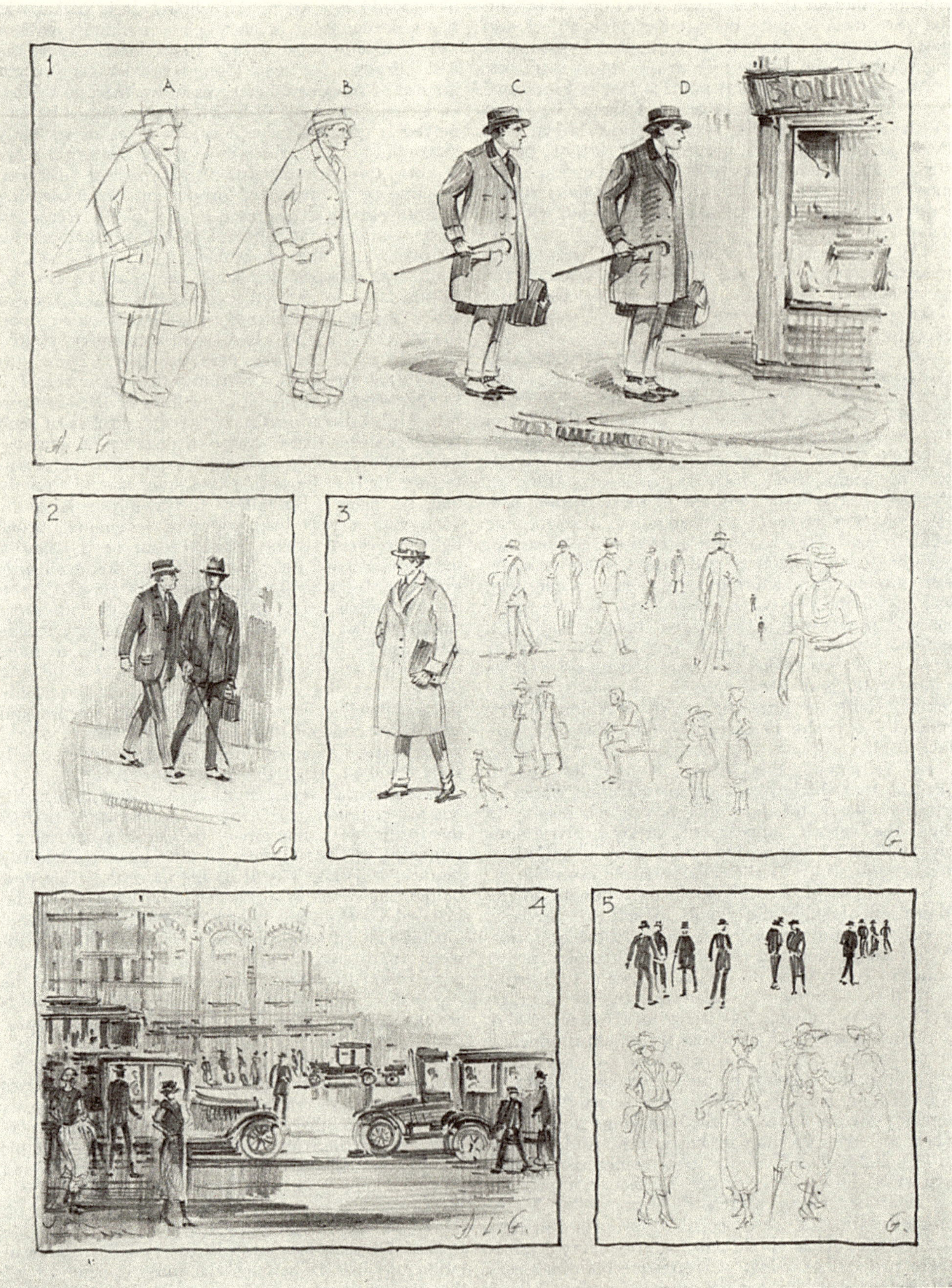

Figure 47. Illustrating Certain Principles Regarding the Representation of Figures as Accessories to Architecture.

they form a part of an architectural setting, and right at the start it is well to state that it is better to omit figures entirely than to draw them poorly. This should not be interpreted to mean that they must be indicated with photographic accuracy —in fact, it is often possible to suggest them satisfactorily in what seems a rather careless manner, omitting or subordinating the features and other detail, especially if the scale is small. It does mean, however, that the first impression gained when one looks at the drawing should be of professional excellence rather than of an amateurish attempt at something beyond one's capabilities. The figures should be correct in size, as they give scale to the architecture itself, and should be arranged in a natural disposition, so grouped that they aid, rather than injure, the unity and balance of the composition; considerable practice is necessary to enable one to do this well. There should be a pleasing variety, too, in their selection, using figures of men, women and children if many people are shown. Choose the number and type, also, that are appropriate to the location of the building. In picturing a railroad station, for instance, show people with suitcases or hand bags, also railroad porters and the like. When drawing an office building have business men, stenographers, postmen, telegraph messengers, etc., with most of the figures in action. At a summer hotel, on the other hand, we would find people dressed for bathing, boating, riding, tennis, golf, and other sports, or leisurely enjoying themselves dressed in appropriate summer clothes. Needless to say, fashions should be up-to-date in such a scene, but by all means avoid the unnatural people often found in the conventional "fashion drawings." Be especially careful not to have the figures too straight and stiff; this is a very common fault. Use care also not to make foreground figures so large or important that they dwarf the architecture or lead the eye from it. Occasionally people so near as to be exceptionally prominent are made slightly smaller than they would actually be, though such liberties should never be taken unless one has sufficient experience to enable him to do so to the best advantage, and a figure beside the building pictured should always be of correct size or a wrong impression of scale will be given. Too many figures spotted around carelessly will destroy balance, so, in composing, plan for the eye to be lead gradually from one group to another. It should not be inferred from this that all drawings demand a number of figures, for this is not true. Sketches of residences seldom need more than two or three at the most and are frequently made with none at all and a single person standing beside any building is enough to give scale and can be done in a very simple, conventional manner. Period costumes are sometimes used for such figures, a Colonial lady or gentleman being shown, for instance, at the door of a Colonial mansion.

Figure 47 shows at 1 the steps sometimes gone through in drawing a figure. At *A* the salient points have been established, at *B* the outline is completed, while *C* gives us the finished result; *D* simply adds a somewhat more sketchy indication of the same person standing before a window, and serves to remind us that the technique used for figures should harmonize with that of the rest of the drawing. At 2 is a quick suggestion of men walking, while 3 and 5 show a number of action sketches, very hastily done. Sketch 4 is a bit of street scene such as might be used as a portion of a large rendering. Perfect drawing and finish is by no means necessary in this sort of work.

Vehicles, automobiles, and similar accessories require no special instructions, as catalogues and other advertising matter give many excellent illustrations which can be adapted to the work at hand. Be sure to draw them in correct perspective in relation to the buildings, and of proper size; neither should you make the mistake of showing any vehicles drawn or parked on the wrong side of the street.

Horses, dogs and other animals require as much skill to draw as do people and unless one is confident of his ability he will do well to omit them entirely or to get assistance from someone with greater dexterity.

The reader is advised to review at this time Chapter VII, Part I, on Life Drawing, and Chapter VIII, Part I, which discusses more fully the sketching of animals.

Chapter XII.
DECORATIVE TREATMENT

WE HAVE mentioned in previous chapters that all pencil drawings are somewhat conventional in treatment, the objects being rendered more according to rule or precedent than by attempting to duplicate nature or fact. Nature shows us color, for instance, which in black-and-white drawings can be suggested only in a somewhat meager manner, and she makes no use of outline, so firmly established by convention in pencil representation. She gives us also such extreme brilliancy of sunlight that it is obviously impossible to adequately portray it on paper, so here too we resort to convention for its suggestion. There are certain conventions, then, that are forced upon us because of our inability to successfully picture some of nature's complexities, but there are many others which are entirely a matter of choice. It is within the power of the skilled artist to approximate, if he desires, the forms and the values (with the exception of the more brilliant ones) of objects in nature, but, mainly because it has been found that such drawings as most closely approach perfection in this direction are usually too photographic in effect to prove pleasing from an æsthetic standpoint, there has always been an attempt to obtain a somewhat individual interpretation rather than mere excellence of depiction. In striving for such expression, artists have developed conventional methods of their own, or have copied from their predecessors and contemporaries such ideas as have strongly appealed to them, with the result that the student now finds unlimited suggestions from which he may select those that he desires, modifying them to suit his problems and his personal tastes. Most draftsmen have a leaning towards some definite type of work;—some like the naturalistic, for instance, while there are others who take greater pleasure in employing a style which is more highly conventionalized, adding a certain decorative quality, perhaps, to all that they do;—who so compose their masses and arrange their lines that regardless of the objects represented this quality is conspicuous. Now the average architectural subject fails to lend itself readily to such treatment, as the more photographic type of work better expresses, from the client's standpoint, the character of buildings, but there are, nevertheless, some classes of drawings in which architecture is prominently shown, but where composition and technique of a decorative nature seem more essential than does a truthful delineation of the architecture itself and its surroundings, and it is this type with which we are especially concerned just now.

Rendering of this sort is used for so great a variety of purposes and is handled in so many different ways that we can hardly do more here than attempt to show its importance, pointing out to the draftsman that his knowledge of sketching and rendering will not be well rounded out until he has given this decorative style his careful consideration. (In this connection we urge him to collect and study many examples by different artists, copying such drawings or portions of drawings as make a strong appeal.)

Among the uses of such drawings may be mentioned the illustration of types of advertising matter in which drawings of buildings, or parts of buildings, are required or the making of magazine covers, the designing of title pages, or the illustration of certain classes of books and articles, such as those pertaining to the purchase or furnishing of the home (and others of similar nature)—or, again, the drawing of decorative headings, marginal sketches and tailpieces.

It should not be supposed from what is said above, that architectural perspectives of proposed buildings for submission to the client cannot be done satisfactorily in a decorative manner, for if the style is not forced the results may be very pleasing without detraction from the subject, and even the more naturalistic type of drawing can be made somewhat decorative in effect, if it seems desirable to do so, by the addition of an ornamental border or lettered inscription or something of that sort. There are many drawings, however, where the architecture is simply a part of the decoration, being sometimes entirely imaginary or perhaps distorted into forms which would be impossible to build or undesirable if built, yet which add nicely to the decorative appearance. In such work the drawing is not a means to an end (as is the average architectural rendering) but is an end in itself, and as its main purpose is frequently to catch and hold the attention, as in advertising work, prominence is therefore often given to such architectural features as are considered quaint and picturesque. Thatched and tiled roofs are popular, for example; as are huge chimneys, windows with shutters of unusual design, flower boxes, lattices, garden gateways, etc.,—birdhouses, weathervanes and sundials, rainwater leaders and leader-heads, door knockers, ornamental hinges, and so on.

It is not only in the selection of these details, however, but it is in their arrangement as well that the picturesque is sought, for the spacing of the windows and doors—in fact all those parts,—often depends more on what looks interesting and attractive than on what would be practical. The search

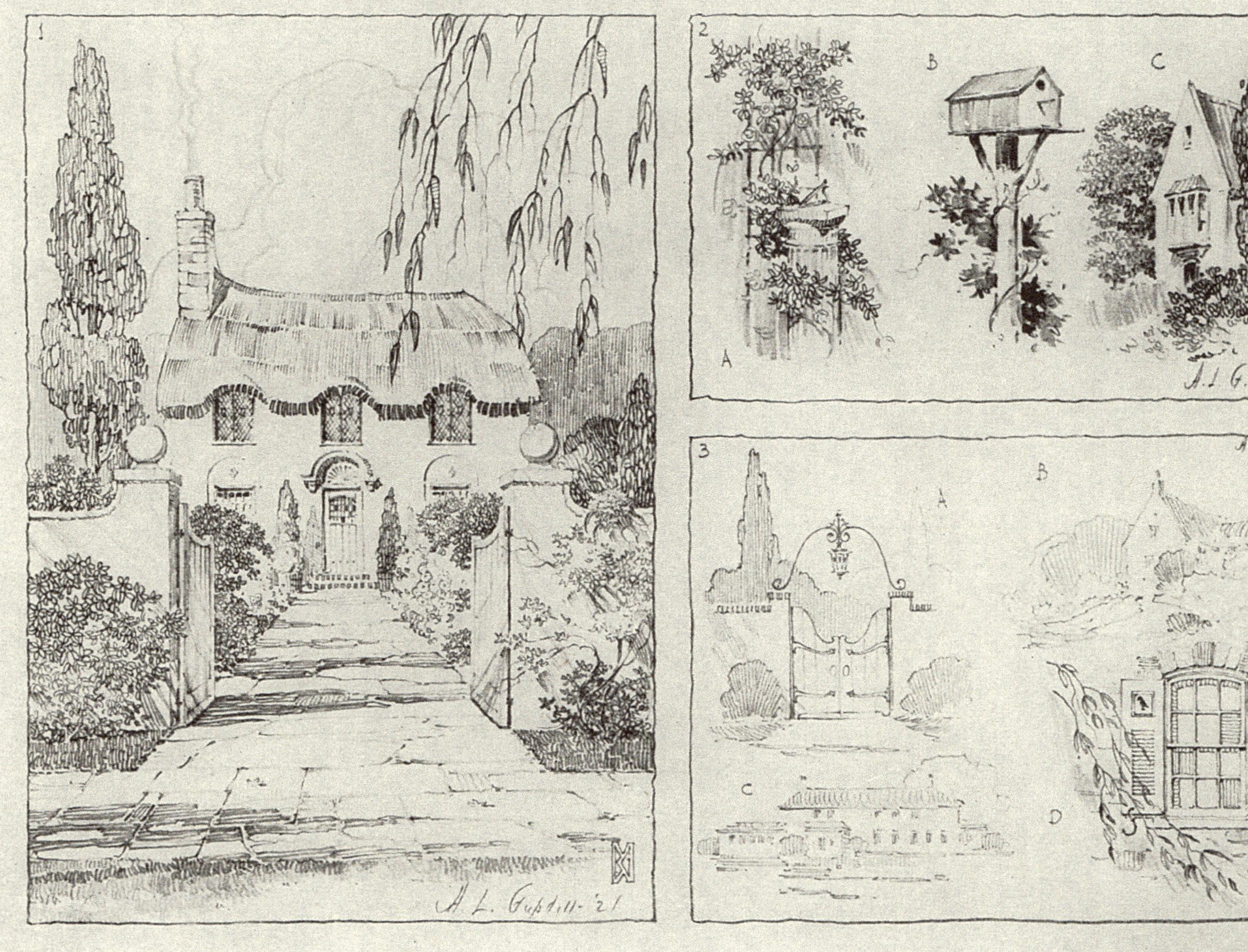

Figure 48. *A Somewhat Decorative Handling of Architecture and Its Accessories.*

for the picturesque is not confined to the architecture, for trees and shrubs of all sorts are utilized, distorted into any shape and arranged in any way that pleases the fancy of the artist. Flowers of unheard-of species grow in curiously fashioned pots or are grouped in beds of fanciful design while clouds are piled in the sky in a manner wholly without precedent in nature. The technique is as varied, too, as the selection, all sorts and kinds of lines being used in every possible way. One should not gain the impression from all this, however, that these things are jumbled together in a haphazard manner, for quite the opposite is true,—the greatest pains being usually taken that the completed whole shall be a beautiful and interesting design, rendered in an attractive manner, and although in much of this work the imagination is given free play, it is by no means permitted to run riot.

Many of these decorative renderings are done in pen-and-ink or wash or some medium other than pencil, but as in nearly every case careful pencil preparation is required, regardless of the medium used for completing the final drawing, the subject seems to fall within our scope. In fact the importance of such preparation cannot be over emphasized. When a decorative sketch is desired the customary method of proceedure is the same as we have explained for other pencil work, for once the artist has conceived his scheme a number of rough sketches are generally made first of all at small scale, from which the best is selected for further study, following which larger scale sketches are drawn, frequently on tracing paper and one over the other, changes and corrections being performed as the work progresses. When the design meets the requirements and satisfies the artist it is transferred to the final paper and completed. The number of studies made from start to finish depends on the skill of the artist and on the kind and size and importance of the problem.

At "1," Figure 48, is a "fine line" pencil sketch of a decorative nature, and yet the naturalistic effect is not in this case wholly lost;—in fact one can gain a clear conception of the building and its environment in spite of the decorative character of the rendering. At "2" and "3" are several other suggestions, showing a somewhat similar treatment of smaller subjects, and in these, too, architecture of a practical nature has been indicated.

Not infrequently artists make decorative sketches just as a pastime, either combining existing elements, or fragments of some definite style, into a decorative arrangement or composing fanciful designs entirely from the imagination. In such projects no limitations of any sort are present unless the designer wishes to impose them upon himself, so he is able to forget the many handicaps that ordinarily restrict him in every direction and find an opportunity to lose himself for the moment in these creations of his imagination.

Uses of Color—Mention pencil sketching or rendering to the average individual and he immediately conjures up in his mind a visualization of the making of the customary type of drawing such as we find in common use, done on white paper, as a rule, and with ordinary graphite pencils. This is only natural, for a large majority of sketches are done with these mediums and in this way, and it is because of the frequency with which they are found that so much has been written in previous chapters referring especially to this everyday sort of representation.

There is, however, another class of work which comes within the scope of our subject yet which differs in many respects from the type just mentioned, and which, in so differing, offers so many opportunities for variety, both in the selection of materials and in the technique employed, that it finds special favor among those who prefer to break away from the commonplace and exercise their abilities in a less restricted field,—one which offers, in fact, unlimited opportunities for individual expression. For it is our present purpose to describe briefly some of the uses of papers of various tints and shades; to touch upon the employment of wax crayons, lithographic pencils and the like; to point out also a few of the advantages of colored pencils, and most important of all, perhaps, to describe some of the many successful combinations of two or more media, such as pencil tinted with water color, water color touched up with pencil, and colored crayon accented with brown ink.

A glance at the appended list (on page 170 concluding this text) which shows some of these combinations, will emphasize the futility of even attempting an adequate exposition of our subject within a single chapter, but if the student desires to acquire a more complete knowledge of some of these inexhaustible possibilities for obtaining effective results, let him study such examples as he finds available, and then take his own tinted papers and his pencils and colors and work out for himself such ideas as make the strongest appeal to him.

First of all it is well to learn what the market affords in the way of materials for such work, for too many artists are ignorant of the numerous kinds of pencils and crayons and papers and the like that have been prepared to serve him. So multitudinous are these offerings, in fact, and so varied, that to recommend any particular ones here might handicap rather than help, for it is best for each student to experiment with all these things himself. As an instance of the wealth of drawing materials at our disposal, inquiry of any large dealer in artist's supplies for black pencils and crayons alone will bring out many sorts, each having its individual characteristics and uses. Some give a shiny and some a dull tint or tone,—some are easily erased while others smear and smudge when rubbed or are practically indelible. There are those which offer resistance to water, too, and others so soluble as to blur or wash off under its application. Then again, the extreme softness of some prevents a firm line while in others brittleness makes a sharp point impossible. Now just as these pencils vary, so also do the numerous colored ones, hence considerable testing is necessary if one desires to ascertain their possibilities and limitations, but once such a knowledge is obtained and along with

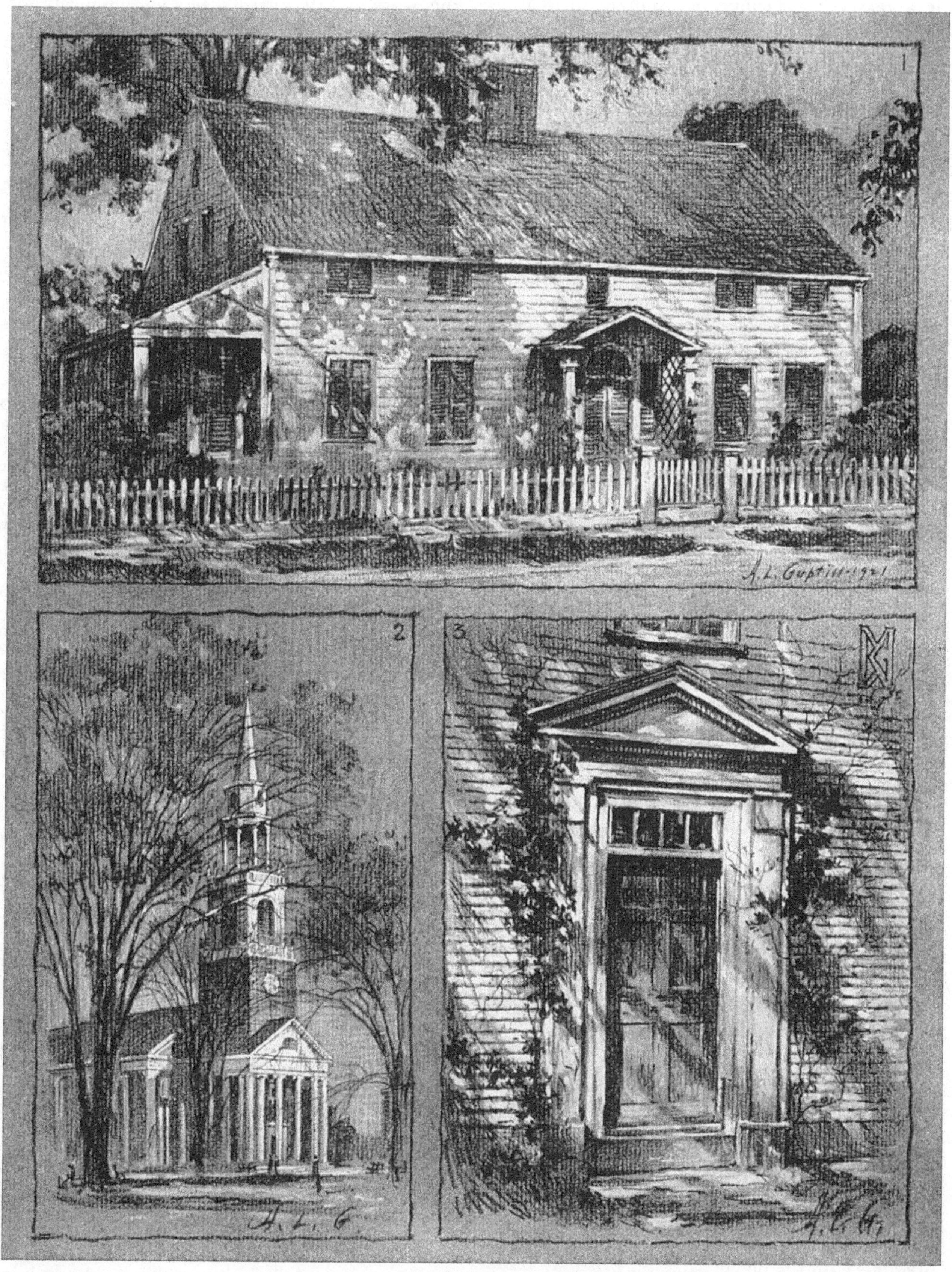

Figure 49. Some Sketches Done with Black and White Pencils on Dark Green Paper, the Highlights Being Sharpened with Chinese White Applied with a Brush.

it a reasonable facility in handling, it will be realized that notwithstanding these differences each kind of pencil or crayon, whether black or white or colored, is capable of serving a useful purpose. It is not only in pencils and crayons that we find a wide diversity, however, for papers are multifarious also, and in addition to the numerous kinds, both white and colored, especially prepared for artists, wrapping paper, cover papers, mat stock and the like are used, even wall paper of some sorts occasionally finding favor. The beginner increases his difficulties, however, if he selects papers which do not permit of considerable erasure. In this connection attention is directed to the fact that erasers have individual characteristics, also, and some which prove satisfactory on certain papers, or for erasing some grades of pencils or crayons, are useless with others, so here again personal experimentation is desirable, seeking all the time for ideal combinations of pencil, paper and eraser.

Now in order that the student who is accustomed to working in the usual manner on white paper may become acquainted gradually with these materials and methods which are new to him, it is suggested that as a first step the same pencils and technique be employed as for this familiar type of drawing, but with some tinted paper such as cream or buff or light gray substituted for the customary white. This brings in little that is different yet the effect gained is often very interesting, and if one cares to go a bit further and the subject seems to suggest it, a few touches of high light may be added with a white pencil or crayon or with Chinese white or some similar water color. Do not forget, however, that water color causes thin paper to wrinkle and buckle out of shape unless mounted, and injures or destroys the gloss of glazed paper, though there is a difference in the appearance of various white pigments when dry, some being flat or dull and others shiny.

As the ordinary pencil line has more or less gloss, some artists prefer, especially when using pencils in connection with other mediums, to employ such kinds as give a dull effect. It is advisable, then, for the student to become familiar with these, so as soon as fairly satisfactory results have been obtained with the usual pencils on the tinted paper, it might be well, before attempting any of the more difficult combinations, to try out, first on white and later on tinted paper, the various black pencils and crayons, making, perhaps, on each sheet of paper used several comparative sketches, for by so doing one can most easily learn the adaptability of each particular pencil to the paper and to the subject represented. Then when numerous experiments have been made with the black pencils on various papers try colored pencils. As their use leads to new difficulties it is best for the beginner to confine his attempts to one or two colors, using a red or brown tone, for example, making an entire drawing with the one pencil. Surprisingly pleasing results are frequently obtained in this manner, the effect being somewhat similar to that of the red chalk drawings often made by the old masters. Whereas white paper may be used for this work, lightly tinted sheets will do nicely too, offering again the opportunity for added highlights if they are felt to be desirable. Though charming sketches are found in which pencils or crayons of many colors have been employed, the beginner should bear in mind that unless he has had training in color harmony or has an excellent innate color sense, the difficulties of combining the various hues will be far from negligible, especially if the paper is not white. For this reason it might be better for him to first turn his attention to some of the more simple combinations of mediums, such as pencil and a wash of monotone. Some of his old drawings might be utilized to advantage in this connection, treating them in different ways. Take one of these, for instance, and run a light wash of yellow ochre or Naples yellow or some other simple tint uniformly over the whole thing, bringing the wash to an even edge a quarter of an inch or so outside the margin line all around. The effect will resemble to some extent that obtained by using paper of a similar tint, with the one exception that the pigment will have a tendency to soften the lines of the pencil, removing more or less of the gloss, and so "fixing" the lines that they will smudge less easily than before. Another scheme is to apply a wash of gray of a tone somewhat like that of the pencil lines themselves to such portions of the drawing as need to be toned down or pulled together. A sky may be grayed, for instance, in order to increase the contrast of a building against it, or a lawn may be simplified by passing a wash from one end to the other, and not only are such results often very pleasing but time can frequently be saved by thus combining the wash work with the pencil, as it is much quicker as a rule to cover a surface with the brush than with the smaller point. Pencils can be used very often in drawing fine detail and the brush then taken up for the larger work, or if this larger work has been done with the pencil but the values seem too light or complicated they may be toned to the desired depth or satisfactorily simplified by wash. For such work ivory black, lamp black, neutral tint, sepia, india ink or any such pigments will do or a gray can be mixed by combining two or more neutralizing colors.

Now just as tints of monotone can be used in connection with pencil work so can tints of several hues, in fact the author has found that a great demand exists among the architects for such renderings, as they afford an opportunity for a suggestion of the colors of the building materials and the surroundings, thus adding greater interest and value. As a rule a drawing to be so tinted is completed in the usual manner in pencil and then very transparent washes of the desired hues are flowed over the various parts. When using this method there are several points worth remembering, and one is that the color should be applied in very light tints rather than in more nearly its full intensity, for the result should count primarily as pencil work, with the tints of secondary importance, and much of the charm is lost if the colors do become so conspicuous as to compete with the pencilling for supremacy. If such prominent color is desired it is

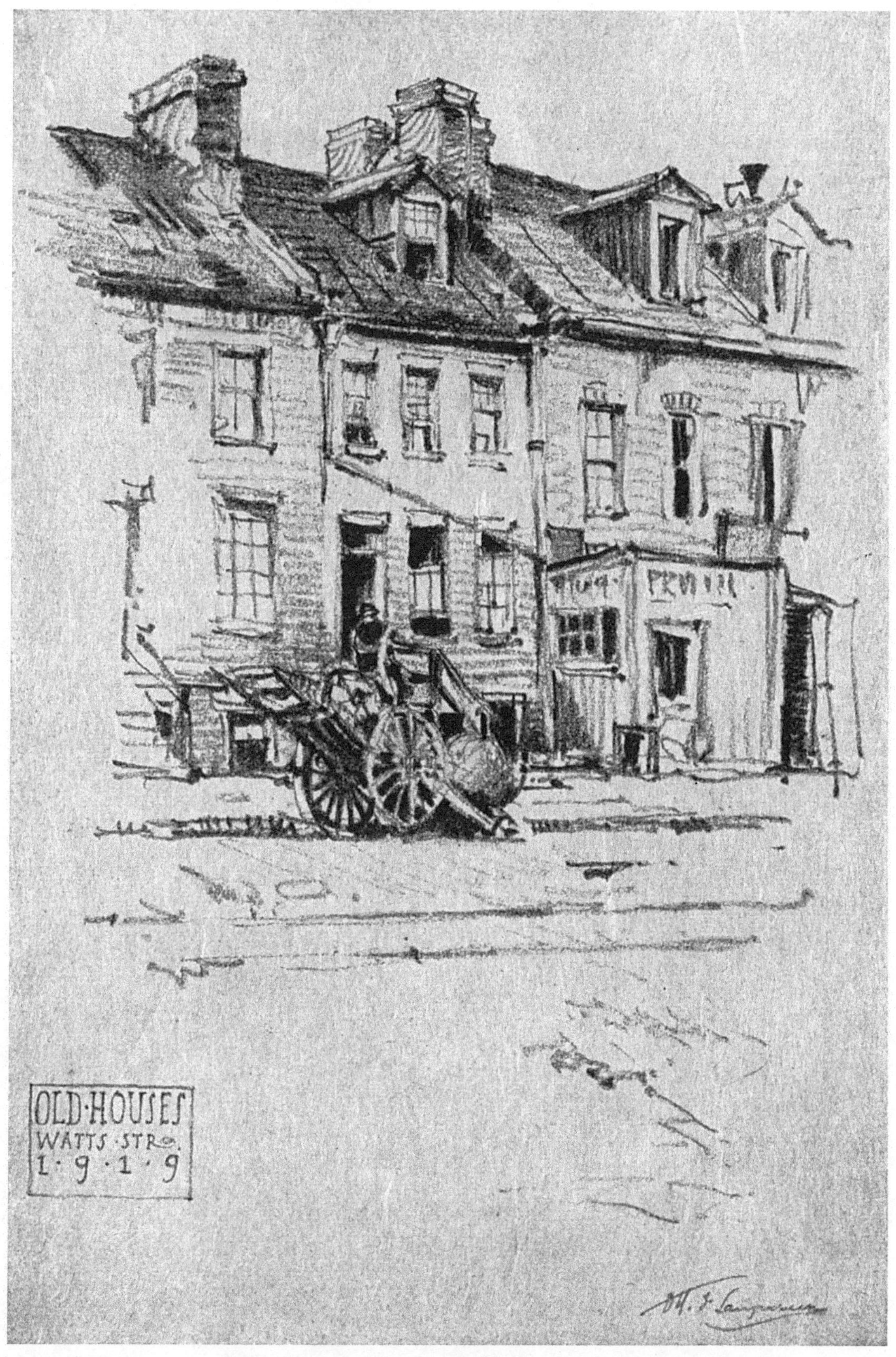

PENCIL SKETCH BY OTTO F. LANGMANN, OLD HOUSES, WATTS STREET, NEW YORK CITY

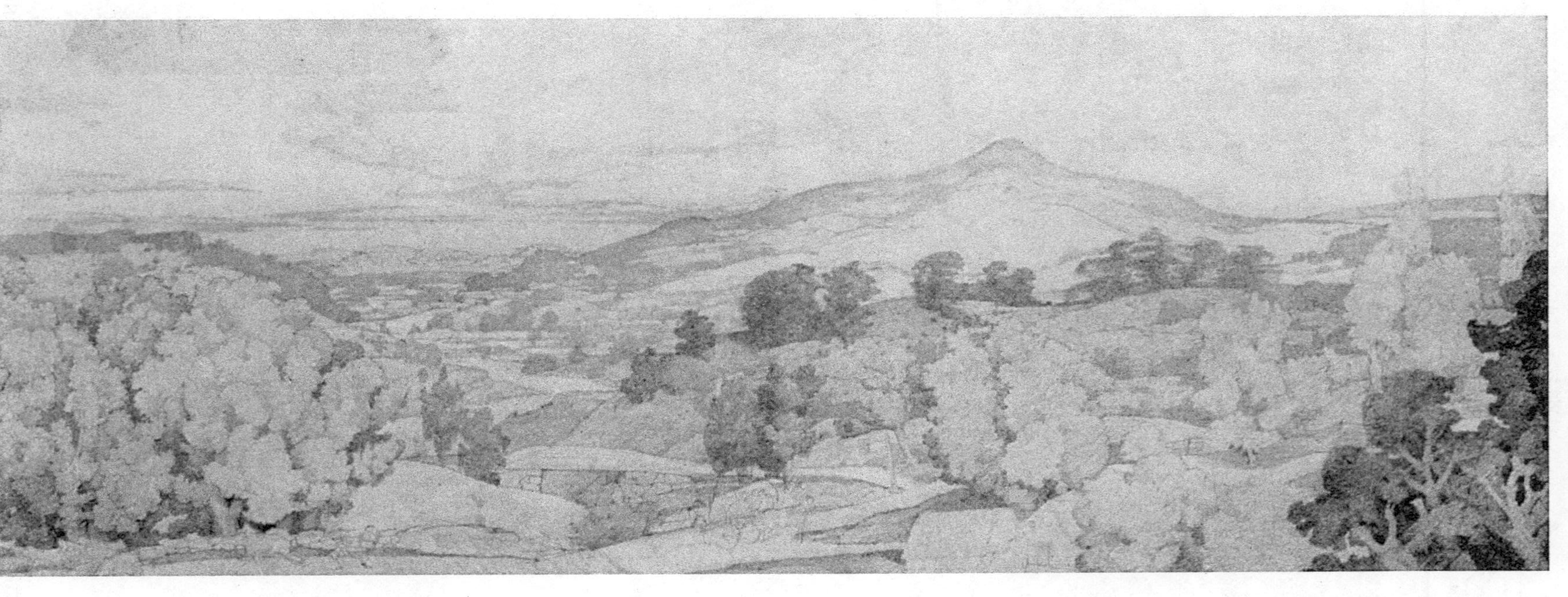

PENCIL STUDY FOR A MURAL PAINTING BY BARRY FAULKNER

better to make the usual sort of water color drawing and be done with it, so subordinating the pencilling that it becomes in itself almost negligible, serving simply as a guide for the color work. Another point is that when tints are to be used, whether of monochrome or varied colors, it is well to first flow one or two washes of clear water over the entire paper, for this will remove the shine of the pencil to a large extent, thus insuring greater harmony between the pencil strokes and brush work, and will at the same time act as a cleansing agent removing superfluous pencil dust and preparing the paper surface for the subsequent tints. Again, as some tints are quite transparent and others rather opaque, a careful choice should be made, the transparent ones being generally considered best for this sort of work. As the chief objection made to tinted pencil drawings is that the shiny lines and dull washes have dissimilar characteristics, it is better, when it is known in advance that washes are to be applied, to select one of the special pencils that gives a dull instead of a glossy line, thus avoiding any unpleasantness from this source. As some pencils such as the lithographic ones offer little resistance to water, however, they are hardly suitable for such work, so if a new kind of pencil is used, tests should be made beforehand to make sure the line will stand washing.

This brings us to another method of combining pencil and color, one which is perhaps less commonly used but which offers at the same time opportunity for excellent results, especially in the making of quick sketches. In this method the object pictured is outlined in pencil in the usual way and washes of water color are added, much as would be done in making the regular sort of water-color sketch. When the general tones have been thus obtained, a pencil which will give a dull line is selected and used for adding accents and finishing touches:—usually this is black but sometimes one or more colored pencils prove more effective. These need not, of course, be proof against water as they are not employed until the surface is dry. The two delightful sketches of interiors by Mr. Otto R. Eggers, on pages 142 and 143, Chapter IX, Part II, were touched up with lithographic pencil after the washes were applied, thus illustrating the method just described. A similar method offers a means of improving such portions of water-color renderings as become muddy, losing their crispness and directness, for under such conditions a few touches or accents of colored pencil or crayon or pastel often do much towards overcoming the difficulties and securing the desired effect. There are, in fact, numerous ways of combining water color and colored pencils pleasingly, washes being sometimes applied over the pencil work, in contrast to the method just mentioned. Occasionally ink lines are added to these others, in fact very effective results can be obtained on tinted paper by sketching in the forms with brown ink, next adding a few washes of color, finally touching up the whole with crisp strokes of black or colored pencils.

Colored pencils alone produce pleasing results also, especially if used on tinted paper or board, and a very satisfactory combination is gray or buff board, brown ink, one or two colored pencils and a white pencil or Chinese white.

So numerous are the possibilities of thus employing several mediums in one sketch that we cannot hope to describe them all here,—in fact, words fail to convey an adequate impression of such subtleties of tone and color, so we must leave the student to perform his own experiments and arrive at his own results. Before closing, though, just another word regarding papers and some of the mediums best suited to special surfaces.

The kid-finish bristol board such as we have previously recommended for pencil work takes light tints nicely and does not warp badly if the entire surface of the sheet is first wet with water. If it should buckle out of shape in spite of this precaution it may be thoroughly dampened after the rendering is entirely completed, and put to press for a few hours between two drawing boards held together with weights. Thin drawing papers are best if mounted before the washes are applied. Then even if they do wrinkle somewhat as they are dampened, they will dry back into shape. Some grades of tracing paper are excellent for wash work if floated or stretched beforehand, or if used without stretching they permit of interesting results of another kind, for if quite thin, colored pencils may be effectively used on the back of the paper, just as is frequently done in preparing house plans, thus permitting the color to show through, or delicate tones of pastel may be rubbed on the front, accented with as many pencil lines as seem necessary. Another useful fact is that regardless of how white in appearance tracing paper may seem to be, Chinese white will always stand out against it distinctly, hence it is useful for highlights. One of the most effective kinds of quick sketches is made by first outlining the masses with brown ink on tracing paper, next pencilling the darker tones in black or such a color as conditions seem to demand, finally adding Chinese white on the lighter portions. Brown ink is recommended for such purposes rather than black as the lines seem less hard and mechanical and harmonize because of their color with the other mediums, and at the same time better represent the hues of such materials as brick, tile, timber work, etc., which are often of a color similar to that of the ink itself.

The illustrations accompanying this chapter show some of the combinations here described but it should be understood that in the processes of reproduction the effect of the originals is somewhat changed, this being especially true of the tints of the papers on which the drawings are made. The three sketches on Figure 49 were all done by the same method on a charcoal paper of a greenish gray hue. This paper was allowed to represent the middle values while the dark tones were made with a black pencil which was purchased as one of a set of colored pencils. The white was done for the most part with pencil, too, being added gradually as the work progressed, but as it proved difficult to keep the point sufficiently sharp for the finer detail some finishing touches of Chinese white were done with a brush, especially in the drawing of the church. The size of the original sheet is 9¾"x13½". Figure 50, below, was drawn on a light gray mat board, being first laid out instrumentally from the plan at a scale of $\frac{3}{16}$" to the foot, then rubbed down with an eraser and rendered with a black pencil giving a dull line. Two washes of water were next applied, brushed well into the pencilled portions each time, as the lines had a tendency to resist or shed the water. Then washes of ivory black were added to the roof, shutters, foliage, etc., and to the shadow tones, after which Chinese white was applied sparingly for the high lights. The white should always be the last thing used in such a case, as it is almost impossible to pass any washes over it without causing messy results. This whole sketch was very quickly done as it measures only 7½"x10½". The charming sketch by Mr. Otto F. Langmann on page 167, presenting a bit of old New York, was drawn in lithographic pencil on a thin, ivory-tinted Japanese paper of fibrous texture. The drawing by Barry Faulkner on page 168 is reproduced from one of his pencil studies for a series of mural paintings forming a continuous landscape around the dining room of the city residence of Mr. Richard Henry Dana, Jr.

The list below is given to show at a glance some of the uses of pencil and some of the most effective combinations of various mediums as used in conjunction with it, and though it is by no means complete it may suggest to the student some ideas for his own experiments.

1. Black pencils or crayons of various sorts on white papers.
2. Black pencils or crayons with washes of gray added.
3. Black pencils or crayons with washes of color added.
4. Black pencils or crayons on tinted papers.
5. Black pencils or crayons on tinted papers with highlights added.
6. Black pencils or crayons on tinted papers with washes of gray, with or without highlights.
7. Same as "6" but with washes of color.
8. Colored pencils or crayons on white or tinted paper.
9. Same as "8" combined with wash or color.
10. Combinations of black, white and colored pencils or crayons on white or tinted paper.
11. Same as "10" with wash or color added.
12. Combinations of pencils with ink or with ink and wash or color on white or tinted paper.

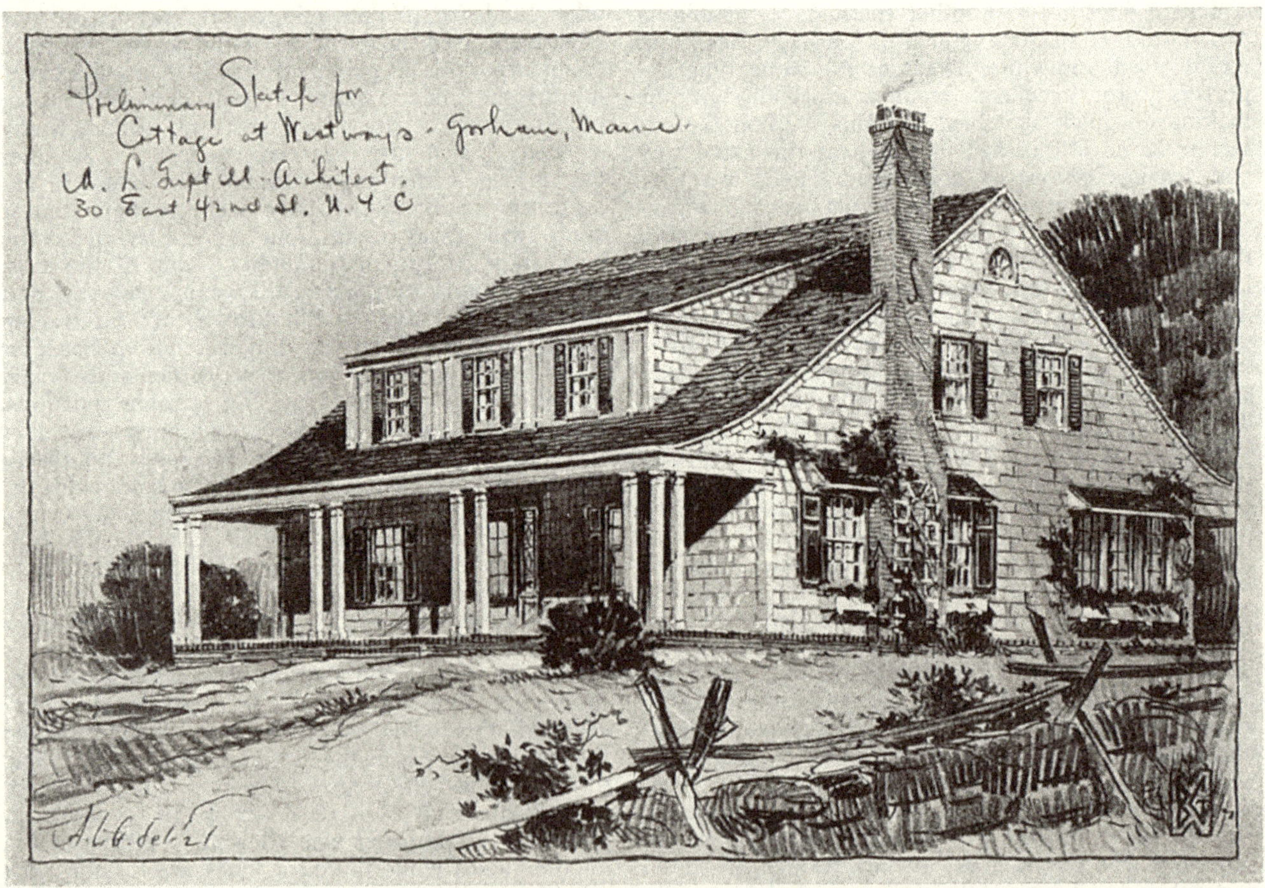

Figure 50. A Sketch on Colored Paper, Done in Pencil and Wash, with Chinese White Sparingly Used.

Chapter XIII.

LARGE BUILDINGS

IN THE preceding chapters the greater part of our space has been devoted to describing methods of sketching or rendering the small type of building such as the average student or draftsman usually desires to draw, so although much that has been contained in them relates also to such larger subjects as office buildings, hotels, theatres, churches and the like, it seems wise to offer some suggestions which apply especially to their handling, supplementing these with a few additional facts not yet discussed in this volume applicable to the treatment of both small and large structures.

When a proposed building of such magnitude as a hotel or court house or railway station is to be represented in perspective there are many architects and clients who prefer to see it done in water color or wash, or, if the drawing is to be reproduced, pen-and-ink is popular because of the ease of getting a good reproduction at comparatively low cost. Pencil, then, is perhaps less in demand as a medium for large subjects than it is for smaller ones, but there is, nevertheless, enough call for it to make its study essential. It should be borne in mind also that the pencil plays a most important part in laying out subjects to be rendered in water color, pen and ink and other mediums,—in fact it is difficult indeed to make an excellent color rendering unless the instrumental pencilling has been very carefully prepared, and it is quite an art to do this well, for certain profiles, lines of division between light and shade, etc., are often best if accented or strengthened, while subordination is necessary in some other parts. When such a layout is complete and before the color is applied, free-hand pencil lines are often added to indicate the brick courses, etc., a texture being thus obtained which could not be gained with the brush alone. Even for a pen drawing where the pencil layout simply serves as a guide for the ink lines it must be prepared with care, though no great attention need be given to the neatness of the draftsmanship as the lines will be erased or obliterated as the pen work progresses.

It is not this pencil preparation for rendering in other mediums which especially interests us at this time, however, but rather the free hand completion of a pencil rendering after the instrumental layout has been made. Just a word first, though, regarding this layout. To begin with, it is of course necessary to select such a paper or board as is known to be satisfactory for the free-hand pencil work,—then in drawing the instrumental lines it is best to use a hard enough pencil to permit later cleaning of the paper with a soft eraser without entirely effacing them, a 2H or 3H answering very well for such a purpose, the choice depending, of course, on the nature of the paper, too hard a pencil or too much pressure forming such deep grooves as to mar the perfection of the finished work or especially those parts of it which are to remain the tone of the paper itself, whereas too soft a pencil will leave hardly enough of a guide to be easily followed after the paper is cleaned. This layout, although it must be accurate, need not be quite so carefully drawn or at least so fully completed as would be necessary for wash or color work, unless, as is sometimes the case, part of the lines are to be left in the finished rendering,—then, of course, extreme care is essential.

Once the layout has been completed it is advisable for the student to make, just as for smaller work, a preliminary study or two, as a means of deciding the values and working out a pleasing composition of the surroundings,—in fact because of the amount of time and labor involved in making a large rendering such preliminaries are even more essential than for smaller problems, and an hour or two spent making them will usually result not only in the saving of several hours in the end but at the same time in better work. (It seems hard, however, to impress this fact on students, who therefore waste much time trying to render without any definite plan in mind). Such studies are usually made on tracing paper directly over the layout and the best selected and saved as a guide for completing the drawing. On work of such magnitude a diminishing glass is often of help in making both the layout and the final as it is possible by its use to reduce the whole to a size easily seen without shifting the eye. Setting the drawing away at a distance of several feet will accomplish the same result.

If the preliminary sketch is well done it will be possible for the student in starting the finished rendering to begin at the top of the sheet and work down, completing the drawing as he goes, with the exception of a few final touches which will probably be necessary at the last moment. In order to do this successfully, however, the preliminary must be carefully worked out, special care being taken to see that there is a center of interest for the entire composition and that unity and balance are obtained, for it is generally true that the larger and more complicated the subject the more likely the student is to be led into overaccenting relatively unimportant parts. As

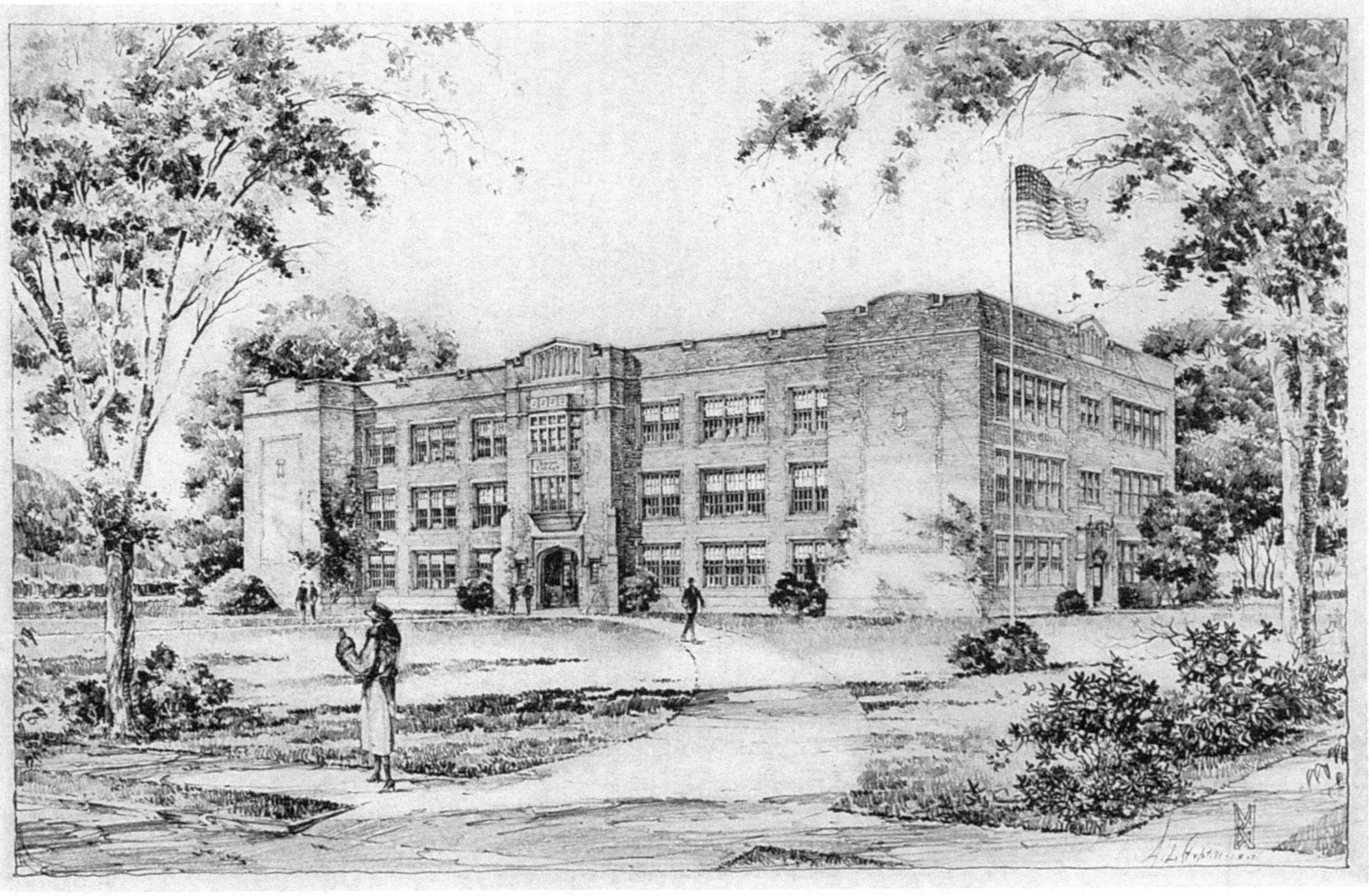

Figure 51. Pencil Rendering of Proposed Building for Harper College, Wichita, Kansas. Edward Forsblom, Architect.

soon as this sketch is completed and "fixed" for preservation the rendering of the final is started, pencils of several grades being prepared beforehand as described in a previous article. Beginning at the top, then, and working as a rule from left to right, a strip an inch or two in height can be completed at one time,—for instance if a balustrade forms the crowning feature of a building this and the cornice beneath might be finished first,—next the upper story,—then the story below and so on down until the street is reached, adding the surroundings as the rest progresses or completing them after the building itself is finished. Finally it may be necessary to go back to touch up here and there, as has just been mentioned above, adding a bit of tone in one place, lifting a little in another, until the results are satisfactory. Some teachers and artists would doubtless criticise this method as not being conducive to the best results but it at least offers the great advantage of reducing the difficulty of keeping the drawing crisp and clean, which means much to the architect, who takes little pleasure in smeared or soiled drawings. Perhaps a more logical method, however, would be to render at the center of interest first as has been mentioned in a former discussion of smaller problems, gradually carrying the work towards the edges, thus building up the entire drawing as a unit, going back over the different parts as often as may prove necessary, to change them or correct them. Whatever method is followed, however, perseverance is the one thing most needed. There seem to be many draftsmen willing to attempt to render comparatively small subjects and who succeed with them nicely yet who shun such buildings as we are considering here, though mere size seldom brings difficulties greater than are found in work of less magnitude, and so should not cause one to refrain from attempting to represent them,—in fact small residences with their irregular plans, sloping roofs, numerous chimneys and the like, to say nothing of their variety of building materials, are often far more difficult in proportion to their size than are the bigger structures. Again, the smaller the building as a general rule the larger the scale at which it is drawn, simple residences being sometimes done, for instance, at a scale of 3/8" or 1/2" to the foot and seldom at less than 1/4", whereas larger buildings are more often 1/8" or 3/32", thus reducing such details as windows to a size too small to require much labor. Of course the greater mass of a big building does make necessary the expenditure of more time and patience than are usually demanded by one which is small, because of the mere effort needed to cover the extensive area of paper, and some such complicated subjects as Gothic cathedrals doubtless call for more skill as well. It is usually lack of persistency rather than lack of skill, however, that causes the failures among attempted renderings of large subjects, though it is nevertheless true, paradoxical though it may seem, that those renderings which are completed by students or draftsmen attempting large subjects for the first time, often show as their greatest fault overstudy rather than lack of study and too much detail rather than too little. Too often every window is indicated with painful precision, while not a brick or stone course is slighted or omitted. Though such conscientiousness about the detail is frequently found, too little attention is given as a rule to the study of the effect as a whole,—it is for this reason that we are laying such stress on the importance of the preliminary study.

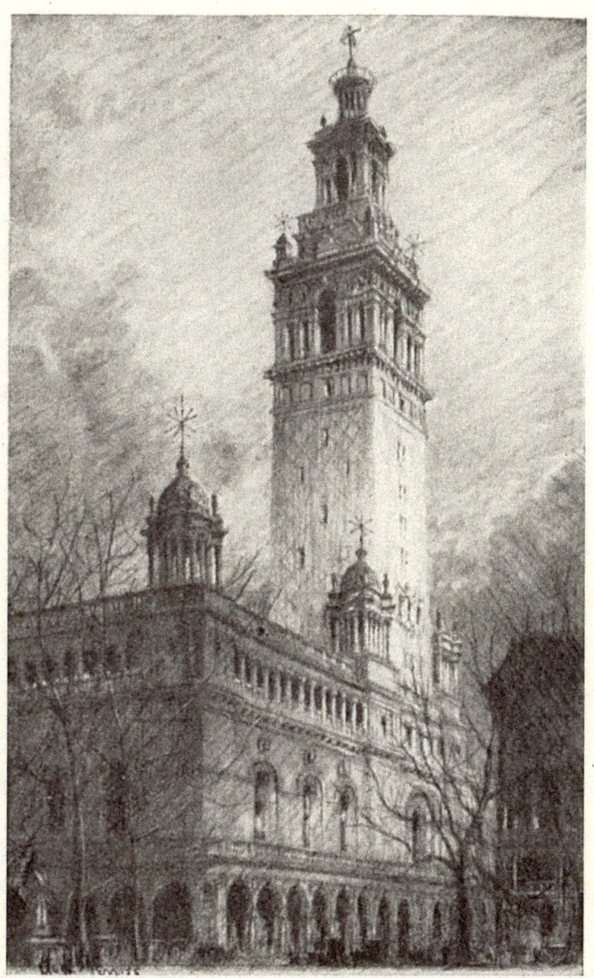

Sketch by Hugh Ferriss. Madison Square Garden, New York. McKim, Mead & White, Architects.

The amount of time spent on a drawing should depend largely on its purpose, a few hours answering for some problems while several days or even a week may be required for others. It should be remembered that most renderings are drawn for a practical reason,—to show the architect or client how a building will look when completed. The drawing has, therefore, a limited and a somewhat temporary value. Naturally, then, the person paying for it can seldom afford a larger amount than the drawing is expected to be worth to him, and this will depend on its purpose. As we have previously explained, some renderings are simply studies to

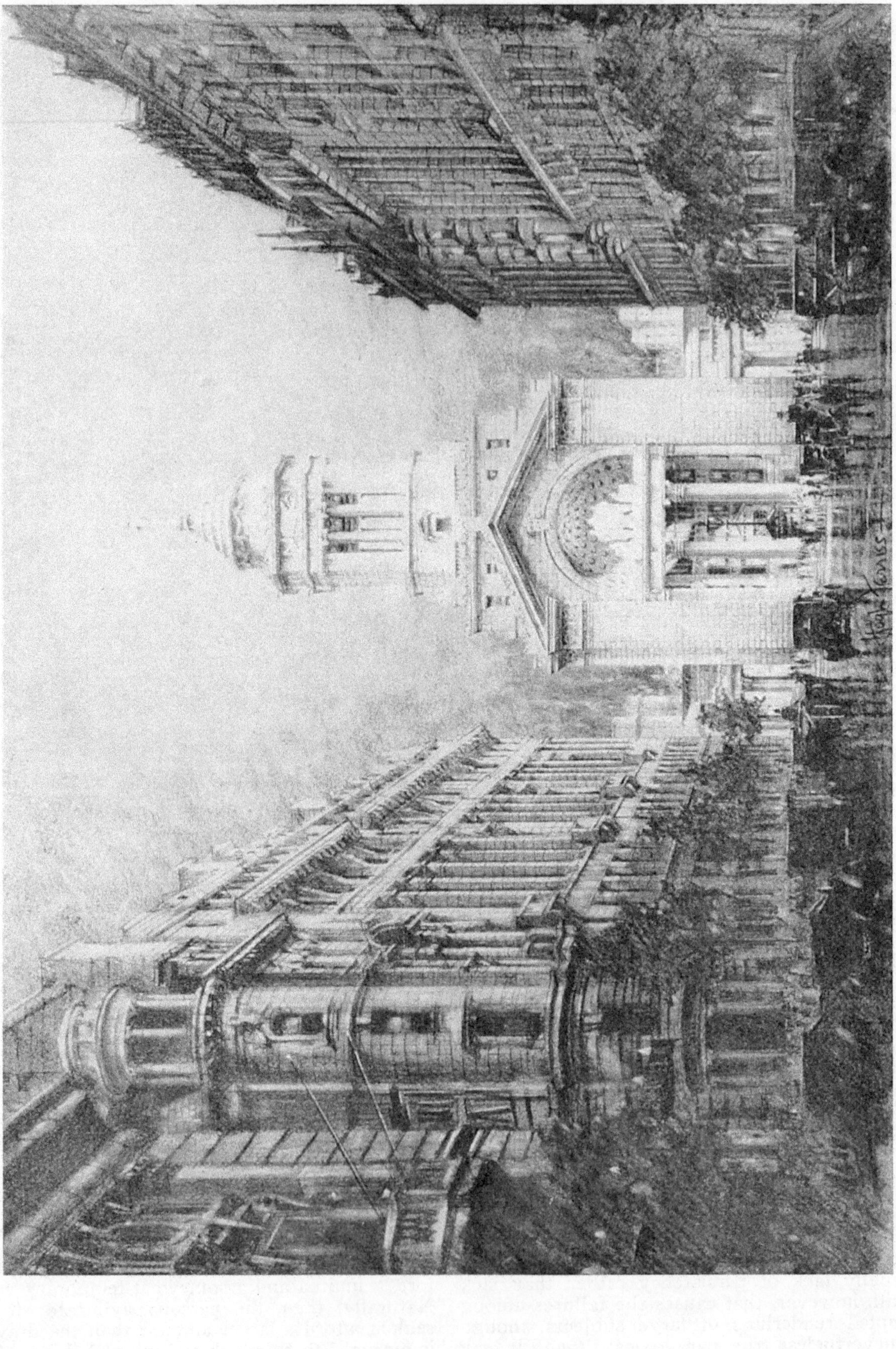

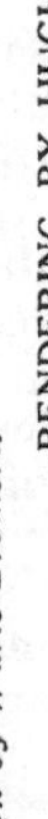

Photograph by Wurts Brothers.

RENDERING BY HUGH FERRISS. BUSH HOUSE, LONDON, ENGLAND. HELMLE & CORBETT. ARCHITECTS

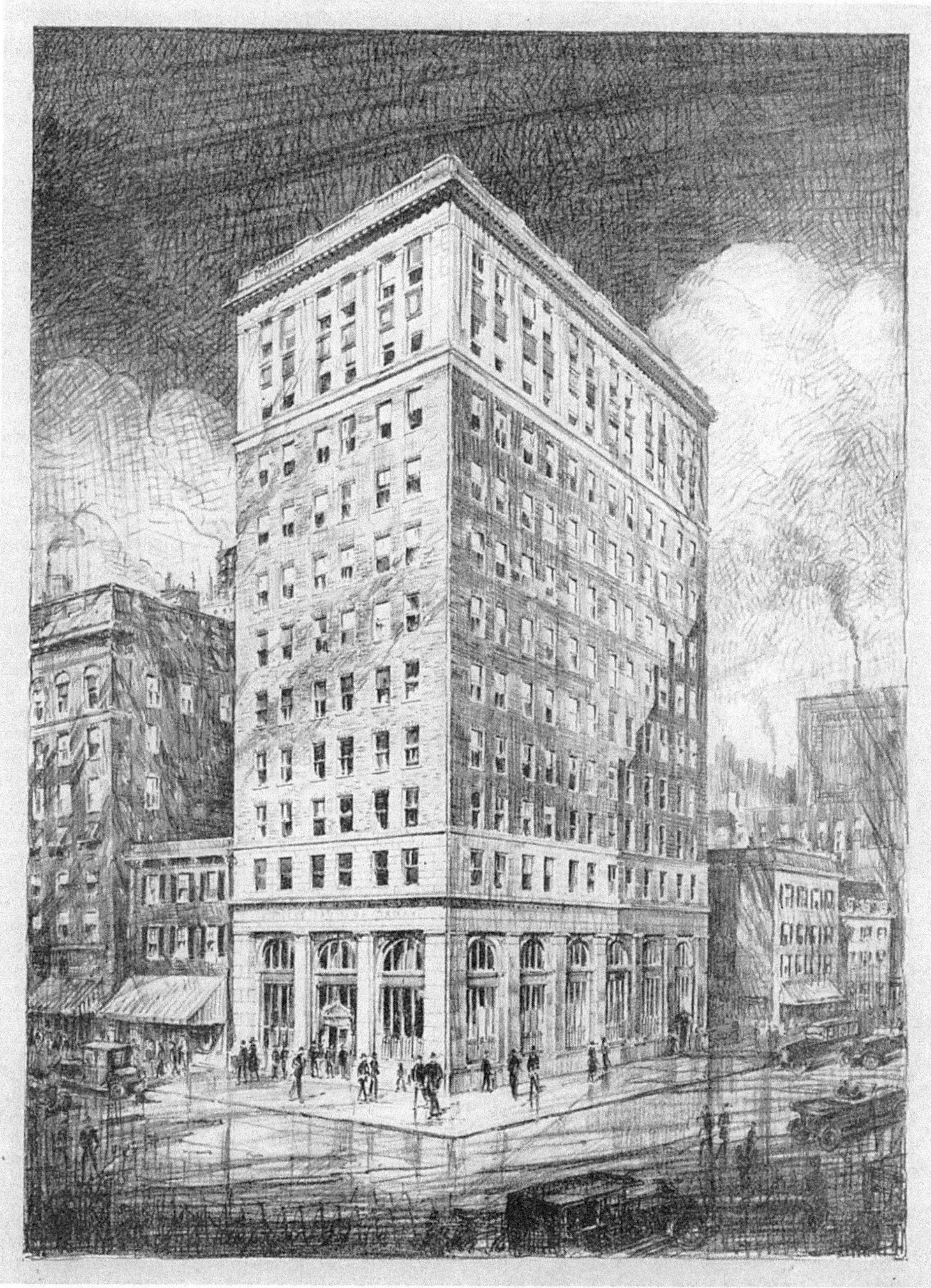

Figure 52. A Quick Sketch Done in Lithographic Pencil on Tracing Paper as a Preliminary Study.

help the architect to visualize his design,—more, perhaps, are to make its appearance clear to the client. Others are submitted to banks as an aid in obtaining loans for building purposes, while some, again, are drawn for publicity or advertising uses, perhaps reproduced in circulars or magazines, the original being exhibited, possibly, in a show window or other conspicuous place. It is evident, then, that the delineator must, as in smaller work, prepare the kind of drawing demanded by his particular problem,—if a rough, quick sketch will answer as well as any other that is the kind to make by all means. It is necessary, therefore, to ascertain all the requirements right at the start. The architect himself is often at fault in not giving the delineator sufficiently plain directions, forgetting that a project which is clear in his own mind is not equally so in the minds of others. Or he will ask, perhaps, for a rough, sketchy drawing, "just a few hours work," and then on seeing it either completed or partially drawn will object emphatically and vociferously to the inaccuracies of incompleteness of this or that small detail. The architect should endeavor to make plain beforehand just what is needed, and the artist should try equally hard in turn to successfully fill the requirements,

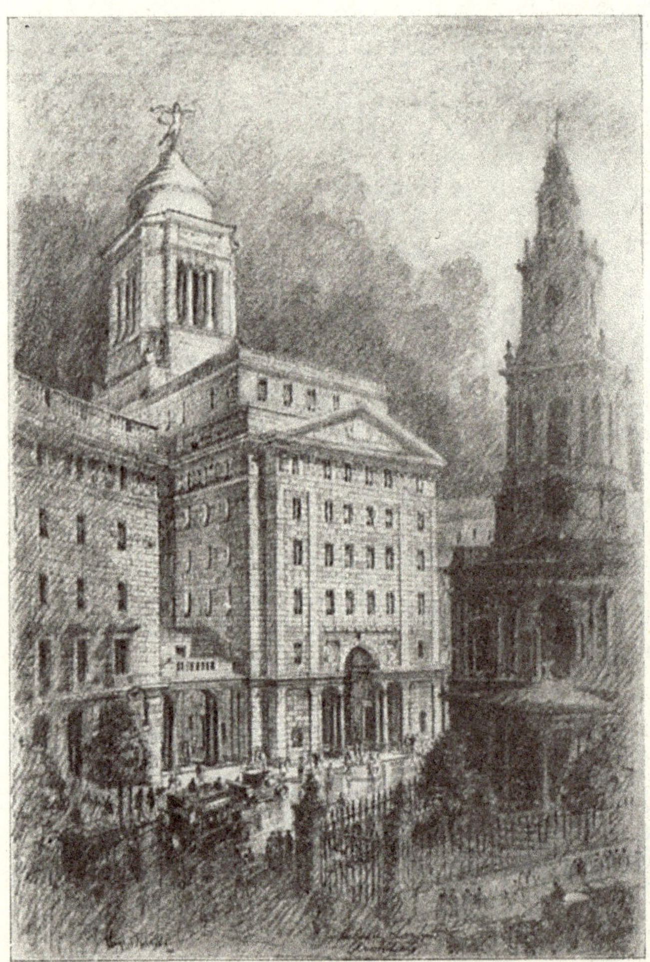

Rendering by Hugh Ferriss. Bush House, London, England. Helmle & Corbett, Architects.

remembering that the architect is the one who is paying for the job. In order to do this it may be necessary for him to be familiar with several kinds of technique, for sometimes very bold drawings will be demanded, strong in contrasts and vigorous in treatment, while again preference will be shown for a more delicate type with the detail more accurately handled. Drawings of the bold type are often on rather rough paper while the others are more frequently done on a smoother surface. There are architects, however, who while they wish the general effect of a rendering to be rather bold, at the same time desire greater accuracy, even in the smaller parts, than can be obtained easily on a rough textured paper. This demand has caused the introduction of a rather interesting trick, the building itself being laid out first of all in the usual way instrumentally on a good quality tracing paper and rendered quite carefully and completely with the desired attention given to the smaller details, nothing being done to the surroundings, however, at this stage. Before they are rendered the tracing paper is loosened from the board and a rather rough sheet of cardboard or paper or even of cloth is put beneath the drawing and the rendering of the entourage then done, the pencil lines on the tracing paper taking an impression of the rough surface below. Then the building itself can be touched up a bit, enough to bring it into harmony with the surroundings, and the tracing mounted on a stiff board, which, if rather rough, will add to the effect desired. This same idea can of course be utilized in the making of drawings of less pretentious subjects, as can another trick which it may be worth while to mention, though it is more frequently used in connection with color work. This trick is borrowed from the printers and consists in running finished renderings, usually done on a fairly smooth paper, through heavy machines containing rollers which are designed to press patterns onto the paper, such surfaces as eggshell, linen, crash, canvas, moire, etc., being obtainable. These surfaces may seem a bit artificial but the idea is handed on for what it is worth. Perhaps it is well as a word of caution to mention that this process often makes the paper slightly smaller, destroying the accuracy of the dimensions.

Then there is one more addition to our list of tricks, this idea having been stumbled upon quite by chance by the author, though the same thing has perhaps been done many times by others. As the muntins and meeting rails of windows, as well as other similar architectural members, are usually left white on small scale pencil drawings, considerable labor is sometimes involved in so darkening the glass or adjacent members as to leave them sharp and clean cut. It has been found that if a pencil drawing is being done on a fairly thick board, such as the illustration boards in common use, it is possible to rule these small members with a clean ruling pen or dull knife point or anything of that nature, pressing a groove into the surface for each white line desired, using care of course that the instrument employed is perfectly clean and that the lines start and stop at just the right points. Then

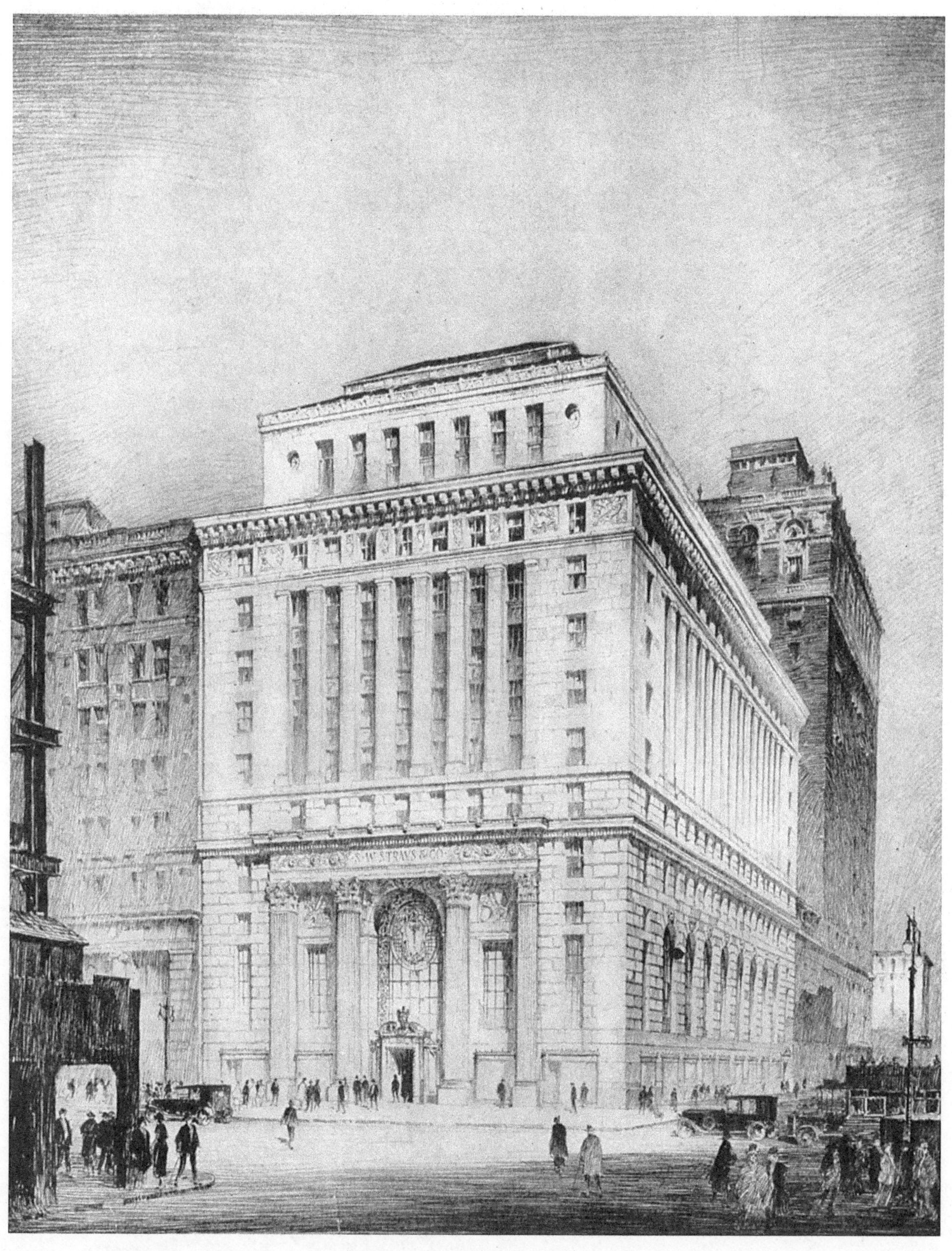

PENCIL RENDERING BY CHESTER B. PRICE. S. W. STRAUS & CO. BUILDING, NEW YORK CITY
WARREN & WETMORE, ARCHITECTS

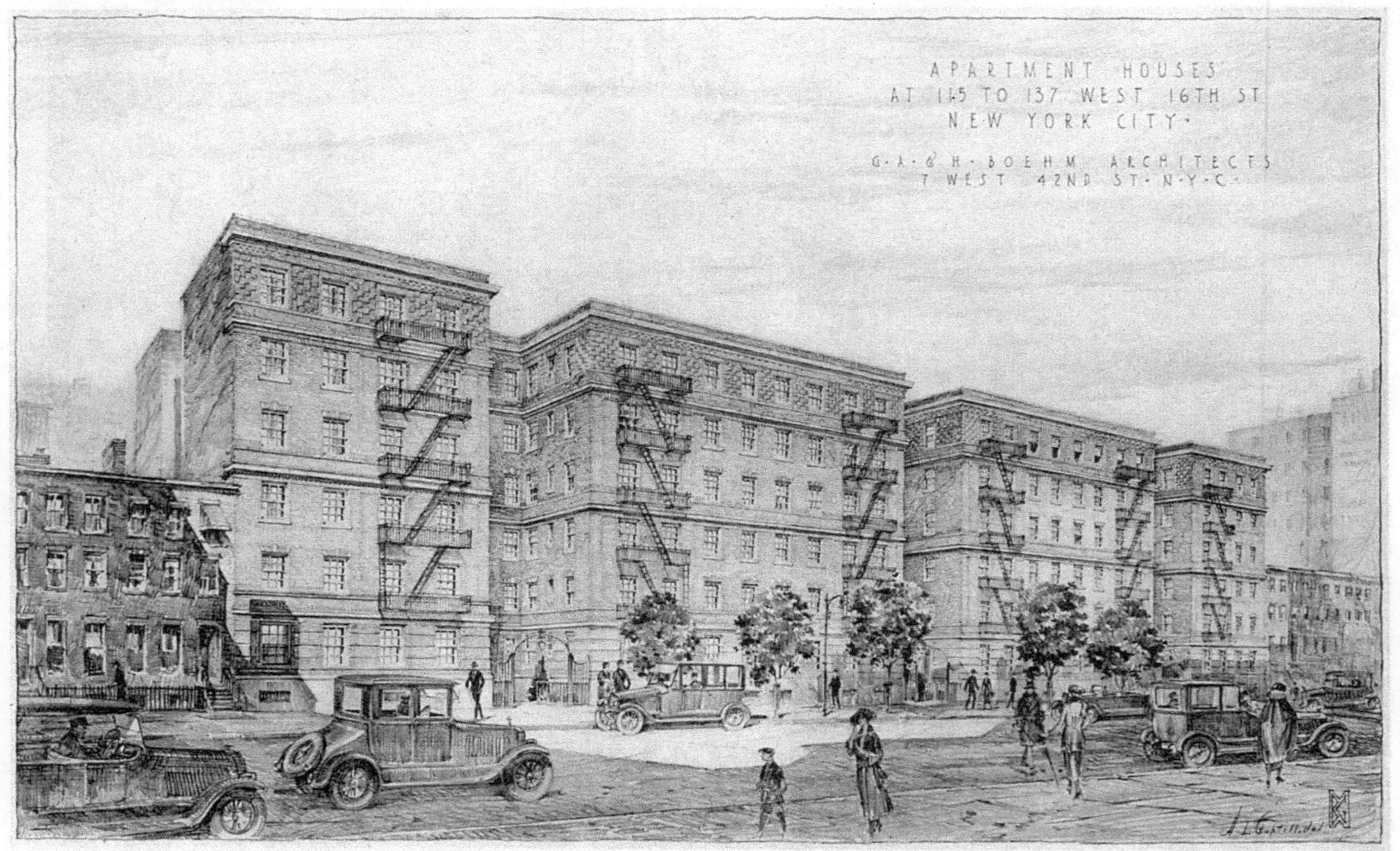

Figure 53. Apartment Houses at 115 to 137 West Sixteenth Street, New York City. G. A. & H. Boehm, Architects. Drawn in Pencil on Kid-finished Bristol Board.

with a little practice one can learn to pass two or three strokes of the pencil over each window, grooves and all, toning the various parts to the desired values, using a similar process wherever the grooves are employed. If the pressure is not too great and the point is rather blunt the pencil will pass over the grooves without darkening them, leaving them instead to appear as white lines. After a day or two or as soon as the paper has become damp (it may be lightly washed or sprayed with water if desired) the grooves themselves practically disappear, simply leaving the white lines. Possibly the greatest objection to this way of working is that the lines so formed sometimes seem a bit too perfect in relation to those drawn more freely with the pencil, yet on drawings at small scale enough time can frequently be saved by this method to make a knowledge of it worth having.

So much in regard to the architectural handling of large buildings. For additional suggestions see the previous chapters of this book, nearly all of which offer something related to our present subject, and study the numerous examples of rendering that have appeared from place to place in the text.

We should not close our discussion of the rendering of large buildings without some reference to the very sketchy and often rather impressionistic type of drawing in which the architecture is treated from the point of view of the artist rather than of the architect, and which, therefore, gives special attention to the effect of the whole and not to the almost photographic representation of the architectural detail common to the work of the architect and the professional delineator. In drawings of this type, for instance, the whole is treated very broadly, some of the windows being merely suggested, perhaps, or omitted entirely, while practically all of the tiny members such as dentils are left out. Such drawings are usually more interesting than the architectural type, partly because more is left to the imagination and partly because of the absence of mechanical perfection of line. (In fact many are made entirely freehand from start to finish). Again, the accessories may be treated with greater freedom as no reason exists for suppressing them,—so all-in-all, when the artist draws architecture the results are better from a purely æsthetic standpoint than those obtained by the average architect or architectural delineator, who is of necessity usually forced to show so much detail (in order to make the design clear to the client) as to prevent the most artistic result.

Then there is another form of work in which large buildings are shown but where they become subordinate to something else. As examples of this we have advertisements of automobiles and clothing and the like, where the buildings are simply a setting or background. Here of course the greatest freedom in their treatment is permissible, the slightest suggestion of the architecture often sufficing.

So much variety is found in all this sort of work that we can hardly do more than mention it here, and bring emphasis to the fact that the outstanding difference between this and the architectural type is, as we have mentioned, the greater freedom used in the former in relation to the latter. This freedom is not confined to the technique but is found in the composition also, and in the general treatment, moonlight or evening scenes, sunsets, rainy day effects and the like being popular. Even though these are not common in architectural work, it would be well for the student of architectural rendering to study all this sort of thing, as much can be learned from it which is adaptable with modifications to his own problems.

Whether the student desires to better his ability to do architectural renderings or whether it is this other work which interests him most, there is no better training in either case than to sketch directly from buildings. It is by making many such sketches as that by Otto F. Langmann on page 181 from the big buildings themselves that one can get a strong grasp on how to handle them.

Now of these various types of drawings our illustrations have been selected from those of an architectural nature. Figure 52, page 175, is the reproduction of a very quick sketch of a proposed building done on tracing paper with a lithographic pencil. Unfortunately this reproduction is reduced from so large a drawing that the values show stronger contrasts in many ways than on the original, making the whole lighting seem somewhat unnatural and artificial. It will serve to show, however, that such a drawing, even though hastily done without preliminary study, conveys the general impression of the proposed structure.

Figure 53, page 178, was done at much smaller scale (⅛-inch to the foot) with ordinary graphite pencils. Both of these illustrations show comparatively simple buildings, simple indeed so far as general mass is concerned, and in presenting them we wish to point out a truth not commonly recognized by the beginner who attempts this sort of work, and this is that it is more difficult to get an interesting representation of simple masses of this type than of buildings having towers or domes or pediments or, in fact, any irregular shaped features. Even the outline drawing of a domed structure is full of interest before the rendering is started, whereas the block forms or skeletons of such buildings as we are picturing here seem very commonplace, which means that greater care must be given to the rendering. Choose, then, for your early practice, structures with domes or towers which will form interesting silhouettes and you will find it less difficult to obtain good results, saving the more simple forms for later practice. This seems strange, perhaps, but it is true.

Figure 51, page 172, was also made at the scale of ⅛″ to the foot, on kid-finished bristol board, and in this case the main lines were drawn instrumentally and left to show in the final result, the free-hand work being added to them. This building, like the others, is very simple in general mass, but because of the trees it was possible to avoid the rather hard and uninteresting outline against the sky which we find in Figure 53.

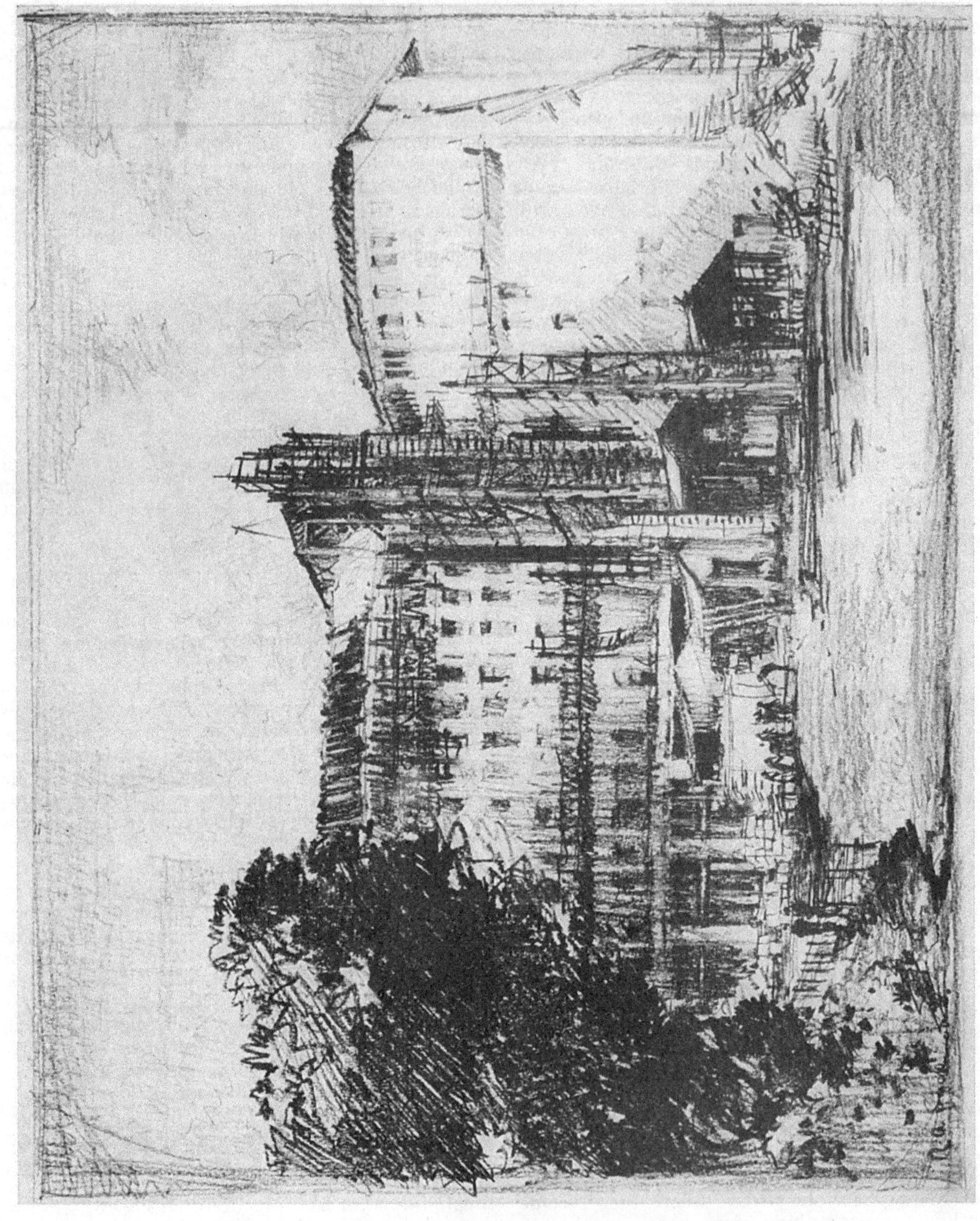

SKETCH BY ROBERT A. LOCKWOOD.

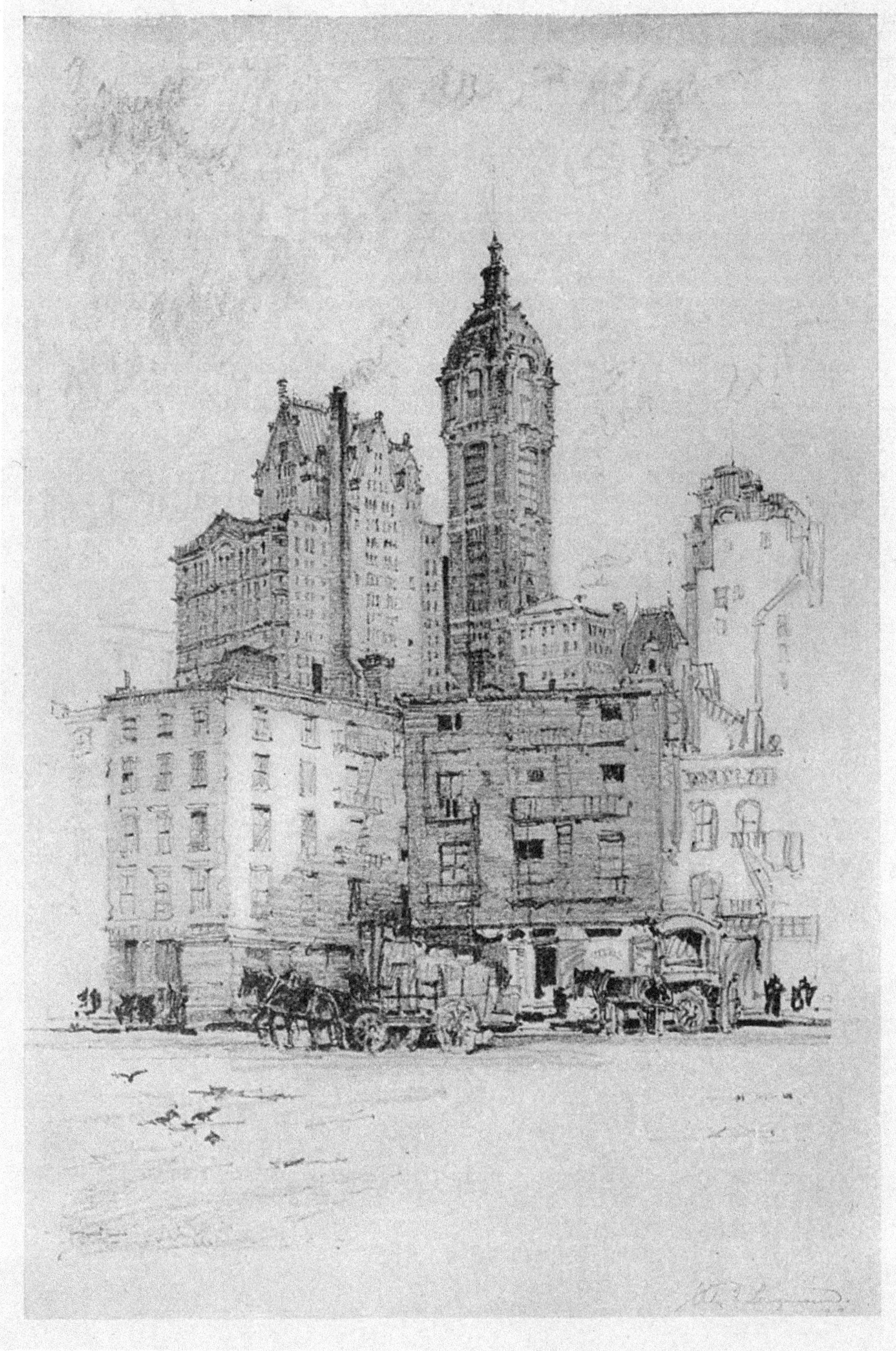

PENCIL SKETCH BY OTTO F. LANGMANN. A BIT OF LOWER NEW YORK FROM WEST STREET

The admirable rendering by Hugh Ferriss of Bush House, London, England, on page 174, was done after the designs for the building had reached a definite stage and as the surroundings were well known it was possible to produce a drawing which conveys a very convincing and realistic impression; one which while showing considerable detail is not without atmospheric effect. A carbon pencil was used for this rendering which was made on a fairly smooth, heavy drawing board. Attention is directed also to the smaller reproductions of masterly renderings by Mr. Ferriss on pages 173 and 176.

On page 177 is an exceptional example of fine line treatment of a large building, by Chester B. Price, the subject being the new structure for S. W. Straus & Co., Fifth Avenue, New York City. Although a close inspection of this reproduction reveals that every essential detail of the architecture has been shown, the drawing has, nevertheless, a remarkable breadth of effect and a most commendable simplicity. Two other drawings of large buildings done by Mr. Price have been reproduced on page 183, opposite, and these, too, are worthy of the most careful study on the part of the student.

The sketch by Robert A. Lockwood on page 180 is a very virile interpretation of a building in course of construction. Subjects of this sort are excellent for the student to attempt.

We have already mentioned the delightful sketch by Mr. Langmann on page 181. This is one of a series which Mr. Langmann has made of interesting groupings of New York buildings, old and new, approaching his subjects in much the same way that the travelling student of architecture sketches buildings and groupings abroad. The original from which this particular reproduction was made is in lithographic pencil on white paper.

Now study and analyze all these various examples carefully and try to obtain others of your own. Copy parts of them, if you wish, but in doing so remember that the amount of reduction in size is considerable, so allow for this while doing your copying. Next go ahead with larger subjects, but in this work as in the sketching of smaller buildings it might be well to make first a number of sketches from photographs, and when larger subjects of an original sort are undertaken do not forget what we have said about the importance of the preliminary study. It is often a good plan, if an architectural rendering of a big building is being attempted for the first time, to select photographs and reproductions of renderings of similar buildings viewed from about the same point, and to keep these around you for study and comparison all the time that you are working on your preliminary study and on the final rendering itself. And above all do not lose your confidence and patience simply because the subject is large.

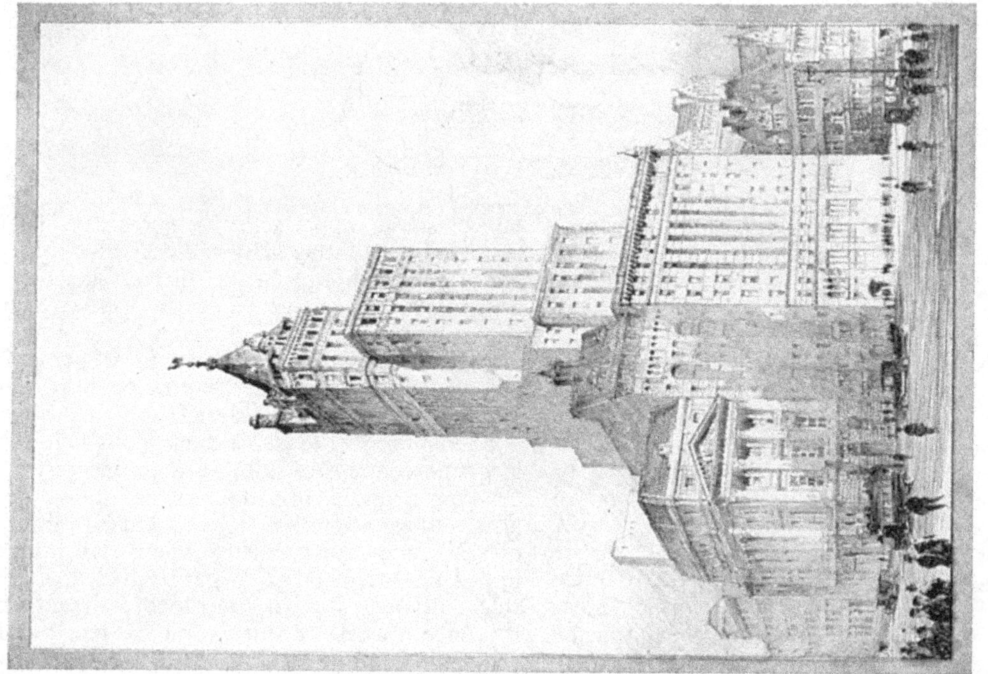

RENDERING BY CHESTER B. PRICE
THE HECKSCHER BUILDING, NEW YORK CITY
WARREN & WETMORE, ARCHITECTS

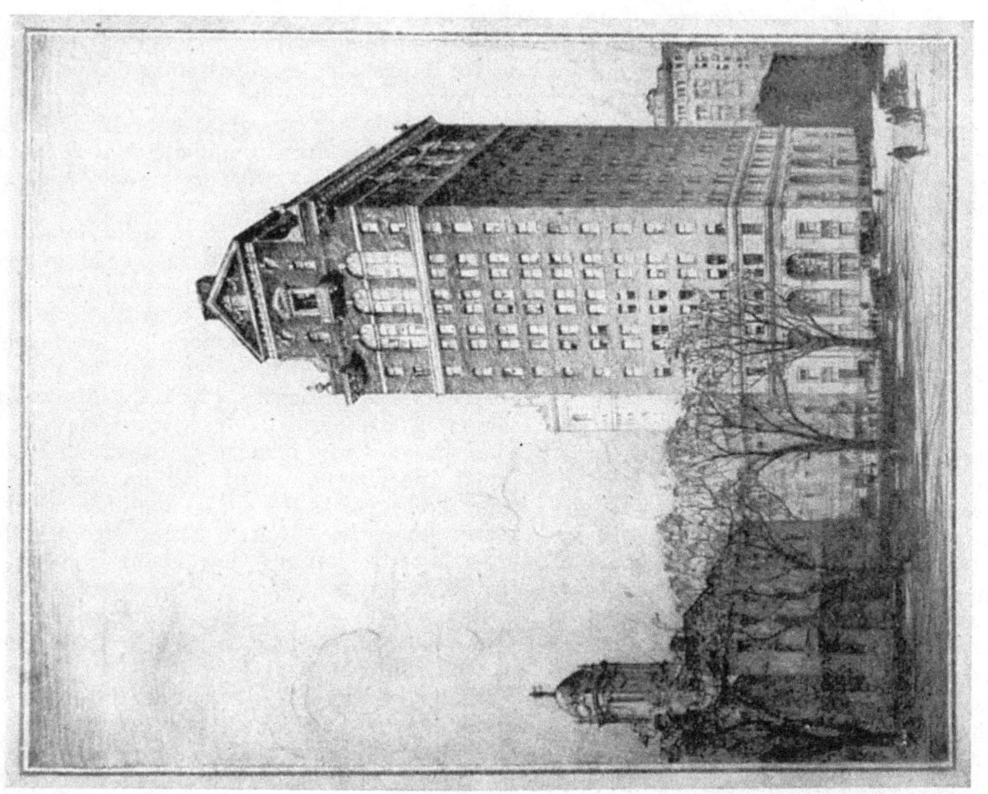

RENDERING BY CHESTER B. PRICE
BUILDING FOR THE HARTFORD CONNECTICUT TRUST COMPANY
BENJAMIN WISTAR MORRIS, ARCHITECT

Chapter XIV.

CONCLUSION

IF ONE desires to learn to draw, let him draw and draw and draw. The author wishes that this message might remain fixed in the mind of every reader of these chapters, for even those who have had the patience to follow them through from the very first to this the concluding one, will profit little by them unless such ideas as have been acquired are put to practice before they are forgotten, as it is only by drawing over and over again until such assimilation has taken place as will enable one to make unconscious use of them, that they will prove of more than partial and transitory value.

Yet it is not enough to draw, without plan or reason, for one gets even through faithful practice far less gain than should be rightfully his, unless he follows a logical system, adopting some scheme which seems best suited to his individual requirements. For what might be logical for one might be illogical indeed for another. There are students, for instance, so imbued with earnestness and enthusiasm, so passionately fond of drawing, that they seize with avidity every hint or suggestion which is offered as an aid to the development of their talent, and who at the same time possess enough common sense to realize their own shortcomings and weaknesses and to direct their own energies to the best advantage in their attempt to overcome them, so planning their study and practice that they move on step-by-step up a road of steady progress. Such men are also occasionally so fortunate as to have the somewhat rare ability of judging correctly the merits of their own work, being able to view it impartially from a wholly unbiased standpoint, acting as their own critics with considerable success.

Needless to say men of this type are scarce, however, the average student falling into one or another of three classes, the first including such as either underrate their own ability or are easily disheartened, the second and largest class consisting of those having a fair amount of ability and confidence coupled with a willingness to work, and with an excellent attitude towards the acceptance of instruction and criticism, the third being made up of a few such vain and self-conceited individuals as hold the egotistical opinion that their work is the acme of perfection, ignoring with thinly masked ridicule the suggestions of their instructors and fellow students, seemingly ignorant or careless of the fact that their attitude of antagonism is deterrent to their own progress.

Now the student of this first class needs a guiding hand and word of encouragement, for once he gains a reasonable amount of confidence in himself and his own ability his advancement is frequently rapid. Such a student should by all means join a class or work under a critic or patron, as otherwise he may lack the necessary incentive to inspire him to the achievement which is possible, and neither should he be discouraged by adverse criticism. Especially if one is self-conscious and supersensitive he should strive to become so thoroughly immersed in his work as to grow forgetful of self and unmindful of unfavorable comment or the gibes of the thoughtless.

Students of the second class, which includes a large percentage of all the men interested in such drawing, should put themselves under instruction also, either attending school (many night schools offer courses for those to whom day attendance is impossible) or, if no organized classes are available, gathering as a group to form a sketch club, meeting once a week or so to compare work and receive criticism from each other or, better yet, from some capable critic engaged for the purpose. Or if it seems impractical to join or form a club or class it is all the more important to work under an able teacher. As far as the architectural draftsman is concerned this should be easy, especially in the larger cities, as capable men may be found in nearly every office, glad to give their services either gratuitously or for reasonable compensation. The choice of a teacher or critic should not be made hastily, however, for it is not enough that he be a skilled artist, for many who draw exquisitely well cannot tell how they do it or what is wrong with another's work. Again some teachers are so dogmatic and opinionated as to try to force their own ideas upon all their students rather than to aid in developing the individuality of each. So make your choice with care, but once you go to a teacher, put yourself under his direction unreservedly, and even though you sometimes fail to agree with him or with his corrections or criticisms, try to get his viewpoint, to see from his eyes, as his vision may be broader than your own. It is not always wise to remain under the instruction of one man for too long a time, however, as there is sometimes a tendency to mimic his style, but it is better, instead, to change after a while, gaining new inspiration and help by the fresh contact.

But we are digressing a bit from our consideration of the three various classes of students so let us return to discuss the third, the conceited lot. Perhaps the less said about them the better, for such men are well-nigh hopeless unless they can be made to see the light, and this is not easy if they are confirmed egotists. But some men are egotists only so far as their drawing ability is concerned, and for these there is hope. This condition is sometimes brought about because friends or members of a student's family or possibly teachers have in their ignorance or in their desire to flatter, heaped

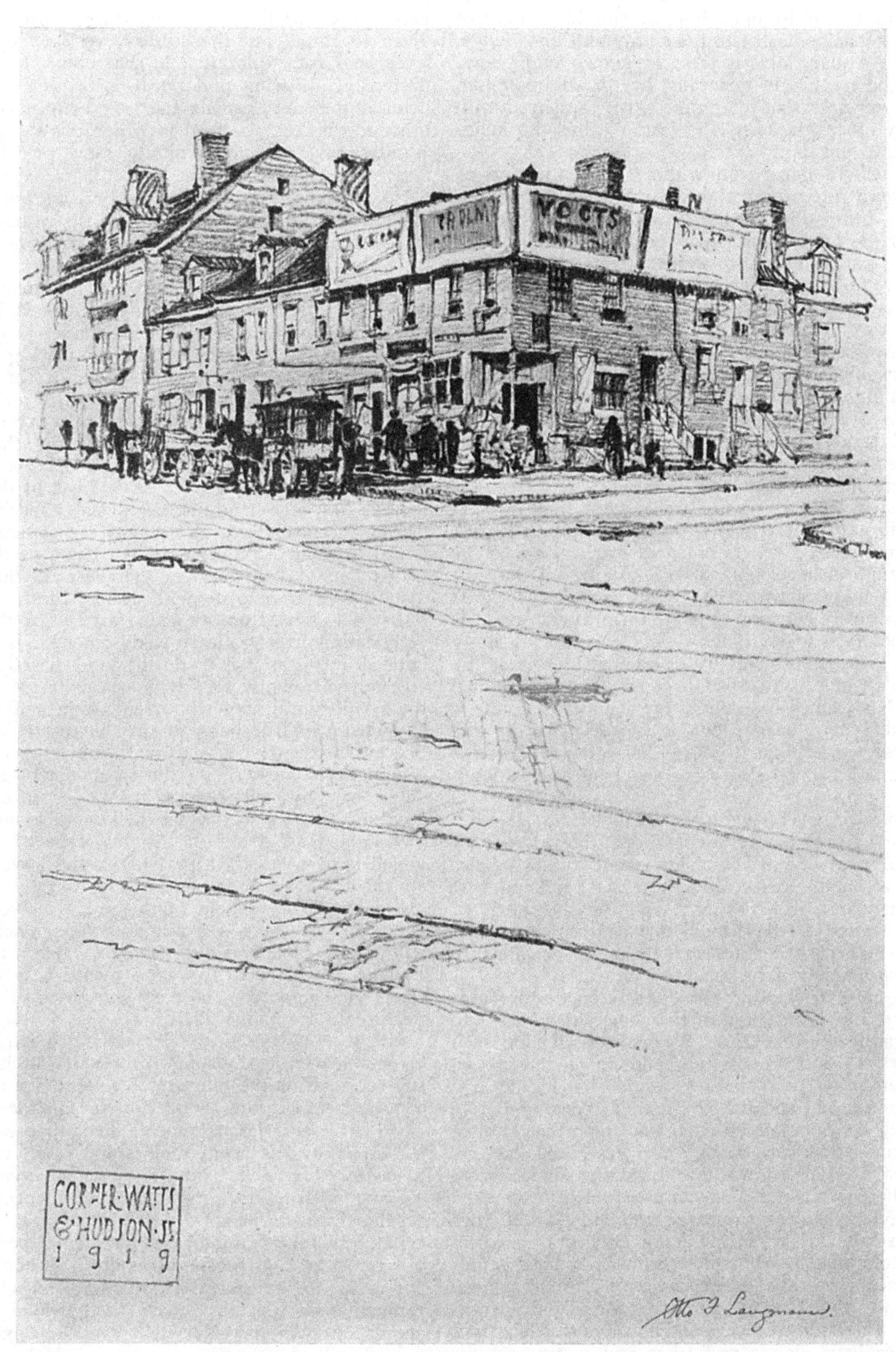

PENCIL SKETCH BY OTTO F. LANGMANN. A BIT OF OLD NEW YORK

unwarranted praise upon him, causing him to arrive at false conclusions as to his ability and knowledge. If such a man joins a class or sketch club, however, the truth will generally be forced upon him sooner or later that his work, when compared with that by others, lacks the perfection which he imagined it to possess.

We should not go on without some mention of the man who earnestly desires to draw but whose efforts bring him little reward. Such a person should try over and over again. Then if after repeated attempts improvement seems as far away as ever, failure may be quite properly attributed to lack of natural ability, in which case it is doubtless better to give up the hope of ever becoming more than mediocre, seeking perhaps to win greater success in some other direction, for even the man of real ability has no easy task to gain recognition. But do not let discouragement deter you from repeated trial, for many who show little promise in their early work persevere until their results show amazing improvement.

The reader can readily understand that in consideration of these many types of men who are studying these chapters, men at various stages of progress and development, too, ranging all the way from beginners with their first problems to men professionally engaged in some form of art work, it is impractical to lay down definite courses of study here. Disappointment has perhaps been felt by some that more actual problems have not been given, but it has seemed best, under the conditions, to offer, instead, general suggestions, hoping to make the student see what things it is essential for him to know, and to point out the way for acquiring such knowledge.

And so in Part I we have discussed among other things the preliminary preparations, the drawing of objects in outline and light and shade, the principles of free-hand perspective, methods of doing cast drawing and life drawing, and the sketching of animals; and we have tried to make the reader see that whether he is interested in art or architecture all such training is of benefit to him.

We have touched here in Part II on the preparation of drawing materials, the choice of subjects to draw and how to begin. We have written on such matters as individual style and method and on different ways of obtaining results in outline and light-and-shade and flat and graded tones, and have devoted considerable space to the important subject of composition with attention to unity and balance. We have discussed working from the object, from the photograph and from nature, and have covered in special chapters the representation of buildings both small and large, including exteriors, interiors and street scenes, while the treatment of their details and accessories has been broad, too, offering suggestions for the handling of furniture and draperies, doors, windows, chimneys and all these smaller parts. Neither have clouds and trees and water and the like been neglected, nor have people and animals as used in connection with building representation. Then to round out the subject we have opened a large field for exploration in the recent chapters on decorative drawing and on uses of tinted papers, colored pencils, pencils used in connection with other media, etc.,—a field in which the student may wander far, constantly finding new pleasure and delight.

So with all this as a background we must leave the reader to map out for himself the course which it seems best for him to pursue, and this, as we have explained, depends wholly on his present stage of progress and his individual requirements. Let each man study himself and his needs. If he lacks the ability to sketch objects in correct proportion, let him spend considerable time in drawing directly from objects themselves, as described in Part I, thus giving special attention to this common weakness. In fact, too much emphasis cannot be given to the importance of such work, especially for the architectural student who so often lays out his proportions instrumentally and to scale, that to do so by the eye in a free-hand manner proves especially difficult. Yet architectural students are sometimes inclined to scoff at object drawing, being of the erroneous opinion that cubes and cylinders and books and dishes have little to do with architecture.

In fact, too often students fail to see that it is fully as important to learn to do other kinds of free-hand drawing as it is to do the kind directly applicable to their own work. It is especially valuable for the architectural man who spends much of his time at instrumental drawing to vary his sketching practice by frequently choosing such subjects as will get him entirely away from the mechanical,—a dilapidated barn or vine-covered ruin, for instance, or anything of this sort which will serve as an aid to "loosening up" from the "tight" type of drawing which is of necessity a part of his day's work. He should try such subjects as the bridge by Mr. Watson on page 86, or the old houses by Mr. Langmann, page 167, or even less ambitious things where the subject is small and few straight lines are found. In such work try to seek and record that which is really vital in a free and easy way, with little attention to the technique itself.

But whether one draws from the geometric forms or still life or cast or figure or some architectural subject, truth is the thing to be sought, for a knowledge of truth is the foundation for all the rest.

So in closing let us repeat, then, that each man should study his needs and straightway commence to correct his faults and overcome his weaknesses, seeking instruction, inviting criticism, comparing results with drawings by others and so striving constantly for greater perfection, remembering that one never reaches the point where it is not possible for him to advance still further,—and let it be remembered, too, that even though one fails to acquire exceptional skill, whatever of dexterity is gained will always prove a source of pleasure and satisfaction.

Art Instruction

THE ART OF ANIMAL DRAWING: CONSTRUCTION, ACTION ANALYSIS, CARICATURE, **Ken Hultgren.** Former Disney animator offers expert advice–with more than 700 illustrations on drawing animals realistically and as caricatures. Line, brush technique, mood, action, and more. Dogs, cats, deer, foxes, rabbits, etc. ix+134pp. 8⅜ x 11. 0-486-27426-8

WAYS WITH WATERCOLOR, **Ted Kautzky.** Simple, direct language discusses color pigments, paper, and other supplies; washes, strokes, and the use of accessories for special effects. Valuable instructions on composition. 125 illustrations, including 37 color plates. 144pp. 8⅜ x 11. 0-486-43954-2

MODELLING AND SCULPTING THE HUMAN FIGURE, **Edouard Lanteri.** Covers modelling from casts, live models; measurements; frameworks; scale of proportions; compositions; reliefs, drapery, medals, etc. 107 full-page photographic plates. 27 other photographs. 175 drawings and diagrams. 480pp. 5⅜ x 8. 0-486-25006-7

THE PAINTER'S METHODS AND MATERIALS, **A. P. Laurie.** Foremost authority on techniques and materials: permanency, pigments, tempera, varnishes, etc. Modern procedures plus insights into classical techniques of the masters. 64 illustrations. 250pp. 5⅜ x 8½. 0-486-21868-6

ETCHING, ENGRAVING AND OTHER INTAGLIO PRINTMAKING TECHNIQUES, **Ruth Leaf.** Comprehensive handbook covers materials and equipment, tools, printing papers, presses, and other essentials. Detailed instructions for etching, engraving, drypointing, collagraphs, tuilegraphs, and the Blake transfer method. Profusely illustrated. 232pp. 8⅜ x 11¼. 0-486-24721-X

THE ANATOMY AND ACTION OF THE HORSE, **Lowes D. Luard.** Easy-to-read text explains the horse as a machine designed for movement, with meticulously rendered sketches of the entire animal supplementing diagrams and color illustrations of the horse's anatomy. 62 b/w illustrations. xiv+146pp. plus 24-page full-color insert. 6½ x 9¼. 0-486-42980-6

LIGHT AND SHADE: A CLASSIC APPROACH TO THREE-DIMENSIONAL DRAWING, **Mary P. Merrifield.** Handy reference clearly demonstrates principles of light and shade by revealing effects of common daylight, sunshine, and candle or artificial light on geometrical solids. 13 plates. 64pp. 5⅜ x 8½. 0-486-44143-1

THE HUMAN FIGURE IN MOTION, **Eadweard Muybridge.** The 4,789 photographs in this definitive selection show human figures–models almost all undraped–engaged in more than 160 different types of action: running, climbing stairs, tumbling, dressing, dancing, etc. 390pp. 7⅞ x 10⅝. 0-486-20204-6

ANIMAL DRAWING AND ANATOMY, **Edwin Noble.** Written and illustrated by a distinguished artist and art instructor, this volume features valuable insights into reproducing accurate images of horses, cows, dogs, sheep, birds, and wild animals. Advice on depicting musculature, hair, feathers, and other obvious physical features, plus action, pose, proportions, and character. 233 drawings. 128pp. 5⅜ x 8½. 0-486-42312-3

PERSPECTIVE MADE EASY, **Ernest Norling.** Perspective is easy; yet surprisingly few artists know the simple rules that make it so. Remedy that situation with this simple, step-by-step book, the first devoted entirely to the topic. Horizon, vanishing point, shade and shadow, and much more. 256 illustrations. 224pp. 5⅜ x 8½. 0-486-40473-0

PAINTING AND DRAWING CHILDREN, **John Norton.** Great children's portraitist covers every aspect of the subject, from getting to know the child to fees and public relations. Full-color layouts show step-by-step evolution of four beautiful portraits. 59 b/w and 40 color illustrations. 176pp. 8⅛ x 11. 0-486-41803-0

DRAWING OUTDOORS, **Henry C. Pitz.** How to draw every major outdoor subject–land, greenery, skies, buildings, people, cities, and more–in all the major drawing media. Many examples from the masters. More than 100 illustrations. 144pp. 8⅛ x 11. 0-486-28679-7

COMPOSITION IN ART, **Henry Rankin Poore.** Learn principles of composition, classical and modern, through analysis of works from Middle Ages to present. 148 illustrations, 9 in color. 104pp. 8⅛ x 11. 0-486-23358-8

THE MATERIALS AND METHODS OF SCULPTURE, **Jack C. Rich.** Exhaustive, profusely illustrated guide to technical aspects of sculpting in stone, metal, wood, and other materials. Tools, techniques, modelling, casting, firing, and much more. 281 illustrations. 512pp. 6½ x 9¼. 0-486-25742-8

HENSCHE ON PAINTING, **John W. Robichaux.** Basic painting philosophy and methodology of a great teacher, as expounded in his famous classes and workshops on Cape Cod. 7 illustrations in color on covers. 80pp. 5⅜ x 8½. 0-486-43728-0

THE ELEMENTS OF DRAWING, **John Ruskin.** Timeless classic by one of the greatest art critics of all time begins with bare fundamentals and offers brilliant philosophical advice. Many practical exercises. 48 illustrations. 228pp. 5⅜ x 8½. 0-486-22730-8

THE ENJOYMENT AND USE OF COLOR, **Walter Sargent.** Color relationships, values, intensities; complementary colors, illumination, and similar topics. Color in nature and art. 7 color plates. 29 illustrations. 274pp. 5⅜ x 8½. 0-486-20944-X

DRAWING THE LIVING FIGURE, **Joseph Sheppard.** Innovative approach to artistic anatomy focuses on specifics of surface anatomy, rather than muscles and bones. Over 170 drawings of live models in front, back, and side views, and in widely varying poses. Accompanying diagrams. 177 illustrations. 144pp. 8⅜ x 11¼. 0-486-26723-7

JOHN SLOAN ON DRAWING AND PAINTING, **John Sloan.** This illustrated, practical record of talks and instructional advice by a member of the "Ashcan School" of American painting discusses line, tone, texture, light and shade, composition, design, space, perspective, and related issues. Wealth of helpful suggestions and exercises. 252pp. 5⅜ x 8½. 0-486-40947-3

SCULPTURE: PRINCIPLES AND PRACTICE, **Louis Slobodkin.** Step-by-step approach to clay, plaster, metals, and stone; classical and modern. 253 drawings, photos. 255pp. 8⅛ x 11. 0-486-22960-2

THE PRACTICE AND SCIENCE OF DRAWING, **Harold Speed.** Classic approach to the dynamics of drawing by brilliant teacher with insights and practical advice on line drawing, mass drawing, visual memory, materials, and much more. 84 plates and diagrams. 296pp. 5⅜ x 8½. 0-486-22870-3

THE PRACTICE OF TEMPERA PAINTING, **Daniel V. Thompson, Jr.** Historical background, step-by-step instruction, materials, permanence. Lucid, careful exposition of all aspects of authentic technique. 85 illustrations. 141pp. 5⅜ x 8½. 0-486-20343-3

A HANDBOOK OF ANATOMY FOR ART STUDENTS, **Arthur Thomson.** Thorough coverage of skeletal structure, muscles, heads, etc. Text supplemented by anatomical drawings, diagrams, and photos of undraped figures. 211 figures, 40 drawings, 86 photos. 459pp. 5⅜ x 8½. 0-486-21163-0

THE WATSON DRAWING BOOK, **Ernest W. Watson and Aldren A. Watson.** Authoritative, stimulating book brims with information on drawing techniques, media, and artistic examples. Technical information and tips on perspective, measure and form analysis, rendering light, shade, and shadow, portrait drawing, figure sketching, and outdoor sketching. 160pp. 8¼ x 10¾. 0-486-42606-8

COMPLETE GUIDE TO WATERCOLOR PAINTING, **Edgar A. Whitney.** Brilliant guide by renowned artist tells all, from basics to creating masterful landscapes, portraits, and figures. Full-color sections follow evolution of seven of the author's own watercolors. More than 100 illustrations, including 37 in color. 176pp. 8¼ x 10¾. 0-486-41742-5

CALLIGRAPHY IN TEN EASY LESSONS, **Eleanor Winters and Laurie E. Lico.** Beginners can get started on the basic Italic hand with this practical guide. Detailed discussions cover spacing, connecting letters; forming words and sentences; drawing "swash" capitals; and more, plus applications–addressing envelopes, making stationery, and transcribing special texts. Numerous b/w illustrations. 112pp. 8⅜ x 11. 0-486-41804-9

PENCIL DRAWING, **Michael Woods.** Complete first course covers basic techniques, line work, shading, tone, perspective, composition, even fixing, mounting, and framing. Engaging, easy-to-follow text enhanced with 155 carefully prepared illustrations. 118pp. 6⅛ x 9¼. 0-486-25886-6

*Write for **free** Fine Art and Art Instruction Catalog to*
Dover Publications, Inc., Dept. ABI, 31 East 2nd Street, Mineola, NY 11501
*Visit us online at **www.doverpublications.com***

Dover Books on Art & Art History

De Re Metallica, Georgius Agricola. One of the most important scientific classics of all time, this 1556 work on mining was the first based on field research and observation and the methods of modern science. 289 authentic Renaissance woodcuts. Translated by Herbert Hoover. Reprint of English (1912) edition. 672pp. 6¾ x 10¾. 0-486-60006-8

The Universal Penman, George Bickham. Famous treasury of English roundhand calligraphy of 1740. Alphabets, decorated pages, scrolls, frames, cupids, and similar material. 212pp. 9 x 13¾. 0-486-20616-5

The Art of Botanical Illustration: An Illustrated History, Wilfrid Blunt. Surveys the evolution of botanical illustration from the crude scratchings of paleolithic man down to the highly scientific work of 20th-century illustrators. With 186 magnificent examples, more than 30 in full color. "A classic"–*The Sunday Times* (London). 372pp. 5⅜ x 8¼. 0-486-27265-6

Idols Behind Altars: Modern Mexican Art and Its Cultural Roots, Anita Brenner. Critical study ranges from pre-Columbian times through the 20th century to explore Mexico's intrinsic association between art and religion; the role of iconography in Mexican art; and the return to native values. Unabridged reprint of the classic 1929 edition. 118 b/w illustrations. 432pp. 5⅜ x 8½. 0-486-42303-4

The Book of Kells, Blanche Cirker (ed.). 32 full-color, full-page plates from the greatest illuminated manuscript of the Middle Ages; painstakingly reproduced from rare facsimile edition. Publisher's Note. Captions. 32pp. 9⅜ x 12¼. 0-486-24345-1

Christian and Oriental Philosophy of Art, Ananda K. Coomaraswamy. Nine essays by philosopher-art-historian on symbolism, traditional culture, folk art, ideal portraiture, etc. 146pp. 5⅜ x 8½. 0-486-20378-6

The Secret Life of Salvador Dalí, Salvador Dalí. One of the most readable autobiographies ever! Superbly illustrated with more than 80 photos of Dalí and his works, and scores of Dalí drawings and sketches. "It is impossible not to admire this painter as writer . . . (Dalí) communicates the snobbishness, self-adoration, comedy, seriousness, fanaticism, in short the concept of life and the total picture of himself he sets out to portray."–*Books*. 432pp. 6½ x 9¼. (Available in U.S. only) 0-486-27454-3

Leonardo on Art and the Artist, Leonardo da Vinci (André Chastel, ed.). Systematic grouping of passages of Leonardo's writings concerning painting, with focus on problems of interpretation. More than an anthology, it offers a reconstruction of the underlying meaning of Leonardo's words. Introduction, notes, and bibliographic and reference materials. More than 125 b/w illustrations. 288pp. 9¼ x 7⅜. 0-486-42166-X

Leonardo on the Human Body, Leonardo da Vinci. More than 1,200 of Leonardo's anatomical drawings on 215 plates. Leonardo's text, which accompanies the drawings, has been translated into English. 506pp. 8⅜ x 11¼. 0-486-24483-0

A Treatise on Painting, Leonardo da Vinci. The great Renaissance artist's practical advice on drawing and painting techniques covers anatomy, perspective, composition, light and shadow, and color. A classic of art instruction, it features 48 drawings by Nicholas Poussin and Leon Battista Alberti. vii+182pp. 5⅜ x 8½. 0-486-44155-5

The Book Before Printing: Ancient, Medieval and Oriental, David Diringer. Rich authoritative study of the book before Gutenberg. Nearly 200 photographic facsimiles of priceless documents. 604pp. 5⅜ x 8½. 0-486-24243-9

Gauguin's Intimate Journals, Paul Gauguin. Revealing documents, reprinted from rare, limited edition, throw much light on the painter's inner life, his tumultuous relationship with van Gogh, evaluations of Degas, Monet, and other artists; hatred of hypocrisy and sham, life in the Marquesas Islands, and much more. 27 full-page illustrations by Gauguin. Preface by Emil Gauguin. 160pp. 6½ x 9¼. 0-486-29441-2

The Geometry of Art and Life, Matila Ghyka. Revealing discussion ranging from Plato to modern architecture. 80 plates and 64 figures, including paintings, flowers, shells, etc. 174pp. 5⅜ x 8½. 0-486-23542-4

A Manual of Historic Ornament, Richard Glazier. Hundreds of detailed illustrations depict painted pilasters from Pompeii, early Gothic stone carvings, a detail from a stained glass window in Canterbury Cathedral, and much more. Unabridged reprint of the 6th edition (1948) of *A Manual of Historic Ornament,* originally published in 1899 by B. T. Batsford, Ltd., London. Over 700 b/w illustrations. 16 plates of photographs. x+230pp. 6⅛ x 9¼. 0-486-42148-1

The Disasters of War, Francisco Goya. This powerful graphic indictment of war's horrors–inspired by the Peninsular War and the following famine–comprises 80 prints and includes veiled attacks on various people, the Church, and the State. Captions reprinted with English translations. 97pp. 9⅜ x 8¼. 0-486-21872-4

Great Drawings of Nudes, Carol Belanger Grafton (ed.). An impressive sampling of life drawings by 45 of the art world's greatest masters displays the styles of figure drawing across five centuries, from Dürer and Michelangelo to Modigliani and Derain. Featured artists include Raphael, Rubens, van Dyck, Hogarth, Constable, Ingres, Gauguin, Matisse, Rodin, and others. Captions. 48pp. 8¼ x 11. 0-486-42766-8

Great Self-Portraits, Carol Belanger Grafton (ed.). Unique volume of 45 splendid self-portraits encompasses pen, ink, and charcoal renderings as well as etchings and engravings. Subjects range from such 15th-century artists as da Vinci and Dürer to a host of 19th-century masters: Whistler, Rodin, van Gogh, Beardsley, and many more–Rembrandt, Rubens, Goya, Blake, Pissarro, and numerous others. 45 b/w illustrations. 48pp. 8¼ x 11. 0-486-42168-6

Hawthorne on Painting, Charles W. Hawthorne. Collected from notes taken by students at famous Cape Cod School; hundreds of direct, personal aperçus, ideas, suggestions. 91pp. 5⅜ x 8½. 0-486-20653-X

Modern Mexican Painters, MacKinley Helm. Definitive introduction to art and artists of Mexico during great artistic movements of '20s and '30s. Discussion of Rivera, Orozco, Siqueiros, Galvan, Cantú, Meza, and many others. 95 illustrations. 228pp. 6½ x 9¼. 0-486-26028-3

Modern Artists on Art, Second Enlarged Edition, Robert L. Herbert (ed.). Sixteen of the twentieth century's leading artistic innovators talk forcefully about their work–from Albert Gleizes and Jean Metzinger's 1912 presentation of Cubist theory to Henry Moore's comments, three decades later, on sculpture and primitive art. Four essays by Kurt Schwitters, Max Ernst, El Lissitzky, and Fernand Léger. 192pp. 5⅜ x 8½. 0-486-41191-5

A History of Engraving and Etching, Arthur M. Hind. British Museum Keeper of Prints offers complete history, from 15th century to 1914: accomplishments, influences, and artistic merit. 111 illustrations. 505pp. 5⅜ x 8½. 0-486-20954-7

Art and Geometry, William M. Ivins. Stimulating, controversial study of interrelations of art and mathematics, Greek disservice and contribution. Renaissance perspective, Dürer and math, etc. 123pp. 5⅜ x 8½. 0-486-20941-5

A Treasury of Bookplates from the Renaissance to the Present, Fridolf Johnson (ed.). 759 of the finest specimens including Dürer, Beardsley, Kent, and others, from many traditions, selected by the former editor of *American Artist.* 151pp. 8⅜ x 11¼. 0-486-23485-1

Concerning the Spiritual in Art, Wassily Kandinsky. Pioneering work by father of abstract art. Thoughts on color theory and nature of art. Analysis of earlier masters. 12 illustrations. 80pp. of text. 5⅜ x 8½. 0-486-23411-8

Point and Line to Plane, Wassily Kandinsky. Seminal exposition of role of line, point, and other elements of non-objective painting. Essential to understanding 20th-century art. 127 illustrations. 192pp. 6½ x 9¼. 0-486-23808-3

Language of Vision, Gyorgy Kepes. Noted painter, designer, and theoretician analyzes effect of visual language on human consciousness: perception of line and form, perspective, much more. Over 300 photos, drawings, and illustrations. 224pp. 8⅞ x 11¼. 0-486-28650-9

Dover Books on Art and Art History

Nineteenth-Century Art

Great Drawings and Illustrations from Punch, 1841–1901, Stanley Appelbaum and Richard Kelly (eds.). Golden years of British illustration. 192 drawings by 25 artists: Phiz, Leech, Tenniel, du Maurier, Sambourne. 144pp. 9 x 12. 0-486-24110-6

Best Works of Aubrey Beardsley, Aubrey Beardsley. Rich selection of 170 boldly executed black-and-white illustrations ranging from illustrations for Laclos' *Les Liaisons Dangereuses* and Balzac's *La Comédie Humaine* to magazine cover designs, book plates, title-page ornaments for books, silhouettes, and delightful mini-portraits of major composers. 160pp. 8⅛ x 11. 0-486-26273-1

The Rape of the Lock, Aubrey Beardsley and Alexander Pope. Reproduction of "ideal" 1896 edition in which text, typography, and illustration complement each other. 10 great illustrations capture the mock-heroic, delicate fancy of Pope's poem. 47pp. 8⅛ x 11. 0-486-21963-1

Salome, Aubrey Beardsley and Oscar Wilde. Lord Alfred Douglas' translation of Wilde's great play (originally written in French,) with all 20 well-known Beardsley illustrations including suppressed plates. Introduction by Robert Ross. xxii+69pp. 8⅛ x 11. 0-486-21830-9

Drawings of William Blake, William Blake. Fine reproductions show the range of Blake's artistic genius: drawings for *The Book of Job, The Divine Comedy, Paradise Lost,* an edition of Shakespeare's plays, grotesques and visionary heads, mythological figures, and other drawings. Selection, introduction, and commentary by Sir Geoffrey Keynes. 178pp. 8⅛ x 11. 0-486-22303-5

Songs of Innocence, William Blake. The first and most popular of Blake's famous "Illuminated Books" in a facsimile edition. 31 illustrations, text of each poem. 64pp. 5¼ x 7. 0-486-22764-2

A Cézanne Sketchbook: Figures, Portraits, Landscapes and Still Lifes, Paul Cézanne. Experiments with tonal effects, light, mass, and other qualities in more than 100 drawings. A revealing view of developing master painter, precursor of cubism. 102 illustrations. 144pp. 8⅜ x 6⅜. 0-486-24790-2

Graphic Works of George Cruikshank, George Cruikshank (Richard A. Vogler, ed.). 269 permission-free illustrations (8 in full color) reproduced directly from original etchings and woodcuts. Introduction, notes. 200pp. 9⅜ x 12¼. 0-486-23438-X

Daumier: 10 Great Lithographs, Honoré Daumier. Works range from early and caustic anti-government drawings in 1831 to last works prior to retirement in 1872. Collection concentrates on liberated women, the French bourgeoisie, actors, musicians, soldiers, teachers, lawyers, married life, and myriad other creations by the "Michelangelo of the people." 158pp. 9⅜ x 12¼. 0-486-23512-2

Degas' Drawings, H. G. E. Degas. Dancers, nudes, portraits, travel scenes, and other works in inimitable style, most not available anywhere else. 100 plates, 8 in color. 100pp. 9 x 12. 0-486-21233-5

The Doré Bible Illustrations, Gustave Doré. 241 detailed plates from the Bible: the Creation scenes, Adam and Eve, horrifying visions of the Flood, the battle sequences with their monumental crowds, depictions of the life of Jesus, and visions of the new Jerusalem. Each plate is accompanied by the appropriate verses from the King James version. 241pp. 9 x 12. 0-486-23004-X

The Doré Gallery: His 120 Greatest Illustrations, Gustave Doré (Carol Belanger Grafton, ed.). Comprising the finest plates from the great illustrator's work, this collection features outstanding engravings from such literary classics as Milton's *Paradise Lost, The Divine Comedy* by Dante, Coleridge's *The Rime of the Ancient Mariner, The Raven* by Poe, Sue's *The Wandering Jew,* and many others. Captions. 128pp. 9 x 12. 0-486-40160-X

Doré's Angels, Gustave Doré. Dozens of the renowned artist's celestial beings, as created for such great literary works as the Bible, Coleridge's *The Rime of the Ancient Mariner,* and Milton's classic, *Paradise Lost.* 75 b/w illustrations. 80pp. 9 x 12. 0-486-43668-3

Doré's Illustrations of the Crusades, Gustave Doré. Magnificent compilation of all 100 original plates from Ichaud's classic *History of the Crusades.* Includes *The War Cry of the Crusaders, The Massacre of Antioch, The Road to Jerusalem, the Baptism of Infidels, the Battle of Lepanto,* and many more. Captions. 112pp. 9 x 12. 0-486-29597-4

Doré's Illustrations for Don Quixote, Gustave Doré. Here are 190 wood-engraved plates, 120 full-page: charging the windmill, traversing Spanish plains, valleys, and mountains; ghostly visions of dragons, knights, and flaming lake. Marvelous detail, minutiae, accurate costumes, architecture, enchantment, pathos, and humor. Captions. 160pp. 9 x 12. 0-486-24300-1

The Rime of the Ancient Mariner, Gustave Doré and Samuel Taylor Coleridge. Doré's dramatic engravings for *The Rime of the Ancient Mariner* are considered by many to be his greatest work. The terrifying space of the open sea, the storms and whirlpools of an unknown ocean, the ice of the Antarctica, and more–all are rendered in a powerful manner. Full text. 38 plates. 77pp. 9¼ x 12. 0-486-22305-1

Gauguin's Intimate Journals, Paul Gauguin. Revealing documents, reprinted from rare, limited edition, throw much light on the painter's inner life, his tumultuous relationship with van Gogh, evaluations of Degas, Monet, and other artists; hatred of hypocrisy and sham, life in the Marquesas Islands, and much more. 27 full-page illustrations by Gauguin. Preface by Emil Gauguin. 160pp. 6½ x 9¼. 0-486-29441-2

Noa Noa: The Tahitian Journal, Paul Gauguin. Celebrated journal records the artist's thoughts and impressions during two years he spent in Tahiti. Compelling autobiographical fragment. 24 b/w illustrations. 96pp. 5⅜ x 8½. 0-486-24859-3

The Disasters of War, Francisco Goya. 83 etchings record horrors of Napoleonic wars in Spain and war in general. Reprint of first edition, plus 3 additional plates. 97pp. 9⅜ x 8¼. 0-486-21872-4

Los Caprichos, Francisco Goya. Considered Goya's most brilliant work, this collection combines corrosive satire and exquisite technique to depict 18th-century Spain as a nation of grotesque monsters sprung up in the absence of reason. Captions. 183pp. 6⅜ x 9⅝. 0-486-22384-1

Great Ballet Prints of the Romantic Era, Parmenia Migel. Sumptuous collection from 1830 to 1860. Taglioni, Elssler, Grisi, and other stars by such artists as Chalon, Grevedon, Deveria, etc. Introduction. 128pp. 9 x 12. 0-486-24050-9

Ornamentation and Illustrations from the Kelmscott Chaucer, William Morris. Beautiful permission-free tailpieces, decorative letters, elaborate floral borders and frames, samples of body type, and all 98 delicate woodcut illustrations. xiv+112pp. 8½ x 12. 0-486-22970-X

William Morris on Art and Socialism, William Morris (Norman Kelvin, ed.). This outstanding collection of 11 lectures and an essay, delivered between 1881 and 1896, illustrates Morris' conviction that the primary human pleasure lies in making and using items of utility and beauty. Selections include: "Art: A Serious Thing," "Art Under Plutocracy," "Useful Work vs. Useless Toil," "The Dawn of a New Epoch," "Of the Origins of Ornamental Art," "The Society of the Future," and "The Present Outlook of Socialism." Introduction. Biographical Note. 208pp. 5⅜ x 8½. 0-486-40904-X

The Renaissance: Studies in Art and Poetry, Walter Pater. One of the most talked-about books of the 19th century, *The Renaissance* combines scholarship and philosophy in an innovative work of cultural criticism that examines the achievements of Botticelli, Leonardo, Michelangelo, and other artists. "The holy writ of beauty."–Oscar Wilde. vi+154pp. 5⅜ x 8½. 0-486-44025-7

Great Lithographs by Toulouse-Lautrec: 89 Plates, H. Toulouse-Lautrec. Exceptional sampling of some of finest lithographs ever. 89 plates, including 8 in full color. 88pp. 9⅝ x 12¼. 0-486-24359-1

A Toulouse-Lautrec Sketchbook, Henri de Toulouse-Lautrec. A superb draftsman whose work–especially his sketches–was graphic in nature, Toulouse-Lautrec produced art of striking originality and power. This little-known volume includes 85 of his most striking early efforts, the majority of them studies of horses. 112pp. 8⅜ x 6⅜. 0-486-43377-3

Renoir: An Intimate Record, Ambroise Vollard. Art dealer and publisher Vollard's splendid portrait of Renoir emerges in a long series of informal conversations with the Impressionist master that reveal intimate details of his life and career. 19 black-and-white illustrations of Renoir's paintings. 160pp. 5⅜ x 8½. 0-486-26488-2

Twentieth-Century Art

FRENCH SATIRICAL DRAWINGS FROM "L'ASSIETTE AU BEURRE," Stanley Appelbaum (ed.). 170 biting, original drawings (8 in full color) from French magazine with an unsurpassed style. Works by Steinlen, Cappiello, Caran d'Ache, Willette, Poulbot, Forain, Vallotton, and Robida–as well as Juan Gris, Jacques Villon, Kees van Dongen, and Frantisek Kupka. 183pp. 9⅜ x 12¼. 0-486-23583-1

THE VIBRANT METROPOLIS: 88 LITHOGRAPHS, George W. Bellows (selected by Carol Belanger Grafton). Brilliantly executed, richly evocative works by one of the most popular American artists of the early 20th century include *Nude in a Bed, Evening; In the Subway; Dempsey Through the Ropes;* and *Base Hospital,* among others. 96pp. 8⅜ x 11. 0-486-42304-2

CHAGALL DRAWINGS: 43 WORKS, Marc Chagall. Superb treasury of images by one of the most distinctive and original artists of the 20th century–from fanciful fiddlers hovering above rooftops to imaginatively conceived depictions of bareback riders and other circus performers. Includes, among other masterworks, *Wounded Soldier, Three Acrobats, Child on a Chair, Nude with a Fan, Peasants in Vitebsk,* and *The Magician.* 48pp. 8¼ x 11. 0-486-41222-9

DRAWINGS FOR THE BIBLE, Marc Chagall. 136 works, 24 in full color, depicting Old Testament subjects. Captions cite the biblical sources of each drawing. Reprinted from a rare double issue of the French arts magazine *Verve.* Publisher's Note. 136pp. 9¼ x 12¼. 0-486-28575-8

50 SECRETS OF MAGIC CRAFTSMANSHIP, Salvadore Dalí. Rare, important volume in which Dalí expounds (in his inimitably eccentric fashion) on what painting should be, the history of painting, what is good and bad painting, the merits of specific artists, and more. Includes his 50 "secrets" for mastering the craft, including "the secret of the painter's pointed mustaches." Filled with sensible artistic advice, lively personal anecdotes, academic craftsmanship, and the artist's own marginal drawings. 192pp. 9¼ x 12¼. (Available in U.S. only) 0-486-27132-3

MODERN ARTISTS ON ART: SECOND ENLARGED EDITION, Robert L. Herbert (ed.). Sixteen of the 20th century's leading artistic innovators talk forcefully about their work–from Albert Gleizes and Jean Metzinger's 1912 presentation of cubist theory to Henry Moore's comments, three decades later, on sculpture and primitive art. Four newly added essays by Kurt Schwitters, Max Ernst, El Lissitzky, and Fernand Léger. 192pp. 5⅜ x 8½. 0-486-41191-5

HOPPER DRAWINGS, Edward Hopper. 44 plates, reproduced directly from originals in the collection of the Whitney Museum of American Art, reveal Hopper's superb draftsmanship and evocative power. Only book devoted exclusively to Hopper's drawings. 48pp. 8¼ x 11¼. 0-486-25854-8

100 DRAWINGS, Gustav Klimt. The finest drawings of the celebrated Austrian artist–mostly nudes and seminudes taken in part from rare portfolios of 1919 and 1964–reveal the dynamics of the line in representing the human figure spontaneously and freely. Introduction. 99pp. 9⅜ x 12¼. 0-486-22446-5

THE SPIRITUAL IN TWENTIETH-CENTURY ART, Roger Lipsey. Compelling and well-illustrated, this study focuses on the works of such renowned painters as Kandinsky, Mondrian, Klee, Picasso, Duchamp, and Matisse. The eloquent text offers insights into the artists' views of spirituality and their approach to work as a form of meditation. 121 black-and-white illustrations. xxvi+518pp. 5⅜ x 8½. 0-486-43294-7

THE ART NOUVEAU STYLE: A Comprehensive Guide with 264 Illustrations, Stephan Tschudi Madsen. Absorbing, exceptionally detailed study examines early trends, posters, and book illustrations, stylistic influences in architecture; furniture, jewelry, and other applied arts; plus perceptive discussions of artists associated with the movement. 488pp. 6½ x 9¼. 0-486-41794-8

THE NON-OBJECTIVE WORLD: THE MANIFESTO OF SUPREMATISM, Kasimir Malevich. One of the 20th century's most profound statements of aesthetic theory, this work defined the artist's radical, non-objective style, which he referred to as Suprematism (the preeminence of emotion in creating works of art). Included here among Malevich's most famous works is the 1913 painting *Black Square on White.* 92 b/w illustrations. 102pp. 8⅜ x 11. 0-486-42974-1

MIRÓ LITHOGRAPHS, Joan Miró. 40 important lithographic prints with line and composition comparable to Miró's friend Picasso. Eerie, droll, technically brilliant and aggressive. 48pp. 8¼ x 11¼. 0-486-24437-7

DRAWINGS OF MUCHA, Alphonse Mucha. 70 large-size illustrations trace Mucha's draftsmanship over more than 40 years: original plans and drawings for "The Seasons," Sarah Bernhardt posters, etc., all displaying marvelous technique. Introduction. 75pp. 9⅜ x 12¼. 0-486-23672-2

MUCHA'S FIGURES DÉCORATIVES, Alphonse Mucha. Figures of women, young girls, and children of both sexes in inimitable style of Art Nouveau master. His last stylebook. 40 plates in original color. 48pp. 9⅜ x 12¼. 0-486-24234-X

GRAPHIC WORKS OF EDVARD MUNCH, Edvard Munch. 90 haunting, evocative prints by first major Expressionist artist: *The Scream, Anxiety, Death Chamber, The Kiss, Madonna on the Jetty, Picking Apples, Ibsen in the Cafe of the Grand Hotel,* etc. xvii+90pp. 9 x 12. 0-486-23765-6

JOSÉ CLEMENTE OROZCO: AN AUTOBIOGRAPHY, José Clemente Orozco. Wealth of insights about great muralist's first inspirations; reflections on his life, on Mexico, on mural paintings; his relationships with other painters, and experiences in the United States. 192pp. 5⅜ x 8¼. 0-486-41819-7

OPTICAL ART: Theory and Practice, Rene Parola. First complete explanation of influential artistic movement: visual perception, psychological phenomena, principles and applications of Op Art, and more. Over 180 illustrations. 144pp. 9 x 12. 0-486-29054-9

PICASSO LINE DRAWINGS AND PRINTS, Pablo Picasso. 44 works from many periods and styles show 1905 circus family, portraits of Diaghilev, Balzac, Cubist studies, etc. 48pp. 8¼ x 11¼. 0-486-24196-3

PICASSO LITHOGRAPHS, Pablo Picasso. 61 works over a period of 35 years. Master artist/craftsman revels in bulls, nudes, myth, artists, actors–all in the purest lithographic line. 64pp. 8¼ x 11¼. 0-486-23949-7

THE COMPLETE GRAPHIC WORK OF JACK LEVINE, Kenneth W. Prescott and Emma Stina-Prescott.. Never-before-published prints of work by major American artist/social commentator. Plate-by-plate commentaries. 84 works in all. 112pp. 9⅜ x 12¼. 0-486-24481-4

RACKHAM'S COLOR ILLUSTRATIONS FOR WAGNER'S RING, Arthur Rackham. By the time he began this work, Rackham (1867–1939) was England's leading illustrator, famous throughout the world for his fantastic interpretations of fairy tales and myths. This, his masterpiece, is regarded by some as the greatest representation of Wagner's drama ever produced. 64 illustrations. 9 vignettes. 72pp. 8⅜ x 11¼. 0-486-23779-6

RACKHAM'S FAIRY TALE ILLUSTRATIONS IN FULL COLOR, Arthur Rackham (selected and edited by Jeff Menges). Superb collection of 55 lovely plates, reproduced from rare, early editions; scenes from *Irish Fairy Tales, English Fairy Tales, Hansel and Gretel, Snowdrop and Other Tales, Little Brother & Little Sister,* and others. 64pp. 8 x 11¼. 0-486-42167-8

PHOTOGRAPHS BY MAN RAY: 105 WORKS, 1920–1934, Man Ray. Here is a treasury of Ray's finest photographic work, arranged in five groupings: general subject, female figures, women's faces, celebrity portraits, and rayographs ("cameraless" compositions, created by resting objects on unexposed film). 105 photos, including one in color. Texts by Ray and others. 128pp. 9⅜ x 12¼. 0-486-23842-3

SCHIELE DRAWINGS: 44 WORKS: Egon Schiele. Treasury of portraits, character studies, nudes, and more, by great Viennese Expressionist. Characteristic focus on inner psychological states and hidden personality traits of subjects. 48pp. 8¼ x 11¼. 0-486-28150-7

CAMERA WORK: A PICTORIAL GUIDE, Alfred Steiglitz (edited by Marianne Fulton Margolis). The most important periodical in the history of art photography was *Camera Work,* edited and published by Alfred Stieglitz from 1903 to 1917. This volume contains all 559 illustrations that ever appeared in its pages, including hundreds of important photographs by the preeminent photographers of the time: Eduard Steichen, Alfred Stieglitz, Paul Strand, Alvin Langdon Coburn, Clarence White, and many others. 176pp. 8⅜ x 11¼. 0-486-23591-2

STEINLEN CATS, Théophile-Alexandre Steinlen. 66 drawings and 8 picture stories of great illustrator's favorite study–cats! 48pp. 8¼ x 11¼. 0-486-23950-0

GODS' MAN: A NOVEL IN WOODCUTS, Lynd Ward. A powerful, passionate novel–told entirely through 139 intricate woodcuts–artist Lynd Ward invented the concept of a wordless novel with this autobiographical account of his struggles with his craft and with life in the 1920s. Top-quality, low-cost republication of a longtime collectors' item. 160pp. 6⅛ x 9¼. 0-486-43500-8